INSIGHT GUIDE

New Zealand

DISCOVERY
CHANNEL

APA PUBLICATIONS
Part of the Langenscheidt Publishing Group

ABOUT THIS BOOK

INSIGHT GUIDE

New Zealand

Editorial

Project Editor
Craig Dowling
Editorial Director
Brian Bell

Distribution

UK & Ireland
GeoCenter International Ltd
The Viables Centre, Harrow Way
Basingstoke, Hants RG22 4BJ
Fax: (44) 1256 817988

United States
Langenscheidt Publishers, Inc.
46–35 54th Road, Maspeth, NY 11378
Fax: (1) 718 784 0640

Canada
Thomas Allen & Son Ltd
390 Steelcase Road East
Markham, Ontario L3R 1G2
Fax: (1) 905 475 6747

Australia
Universal Press
1 Waterloo Road
Macquarie Park, NSW 2113
Fax: (61) 2 9888 9074

New Zealand
Hema Maps New Zealand Ltd (HNZ)
Unit D, 24 Ra ORA Drive
East Tamaki, Auckland
Fax: (64) 9 273 6479

Worldwide
**Apa Publications GmbH & Co.
Verlag KG (Singapore branch)**
38 Joo Koon Road, Singapore 628990
Tel: (65) 6865 1600. Fax: (65) 6861 6438

Printing

Insight Print Services (Pte) Ltd
38 Joo Koon Road, Singapore 628990
Tel: (65) 6865 1600. Fax: (65) 6861 6438

©2003 Apa Publications GmbH & Co.
Verlag KG (Singapore branch)
All Rights Reserved
First Edition 1984
Sixth Edition 1998
Updated 2002; Reprinted 2003

CONTACTING THE EDITORS
We would appreciate it if readers
would alert us to errors or out-
dated information by writing to:
**Insight Guides, P.O. Box 7910,
London SE1 1WE, England.
Fax: (44) 20 7403 0290.**
insight@apaguide.demon.co.uk
NO part of this book may be reproduced,
stored in a retrieval system or transmitted
in any form or means electronic, mechanical, photocopying, recording or otherwise, without prior written permission of
Apa Publications. Brief text quotations
with use of photographs are exempted
for book review purposes only. Information has been obtained from sources
believed to be reliable, but its accuracy
and completeness, and the opinions
based thereon, are not guaranteed.

www.insightguides.com

This guidebook combines the interests and enthusiasms of two of the world's best known information providers: Insight Guides, whose titles have set the standard for visual travel guides since 1970, and Discovery Channel, the world's premier source of non-fiction television programming.

Insight Guides' editors provide practical advice and general understanding about a destination's history, culture, institutions and people. Discovery Channel and its website, www.discovery.com, help millions of viewers explore the world from the comfort of their homes, and encourage them to explore it first-hand.

How to use this book

The book is structured to convey a full understanding of the country and its culture and to guide readers through its various sights and activities:

◆ To understand New Zealand today, you need to know something of its past. The **History** and **Features** sections cover the country's people and culture in lively, authoritative essays written by specialists.

◆ The main **Places** section provides a full run-down of all the attractions worth seeing. The principal places of interest are coordinated by number with full-colour maps.

◆ The **Travel Tips** listings section provides a convenient point of reference for information on travel, hotels, restaurants, sports and culture. Information may be found quickly by using the index printed on the back cover flap – and the flaps are designed to serve as handy bookmarks.

◆ **Photographs** are chosen not only to illustrate geography but also to convey New Zealand's many moods and the activities of its people.

The contributors

This fully revised edition of *Insight Guide: New Zealand* builds on the original edition, compiled by a team of top local writers and photographers, and led by one of the country's best-known writers and broadcasters, **Gordon McLauchlan**. He has written several historical and biographical works, including *New Zealand Encyclopedia*.

David McGill, author of *The Other New Zealanders*, a book on minorities, wrote the Melting Pot, Wellington and Antarctica chapters. **Michael King** (pre-European history and Modern Maori) has been a journalist, teacher and broadcaster. His books include *New Zealanders at War* and *Being Pakeha*. **Janet Leggett**, author of *Hamilton*, a book on her home city, wrote the Waikato chapter.

John Harvey, editor of Palmerston North's *Evening Standard*, wrote on Manawatu and Wanganui. The Poverty Bay and Hawke's Bay chapter were written for the first edition by **Geoff Conly**.

John Goulter, a native of Christchurch, wrote the chapters on that city and on farming. Several South Island stories, including Canterbury, Westland and Central Otago, were produced by two of New Zealand's top tourism writers, **Les Bloxham** and **Robin Charteris**. Southland and Fiordland, along with Stewart Island, were covered by **Clive Lind**, author of a number of books on the history of Southland. **William Hobbs**, a writer and broadcaster, compiled the Nelson/Marlborough story.

Also contributing were **Phil Gifford**, a prolific sports commentator, and **Katherine Findlay** (Cultural Scene), director of *Kaleidoscope*, a local TV arts programme. **Terence Barrow** (Maori Art) is the author of *An Illustrated Guide to Maori Art*.

John Costello wrote about New Zealand horse racing. **Jim Wilson** (Outdoor Adventures) is an academic and mountaineer. **Jack Adlington** wrote on Northland, **Joseph Frahm** was responsible for Coromandel and the Bay of Plenty, and the chapter on Rotorua is by **Colin Taylor**. **Wendy Canning** did a wide range of background research for the book.

In 1998, the new sixth edition was checked and updated by journalist **Craig Dowling**, with **Stefan Huy** contributing some new sections, including the picture spread on Maori art. **Natalie Minnis** brought the new elements together while **Helen Partington** proof-read the text.

In 2002, Auckland-based freelance writer **Jane Wynyard** updated the book and compiled a brand new Travel Tips section.

Map Legend

	National Park/Nature Reserve
	Ferry Route
✈	Airport
🚌	Bus Station
P	Parking
ℹ	Tourist Information
✉	Post Office
✝	Church/Ruins
	Mosque
✡	Synagogue
	Castle/Ruins
∴	Archaeological Site
∩	Cave
★	Place of Interest

The main places of interest in the Places section are coordinated by number with a full-colour map (e.g. ❶), and a symbol at the top of every right-hand page tells you where to find the map.

New Zealand

CONTENTS

Maps

Introduction

History

Features

AOTEAROA

New Zealand – Aotearoa to the Maori – is home to stunning landscapes, adventure sports and fascinating mythology

This is New Zealand. *Haere mai*. Welcome. Welcome to a land of majestic snow-capped peaks and unexplored rain forests, of pristine lakes swarming with trout and turquoise ocean bays speckled with wooded isles, of glaciers and fiords, geysers and volcanoes. It is a land of kauri forests and kiwi fruit plantations, of modern cosmopolitan cities and backcountry sheep stations, of the flightless kiwi and the prehistoric tuatara. It is a land of rugby fields and ski fields, of barbecues and bungee jumping. It is a combination of a land that time forgot, and a land that is difficult to forget. Perhaps most important of all, it is the land of the Maori.

Anthropologists tell the story of a remarkable migration as the Polynesian ancestors of the Maori moved through the Pacific, arriving on these islands by outrigger canoe in about the 8th century AD. Maori legend tells a much more evocative story, about the birth of all life in the stillness of a long dark night, Te Po, from the primordial parents – Rangi, the sky father, and Papa, the earth mother.

Tane, the god of the forests and their eldest son, pulled himself free of his parents in the darkness and with great effort, over a long period of time, pushed them apart. He decorated Rangi with the sun, moon and stars, and Papa with plant and animal life, thereby flooding this new universe with light and colour. But Rangi's sorrow at the parting from his mate caused tears to flood from his eyes, filling her surface with oceans and lakes.

Today, it is not hard to understand why New Zealanders, Maori and Pakeha (the name given to descendants of European settlers) have such a strong attachment to their native land. The waters of Rangi's tears have contributed to a recreational wonderland perhaps unrivalled anywhere.

From essays written by experts in their field, learn about what makes New Zealanders who they are. Learn about the Maori and how they adapted their Polynesian culture to suit the new conditions of the land they called Aotearoa. Learn about Maori art and the current renaissance of their language.

Read about the European voyages of discovery that opened New Zealand up to the outside world, and then discover for yourself New Zealand wine and foods, art and culture. Discover life on New Zealand farms. Discover the great New Zealand outdoor lifestyle. Discover what has changed and what has stayed the same.

PRECEDING PAGES: various Kiwi transports of delight – by boat into fiordland; by jeep on to Northland's Ninety Mile Beach; by skiplane on the glacier at Mount Cook; and by Shotover Jet around the very ragged rocks.
LEFT: Pohutu Geyser at Rotorua.

Decisive Dates

Prehistoric times

130 million years ago The landmass that will eventually contain New Zealand breaks away from New Caledonia, Eastern Australia, Tasmania and Antarctica.

80 million years ago New Zealand physically independent, splitting from Gondwana as the Tasman Sea begins to form.

60 million years ago New Zealand reaches its present distance from Australia of more than 1,500 km (930 miles).

Traders and explorers

AD 950 First Polynesians arrive in New Zealand, led, according to tradition, by the voyager Kupe, who names the country Aotearoa, or Land of The Long White Cloud, and later returns to his native Hawaiiki.

1300s A wave of immigrants arrive, it is said, from Hawaiiki, in 12 outrigger canoes. They bring taro, yam, kumara (sweet potato) and the rat and the dog.

1642 Abel Tasman, of the Dutch East India Co., becomes first European to sight land. Names it Nieuw Zeeland.

1769 Englishman Capt. James Cook is first European to land and explore New Zealand.

1791–2 Deep-sea whaling begins.

1814 Church Missionary Society (Anglican) begins at Rangihoua, Bay of Islands.

1818 "Musket Wars" begin as Maori appropriate muskets from Europeans. About 20,000 people killed in 12 years of inter-tribal conflict.

1837 200 British settlers petition their monarch about lack of order.

1839 Capt. W.B. Rhodes establishes first cattle station on the South Island, at Akaroa.

Colonialisation

1840 First colony of New Zealand Company settlers reaches Port Nicholson and establishes settlements at Wanganui, New Plymouth, Nelson and Wellington.

1840 Capt. William Hobson arrives in the Bay of Islands and announces himself as Lieutenant-Governor.

1840 Some 50 Maori chiefs sign the Treaty of Waitangi, ceding sovereignty to the Queen. In return the Queen guarantees the Maoris possession of the lands, forests, fisheries and other property.

1840 Capt. Hobson proclaims British sovereignty over the whole country and chooses Auckland as New Zealand's capital.

1844 Hone Heke, first Maori to sign the Treaty of Waitangi, cuts down its symbol, the flagstaff at Kororareka, three times, and sacks and burns the town, in protest over land disputes. About 1,000 Maoris take arms against the British.

1848 Otago settled by a community of Scottish farmers.

1850 Canterbury settled.

1852 The Constitution Act divides the country into six provinces.

1852 Colonisation of Taranaki begun by the Plymouth Company.

1853 Maori King movement takes off, centred in the Waikato-Manipoto tribes, designed to protect tribal land.

1856 New Zealand becomes a self-governing British colony. Gold rush and land struggles.

1860 Wiremu Kingi's claim to the Waitara starts the Maori Land Wars; vast tracts of land are confiscated from rebel tribes.

1861 Otago gold rush begins when Gabriel Read makes discovery at Blue Spur, Tuapeka.

1865 Wellington becomes capital.

1867 Maori given the vote.

1868 Raids from Maori leaders Titokowaru and Te Kooti throw the colony into crisis.

1869 Te Kooti defeated at Ngatapa.
1870 First rugby match in New Zealand.
1877 Treaty of Waitangi ruled "a simple nullity" by Chief Justice Prendergast.
1877 Free compulsory education introduced.
1882 First refrigerated agricultural produce cargo dispatched to England.
1886 Mount Tarawera erupts. 153 lives lost.

Social reforms and world wars

1890 Liberal Party under John Ballance introduce new laws regulating conditions in factories; libraries and schools built.
1893 Women given the vote, 25 years before Britain and the USA.
1896 Maori population down to 42,000 (from 100,000 in 1769) because of disease.
1898 World's first old-age pension for men introduced by Liberal Richard Seddon.
1899–1902 NZ troops fight in Boer War.
1901 Cook Islands annexed by New Zealand.
1907 New Zealand promoted from a colony to a Dominion.
1908 Ernest Rutherford awarded Nobel Prize for Chemistry.
1914 World War I. New Zealand casualties are the highest per capita of any Allied country.
1918–19 Influenza epidemic hits New Zealand, with the loss of 6,700 lives.
1938 Health care and social security systems introduced.
1939 World War II. New Zealand suffers heavy losses.
1941 War in the Pacific brings threat of Japanese invasion.
1947 New Zealand becomes fully independent.
1950 New Zealand troops sail for Korea.
1951 New Zealand signs the ANZUS defence alliance with Australia and the United States.
1953 New Zealander Edmund Hillary and Nepal's Sherpa Tenzing become first to reach summit of Mount Everest.
1953 Tangiwai Bridge collapse causes New Zealand's worst train disaster.
1965 New Zealand troops sent to Vietnam.
1968 MV *Wahine*, an overnight passenger ferry, is wrecked on a reef near Wellington Harbour in a storm. 51 die.
1971 New Zealand joins South Pacific Forum. Economic trouble and strife.

PRECEDING PAGES: Rotorua mineral lakes. **LEFT** and **ABOVE RIGHT:** New Zealand women, then and now.

1973 Britain joins Common Market. Two years later, amid mounting oil prices, New Zealand has a crippling balance of payments deficit.
1974 Christchurch hosts the Commonwealth Games.
1975 Parliament passes the Treaty of Waitangi Act, establishing a tribunal to investigate claims.
1983 Closer Economic Relations Agreement with Australia.
1985 Greenpeace ship *Rainbow Warrior*, protesting against French nuclear testing, is bombed by French secret agents in Auckland.
1985 Sir Paul Reeves sworn in as first Maori Governor-General.

1985 Welfare state dismembered in drastic programme of economic reform.
1985 Government bans visits by ships carrying nuclear weapons.
1990 Auckland hosts Commonwealth Games.
1993 Proportional representation election system, MMP, introduced.
1995 New Zealand wins the America's Cup.
1997 National Party's Jenny Shipley becomes New Zealand's first woman Prime Minister.
1999 New Zealand hosts APEC summit and America's Cup yachting regatta. Labour Party's Helen Clark is elected as Prime Minister.
2001 World-premiere of *Lord of the Rings*, directed by New Zealand director Peter Jackson.

ARRIVAL OF THE MAORI

In around AD *800, Polynesian settlers arrived in New Zealand.*
There they evolved a sophisticated and highly organised culture

Apart from Antarctica, New Zealand was the last major land mass to be explored by people. These earliest Pacific navigators preceded those from Europe by some 800 years. They were "Vikings of the sunrise" and their descendants came to be called Maori.

Few subjects have been the source of more controversy than the origins of the Maori. Nineteenth-century scholars devised bizarre theories. Some asserted Maori were wandering Aryans, others believed that they were originally Hindu, and still others that they were indisputably a lost tribe of Israel. Interpretations of evidence in the 20th century have been more cautious. The current consensus among scholars is that Maori were descendants of Austronesian people who originated in Southeast Asia. A few authorities dispute this. Minority opinions have suggested they came from Egypt, from Mesopotamia or from South America.

Linguistic and archaeological evidence establishes, however, that New Zealand Maori are Polynesian people; and that the ancestors of the Polynesians sailed into the South China Sea from the Asian mainland some 2,000 to 3,000 years ago. Some went southwest, ultimately to Madagascar; others southeast along the Malaysian, Indonesian and Philippine island chains.

Early nautical words

What appears to have inspired these vast journeys was the introduction of the sail to Southeast Asia and the invention of the outrigger. In the Austronesian languages shared by the people of the Pacific and the Southeast Asian archipelagos, the words for sail, mast, outrigger float and outrigger boom are among the most widespread and therefore among the oldest.

The Pacific Austronesians who made their way along the Melanesian chain of islands, reaching Fiji by about 1300 BC and Tonga before 1100 BC, left behind fragments of pottery with distinctive decorations. This pottery has been called Lapita, and the same name has been given by archaeologists to the people who made it. With their pottery they also carried pigs, dogs, rats, fowls and cultivated plants. All of these originated on the mainland of Southeast Asia, except the kumara, a sweet potato

which originally came from South America.

Polynesian culture as recognised today evolved among the Lapita people in Tonga and Samoa. It was from East Polynesia, possibly from the Society or Marquesas Islands, that a migration was eventually launched to New Zealand. The East Polynesian characteristics of early Maori remains, the earliest carbon dates and the rate of growth and spread of the Maori population all indicate that a landfall was made in New Zealand around AD 800.

The land was unlike anything that Polynesians had encountered elsewhere in the Pacific. It was far larger – more than 1,500 km (over 900 miles) from north to south – and more varied

LEFT: a Maori chief as depicted by Sydney Parkinson, an artist on one of Cook's expeditions.
ABOVE RIGHT: Maori feather box.

than islands they had colonised previously. Mountains were higher, rivers wider. It was temperate rather than tropical and sufficiently cold in much of the South Island to prevent the growing of traditional crops. They had to adapt to a range of climatic conditions they had never previously experienced. Other than bats, there were no mammals ashore until the ancestors of the Maori released the rats *(kiore)* and dogs *(kuri)* they had brought with them. They probably also brought pigs and fowls. These animals did not survive, but the ancestors of the Maori did, showing great fortitude and adaptability.

The lack of meat was compensated for by an abundance of seafood: fish, shellfish, crayfish, crab, seaweed and sea-eggs. There were also aquatic mammals: whales, dolphins and seals. The land provided fern root that offered a staple food (though it had to be heavily pounded), and there were nearly 200 species of bird, many of them edible. Inland waterways contained additional resources: waterfowl, eel, fish and more shellfish.

To all these the immigrants added the cultivated vegetables they had carried with them: taro, kumara, yam, gourds and the paper mulberry. For meat, in addition to birds, fish and sea mammals, there were limited supplies of dog and rat.

HIGH-QUALITY MATERIALS

The New Zealand forests had larger trees than Polynesians had seen previously. With these they built bigger dugout canoes and evolved a tradition of carving. Later, they used wooden beams in their houses. Materials such as raupo and nikau made excellent walls and roofs. Flax plaited well into cords and baskets and provided fine fibre for garments. There was stone for adzes and drill points, bone for fish-hooks and ornaments, and obsidian for flake knives. With these materials, the New Zealand Polynesians developed one of the world's most sophisticated neolithic cultures.

Perhaps the most spectacular of the new country's resources was the huge flightless bird, the moa. There were several species, ranging from the turkey-sized *anomalopteryx* to the gigantic *dinornis maximus*, several times larger than ostriches or emu. They offered a food supply on a scale never before encountered in Polynesia, other than when whales were cast ashore. Some early groups of Maori based their economy around moas in areas where the birds were relatively plentiful, until extensive hunting eventually led to their extinction.

The history of the first colonists, from the time of their arrival until the advent of Europeans, is a history of their adaptation to the environment – the matching of their skills and cultural resources to it, and the evolution of new features in their culture in response to the conditions that the environment imposed.

Maori life

Ethnologists recognise two distinguishable but related phases in that culture. The first is New Zealand East Polynesian, or Archaic Maori, displayed by the archaeological remains of the earliest settlers and their immediate descendants. The second is Classic Maori, the culture encountered and recorded by the earliest European navigators to reach the country. The

regional variations were apparent in the details and traditions of the culture, the most important features were practised throughout the country.

Competitive tribalism, for example, was the basis of Maori life. The family and *hapu* (sub-tribe) were the unit of society that determined who married whom, where people lived, where and when they fought other people and why. Tribal ancestors were venerated, as were gods representing the natural elements (the earth, the sky, the wind, the sea, and so on). The whole of life was bound up in a unified vision in which every aspect of living was related to every other. And the universal acceptance of concepts such

process by which the first phase evolved into the second is complex.

What is certain, however, is that by the time James Cook observed New Zealand in 1769, New Zealand Polynesians had settled the land from the far north to Foveaux Strait in the south. The language these inhabitants shared was similar enough for a speaker to be understood anywhere in the country, although dialectal differences were pronounced, particularly between the North and South Islands. While

LEFT: Maori fort (known as a *pa*), a reminder of a warlike race. **ABOVE:** early depiction of the traditional greeting, the *hongi*.

as *tapu* (sacredness), *mana* (spiritual authority), *mauri* (life force), *utu* (satisfaction) and a belief in *makutu* (sorcery) regulated all aspects of life.

Maori hierarchy

Maori society was stratified. People were born into *rangatira* or chiefly families, or they were *tutua* (commoners). They became slaves if they were captured as a consequence of warfare. Immediate authority was exercised by *kaumatua,* the elders who were family heads. Whole communities, sharing a common ancestor, were under the jurisdiction of the *rangatira* families whose authority was in part hereditary and in part based on past achievement. Occasionally federations of *hapu* and tribes would come together and join forces under an *ariki* (paramount chief) for joint ventures such as waging war against foreign elements, trading or foraging for resources. The most common relationship among even closely related *hapu*, however, was fierce competition.

Communities ranging from a handful of households to more than 500 lived in *kainga* (villages). These were usually based on membership of a single *hapu*. The *kainga* would be close

COPING WITH SCARCITY

When items of food became scarce in a *kainga* or *pa*, they had a *rahui*, or prohibition, laid on them to conserve precious supplies.

food growing and (in areas where fighting was common) warfare. Cultivation and foraging were carried out by large parties of workers, seasonally.

Warfare was an important feature of Maori life in most parts of the country. It was sometimes conducted to obtain territory abundant in food or other natural resources (for example, stone for tool-making); sometimes to avenge insults, sometimes to obtain satisfaction from *hapu* whose members had allegedly transgressed the social

to water, food sources and crops. Some settlements, called *pa*, were fortified. More often the *kainga* were adjacent to hilltop *pa*, to which communities could retreat when under attack.

Defensive settlements

Maori *pa* were elaborately constructed with an interior stronghold, ditches, banks and palisades. Some proved impregnable; others were taken and lost several times in the course of a lifetime. Some scholars speculate that primary function of hilltop *pa* was to protect kumara tubers from marauders.

Communal patterns of life in Maori settlements were organised around food gathering,

code; and sometimes as a result of serious disagreements over control or authority.

Prior to the introduction of the musket, however, most warfare was not totally destructive. It often involved only individuals or small raiding parties, and ambush or short, sporadic attacks. Even when larger groups met in head-on confrontation or siege, the dead rarely amounted to more than a few score. Most battles occurred in summer and, except when a migration was under way, fighting was rarely carried on far from a tribe's home territory.

For individual men, as for tribes, the concept of *mana* (respect) was paramount. An individual's *mana* was intensified by victory, and diminished by defeat. Courage and combat skills were also essential ingredients in initiation, and in acceptance by male peers, especially in the case of chiefs. Favourite weapons were *taiaha* (long wooden-bladed swords) and short clubs known as *patu* and *mere*.

Non-combatants were able to achieve high standing in the arts, or in the exercise of esoteric powers as *tohunga* (priests or experts). With no written language, the indigenous Maori relied on sophisticated oral traditions. Considerable mana was bestowed on the best orators. An ability to carve was also highly regarded and the working of wood, bone and stone reached

heights of intricacy and delicacy in New Zealand seldom seen elsewhere. The best wood-carving was seen on door lintels, house gables and canoe prows, and in stone and bone in personal ornaments such as *tikis*, pendants and necklaces. The most prized material for carving was *pounamu* (New Zealand jade or greenstone), the search for which led Maori to some of the most inhospitable parts of the South Island. *Pounamu* was valued for its hardness and the sharpness of the edges which could be fashioned from it. More than just a resource, it

ABOVE LEFT: idealised view of Maori by Sydney Parkinson.
ABOVE: Parkinson's portrait of a Maori warrior.

holds mystical associations. Like the other Polynesians, the Maori had no access to metals.

With animal skins also unavailable, Maori weavers fashioned intricate ceremonial clothing from feathers, flax and other materials.

Personal decoration in the form of *moko* (tattooing) was also a feature of Maori art. Men were marked primarily on the face or buttocks, women largely on the face and breasts. The Maori usually used a straight rather than a serrated blade. This left a grooved scar which looked more like carving than tattooing.

In spite of competition, warfare and tribal demarcations among Maori, trading was also extensive. South Islanders exported greenstone to other parts of the country for use in *patu*, chisels and ornaments. Bay of Plenty settlers distributed high-quality obsidian from Mayor Island. Nelson and D'Urville Island inhabitants quarried and distributed argillite. Food that was readily available in some districts but not in others, such as mutton birds, was also preserved and bartered. People travelled long distances for materials and food delicacies. Although ocean-going vessels disappeared from New Zealand by the 18th century, canoes were still widely used for river, lake and coastal transport.

Land of the Long White Cloud

Medical examination of pre-European remains reveals that few Maori lived beyond the age of 30. From their late twenties, most people would have suffered considerably as a consequence of arthritis, and from infected gums and loss of teeth brought about by the staple fern-root diet. Many of the healthy-looking "elderly" men, on whose condition James Cook commented favourably in 1770, may have been, at the most, around 40 years of age.

Such were the contours of Maori life that Cook and other navigators encountered towards the end of the 18th century. The population was probably some 100,000 to 120,000. Having been so long separated from other cultures, Maori had no concept of nationhood. However, they were fiercely assertive of the identity that they took from their ancestry and *hapu* membership. To that extent they led a tribal existence, but one thing they did share strongly, no matter which tribe they were born to, was a deep and profound affinity with the land and its bounty. They called the land Aotearoa – "the land of the long white cloud".

VOYAGES OF DISCOVERY

A Dutchman searching for a "Great Southern Continent" first stumbled upon
New Zealand in 1642 – but it was another 130 years before any European returned

The southern Pacific was the last habitable part of the world to be reached by Europeans. It was then only gradually explored at the end of long-haul routes down the coast of South America on one side and Africa on the other. Once inside the rim of the world's largest ocean, seafarers faced vast areas to be crossed, always hundreds or thousands of miles away from any familiar territory. So it required not only steady courage to venture into this region but a high degree of navigational skill.

The countries of the South Pacific – tucked down near the bottom of the globe – were left to the Polynesians for nearly 150 years after the Europeans first burst into the Western Pacific. And then New Zealand was left alone for another 130 years after the Dutchman Abel Janszoon Tasman first sighted its coast in 1642.

It was left to the Englishman James Cook to put the South Pacific firmly on the world map. A famous New Zealand historian and biographer of Cook, Dr J.C. Beaglehole, wrote of the three great Cook voyages: "... his career is one of which the justification lies not so much in the underlining of its detail as in the comparison of the map of the Pacific before his first voyage with that at the end of the century. For his was a life consistent and integrated; to a passion for scientific precision he added the inexhaustible effort of the dedicated discoverer..."

The Dutch traders

European knowledge of the Pacific Ocean had gradually expanded during the 16th and 17th centuries following the first view of it by Vasco Nuñez de Balboa from the Isthmus of Panama in 1513. Spanish and Portuguese seafarers such as Magellan and Quiros, and England's Francis Drake, made their epic expeditions. The Spanish were motivated by their zeal to claim converts for the Catholic Church as well as the search for rare and precious metals and spices.

PRECEDING PAGES: a 1990s replica of Cook's *Endeavour.*
LEFT: Captain Cook arrives in New Zealand in 1769.
ABOVE RIGHT: Cook's ship, the *Endeavour.*

But towards the end of the 16th century, the Dutch emerged as the great seafaring and trading nation of the central and western Pacific. They set up a major administrative and trading centre at Batavia (now Jakarta) in Java early in the 17th century, an operation dominated by the Dutch East India Company. For 200 years the

Dutch were a power in the region, though for most of that period, voyages of exploration were incidental to the activities of trade.

The Dutch ships eventually found that by staying south after rounding the tip of Africa at the Cape of Good Hope and catching the consistent westerlies almost as far as the western coast of Australia, they could make the journey to Java more quickly than by adopting the traditional route – sailing up the east coast of Africa and then catching seasonal winds for the journey eastwards. And so islands off the west coast of Australia and stretches of the coast itself began to be noted on charts but were not yet recognised as the western side of a huge continent.

Then an ambitious governor of Batavia, Anthony van Diemen, showed a more imaginative interest in discovering new lands for trade than most of his predecessors.

Tasman's visit

In 1642 Tasman was chosen by van Diemen to lead an expedition south, to be accompanied by a highly competent specialist navigator, Frans Visscher. The proposed voyage would take them first to Mauritius, then southwest to between 50 and 55 degrees south in search of the great southern continent, Terra Australis Incognita. The expedition, aboard the vessels

Farewell into what is now known as Golden Bay.

Tasman's first and only encounter with the Maori was disastrous. When a canoe rammed a small boat travelling from the *Zeehaen* to the *Heemskerck*, fighting broke out and there was loss of life on both sides. Tasman called the place Massacre Bay and headed north again, not realising that he was inside the western entrance to Cook Strait. A voyage eastwards of only a few miles would have shown him that he was not on the edge of a continent but in the centre of two islands. He did not land again.

Tasman's voyage was not regarded as a major success immediately but ultimately he was

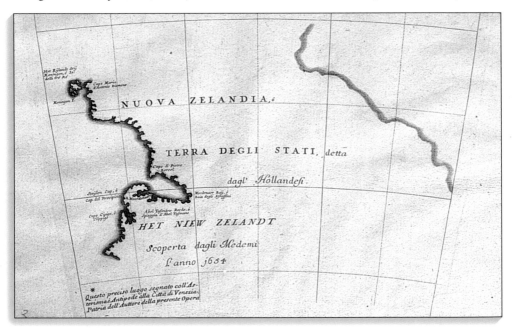

Heemskerck and *Zeehaen*, was then to come eastwards if no land had been found to impede their progress and to sail across to investigate a shorter route to Chile, a rich trading area and the monopoly of the Spanish. The expedition went only as far as 49 degrees south before turning eastwards, whereupon it made two great South Pacific discoveries – Tasmania (or van Diemen's Land, as he named it) and New Zealand (or Staten Landt).

On 13 December 1642, Tasman and his men saw what was described as "land uplifted high", the Southern Alps of the South Island, and in strong winds and heavy seas sailed northwards up the coast of Westland, and rounded Cape

given his due for a gallant and well-recorded journey of exploration.

Cook's oyster

Within a year or two, other navigators had discovered that New Zealand could not be attached to a huge continent which ran across to South America. The name was therefore changed from Staten Landt (the Dutch name for South America) to New Zealand, after the Dutch province of Zeeland.

But it was left to James Cook to open up the South Pacific like a huge oyster and reveal its contents. The son of a Yorkshire labourer, Cook was born in 1728. He served as an apprentice seaman on a collier, and then volunteered as an able seaman with the Royal Navy during the Seven Years' War. He helped survey Canada's St Lawrence River, an essential preliminary to the capture of Québec by General James Wolfe, and he enhanced an already growing reputation as a marine surveyor by charting the St Lawrence and parts of the Newfoundland and Nova Scotia coasts. In 1766, he observed an eclipse of the sun; both the Royal Society and the Admiralty were impressed with his report.

It was primarily to observe the transit of the planet Venus over the disc of the sun in June 1769 that he was dispatched in 1768 to the

South Seas in a 368-ton bark built in Whitby, *Endeavour*. He was instructed to sail to Otaheite (Tahiti) for the transit and then to sail southwards as far as 50 degrees south latitude on another search for the great southern continent, fixing on the map the positions of any islands he might incidentally discover.

Cook rounded Cape Horn and entered the Pacific Ocean for the first time on 27 January 1769. After observing the transit of Venus and investigating other islands in the group which

LEFT: based on Dutch explorations, a chart published in 1690 by Vincenzo Coronelli shows Cape Maria van Diemen (North Island). **ABOVE:** Tasman.

MAPPING MISTAKES

Cook made two major errors: attaching Stewart Island to the mainland as a peninsula, and mapping Banks Peninsula as an island.

he named the Society Islands, he sailed south and then westwards. On 6 October, a ship's boy, Nicholas Young, sighted the east coast of the North Island of New Zealand where it is today called Young Nick's Head.

Two days after this first sighting of what he knew to be the east coast of New Zealand, the land reported by Tasman, the *Endeavour* sailed into a bay where smoke could be seen – a clear sign that there were inhabitants. Their first visit ashore ended with violence when a band of Maori attacked four boys left guarding the ship's boat; one of the attackers was shot dead.

It was discovered that a Tahitian chief on board the *Endeavour*, Tupaea, could converse with the Maori in his own tongue. He was taken back ashore with Cook the next morning. But the Maori were in a threatening mood and Cook ordered one of them shot to make them retreat. That afternoon, the firing of a musket over a canoe (to attract the attention of its occupants) brought an attack on the ship's boat from which the shot had been fired; to repel the canoe, three or more Maori were shot. Cook had learnt quickly that the inhabitants of this country were powerful, aggressive and brave. He called the place Poverty Bay because he could not find the supplies he wanted.

First friendly encounter

The *Endeavour* sailed south into Hawke's Bay, and then north again around the top of East Cape. It spent 10 days in Mercury Bay, so called because an observation of the transit of the planet Mercury was made there. In Mercury Bay, for the first time, the explorers made friends with the local Maori and traded trinkets for supplies of fish, birds and clean water. They were shown over the Maori settlement and inspected a nearby fortified pa which greatly impressed Cook.

The expedition circumnavigated New Zealand and with brilliant accuracy made a chart of the coastline which proved basically reliable for more than 150 years.

Cook and his crew spent weeks in Ship Cove, in a long inlet which he called Queen Charlotte

Sound, on the northern coast of the South Island, refurbishing the ship and gathering supplies. The stay gave the two botanists aboard, Joseph Banks and Daniel Solander, a wonderful opportunity to study closely the flora and fauna of the area. While the ship was being cleaned, the boats did detailed survey work.

The *Endeavour* left for home at the end of March 1770, sailing up the east coast of Australia, through the Dutch East Indies and then rounding the Cape of Good Hope to complete a circumnavigation of the world. The expedition was an extraordinary feat of seamanship, putting New Zealand firmly on the map and

vessel was known to have gone before; he was unlucky, however, in that he did not become the first person ever to see the Antarctic continent.

It was to Dusky Sound in New Zealand that Cook repaired for rest and recovery after the extreme hardships faced by his crew in the southern ocean. During the seven weeks his expedition was there, the crew set up a workshop and an observatory, and restored their health with spruce beer (to defeat scurvy) and the plenitude of fish and birds. They made contact with a single family of Maori in an area which was never thickly populated, then or now. They planted seeds on the shore of the sound,

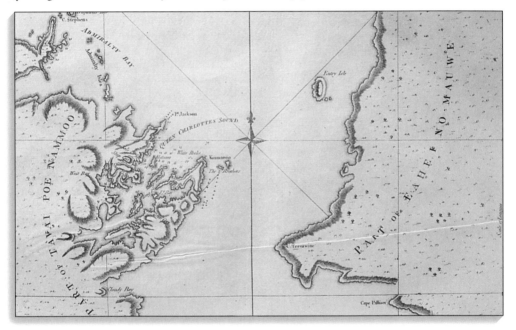

gathering a huge amount of data. Cook seemed to personify the Great Discoverer as defined by his biographer, Beaglehole: "In every great discoverer there is a dual passion – the passion to see, the passion to report; and in the greatest this duality is fused into one – a passion to see and to report truly." Cook's first voyage was one of the most expert and detailed expeditions of exploration in all history.

Antarctic R & R

Cook twice again led expeditions into the Pacific – from 1772 to 1775 and from 1776 to 1780. During the second of these, he twice took his ship south into the Antarctic Circle where no

and then sailed for their favourite anchorage in Ship Cove at the other end of the South Island.

On Cook's way home from New Zealand during his second voyage a few years laster, he gave pigs, fowls and vegetable seeds to Maori near Hawke's Bay before he again sailed for Ship Cove to a rendezvous with another vessel of the expedition, *Adventure*.

On his third voyage, Cook came again to New Zealand, and to his home away from home at Ship Cove. By now he had a friendship with some of the local Maori that had lasted nearly 10 years. In his journals, he referred to the Maori as "manly and mild" and wrote that "they have some arts among them which they execute with great judgement and unwearied patience." By then he had done such a thorough job of charting the coasts of New Zealand that there was little else for explorers to discover without going inland. But a number of navigators followed during the remaining years of the 18th century – Frenchmen de Urville (who arrived only two months after Cook first set foot in New Zealand), du Fresne and d'Entrecasteaux; an Italian, Malaspina, who commanded a Spanish expedition; and George

COOK'S DEMISE

Captain Cook was killed in January 1778 in Kealakekua Bay, Hawaii after a series of thefts from his expedition led to a skirmish with locals.

it wasn't long before the seals were in short supply and the ships had to go farther south to the sub-Antarctic islands.

Next came the whalers at the turn of the century, some of them driven from the Pacific coast of South America because of the dangers there brought about by the war between Spain and Britain. Ships from Britain, Australia and the United States hunted the sperm whale in this region and visits brought their crew-members into frequent contact with the Maori of North-

Vancouver, who had served with Cook.

In 10 years, within the decade of the 1770s, Cook and his contemporaries had opened up the Pacific entirely and, in 1788, Sydney was established as a British convict settlement. Traders were soon based there, ready to extract whatever valuable goods they could find.

The first Europeans to make an impact on New Zealand, however, were the sealers, with the first gang put ashore on the southwest coast of the South Island in 1792. There was a brief boom in the early years of the 19th century but

LEFT: a map of Cook Strait from Cook's expeditions.
ABOVE: an English explorer is greeted by Maoris.

land at Kororareka (later renamed as Russell).

At first, relations between Europeans and Maori were peaceful and friendly. But visits were infrequent for a few years after the burning of a vessel called the *Boyd* in 1809 and the massacre of its crew. This was a reprisal against previous punishment of high-born Maori seamen by Pakeha (European) skippers.

The inland exploration of New Zealand took place mostly during the second quarter of the 19th century, mainly in those parts which were fairly accessible from the coast. Vast areas of the interior of the South Island, however, were not successfully explored by Europeans until this century.

HARRIETT
HEKI'S WIFE

HEKI

KAWITI

THE WARRIOR CHIEFTAINS

of

NEW ZEALAND

by Jos.ᵗ J. Merrett

Drawn on Stone by W Nich.ˢ

SETTLEMENT AND COLONISATION

The colonisation of New Zealand was debated and fought over
by Maori, missionaries, politicians, settlers and land speculators

The bleak experiences of Abel Tasman – and the much more successful endeavours of James Cook nearly 130 years later – had no immediate impact on the future of the two main islands. The Dutch were preoccupied with getting all they could out of the Indonesian archipelago; the British were concerned with consolidating and expanding their trading territories in India. New Zealand, it seemed, had little to offer a colonial power.

Australia's "Botany Bay", not so far across the Tasman Sea, was established as a penal settlement in 1788 as a direct result of America's victory in the War of Independence (and as a by-product of Cook's voyages), but the Land of the Long White Cloud was mostly ignored.

Sealskins and whale oil

As the 19th century opened, with Europe engulfed in the Napoleonic Wars, demand increased for commodities such as sealskins and whale oil. Seals and whales were plentiful in New Zealand waters, and skippers from Port Jackson (Sydney's harbour) and the newer settlement of Hobart, in Van Diemen's Land (Tasmania), wasted no time in putting to sea.

Many skippers found a convenient watering-hole at Kororareka (now Russell) in the Bay of Islands. The anchorage there was calm and well-protected and there was a ready supply of kauri wood for spars and masts.

Kororareka, with its new European arrivals, rapidly became a lusty, brawling town; the missionaries who arrived there damned it as the "hell-hole of the Southwest Pacific". The newcomers carried dangerous baggage which in time completely eradicated some of the Maori tribes and *hapu*, and seriously affected others: muskets, hard liquor or "grog", prostitution, and a host of infectious diseases – many of which could prove fatal – to which the Maori had

never previously been exposed and therefore had no natural resistance.

Isolated hostilities occurred in the early decades of the 19th century, such as the burning of the brig *Boyd* and the killing and eating of its crew in Whangaroa Harbour in 1809.

Despite such ugly episodes, contacts between

Maori and Pakeha (Europeans) remained essentially peaceful. A barter trade flourished, the Maori trading vegetables and flax for a variety of European trinkets, tools and weapons (including, of course, the musket). The Maori helped cut down giant kauri trees and drag the trunks from bush to beach; they crewed on European sealing and whaling vessels; they were physically strong and vigorous; and they were also proud – a fact overlooked by most Europeans.

In 1817, mainly in response to lawlessness in the Bay of Islands, the laws of the Colony of New South Wales were extended to include New Zealand.

PRECEDING PAGES: Abel Tasman is attacked by Maoris at Massacre Bay. **LEFT:** Honi Heke with his wife, Harriet, on his right and Chief Kawiti on his left.
ABOVE RIGHT: Samuel Marsden, the "flogging parson".

Around this time, the Reverend Samuel Marsden arrived from New South Wales. Marsden is still reviled in Australia as the "flogging parson", a result of his tenure as a magistrate at Port Jackson. Kiwis see him in a different light, as the man who introduced Christianity to New Zealand.

A dedicated evangelist, he believed that missionary tradesmen would not only encourage the conversion of Maori to Christianity but also develop their expertise in carpentry, farming and European technology.

NOTABLE MISSIONARY

William Colenso arrived at Paihia in 1834 and set up a printing press that played a major role in the development of Maori literacy.

By 1830, Maori were involved in export trading. In that year 28 ships (averaging 110 tonnes) made 56 cross-Tasman voyages, carrying substantial cargoes, including tonnes of Maori-grown potatoes, mainly to Sydney.

The inclusion of New Zealand within the framework of the laws of New South Wales had still not made New Zealand a British colony, nor did the legislation prove very effective. The governors had no way of proving charges nor of enforcing their authority while a ship was

Kororarika Bay of Islands N.Z. 1836

But the missionary-tradesmen-teachers in whom Marsden had placed his faith were in fact an ill-assorted bunch who could hardly be regarded as a civilising, evangelising force by the people they had come to convert. With so many of them involved in gun-running, adultery and drunkenness it is not surprising that 10 years passed before the first Maori baptism. Not until the 1820s did the Maori begin to find Christianity an attractive proposition.

The missionaries did accomplish some good. Thomas Kendall was instrumental in compiling the first grammar and dictionary of the Maori language, and in 1820 accompanied two famous chiefs, Hongi and Waikato, to Britain.

in New Zealand waters, and they had no authority over foreign vessels and their crews.

The early missionaries did not want to see New Zealand colonised. They hoped to be allowed to spread what they saw as the benefits of Christian civilisation among the Maori, leaving them uncorrupted by the depravity introduced to earlier colonies by European settlers and adventurers.

But many British people believed that organised and responsible settlement would be able to avoid the disasters inflicted by Europeans upon indigenous peoples of other countries. The most influential proponent of this view was Edward Gibbon Wakefield.

On a less idealistic level, there was also pressure among Britons for new colonies with land for settlement, and the notion that if Britain did not take sovereignty over New Zealand and populate it with European immigrants, some other colonial power – most probably France – would do so. In retrospect, it seems doubtful that the French had any specific designs upon New Zealand.

The "home government" remained steadfastly irresolute, and the issue of colonisation was allowed to drift. By the 1830s, the scramble for land was in full swing – a scramble that was to produce tragic results within 20 years.

The Maori had no concept of permanent, private ownership of land. Their land was held by tribes who traditionally inherited it. A chief's authority was generally strong enough to have a sale accepted by most members of the tribe – but even this could be complicated by conflicting claims of ownership among tribes or sub-tribes, and such claims could involve very large areas. Many land transfers between Pakeha and Maori led to conflicts in the 1860s; some of them are still being legally contested today.

LEFT: Nelson Haven in Tasman Bay, by Charles Heaphy in 1841. **ABOVE:** Edward Gibbon Wakefield, who founded the Colonisation Society.

There was also the problem of what was being bought. The settlers, and the rapacious speculators in Britain, thought they were buying outright freehold land; in many cases, the Maori believed they were merely leasing their lands for a fee.

The missionaries were not skilled in matters of British law, and certainly not in the area of land conveyancing. Nor were they renowned as administrators and they did not want to become involved because of their professed anti-settlement beliefs. The time had finally come for government intervention, however reluctant.

In 1833, with the arrival in the Bay of Islands of James Busby as British Resident, the move was made. The notion of "Resident" was vague. A Resident, in most cases, had the full backing of His or Her Majesty's Government as a diplomat representing British interests in a territory that had not yet been annexed by the Crown. He could advise local chieftains, he could cajole – but he had no real power.

Busby did what he could. He attempted to create some unity and overall sovereignty among the disparate Maori by formally establishing a confederation of Maori chiefs, and then in 1835 he proposed that Britain and the United Tribes of New Zealand should agree to an arrangement under which the confederation would represent the Maori people and gradually expand their influence as a government while the British government, in the meantime, administered the country in trust.

Busby won personal respect from the Maori. Even so, he keenly felt his own impotence and knew he could never achieve law and order without the backing of some adequate force.

The Wakefield Scheme

In the course of the 1830s it had become obvious that land buying was going to cause serious trouble. Speculators were gambling on Britain taking over and settling the country, while Busby, the British Resident, was powerless to prevent such "deals" from taking place. Colonisation, in fact, was developing a kind of inevitability. In 1836, Edward Gibbon Wakefield told a committee of the House of Commons that Britain was colonising New Zealand already, but "in a most slovenly and scrambling and disgraceful manner".

In 1837, at the behest of the government of New South Wales, Captain William Hobson, commanding HMS *Rattlesnake*, sailed from Sydney to the Bay of Islands to report on the situation. Hobson suggested a treaty with the Maori chiefs (which Busby thought he had already achieved) and the placing of all British subjects in New Zealand under British rule. Hobson's report provoked a response, but without Wakefield's influence there might not have been such an outcome.

Wakefield disliked the results of colonisation in the United States, Canada, New South Wales and Tasmania. He believed that if land was sold at what he called "a sufficient price" to "capitalist" settlers, labourers among the immigrants would not disperse thinly but would stay in the new communities working for landowners – at least for a few years until they could save enough to buy land for themselves at the "sufficient price" and employ more recently arrived immigrant labour.

Land prices were crucial to Wakefield's system, and New Zealand his testing ground. Unfortunately he underestimated the aspirations of immigrant labourers who were prepared to suffer extreme isolation in order to farm their own land, and he did not foresee the readiness with which "capitalists" would move out of the centralised settlements to areas they considered more profitable.

During the late 1830s and early 1840s Wakefield helped establish the New Zealand Company. This became a joint stock company so that the people involved would bear the costs of establishing the settlements they planned.

The Treaty of Waitangi

Around this time the British government at last responded to the anti-colonial feelings of the missionary groups. Britain decided that the Maori should be consulted on their own future, and that their consent should be given to the annexation of their country. The result was the Treaty of Waitangi, signed at the Bay of Islands on 6 February 1840 by Lieutenant-Governor William Hobson on behalf of the British government. The treaty was later taken to other parts of the country for signing by most of the Maori chiefs.

Ironically, the treaty was never ratified. Within a decade the Chief Justice, Sir William Martin, ruled that it had no legal validity because it was not incorporated in New Zealand's statutory law. The second irony is that the

date of the original signing of the treaty is now said to be the "founding day" of New Zealand as a British colony, the opposite of what the missionaries had hoped to achieve.

The treaty itself remains a bone of contention. The text of the document was written in English, apparently amended by Hobson after it was first explained to the assembled Maori leaders. A rather loosely translated version in Maori was signed by most of the Maori leaders. The Maori had put much faith in advice from the missionaries, being told that they were signing a solemn pact, under which New Zealand sovereignty was being vested in the British Crown in return

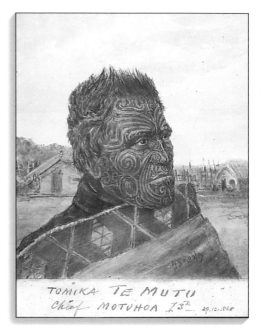

TOMIKA TE MUTU
Chief MOTUHOA Is. 29.12.1865

for guarantees of certain Maori rights. Many Europeans (and also Maori) genuinely believed this, and for some years the British government upheld the agreement.

It is almost impossible now to regard the treaty objectively. In the context of its time it was an example of enlightened respect for the rights of an indigenous population. But because it was never ratified, and never truly honoured by the white settlers hungry for land, it is easily construed these days as an expedient fraud and is the focus of some civil dissent.

The formal British annexation of New Zealand implicit in the 1840 Treaty of Waitangi was quickly followed by the arrival of the first ships carrying immigrants organised by Wakefield's New Zealand Company. The *Tory*, despatched from England before the treaty had been signed and arriving early in 1840, carried a batch of immigrants who were to settle in Wellington. The Wanganui district received its first settlers shortly afterwards, and in 1841 a subsidiary of the Company, based in Plymouth, England, and drawing emigrants from Devon and Cornwall, established New Plymouth.

The South Island was not ignored. Captain Arthur Wakefield, one of Edward's many brothers, arrived at Nelson in 1841 and was followed by 3,000 settlers in 1842.

occasions, and once sacked the entire town as Pakehas scampered off into the woods or took to boats.

George Grey, who arrived as Governor in 1845, called in the army to suppress Hone Heke. With the help of Maori dissidents who refused to support Heke, Grey won the day.

Such open conflict did not encourage emigration. The New Zealand Company went into a decline. It eventually became almost bankrupt in the late 1840s, surrendered its charter, and handed over to the government some 400,000 hectares (about 1 million acres) of land for which about $500,000 were due; the New

In the Bay of Islands, the events in the south were having their repercussions. Hone Heke, a signatory to the Treaty of Waitangi, had become more than disenchanted with the treaty's implications. Although Kororareka (Russell) had been the de facto "capital" of New Zealand before the signing of the treaty, Lieutenant-Governor Hobson decided that Auckland should be the site of the new country's capital. Trade from Russell declined and Hone Heke got fractious. He and his warriors demolished the flagpole (symbol of royal authority) on three

LEFT: Tomika Te Mutu, chief of Motuhoa Island.
ABOVE: stagecoach fording a North Island stream.

THE WAIRAU MASSACRE

Despite (or perhaps because of) the Treaty of Waitangi, land claims soon became a matter of bitter dispute. In 1843, Arthur Wakefield led a party of armed Nelson settlers into the fertile Wairau Valley. He contended that the land had been bought by the Company from the widow of a European trader, who had given the Maori a cannon in exchange. The local chief, Te Rauparaha, and his nephew, Rangihaeata, thought otherwise. When the two sides met, violence broke out. Te Rauparaha's wife was shot and the Maori killed 22 of the Pakeha, including Wakefield.

Zealand Company was finally dissolved in 1858.

Even with the writing on the wall in its last decade of operation, the New Zealand Company remained active, lending its organisational support to members of the Scottish Free Church who established Dunedin in 1848, and to the Anglicans who founded Christchurch in 1850 and quickly opened up the excellent pasturelands of the Canterbury Plains. More and more new settlers imported sheep, mostly merinos, from Australia. What became New Zealand's principal economic asset was soon under way: sheep-farming on a large scale, at first purely for wool, later for lamb and mutton.

Edward Wakefield, architect-in-absence of planned settlement, eventually arrived in New Zealand for the first time in 1852, the year in which the colony was granted self-government by Britain. He achieved much, but at the same time lived long enough (he died in 1862) to see that his ideal of cohesive but expanding communities, complete with "capitalists" and "labourers", was not viable. The immigrants didn't necessarily make the choice for "town life", and many left the infant settlements to establish – or, at least, attempt to establish – agricultural or pastoral properties well beyond the confines of the towns. But, thanks largely to Wakefield's efforts, the settlement and colonisation of New Zealand were achieved in a more orderly manner than had been the case, several decades earlier, in Canada and Australia.

The New Zealand Wars

The new colony, however, was facing problems. There had been a great deal of speculation in land sales, and many Maori were beginning to realise this: land was being sold for as much as 20 times what they had been paid for it.

A direct result of this injustice was the election in 1858 of a Maori "king" by tribes in the centre of the North Island. There had never been such a title among the Maori, who owed their allegiance to a tribe or sub-tribe, but it was hoped that the *mana* (spiritual authority) of a king, uniting many tribes, would help protect their land against purchase by the Pakeha. It didn't work out that way.

In Taranaki, another group of tribes rose up against the government in June 1860 following a blatantly fraudulent land purchase by the colonial administration, the Waitara Land Deal. British regular troops, hastily assembled, were virtually annihilated south of Waitara.

For the next few days, the North Island was ablaze with clashes between Maori and Pakeha. The "Second New Zealand War" (remembering the outbreaks in 1840) was marked by extraordinary courage on both sides. The conflicts were frequently indecisive, but bloody. On the Pakeha side, the brunt of the early fighting, until 1865, was borne by British regular troops, 14 of whom received Britain's highest battle honour, the Victoria Cross.

Between 1865 and 1872 (which was the "official" end of the war, though there was sporadic fighting until the formal surrender of the Maori king in 1881), locally raised militia and constabulary forces played an important role – assisted by some Maori tribes that had decided not to join the Maori king's confederation.

Despite war, the prospects of the country continued to improve. The discovery of gold in the South Island led to a fresh influx of migrants in the early 1860s; the capital was moved from Auckland to Wellington in 1865; and the pursuit of pasture was opening up vast tracts of the country.

LEFT: reverse side of the New Zealand Cross, awarded during the New Zealand Wars. **RIGHT:** one of the many settlers lured by the discovery of gold.

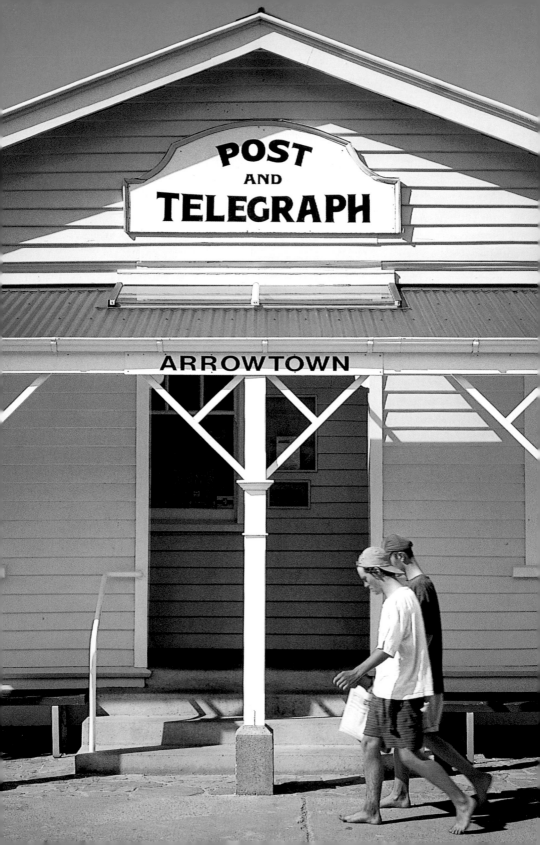

A NEW NATION

The 20th century has seen a series of economic, social and political challenges for the people of New Zealand

Progress towards full independence from Britain began almost as soon as the Maori-Pakeha land wars began to settle down. An economic boom in the 1870s was sparked by Sir Julius Vogel, who as colonial treasurer borrowed heavily overseas for public works construction, notably railways. A flood of immigrants followed, mainly from Britain but also from Scandinavia and Germany.

But Vogel miscalculated the negative impact of his borrow-to-boom credo. In 1880, New Zealand narrowly averted bankruptcy. Within a few years, wool and grain prices dropped so hard that depression set in and unemployment spread rapidly. In 1888, more than 9,000 settlers left the colony, most of them for Australia, which had remained relatively prosperous.

The years of hardship may have had something to do with the emergence of New Zealand as one of the most socially progressive communities in the world. Free, compulsory and secular public-school education was created by law in 1877; two years later, every adult man – Maori as well as Pakeha – won the right to vote.

Lamb for the world's tables

There were some other signs of hope, too, with a new industry emerging that was to help the country make its way in the world for years to come. In 1882, the refrigerated vessel *Dunedin* was loaded with sheep's carcasses; it arrived in England three months later. The voyage was an arduous one, but the meat arrived safely and profits in England were much higher than they would have been for the same meat back in New Zealand. Farmers then began to breed sheep for meat as well as wool, and the frozen meat industry became an economic staple.

In the waning years of the 19th century, a barrage of social reforms was fired by a new Liberal Party government headed by John Ballance.

Sweeping land reforms were introduced, breaking down the large inland estates and providing money for first mortgages to put people on the land. Industrial legislation provided improved conditions for workers, as well as the world's first compulsory system of industrial arbitration. The aged poor were awarded a pension. And for

the first time anywhere (with the exceptions of tiny Pitcairn Island and the American state of Wyoming), women were granted the right to vote on an equal basis with men.

The principal minds behind these great social reforms were William Pember Reeves, a New Zealand-born socialist, and Richard John Seddon, who became prime minister when Ballance died in 1893. Seddon's legendary toughness and political judgement gave him enormous power within the party and in the country.

The burgeoning frozen meat industry and the expansion of dairy exports in the early 20th century saw the affluence and influence of farmers grow. New Zealand politely refused an invita-

---

PRECEDING PAGES: the united colours of modern New Zealand. **LEFT:** the tranquillity of a rural post office. **ABOVE RIGHT:** Richard John Seddon, much admired prime minister from 1893 until his death in 1906.

tion to become a part of the new Common-wealth of Australia and was subsequently upgraded by the British Empire from "colony" to "dominion". The new Reform Party squeezed into power in 1911. New prime minister William Massey was himself a dairy farmer; his election helped consolidate New Zealand's position as an offshore farm for Britain.

World wars and depression

War brought a new sense of nationalism to New Zealand while at the same time reinforcing the country's ties to Britain. Between 1914 and 1918, 100,000 men joined the Australia-New

the nearby Pacific campaign, others in North Africa, Italy and Crete. More than 10,000 died.

American writer James A. Michener once claimed that the bravest soldier in each of the world wars was a New Zealander – Bernard Freyberg in the first and, in the second, Charles Upham, "a stumpy square-jawed chap" whose "behaviour under fire seems incredible". Upham is only the third member of the armed forces to have won the Victoria Cross twice.

Back home, a successful economic stabilisa-tion policy and full employment made the 1940s a decade of relative prosperity. The country emerged from the war with a developed sense

Zealand Army Corps (ANZAC) forces fighting with the Allies in Africa and Europe.

The Great Depression of the 1930s was hard on New Zealand. Curtailed British demand for meat, wool and dairy products led to severe unemployment and several bloody riots.

The new Labour Party swept into power in 1935 and took advantage of the resurgent world economy to pull the nation out of the doldrums. Under prime minister Michael Savage, the nation again moved to the forefront of world social change, establishing a full social security system. Savage led New Zealand into World War II. This time, nearly 200,000 Kiwis were called to battle, many of them under Gen. Douglas MacArthur in

WORLD WAR I

By the time World War I had ended, almost 17,000 New Zealanders had lost their lives. Indeed, the casualties were out of all proportion to the country's population, then about a mil-lion. The futility was underscored by the debacle on Turkey's Gallipoli Peninsula, from 25 April 1915 (a day now marked in memoriam as "ANZAC Day") until British naval evacuation some eight months later; the affair cost the lives of 8,587 Anzacs. Somehow this heroic tragedy, dramatised years later in Peter Weir's film *Gal-lipoli*, gave New Zealand a new identity within the British Empire.

of nationhood. It was an appropriate time, in 1947, for the government to adopt the Statute of Westminster and formally achieve full independence from Britain.

The Labour Party, however, had by then lost its vigour and its defeat in 1949 ended an era. The victors were the National Party, who ran on a platform extolling private enterprise.

The 1950s began with a political tremor as a new National Party government abolished the Legislative Council, the upper house of the national Parliament. New Zealand became one of the few democratic nations with a unicameral legislature. This gave inordinate power to

End of isolation

The first post-war revolution, however, came with the end of isolation. Before mass travel became a possibility, hotels shut at 6pm, restaurants were forbidden to sell liquor and a rigid 40-hour, five-day working week meant shop hours were strictly controlled and most families spent weekends at home. Society remained in that time warp until, in the 1950s, when passenger ships began their trade again. Thousands of young Kiwis went away for their "OE" (overseas experience), almost always to London, and for the first time could compare their society with the old world.

the executive – a Cabinet made up from members of the ruling party. The power to change the law dramatically and within hours enabled the Labour Party to transform the nation's economy – and its whole social structure – in 1984–90.

One of the first actions taken by the unicameral House was the ratification of the ANZUS (Australia-New Zealand-United States) security pact in 1951. This was a clear indication by New Zealand and Australia that they had to look away from Britain to meet their defence requirements.

ABOVE LEFT: even the Cook Islands (here marking ANZAC Day) sent soldiers to war in Europe. **ABOVE:** visits from Britain's Royal Family are still well received.

Air travel and advances in telecommunications in the 1960s and '70s led to radical changes in this narrow, closed, highly controlled society. By the 1980s, shops were staying open to offer extended services into the evenings and weekends, most restrictions were lifted from hotels and taverns, New Zealand wines began to rank with the world's best, and restaurants and cafés made eating-out part of the national culture. On the back of such sophistication, tourism has boomed.

The transition has not always been smooth. In the early 1970s New Zealand began grappling with the problem of diversifying both its production away from bulk commodities and its markets away from Britain. When oil prices soared, debt began to pile up as both Labour and National administrations borrowed and hoped primary production prices would pick up. It was a matter of marketing. But marketing was something New Zealanders had never needed to do. They had lived well for so long, by the relatively simple process of farming well, that the British jump into the European Economic Community (EEC) in 1973 left them in confusion.

Tumultous times

During the 1970s, sheep numbers rose past 70 million for the first time as farmers received ly (up to 17 percent) that farm costs skyrocketed and the Muldoon ministry humiliatingly had to bolster subsidies to New Zealand farmers. All the regulation and readjustment caused an agony of doubt about the short-term future of the economy. By 1984, unemployment had reached 130,000 and the national overseas debt stood at NZ$14.3 billion.

But when a new Labour government came to power towards the end of 1984, farm and other production subsidies were withdrawn virtually overnight, import licences abandoned, wage structures dismantled and a broad policy of economic laissez-faire put in place.

SHOULD AULD ACQUAINTANCE BE FORGOT?

state payments to boost stock numbers. Primary industry was widely subsidised and manufacturing tightly protected in 1975–84.

The trade barriers imposed on Britain by EEC membership, combined with rocketing oil prices, sent the cost of industrial goods sky high.

Led by Sir Robert Muldoon, the National government doubled the tight measures imposed by Labour on immigration, imports and the dollar. Muldoon, a pugnacious man, provoked the anger of trade unionists by imposing a wage freeze, but held his line in the face of numerous strikes and demonstrations.

By the end of the '70s and the beginning of the '80s, internal inflation was raging so strong-

Another change came in the area of foreign affairs, with New Zealand ready at last to assert herself on the international stage. During the 1960s, as France began stepping up a campaign of nuclear testing in its Polynesian possessions, there were several mass demonstrations.

A strong anti-nuclear feeling reached its peak in New Zealand when the Labour government refused nuclear-armed or nuclear-powered US naval vessels entry to New Zealand ports. The Americans insisted on their right as allies under the ANZUS Pact and broke off all defence arrangements with New Zealand.

Labour, under David Lange, pledged to set up a 320-km (200-mile) nuclear-free zone around the shores of New Zealand, and to renegotiate the 33-year-old ANZUS security pact to force the United States to keep nuclear armaments out of New Zealand ports.

Division within the Labour government on other issues had grown so wide, however, that Lange resigned in 1989. After the 1990 election, the new prime minister, Jim Bolger, quickly made it clear his government would stay with economic deregulation. In the mid-1990s the New Zealand economy began to recover and the gov-

No Nukes

In 1990, overwhelming public opinion forced the new National government to maintain the Lange government's anti-nuclear stance.

In 1983, the two governments signed the CER (Closer Economic Relations) pact, and by the beginning of the 1990s, free trade was virtually in place across the Tasman Sea, with only some services still not completely liberated.

Both New Zealand and Australia have also turned their economic attention northwards to the burgeoning economies of Asia. Japan is now New Zealand's second biggest market (behind Australia). More than one third of exports go to Asian markets – more than to North

ernment eased up slightly on its expenditure and its tight monetary policy.

Early in the post-war period, New Zealand had realised that its best economic hope for the future was some sort of pact with Australia. In 1965, the New Zealand Australia Free Trade Agreement (NAFTA) was signed. The plan was gradually to dismantle trade barriers between the two countries, but progress was slow and a better agreement was needed.

America and Europe combined – and almost one third of imports come from Asia. Japan and Singapore have long been trading partners but business is building up with Korea, Thailand, Malaysia, Indonesia, Taiwan and China.

The Maori issue

During the 30 years of social and economic turbulence since the 1960s, New Zealand has proved to be one of the most stable democracies in the world. But there has always been a festering sore beneath the surface, caused by injustices to the Maori over a century ago.

The 1984–90 Labour government acknowledged the validity of Maori claims for land,

ABOVE LEFT: Britain's entry into the EEC (now known as the European Union) was a serious blow to New Zealand's economy.

ABOVE: campaigners for a nuclear-free policy.

fishing grounds and other assets that the Maori insist were illegally taken from them. Their claims are based on the 1840 Treaty of Waitangi.

The Labour government set up the Waitangi Tribunal to consider specific Maori claims, and its work continued under the National government. Many land claims were conceded, particularly where the land was held by the government, and a major fishing concession was awarded to the Maori.

Although there is a consensus that redress is due, a great deal of tension has prevailed over particular Waitangi claims. That tension has spilt over on several occasions. The landmark tree on

One Tree Hill in Auckland *(see page 149)* was attacked; another activist took to the America's Cup yachting trophy with a sledge-hammer, claiming it was a symbol of Pakeha elitism.

Progress towards settlement of land claims continues and is high on the political agenda, but whatever progress is made will fail to please everyone, and tension is likely to continue. The difficulties, however, are seen by many as the growing pains of a new nation.

Cosmopolitan influences and the new economic infrastructure have dramatically re-oriented social attitudes. Whereas for 150 years there was a national sense of egalitarianism, many now believe that to hold its place in the

world the country and its people must work harder and compete more fiercely, both in the domestic market and overseas. This has brought about a growing division between rich and poor – and a new volatility in national politics. The old, narrow division between the two political groupings, neither of them far from the centre, no longer seems wide enough to contain national aspirations.

Electoral reform

Dissatisfaction with the rapid pace of change and with the performance of recent governments was expressed in a referendum on electoral reform. In 1993, the country voted to scrap traditional first-past-the-post elections in favour of a proportional system. Many worried that this would further fragment the structure of political parties – and to an extent it has.

In the 1996 elections, the National Party, led by Jim Bolger, won 44 seats in the 120-member house, while the Labour Party won 37. The New Zealand First Party, having won 17 seats, including four Maori seats off Labour, held the balance of power and emerged as the coalition partner in a new government with the National Party. The situation turned volatile after 1996, with change becoming a constant theme in politics.

In December 1997, Jenny Shipley became the country's first female prime minister, replacing Jim Bolger as leader of the National Party. However, weakened by the break-up of her coalition party and a floundering economy, Shipley lost the 1999 elections to a Labour Party-led coalition, helmed by another woman, Helen Clark. Clark's tough-as-nails approach, helped by a strong domestic economy and lower unemployment rate helped clinch her and the Labour Party a second term at the most recent elections held in 2002.

Despite the vagaries of politics and the economy, there is much about Kiwi life at home that has remained unchanged. New Zealand and New Zealanders have been remade, but the country remains relatively clean, green and uncluttered, and by far the majority still relish the outdoor life of beach and barbecue, or tramping and camping – or simply enjoying that flower and vegetable garden most still have surrounding their suburban homes.

Above left: Labour Party's Helen Clark.
Right: keeping fit in Wellington's modern Civic Square.

THE MELTING POT

Maori, Pacific Islanders and Pakeha are evolving a culture
that is distinctively New Zealand in character

The idea persists that the archetypal Kiwi is a country person – a farmer: dogs at heel, face burnished by the nor'wester, eyes creased against the hard light of the afternoon, peering into the hills for sheep to muster. Perhaps this is because of New Zealand's traditional image as a producer of meat, wool, dairy and horticultural commodities.

In reality, the New Zealander is an urbanite. More than 2 million of the 3.9 million New Zealanders live in or on the perimeter of major cities; there are more people living in Greater Auckland's urban area than in the whole of the South Island. About 90 percent of New Zealanders live in towns of more than 1,000 people.

The majority of the Pakeha (Europeans) who began to populate New Zealand less than 200 years ago were of British origin. Today, close to 80 percent of New Zealanders are of European origin, overwhelmingly from Britain but also from the Netherlands, Croatia and Germany. Maori make up around 13 percent and Pacific Islanders 5 percent. There is also a significant Asian population.

Beginning with the Chinese in the last century and followed by Scandinavians, Germans, Dalmatians, Greeks, Italians, Lebanese, refugees from Nazi-occupied Europe and from more recent tragedies in Indo-China and Africa, there has been a steady flow of immigrants into New Zealand. Since 1990, immigration from Hong Kong, Taiwan and Korea has more than doubled and people of Asian origin have become common in the larger cities.

Migrations

The first great Polynesian migration to this country took place over 1,000 years ago, when Maori began arriving after epic canoe journeys across the Pacific. The second wave of migration was Polynesians from homelands scattered across the Pacific from Tonga in the west to the Cook Islands in the east.

Pacific Islanders currently represent around 4 percent of the population. Most of the immigrants have arrived since the 1960s, their numbers jumping from 14,000 in 1961 to 200,000 in 1996. This second migration had its small

beginnings when Pacific Islanders were brought to New Zealand for training by missionaries. After World War II the islanders came in to fill labour shortages. Once settled, they brought in their families, forming links that extend into virtually every village in the Cook Islands, Western Samoa, Niue, the Tokelaus and Tonga.

Western Samoans make up almost half the numbers of Pacific Islanders here; the Cook Islanders, who have New Zealand citizenship, make up a fifth. In the case of Niue and the Tokelaus, more live in New Zealand than on their home islands. Two-thirds of the Pacific Islanders live in Auckland, many congregated in the southern suburbs.

PRECEDING PAGES: an interesting mix at the helm of a nation; Haka party put on a show. **LEFT:** traditional dances and ethnic costumes survive in local celebrations. **ABOVE RIGHT:** a modern Maori warrior.

The Samoans

As well as being the largest Island group in New Zealand, the Samoans have maintained a stronger church and extended family system than the Cook Islanders. All of Sunday is given over to church attendances, whether Catholic, Presbyterian, Methodist, Congregationalist, Assembly of God, Seventh Day Adventist or Mormon. Full-throat singing and the language are the emphasis of the church activity.

The matai or chief system has not fared so well, its role tend-

ballers excel in their sport in New Zealand. Many of the rugby players have taken their talents back to aid the Western Samoan national team onto the international rugby stage. Now, too, Tongan and Fijian players are regulars in provincial New Zealand teams and some have stepped up to the All Blacks.

DIVERSE METROPOLIS

Many Pacific Islanders live in Auckland, which, together with its Maori numbers, makes it the world's biggest Polynesian settlement.

Cooks, Tongans and others

Many New Zealanders have trouble distinguishing Cook Islanders from indigenous Maori. To see the distinctive language,

ing to be taken over by the churches. One problem of adjustment in New Zealand has been the workplace, which has reversed the traditional Island role by promoting young people and rejecting the older, respected matai. The problem has been compounded by a vigorous work ethic, the man of the house toiling during the day and on any shift work available, the woman at night. This pays much more than the rent, with tithes to the church and money remitted to the extended family back home. Half of Samoa's foreign exchange comes from cash payments from relatives abroad.

Another outlet for their endeavours has been the sports field. Samoan rugby players and net-

culture and dance of the 27,000 resident here, you would have to attend Cook Island church services or social gatherings in such places as Otara, Porirua, Napier and Hastings, or Rotorua and Tokoroa, where many work in the forest industry. Of course, the Cook Islanders might well remind you that several of the great migrating canoes came from the Cooks to New Zealand and that Maori is but a dialect of the parent Cooks language.

The distinctiveness of the Tongan community in New Zealand was defined back in the 1950s when Queen Salote founded the Tongan Society in Auckland, to bring people together and organise social functions. Tongans have since spread around the country. The church has been the major meeting point in the dispersal, particularly the Wesleyan, Free Tongan and United churches. Here Tongans have divided where possible into the same village groups as those back home.

Although the United Nations helped nudge New Zealand into giving Niue independence in 1974, the majority of Niueans choose to live in New Zealand, because their island is too small to support them. The 10,000 Niueans here retain their language and identity largely within their church congregations.

The low-lying Tokelaus have been almost

attitudes towards Pacific Island immigration. A clamp down by the Muldoon Government in the 1970s caused tensions to rise amid claims of racism. A more positive immigration bias in recent times can be seen in the doubling of Tongan numbers here in the last five years to more than 18,000. Government projections expect a doubling of the Pacific Islands population in the next 30 years.

The Celtic question

Immigration policy has often been influenced by prejudice. During the 19th century, Catholic Irish were mostly excluded from the first gen-

wiped out by hurricanes several times, and New Zealand has been their sanctuary. The Tokelauans are among the most celebrated storytellers in the Pacific, which has sustained their morale amidst fragile atoll life.

The largely Melanesian Fijians have been more recent arrivals to New Zealand. Small communities have become established in Auckland and Wellington, doubling to almost 3,000 in the last five years. Fiji Day is a good time to see their celebrated dancing.

Successive governments have taken different

LEFT: couple from the Cook Islands. **ABOVE:** Polynesians are often employed to do heavy manual work.

eration of settlement. The policy was swept away by the gold rush of the 1860s, which saw just about every nationality on earth pour into New Zealand. The Irish accounted for a quarter of the population of the West Coast.

Generally the Irish have been absorbed into the Pakeha mainstream and many have risen to prominence in the political sphere. Richard John Seddon first made his voice heard on the West Coast, where the Irish still have a strong presence. He went on to become the country's most pugnacious prime minister. Robert Muldoon, of Irish-Liverpudlian extraction, emerged out of another significantly Irish settlement, Auckland, to become prime minister in the mid-1970s and early 1980s. Jim Bolger, dominant in National Party politics through much of the 1990s, also has strong Irish roots.

Almost one quarter of the country are of Scottish Presbyterian descent. Their influence is most visible in Dunedin where kilts fly and bagpipes drone whenever a Scottish sporting team comes to the city. Scottish and Caledonian piping and Highland dancing societies are common throughout the country.

Asian increase

The 1990s saw a policy change to actively encourage Asian immigration to New Zealand.

The Chinese have experienced the biggest swing in policy, from when the first Chinese came in the gold rushes. Those Chinese who did not strike gold and were marooned here were characterised by prime minister Seddon as "undesirable" and denied an old age pension.

Many Indians in recent times have fled from a period of political discrimination in Fiji. Indians began coming from Gujarat province around Bombay from the 1920s. The first Indian here was a Sikh, and there is a small Sikh temple outside Hamilton. Many Indians here are Muslim rather than Hindu, and this is reflected in the Islamic Centre built in Auckland. Several

This came about partly with the new recognition of New Zealand's place in the Pacific region, and partly for financial reasons as the country sought to encourage foreign investment.

Many migrants have come from Hong Kong, unsure of their future under Chinese rule. Each had to bring in at least half a million dollars. They were the culmination of a decade in which New Zealand saw its largest ever Asian migration. Chinese, including many from Taiwan, doubled in just five years to almost 38,000. Indians more than doubled in the same period to 27,000, almost the same for the total of other Asian races such as Vietnamese, Cambodians, Japanese, Thais, Malaysians and Filipinos.

hundred families of mostly Buddhist Sri Lankans have also settled here in recent years.

Jews and other Europeans

Jewish merchants have been among the leading citizens in the main centres. One of the earliest to make his mark was treasurer – and later, prime minister – Sir Julius Vogel. In the 1870s he borrowed money from London contacts such as the Rothschilds to finance the great leap forward, bringing in 100,000 immigrants from Europe to develop the road and rail networks.

Perhaps the most successful of Vogel's immigrants were the 5,000 Danes and Norwegians who cut down the forests of the lower North

Island and settled such places as Norsewood and Dannevirke. Eventually 10,000 arrived, settling as quietly into the monoculture as the 1,000 Swiss dairy farmers who were persuaded by Swiss wanderer Felix Hunger to settle the other side of the North Island in the latter half of the 19th century.

German migrants came to New Zealand at the same time as the British and have been coming ever since, except during the two world wars. Once war ended in 1945, New Zealand was recruiting migrants in

ZEELAND TO ZEALAND

The biggest postwar surge was 30,000 Dutch, who left the limited opportunities of their small country in favour of the boom times here.

gum in the north. When the gum ran out they turned to making wine. Ironically they were lumped in with the Germans when World War I broke out and suffered local bully-boy behaviour and prejudice. They persisted, some helping to establish New Zealand's wine industry, initially in the Auckland area. Their names continue to dominate the industry.

Another big name in the wine industry is Corbans, but the family is Lebanese, and typical of many prominent in New Zealand business.

Austria and Germany. The spick and spartan little white wooden Lutheran churches around New Zealand testify to their presence.

The 3,000 Italians who made their own way here around the end of last century, mostly from the Sorrento and Stromboli areas, took up their familiar work as fishermen and tomato growers. The Wellington suburb of Island Bay is still known as Little Italy.

Also at the end of the 19th century, around 1,000 Dalmatians fled the Austro-Hungarian army and joined the British digging for kauri

FAR LEFT: two faces of the melting pot.
ABOVE: celebrating Eastern European origins.

Greeks, Serbs and Croats

The Greeks have trickled here in the same chain migrations as the Italians, and mostly stayed where they arrived, in inner Wellington. However, their presence is flamboyantly apparent around the magnificent Greek Orthodox church. Considerations of community have triumphed over those of climate, and Wellington has benefited over the years. In Masterton, a local church has been converted into the glories of Greek Orthodox iconography.

The only thing to compare with it is the iconostasis or great carved altar of the Romanian Orthodox church in the Wellington suburb of Berhampore, focus for a small Romanian congregation. A few hundred metres away is one of two Serbian churches in Wellington, while several hills away the Croatian community is gathered around its priest, who himself moved across town to join these political refugees from the former Yugoslavia.

Two Yugoslav clubs once opposed each other across an Auckland street, reflecting different waves of migrants. The older Dalmatians have been here long enough to inspire the local ethnic stories of Amelia Batistich. Likewise, Yvonne du Fresne has written her Huguenot/Danish stories in the Manawatu, and Renato Amato was a promising Italian Kiwi writer.

A one-off group of 733 war-orphaned Polish children was given sanctuary here in 1944 following the efforts of prime minister Peter Fraser's wife, Janet. Most of them settled in Wellington, and more than 5,000 Polish refugees followed.

Post-war refugees included Czechs and Slovaks, and in 1968 several hundred more political refugees followed the crushing of the Prague Spring. The other Soviet invasion of a satellite, of Hungary in 1956, brought 1,000 Hungarians here. At least as many Russians have found their way as piecemeal post-war political refugees, many of them Jewish.

More than 7,000 Indo-Chinese "boat people",

fleeing conflict there from the mid-1970s, have accounted for more than 90 percent of refugees in recent times. Small numbers of Russian Jews, Chileans, East Europeans and Assyrians make up the remainder. The Cambodians, Vietnamese and Laotians have been processed through the Mangere immigration centre and helped into jobs around the country.

Following a similar path to a new life have been refugees from wars in Africa. Somali communities, for example, are gradually becoming established in different parts of the country.

Migration has transformed New Zealand's urban areas since the mid-1970s into places with a cosmopolitan diversity most evident in the array of restaurants and delicatessens. While beer hangs on to the declining stakes of the roast leg of lamb Kiwi tradition, earlier migrants have ensured that we have wine to drink with our ethnic meals. And along with rugby and horseracing, Chinese dragon-boat races are increasingly popular events in Auckland and Wellington. New Zealand is officially bi-cultural, but effectively multicultural.

The future

Some would say the melting pot has come about more through accident than design. It was only in the 1980s that New Zealand moved officially from a virtually "white only" immigration policy to one of positive discrimination towards Asian and Pacific migrants. This is already having an impact on the country's social structure.

The "melting pot" ideal still has several issues to resolve, as New Zealand enters the 21st century. Many Maori have expressed concern about the balance between them and the new settlers and some tension has emerged. Maori have sought more consultation on immigration policy and they strongly supported the New Zealand First political party, which campaigned on an anti-immigration platform, in the 1996 election. The primary target of Maori concerns has been the Asian community. They are angered by Asian ownership of New Zealand land while their own land claims under the Treaty of Waitangi have not been resolved. At the same time, Asians who have settled in New Zealand claim they are being unfairly targeted.

ABOVE LEFT: a Thai vendor of rattan in New Zealand.
RIGHT: southern South Island still has strong Scottish links.

MODERN MAORI

Gradually, Maori are gaining a higher profile in all aspects of New Zealand life.
And non-Maori are showing increasing respect for traditional Maori beliefs

If one person has been more responsible than any other for the survival of Maori culture into modern times, it must be the great parliamentarian from the east coast of the North Island, Sir Apirana Ngata (1874–1950). The extent of his contributions to Maoridom make him a figure of enormous significance. By the late 1920s, knighted and made Minister of Native Affairs, Ngata had devised legislation to develop Maori land, established a caring school at Rotorua and initiated a work programme for the building of Maori community facilities.

Working with Ngata to implement national policy at a local level was a group of community leaders including Princess Te Puea Herangi of Waikato (1883–1952). Te Puea was for 40 years the force behind the Maori King Movement, which had grown out of the Maori-Pakeha wars of the 1860s. She raised the morale of her people, revived their cultural activities, built a model village at Ngaruawahia which became the nerve centre of the King Movement, and established thousands of Waikato Maori back on farm land. She also won a wide degree of Maori and Pakeha acceptance for the institution of the Maori kingship, which had previously been regarded with suspicion outside Waikato. Turangawaewae Marae at Ngaruawahia became and remains a focal point for national Maori gatherings.

Today Te Puea's great-niece, Te Arikinui Dame Te Atairangikaahu, keeps the movement alive and commands the direct allegiance of about 100,000 Maori and the respect of the rest.

Rise in living standards

Further consolidation for the Maori people came with the election of a Labour government towards the end of the Great Depression in the 1930s. Labour's welfare programme did more to lift Maori standards of living than any previous measures and ensured the physical survival of the Maori race which had been threatened by

LEFT: the late Sir James Henare, noted Maori leader.
ABOVE RIGHT: a welcoming smile.

diseases introduced by European settlers. The Maori electorate acknowledged this fact by returning only Labour Members of Parliament until New Zealand First gave them another option in the 1996 election.

Following World War II, however, there was a major shift in Maori society. The decline in

rural employment coincided with a rapid expansion of secondary industry in urban areas, which brought Maori into the cities in increasing numbers. In 1945, for example, more than 80 percent of Maori still lived in rural settlements. By the 1980s the figure was less than 10 percent. For the first time, Maori and Pakeha New Zealanders had to live alongside one another.

This new relationship brought difficulties. Maori faced discrimination, some of it obvious, some of it more subtle. Not having had ready access or encouragement to further their education, many of the new urban Maori became trapped in low-paying jobs. Housing conditions were poor, and that led to stereotyping that further hindered their prospects for employment. It was a different world, harsh and lacking the support network that, in the rural environment, was offered by the extended family. Many born in the new environment, struggling for identity and direction, reacted in a strongly anti-social manner. The Maori crime rate increased, adding further to a negative Maori stereotype.

The problems, however, have been recognised, and progress has been made in the past few decades. The education system in New Zealand has gradually adapted to the new demands. *Kohanga Reo* (language nests) have been set up to expose pre-school Maori to Maori language and culture. The school curriculum better reflects the importance of Maori culture to the New Zealand way of life. Programmes have been established to encourage Maori to carry their education through to university, and several new laws ban discrimination in the work place. Legal aid and translation facilities are now available through the courts, and Maori, now officially the country's second language, is occasionally spoken in parliament.

Despite these positive moves, poverty remains a problem for Maori in many areas, and Maori still make up a disproportionate part of the prison population. That has led some com-

THE HUI, A TRADITIONAL MAORI GATHERING

At the start of a *hui*, visitors are called on to the *marae* with a *karanga* – a long, wailing call, performed only by women, that beckons the living and commemorates the dead. Answering the call, the visitors enter the *marae* led by their own women, who are usually dressed in black. Then follows a pause and a *tangi* (ritual weeping) for the dead. This is succeeded by the *mihi* (speeches) of welcome and reply, made by male elders.

At the end of each speech, the orator's companions get to their feet and join him for a *waiata* (song), usually a lament. These formalities over, the visitors come forward and *hongi* (press noses)

with the locals and are absorbed into the ranks of *tangata whenua* for the remainder of the function.

The food served on such occasions is special: meat and vegetables are cooked in a *hangi* or earth oven. There will be a preponderance of seafood, with delicacies such as shellfish, kina (sea egg), eel and dried shark. Fermented corn is a speciality, as is titi (muttonbird). The bread offered is likely to be rewena (a scone-like loaf) or another variety similar to fried doughnuts. Far more than in Pakeha society, eating together is a ritual means of communicating goodwill. Acceptance of such hospitality is often considered as important as offering it.

mentators to suggest the social problems are deep rooted, perhaps going back as far as the colonisation of New Zealand by the Europeans.

The major institution devised to help Maori recover lost ground is the Waitangi Tribunal, established in 1975. This allows Maori to claim compensation – in the form of land, cash or fishing quotas – for resources unfairly taken as a consequence of the European colonisation of New Zealand. Based on the 1840 Treaty of Waitangi, the tribunal has done more than any other measure to address Maori grievances.

Maori today are far more likely to be seen in the work place alongside Pakeha. Maori are

After the opening formalities *(see below left)*, the *hui* will be taken up with public and private discussion of matters of local, tribal and national Maori interest. It will also include community eating, singing and religious services. The participants sleep in the large meeting house or hall, where discussions often go on until the early hours of the morning.

Maori weddings, twenty-first birthday parties, christenings or funeral ceremonies are also quite different in character from those of the Pakeha counterpart. They will include speeches in Maori, Maori songs, Maori proverbs, and an impressive openness about expressing feelings.

going into business and the professions in increasing numbers, and their political power has increased with the advent of proportional representation.

In all aspects of New Zealand life, the Maori profile is growing and a positive stereotype is replacing the old, negative one.

The *hui* offers the most revealing and most moving glimpse of the Maori being Maori. It will usually be held on a *marae* (a courtyard in front of a meeting house) under the supervision of the *tangata whenua* or host tribe.

ABOVE LEFT: the *hongi,* formal Maori greeting.
ABOVE: war canoes, still in ceremonial use.

Maori values, too, pulsate beneath the cloak of Western appearances. Concepts such as *tapu* (sacredness), its opposite, *noa, wairua* (things of the spirit) and *mana* (authority), all persist in modern Maori life.

The fact that the country's two major races now live shoulder to shoulder means that non-Maori are having to show increasing respect for Maori ritual, and for places that are *tapu* (sites of sacred objects, historic events or burials) according to Maori beliefs. Maori ceremonials – especially the *hui* (gathering), the *tangi* (mourning) and *karakia* (prayer) – are increasingly honoured by Pakeha. It is hoped the benefits are there for both races.

MAORI ART

Maori works of art are not only beautiful to look at, but also reveal a great deal about their society's beliefs, history and social structure

The classic art of New Zealand Maori is an unsurpassed Pacific tribal art. Many creative styles and much skilled craftsmanship yielded, and continue to yield, objects of great beauty. To appreciate the achievements of Maori arts and crafts, it is invaluable to have an understanding of the materials used, the techniques of crafts, design and symbolism, and the economic, social and religious requirements that inspired the making of art objects.

The working of wood, stone, bone, fibre, feathers, clay pigments, and other natural materials by skilled craftspeople is at the basis of Maori art and craft, with the carving of wood perhaps the most important craft of all. Canoes, storehouses, dwellings, village fortifications, weapons, domestic bowls, and working equipment were made of wood; Maori culture was basically a wood culture.

Craft categories and art eras

Maori craft objects were of three distinctive categories. The first was communally owned objects, such as war canoes. The second category was intimate things for personal use, such as garments, greenstone ornaments, combs, musical instruments and indelible skin tattoos. The tools of the carver, lines and fishhooks of the fisherman, gardening tools of the field worker, and snares and spears of a fowler were usually made by the users and should be included in this category. The last category was the artefacts of ritual magic kept under the guardianship of priests *(tohunga)* – godsticks, crop gods, and anything else used in ceremonial communication with gods and ancestral spirits. Such things were often elaborate versions of utilitarian objects; an ordinary digging stick, for example, was ornately carved in its ritual form.

Periods of Maori art merge, yet there are four distinctive eras with characteristic features: Archaic, Classic, Historic, and Modern. The Archaic Maori, or moa hunters, were the immediate descendants of the Polynesian canoe navigators who first settled New Zealand. For centuries they survived by hunting, fishing and foraging land and sea. Their art work, including carvings and bone and stone work, is characterised by austere forms that, as pure sculpture, can surpass much of the later work.

In time, the cultivation of the sweet potato (kumara) and other crops, along with an advanced ability to exploit all natural resources of forest and ocean, allowed a settled way of village life. With it there came food surpluses, a tightly organised tribal system, and territorial boundaries. These people have been called the Classic Maori. Because of the changes within Maori society, it became possible to support dedicated craftspeople within the community.

The Historic period of Maori art underwent rapid changes due to the adoption of metal tools, Christianity, Western fabrics, newly introduced crop plants, muskets and cannon. After 1800, warfare became particularly horrible as the first tribes to possess muskets descended on traditional enemies still armed with clubs and spears.

Arawa (Flower of the Arawa), first erected at Maketu, Bay of Plenty, in 1868, is in the Auckland Museum (*see page 330*). The great days of the *pataka* ended, yet communal meeting houses became increasingly useful during the Historic period. Indeed, they became the focal point of Maori social life and of a Maori art revolution.

The fourth period of Maori art, the Modern, was under way before 1900, and remains with us. The great rise in interest in Maori culture (*Maoritanga*) in recent decades is in step with a renaissance of Maori culture. The roots of this Maori art resurgence reach well back into the 19th century, yet it was the early 20th-century

Representation of A WAR CANOE of NEW ZEALAND, with a View of Gable End Foreland

Palisaded villages (*pa*) were no longer defendable so they were duly abandoned. The great war canoes also became useless as the gunpowder weapons changed the strategy of battle. Large storehouses were built as the new potato crops and the acquisition of foreign goods ushered in a new type of economy. These structures themselves became obsolete as Western-style sheds and barns proved more practical.

Fine storehouses (*pataka*) of this era have been preserved in museums. One, Puawai-o-te-

PRECEDING PAGES: inside a Waitangi meeting house. **ABOVE LEFT:** a Maori *koru* symbol used as a logo for Air New Zealand. **ABOVE:** a Maori war canoe.

leaders, notably Sir Apirana Ngata and Sir Peter Buck (Te Rangi Hiroa), who advocated the study and renewal of Maori art. The meeting house proved an ideal, practical medium.

Well-dressed warriors

Maori society and the arts have always been associated with fighting chiefs who exercised their hereditary rights in controlling tribal affairs. They were always the best dressed, ornamented and accoutred; tribal prestige (*mana*) depended on these leaders.

Society as a whole was an autocratic hierarchy. Individuals belonged to extended families (*whanau*) which in turn clustered to form sub-tribes *(hapu)* which were allied as tribes through blood ties. Genealogical trees led back to ancestral canoes *(waka)*, the names of which provided tribal names.

Society was divided into two classes, which overlapped to some degree. The upper class was composed of the nobles *(ariki)* and the generals or chiefs *(rangatira)*. The majority lower class was made up of the commoners *(tutua)*. Outside these classes were the slaves *(taurekareka)* who held no rights. These unfortunates did menial work and sometimes died as sacrificial victims or to provide food when special events required human flesh.

People dressed according to rank, yet when engaged in daily routine work both high and low classes used any old garments. Men and women wore a waist wrap, plus a shoulder cloak when weather or ceremony required. Prepubescent children usually went about naked. On attaining adulthood, it was considered indecent to uncover the sexual organs.

The special indication of rank was facial tattoo. Tattooists were well paid, proportionate to their skill, in goods and hospitality. Men were tattooed over the whole face in painful, deep-grooved cuts made by birdbone chisels dipped in a sooty pigment, which looked blue under the skin. Northern warriors often had additional tattoos over buttocks and thighs. Women were deeply tattooed about lips and chin, but the lips were made blue by the use of comb-type "needles". The remarkable art of the tattooist can still be seen on Maori mummified heads. Traditionally, the heads of enemies were taken home to be reviled but those of kinsfolk were preserved to be mourned over. Mummification was by a process involving steaming, smoking and oiling, and heads so treated remained intact and retained hair, skin and teeth. Out of respect for Maori beliefs, such heads are rarely shown as exhibits in museums, and there is currently strong pressure by Maori for the return of mummified heads held by overseas museums.

Tattooists and other craft specialists were generally drawn from the higher ranks and were respected priests. Skill in craft work was honoured by chiefs and commoners alike, and even the nobles turned their hands to creative art work. High-ranking women enjoyed making fine garments and chiefs often filled in leisure hours with carving chisel in hand, working on a box or some other small item.

Art for warriors and gods

A well-appointed warrior was not fully dressed without his weapons: a short club thrust into his belt and a long club held in hand. Weapons were always kept near, mostly for the practical purpose of defence, as a stealthy, sudden attack on an unsuspecting foe was admired. Weapons were essential in the practice of oratory as they were flourished to stress the points of a speech.

Religious inspiration in Maori art was based on the prevailing beliefs about gods and ancestral spirits. In pre-Christian times supernatural beings were believed to inhabit natural objects. Rituals and chants were thus necessary to ensure the successful pursuit of any task.

People, handmade items and natural objects were all thought to have an inner psychic force called *mana*. This key idea is essential to the understanding of Maori art and behaviour. *Mana* has many shades of meaning, such as prestige, influence, authority, and most significant, psychic power. *Mana*'s presence was traditionally manifested in efficiency or effectiveness, such as a warrior's success in a battle or a fishhook's fish-catching ability. *Mana* increased with success or decreased through improper contact or pollution. If a chief or his possessions were touched by a person of lower rank, then there was pollution and *mana* was diminished.

In traditional Maori society the sexes were kept apart in all their craft activities. While men worked the hard materials of wood, bone and stone, women followed crafts using soft materials such as flax strips (as in mat and basket plaiting) or they prepared flax fibres used in making garments and decorative *taniko* borders. It was believed women were created from the earth by Tane. The first man was a direct spiritual creation of the god Tu. Thus it was said that women were *noa* – non-sacred – and the male, conversely, a sacred *tapu* being. This put females in a subservient position which precluded them from high religious practices and from crafts and activities in which high gods and ancestral spirits were directly involved. Women were not allowed to approach men working at their crafts. This was the law and severe punishment followed any infringement.

Chiefs and priests had the highest status; they attained their positions only after a long apprenticeship with training in religious rites.

Art also had peaceful ends. Wooden stickgods *(tiki wananga)*, bound with sacred cords and dressed in red feathers, were used by priests when communicating with gods and ancestral spirits to protect the welfare of the tribe. Stone crop gods *(taumata atua)* were placed in or near gardens to promote fertility in growing crops.

Remarkable wooden burial chests of *tiki* form, hollowed out and backed with a slab door, were used to contain the bones of the deceased. Maori burial practice, at least for persons of rank, required an initial burial, then a recovery of the bones a year or two later when a final, ceremonial burial would take place. The spirit of the deceased was thought to journey to Cape Reinga, at the North Island's northern tip, where it plunged into the sea, en route to the ancient homeland of Hawaiki. Burial chests often have a canoe-like form; some even possess a central keel ridge. These magnificent chests, concealed in caves or in other hidden places, were found in the Auckland districts and many have been preserved in museums.

Monuments and cenotaphs of various forms were erected in memory of the dead. Some were posts with carved *tiki* while others took the form of canoes buried in the earth deeply enough to stand vertically. Posts were also erected to mark tribal boundaries and to commemorate momentous events.

Maori motifs

Maori art can appear as a disordered jumble. However, an understanding of the small number of symbols and motifs used reveals orderliness. The human form, dominant in most compositions, is generally referred to as a *tiki* and represents the first created man of Maori mythology. *Tiki* represent ancestors and gods in the sculptural arts, and may be carved in wood,

LEFT: a Maori king with elaborate facial tattoo.
ABOVE RIGHT: a Maori woman with a decorated gourd.

PRECIOUS POSSESSIONS

The possessions of the Maori demonstrate their most exquisite art work. Combs, feathered garments, treasure boxes, cloak pins, greenstone ornaments (including *hei-tiki,* ancestral pendants) and weapons were often given a "personal touch" to reflect the *mana* (authority) of their owner. Wooden treasure boxes *(wakahuia)* were made to contain precious items such as greenstone ornaments or feathers. These lidded boxes, designed to be hung from house rafters, were ornately carved on all sides, especially on the underside as they were often looked at from below.

bone or stone. The nephrite (greenstone) *hei-tiki* is the best known of ornaments. In ceremonial meeting-house architecture, ancestral *tiki* were carved on panels supporting the rafters or on other parts of the structure. They were highly stylised with large heads to fill in areas of posts or panels. This design also stressed the importance of the head in Maori belief. The head was, along with the sexual organs, the most sacred part of the body.

Sexual organs were often exaggerated in both male and female carved figures and both penis and vulva were regarded as centres of potent magic in promoting fertility and protection.

Tiki figures often have slanted, staring eyes, clawed hands with a spur thumb, a beaked mouth and other bird-like features. These bird motifs were superimposed on the basic human form to create a hybrid – a bird-man – and probably stemmed from the belief that the souls of the dead and the gods used birds as spirit vehicles.

The *manaia*, another major symbol, is a beaked figure rendered in profile with a body that has arms and legs. When it is placed near *tiki* it appears to bite at them about the head and body. Sometimes *manaia* form part of the *tiki* themselves and often alternate with *tiki* on door lintels. They may represent the psychic power

Small birth figures were placed between the legs or on the bodies of *tiki* representing descending generations. The bodies of panel figures were often placed in the contorted postures of the war dance. The out-thrust tongue was an expression of defiance and of protective magic.

Local styles of carving differ in many respects. The figures of the east coast Bay of Plenty region are square while those of Taranaki and Auckland districts are sinuous.

The Maori *tiki* carver provided material objects to serve as the vehicles of gods and ancestral spirits. Some post figures are portraits depicting an individual's tattoo, though most are stylisations of beings not of the mortal world.

of the *tiki*. In form, it is a bird-man or lizard-man. Lizards made rare appearances in Maori woodcarving and other sculptural arts.

Whales *(pakake)* and whale-like creatures appeared on the slanting façades of storehouses. The head part terminates at the lower end in large, interlocking spirals representing the mouth. Some fish, dogs and other creatures occurred in carvings, but on the whole they are rare; there was no attempt to depict nature in a naturalistic way.

Marakihau, fascinating mermen monsters of the taniwha class (mythical creatures that lurked in river pools and caves), appeared on panels and as greenstone ornaments. *Marakihau* were probably ancestral spirits that took to the sea and are depicted on 19th-century house panels with sinuous bodies terminating in curled tails. Their heads have horns, large round eyes and tube tongues, and were occasionally depicted sucking in a fish. *Marakihau* were supposedly able to swallow canoes with their crews.

Painted patterns can be seen on rafter paintings and are based on a curved stalk and bulb motif called a *koru*. Air New Zealand uses a *koru* as the company logo.

CHANGE IN METHOD

When Europeans introduced metals, the old stone tools were cast aside in favour of iron blades, which altered carving techniques.

was lashed to a short wooden handle. Stone-pointed rotary drills and various wooden wedges and mallets completed the Maori stone-age tool kit.

The introduction of oil-based paints quickly ousted the old red ochre pigment *(kokowai)*, which can be seen today only in traces on older carvings. The later practice of overpainting old carvings with European red paint was unfortunate in that it obliterated much patination and often the older ochres, resulting in the loss of much poly-

Stone and bone

The tools and materials of the Maori craft work were limited to woods, stone, fibres and shells; metal tools did not exist. Adzes, the principal tools of woodcarvers, were made of stone blades lashed to wooden helves. Adzing art was basic to all traditional Maori wood sculpture. Forms were first adzed, then chisels were used to give surface decoration. Greenstone was the most valued blade material. Chisels had either a straight-edged or gouge-type blade which

---

ABOVE LEFT: Maori woodcarver Keri Wilson working on wood. **ABOVE:** detail of sculpture from Ohinemutu village in Rotorua.

chrome-painted work of the Historic period.

The relatively soft yet durable totara and kauri trees, the latter available only in the warm, northern parts of the North Islands, were favoured by the carvers. Hardwoods were also abundant. The nephritic jade *(pounamu)*, known today as greenstone, was valued as a sacred material. Found only in the river beds of the Arahura and Taramakau on the West Coast of South Island, this rare commodity was widely traded. Greenstone is of such a hard texture it cannot be scratched by a steel point. To work it in the days before the diamond cutters of the lapidary was laborious. The worker rubbed away with sandstone cutters to abrade a greenstone piece into the form of a pendant, *hei-tiki*, weapon or some other object.

Bone was used in many ways. Whalebone was especially favoured for weapons, while sperm-whale teeth made fine ornaments and dog hair decorated weapons and cloaks. The brilliant feathers of New Zealand birds were placed on cloaks in varied patterns. The iridescent *paua* (abalone) shell was used as inlay in woodcarving, and textile dyes were made from barks. A deep black dye was obtained by soaking fibres in swamp mud.

Flax plants were used by Maori in many ways. Green leaf strips could quickly be made

into field baskets or platters, or could be water-soaked, pounded and bleached to produce a strong fibre for warm garments, cords and ropes. Maori war canoes, houses and foodstores were assembled using flax cord. Metal nails did not exist, and the Maori did not use pegs as wooden nails.

Communal meeting houses

Ornate meeting houses *(whare whakairo)* played a vital role in the 19th century in providing places to congregate for social purposes, although most of the bigger gatherings were held in the large open area *(marae)* in front of the principal houses. It was on the *marae* that

the common problems and issues affecting the tribe were resolved through formal meetings *(hui)*. The ravages of foreign diseases, destruction and loss of lands and the fighting with settlers placed a huge strain on the Maori population and that was reflected in the large number of meeting houses built. To this day many can be seen throughout the North Island.

After the arrival of the Europeans, meeting houses were often constructed with the aid of steel tools and milled timbers. In due time, corrugated iron roofing was added and Western architectural ideas, combined with Maori concepts of building, proceeded into the 20th century, culminating in the modern community halls. Sometimes the house of a chief would serve as a meeting house, though carvings were small and lightly decorated. In the 1900s, highly ornamented meeting houses continued to be the focus of Maori social activities.

Often, important Maori buildings were named after an ancestor and symbolised the actual person; the ridge pole represented the spine, the rafters were his ribs, and the façade boards, which at times terminated in fingers, were his arms. At the gable peak was the face mask. Some tribe members still believe that when they enter a particular house they are entering the protective body of their ancestor.

Many communal houses can be visited. A fine example is Tama-te-Kapua at Ohinemutu, Rotorua, built in 1878. While Maori meeting houses are often on private property, visitors are welcome with prior permission.

Maori music

Music plays a major role in Maori life. Flute-like wind instruments were fashioned by Classic Maori from wood, whalebone and even stone. Traditional chants and songs *(waiata)* are an important feature of ceremonies such as funerals *(tangi)* and weddings, as is Maori dance. Maori dance is both rhythmic and physical, with the beat added by the slapping of chest and thighs with the hand, foot stamping, or sometimes by the hitting of sticks. Drums were unknown. "Concert Parties" now take part in competitions each year to find the best, and some groups travel the world to perform.

ABOVE LEFT: Maori carving from the Anglican church in Tikitiki. **RIGHT:** sketch of a *moko* (facial tattoo) in Hawke's Bay Museum.

Names of Tatus

V Shape centre fo[r]

Bands on forehea[d] and temples TI[W]

where these in made o[r] the eyelids ?

ornament on l[o] of Tiwhana a[t] corner of eyel[id] PU

ornament over between the KOH

double spiral upper part of N

notching do[wn] nose. Whak

double spirals nostrils Pong[a]

pattern over Lip H

Both Lips tat[t] Ngutu pu

Pattern on the Kau

8 Bands from [t] to chin patter[n] RERE

stab on the outer B centre of the C

SPIRAL on the upper cheeks
KOWIRI →

lines of above, just under the eyes

THE CULTURAL SCENE

New Zealanders have wasted no time in making their mark

in the visual arts, poetry, music, film and architecture

Sheep should not necessarily be regarded as New Zealand's greatest export. Its artists have also made their mark on the wider world. Two of the most famous, writer Katherine Mansfield and painter Frances Hodgkins, were prophets without honour in their own country. But with the increased speed of travel and the sophisticated communications of the "information super-highway", local artists have more recently been able to make an international impact while staying at home. Over the past decade New Zealand arts and crafts have begun to carve out their own identity – one with its roots in the South Pacific. A tradition of artistic mimicry has given way to a new Kiwi self-confidence expressed perhaps most strongly in literature, film and theatre. Opera diva Kiri Te Kanawa, once a more familiar sight in Milan than Masterton, now makes regular trips back to New Zealand to perform. Writers such as Witi Ihimaera, Albert Wendt, Patricia Grace and Keri Hulme are all international figures and "ours".

Geographical isolation has become a "plus" as more artists and musicians feel they can live and work here, yet extend the audience for their work beyond New Zealand shores.

Fine arts

The locals have not always been receptive to art. In 1982, the McDougall Gallery in Christchurch planned to spend $10,000 on a painting by Colin McCahon, arguably the country's most significant and contentious painter, and there was outrage. But McCahon (1919–87) has been deified in the last decade. His paintings fetch high prices and are held in many international collections. He painted in virtual seclusion, accustomed to a high level of incomprehension of his work which embraced the pre- and post-modern, the religious, the abstract and a love of the land. McCahon was never part of any "ism", but his work has had tremendous influence.

PRECEDING PAGES: a potter's workshop. **LEFT:** Dame Kiri Te Kanawa performs. **ABOVE RIGHT:** Maori dancers.

A contemporary of McCahon is Gordon Walters, an artist who investigates the relationship between a deliberately narrow range of forms, mostly the *koru* or fern bud. The interpretation of this local Maori symbol in a recognisably European abstract style, which has much in common with Klee or Mondrian, gives Wal-

ters' work a distinctively New Zealand flavour.

Auckland's Aotea Centre has a permanent collection of modern New Zealand art, and many dealer galleries exhibit the work of upcoming and established international New Zealand artists such as Sir Toss Woollaston, Gretchen Albrecht, Pat Hanly and Ralph Hotere.

Increasingly, New Zealand visual artists have allied themselves with political causes or movements. The works of Maori women such as Robyn Kahukiwa, Kura Te Waru Rewiri and Shona Rapira Davies demonstrate a concern for the land, *whanau* (family), anti-racism and anti-sexism, and reflect the resurgence of Maori pride and values.

Len Lye (1901–80) may yet be the greatest expatriate New Zealand artist. He won an international reputation as a pioneer of direct film techniques (scratching images directly on to celluloid) and as a kinetic sculptor. Several of his works are to be found at the Govett-Brewster Gallery in New Plymouth, which specialises in the work of New Zealand sculptors.

Prose and poetry

"I made my first story on the banks of the Mataura River after a meal of trout and billy tea: 'Once upon a time there was a bird. One day a hawk came out of the sky and ate the bird. The

maera, Patricia Grace and Albert Wendt, have arguably had the biggest impact on the New Zealand literary scene in the 1980s and '90s. Keri Hulme achieved worldwide literary status with her Booker Prize-winning novel, *The Bone People*, in 1985 and continues to write from her home in the South Island.

Music

Rock musicians from New Zealand no longer have to go to Australia, or be considered Australian, to make it on the world stage. Crowded House became an international act while still recording in New Zealand and seeking a "New

next day a big bogie came out from behind the hill and ate up the hawk for eating up the bird.' The story's not unusual told by a child of three. As I still write stories I'm entitled to study this and judge it the best I've written."

So said novelist Janet Frame in the literary magazine, *Landfall*. Her love of writing was nurtured as a child living in a poor South Island family. Born in 1924, Frame has published over 20 novels, four collections of stories, poetry and children's books and three volumes of autobiography – *To the Island, An Angel at My Table,* and *The Envoy From Mirror City*.

Apart from Janet Frame, Maori and Pacific Island post-colonial novelists, such as Witi Ihi-

POETIC LICENCE

One of New Zealand's most colourful poets was James K. Baxter (1926–72). He left his family to set up a commune at Jerusalem, a small Maori settlement on the Whanganui River. Here he lived as a self-appointed guru, spurning materialism and churning out verse. An excerpt from James K Baxter's poem "In Praise of the Taniwha".

Te Ra is on his throne; the girdle of clouds is lifting –
E Koro, you who lie in your nest below the bridge,
In my old coat I wander out to walk on the river
bank and praise the world Te Matua is making.
The ancient One, whose sign is that pure disc in
the sky –

Zealand" sound. Pauly Fuemana was a huge sensation with his hit "How Bizarre". Though many radio stations still pump out predominantly foreign pop music, local musicians' chances of air time have increased. Artistes like Bic Runga, Dave Dobbyn, Pacifier and King Kapisi produce a distinctly local sound.

Classical music-lovers are well served by the New Zealand Symphony Orchestra and regional orchestras in the four main centres and there is a flourishing chamber music and jazz scene. Opera has made a real comeback in New Zealand. World-class productions are regularly staged in the main centres, each of which has its

works, *The End of the Golden Weather* and *The Pohutukawa Tree*, many times in theatres and country halls up and down the land.

Fellow-playwright Roger Hall has enjoyed enormous success with his plays *Middle Age Spread* (which was performed in London's West End) and *By Degrees* among others.

Film

In recent years New Zealand directors have certainly made their mark, in particular, Peter Jackson, award-winning film director of the acclaimed film *Lord of the Rings*. Jackson, who lives in Wellington, filmed the epic trilogy –

own opera company. Performances by Dame Kiri Te Kanawa, Dame Malvina Major and Sir Donald McIntyre guarantee packed houses.

Theatre

Professional theatre is alive and well in New Zealand's major cities. The playwright to whom New Zealand actors and writers owe a great debt is Bruce Mason (1921–82). He was a one-man theatrical band whose source material was purely local. Mason performed his classic

LEFT: a self-drive water sculpture on the Coromandel Peninsula. ABOVE: the good guys and the baddies from Peter Jackson's acclaimed *Lord of the Rings*.

using international and local actors and crew – entirely on location in New Zealand. Although she is now based in Australia, New Zealanders claim Jane Campion, director of the hugely successful film *The Piano*, as their own. *Once Were Warriors* by Maori director Lee Tamahori, featuring an all-Maori cast, enjoyed box office success and several awards.

The feature film industry has enjoyed considerable success since the late 1970s, starting with Roger Donaldson's *Sleeping Dogs*, which starred Sam Neill. The industry received a considerable boost from the New Zealand Film Commission and many local smash hits have followed. They include Geoff Murphy's *Good-*

bye Pork Pie, Vincent Ward's *Vigil* and Harry Sinclair's *Topless Women Talk About Their Lives*. Recent decades have also seen the rise of a new generation of female film makers such as Merata Mita, Sima Urale, Gaylene Preston and Alison McLean.

Dance

The backbone of dance in New Zealand is still ballet, and each week thousands of girls and boys do their pirouettes and *pliés* and dream of a place at the New Zealand School of Dance or the Royal New Zealand Ballet in Wellington.

The Royal New Zealand Ballet does a good

job of maintaining a balance between commercial survival and artistic relevance. The survival of contemporary dance is precarious too. For many years Mary-Jane O'Reilly's Limbs dance company showed New Zealanders a different way of dance. Limbs has been succeeded by Douglas Wright and Michael Parmenter, two local contemporary dancers and choreographers.

Pottery

Pottery is rapidly becoming one of the country's most developed art forms. It first flourished after the second world war, with immigrant potters taking advantage of the country's rich clays. The beauty and isolation of areas like Nelson

and the Coromandel Peninsula also suited the alternative lifestyle that pottery offered.

Barry Brickell in Coromandel, Harry and May Davis of Crewenna and the Lairds of Waimea Potteries (both in Nelson) trained many contemporary potters. Helen Mason on the east coast inspired a generation of young Maoris. Len Castle of Auckland, with his emphasis on simple forms and "clay for clay's sake", was one of the first full-time potters.

Weaving and carving

In a nation of so many sheep, it's hardly surprising that spinning, weaving and the fibre arts are very high on the craft profile. Many weavers are moving into spectacular "art" tapestries, some of them multi-dimensional. There has also been a revival of the Maori art of flax weaving led by weavers such as Rangimarie Hetet and Emily Schuster. Others have created Maori-inspired works which are highly contemporary.

A number of craftspeople, both Maori and Pakeha, now carve wood, bone and the traditional greenstone *(pounamu)* to create their own designs or imitate traditional Maori ones. Auckland's Te Taumata Gallery and Fingers jewellery co-operative display examples of this.

Architecture

New Zealand is a laboratory for the student of architecture who, with care, can observe every style from Renaissance, Gothic, Victorian and Bauhaus to "nouveau concrete".

While the glass towers of Auckland, the Aotea Centre and Sky City are rather dubious tributes to the work of late 20th-century architects, Wellington's cityscape is probably the best example of the work of contemporary architects. Architect Ian Athfield, whose style amounts to a one-man revolution, has been instrumental in erecting or rebuilding some of the capital's more spectacular buildings. His public library adjoins the Michael Fowler Centre (designed by Miles Warren) and the Wellington City Art Gallery to provide a unified and flowing cultural "heart" to the city. The Museum of New Zealand – Te Papa Tongarewa – reflects the influence of design which has its roots in Pacific culture.

ABOVE LEFT: a colourful display on the Coromandel Peninsula.
RIGHT: artist at work, Wellington Sculpture Festival.

FOOD AND WINE

*Over the past few decades, New Zealand has undergone a revolution in its food
and drink. Today its chefs and fine wines are in demand across the globe*

Gone are the days when farmers' wives were asked to "bring a plate" to social get-togethers while their menfolk set up the beer keg. Yet while those clingfilm-wrapped platters of asparagus rolls, savoury cheese balls and Anzac biscuits have gone out of style, they haven't been totally scorned. Instead, pioneer recipes that use local ingredients to modify traditional English dishes have been added to the cuisines of other ethnic groups – Maoris, Italians, Fijians, Taiwanese, Vietnamese, Thais and Tamils. Each wave of New Zealand immigrants has contributed new ingredients and ideas to the pot. The result is a fresh Pacific rim cuisine distinct from that of Australia or the West Coast of the United States. New Zealand food at every level is a savoury jumble of flavours. Order a plate of chips from a bar menu and the chances are they'll be cut from kumaras – Maori sweet potatoes – then served with a Thai chili sauce or heaped portion of South Island oysters and pumpkin mayo.

New Zealanders have come to appreciate the worth of their natural ingredients – fresh and usually organic – whether it be wild venison, rainbow trout, cheeses or traditional Maori foods such as greenshell mussels and mutton birds. Poor man's tucker in this land of plenty has been remarketed as gourmet products for export. The humble Chinese Gooseberry became a kiwi fruit and the darling of 1980s nouvelle cuisine menus, while, more recently, the tree tomato re-emerged as a *tamarillo*, a hot and spicy fruit to accompany meat dishes.

BYO – Bring Your Own – restaurants are everywhere. You can spend an afternoon wine tasting in the vineyards, and then take your favourites along to the restaurant of your choice.

At least once during your visit, do as the locals do and catch your own dinner. Borrow hook and line and fish for snapper from the pier at Tutukaka in Northland; follow families of Pacific islanders to Auckland's Cockle Bay at low tide and gather bucketfuls of fresh cockles to bake over an open fire; or collect mussels for your own thermal bake at Hot Water Beach on the Coromandel, where boiling water gushes from the hot sand. Dig a small hole to cook dinner while you soak in a larger (cooler) pit that you've dug earlier – a DIY jacuzzi.

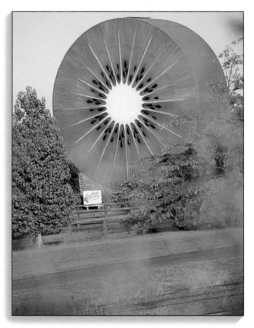

Regional specialities

Because New Zealand is small, with an efficient transport system, most regional delicacies can be obtained around the country, including:

- **Whitebait**, the tiny infant stage of several fish species, caught in nets at tidal river mouths, mostly on the West Coast of the South Island and in the Waikato River in the central North Island. These are usually served whole as egg-bound fritters.
- **Bluff oysters**, from the bottom of the South Island. Similar to French Belons, and equally flavoursome.
- **Kumara**, the much-loved indigenous sweet potato. Delicious boiled, steamed, baked or

LEFT: Pacific Rim cuisine in the open air.
ABOVE RIGHT: glorifying the national fruit.

mashed. Also a popular component of the *hangi*, a Maori feast cooked in an earth oven.

• **Greenshell mussels**, different from the black-shelled varieties found overseas. Inexpensive, they are usually sold live in supermarkets.

• **Paua**, the local abalone, has a rather unappetising green/black colour, but tastes wonderful when quickly cooked.

• **Tuatua**, local clams, are often chopped and used in fritters.

• **Pipi** are similar to tuatua, and usually found in coastal estuaries.

land. Most, by far, make less than 200,000 litres (45,000 gallons) each year. Only three – Montana, Villa Maria and the House of Nobilo – produce over two million litres (450,000 gallons).

Each of the "Big Three" companies produces wine under a number of other names – Montana, for example, produces wines under an array of different labels, Corbans, Lindauer, Robard & Butler, Timara and Longridge, among others; while Villa Maria bottles wines under the Vidal and Esk Valley labels.

BYO BOTTLE

At many establishments, patrons can take along their own favourite wines, which will be opened for a small "corkage" fee. Look for "BYO" (Bring Your Own) in the restaurant's publicity.

Wines

New Zealand wines that have made it big overseas include Marlborough's Cloudy Bay Sauvignon Blanc and West Auckland's Kumeu River Chardonnay. The Cloudy Bay is what Marlborough Sauvignon Blanc is all about – intensely aromatic, superbly refreshing and reeking of sunshine. The Kumeu River is made in more of a French style than many New Zealand Chardonnays (winemaker Michael Brajkovich MW was trained in France). Reds and bubblies are catching up, however, with some brands winning top prizes in international wine challenges and competitions abroad.

There are around 250 wineries in New Zea-

New Zealand's range of latitudes is equivalent to that of other fine wine regions – the Rhine, Alsace, Burgundy and Bordeaux. The country is regarded as a cool climate region partly because of its narrowness, and the consequent maritime influence.

It is interesting to compare the climate with that of other grape growing regions. This is best done by measuring the Degree/Days. This system, first developed in California, measures the number of times each year that the temperature exceeds a certain figure. The actual formula is quite complex, but essentially, the higher the number, the warmer the region.

Using this system, Auckland, with a

Degree/Days reading of 1601, is almost identical to the Napa Valley, with 1600. Hawke's Bay has 1362, Bordeaux comes in at 1328. Burgundy at 1278 is close to Gisborne, with 1206, and Coonawarra, in South Australia, is just above Marlborough's 1123 with 1206. At 923, Canterbury is close to Champagne, with 1011, while Central Otago, on 908, is a little lower than Geisenheim, in Germany, with 994.

Major wine producing regions

Grapes are grown from the top of the North Island to the bottom of the South. Try the wines from these major regions:

• **Auckland** is difficult because of high humidity, but capable of producing good, solid reds, particularly based on Merlot, and excellent Chardonnay and Sauvignon Blanc. Waiheke Island, in Auckland's Hauraki Gulf, produces some of the most exciting Cabernet/Merlot blends in the country.
• **Hawke's Bay** produces excellent Cabernet/Merlot and Chardonnay; Sauvignon Blanc that is less aromatic than its Marlborough cousin, but equally enjoyable; and crisp, floral Riesling.
• **Gisborne** is known as a bulk growing region, but also home to some excellent, full-flavoured Chardonnay and Chenin Blanc, and aromatic Gewürztraminer. Merlot produced in this area also shows promise.
• **Martinborough/Wairarapa** is developing as the natural home of Pinot Noir. Also produces top Chardonnay, good Riesling and a tiny amount of the country's best Pinot Gris.
• **Marlborough** is famous for Sauvignon Blanc, but also capable of producing excellent Riesling and elegant, citric Chardonnay. Cabernet-based wines are often green and vegetal, but when Merlot dominates they are considerably better. Also home to many of the country's best Méthode Champenoise sparkling wines.
• **Nelson** is tiny in production terms, and climatically similar to Marlborough. Produces good Riesling, Chardonnay, Sauvignon Blanc and Pinot Noir.
• **Canterbury/Waipara** makes good Riesling, occasionally excellent Pinot Noir, and top dessert wines.
• **Central Otago** is good for Riesling, Chardon-

ABOVE LEFT: casual dining at an Auckland eatery.
ABOVE RIGHT: oranges growing in the Bay of Plenty.

nay and Pinot Noir. Very cold, so high acids can make the wines fierce in their youth, but excellent prospects for the cellar. Potentially great for Méthode Champenoise.

Grape varieties

New Zealand vineyards are planted with most of the classical grape varieties of Europe. Since the late 19th century, winemakers have been testing out grape varieties to see which best suit particular regions.

• **Chardonnay** is the great white grape of Burgundy, but it has adapted well to New Zealand

conditions. Left to its own devices, it has a citric, melon-like flavour, but many winemakers ferment and age it in barrels, and put at least a percentage of each batch through a malolactic fermentation to convert its sharp malic acids to softer lactic acids. The wine then takes on the flavours caused by these techniques – barrel fermentation adds a grainy mealiness, rather like toasted muesli, and wood ageing gives it spiciness and, sometimes, a hint of vanilla.
• **Sauvignon Blanc** is the "biggie" of the New Zealand wine export scene. It has done exceptionally well in overseas competitions because it stands out in any crowd. New Zealand Sauvignon, particularly if it comes from Marlbor-

ough, is fiercely aromatic, with a bouquet likened to cut grass or freshly cut capsicums. Hawke's Bay Sauvignon Blancs are less aromatic but have a tropical fruit character that often gives them more depth on the palate.

• **Gewürztraminer** is the most distinctive grape variety of them all, with a super-spicy bouquet reminiscent of lychees and cloves. Many of the best come from Gisborne, but Dry River's Neil McCallum makes a startlingly good one at his Martinborough winery. Gewürztraminer can suffer from a bitter finish when it is fermented out to dryness, and for this reason many winemakers leave in a touch of residual sugar.

• **Riesling** has traditionally been a bit of a wallflower, but its sales have been picking up in recent years. It is a gentle variety, with a floral, lightly scented bouquet and fruity taste. It can be made bone dry, but often has a touch of sweetness. It is also used to create super-sweet dessert wines.

• **Chenin Blanc** is often seen in the company of other varieties. That's because its naturally high acidity has the ability to add zing to wines that might otherwise suffer from excess flab. But in the right hands it can turn into wonderful wine with rich flavours and the sort of complexity normally found in top Chardonnay.

• **Müller-Thurgau** The grape is a modern Ger-

man cross between Riesling and Sylvaner, and is nearly always made slightly sweet. It has introduced thousands of people to the potential pleasures of the grape.

• **Pinot Gris**, originally from Alsace, is an up-and-coming variety in New Zealand. At its best, it produces wine with delightfully grainy character and a lot of honest flavour.

• **Cabernet Sauvignon** is well-suited to New Zealand. In most years, it performs best in Hawke's Bay and Waiheke Island but good examples can also come from West Auckland, and as far south as Nelson. Many local examples are blended with Merlot and Cabernet Franc, just as they are in France.

• **Merlot** was first used in New Zealand to fill what was seen as a "flavour hole" in the mid-palate of local Cabernet Sauvignon, but now more and more winemakers are bottling it on its own. Although Cabernet is regarded as the great red grape of Bordeaux, in fact there is more Merlot grown there than any other variety. Merlot ripens up to three weeks earlier than Cabernet, so it is a much better choice for regions that suffer from autumn rain. It has leather/coffee/tobacco characters, often likened to the smell of an old British gentleman's club.

• **Pinotage**, grown only here and in South Africa, has traditionally made light, vaguely peppery reds of no great interest, but a handful of makers have recently rediscovered it, and are getting better results.

• **Pinot Noir**, which is the grape of red Burgundy and is notoriously difficult to grow, has become the ultimate challenge for a number of local winemakers. It seems to behave best in the Wairarapa and Central Otago, but good examples have also been made in Marlborough and Hawke's Bay. Pinot Noir has variously been described as being like strawberries, cherries or mushrooms; it can also develop "barnyard" aromas that some people find off-putting.

Méthode Champenoise

Most are made from Marlborough grapes, and this province has been chosen for sparkling wine production by two Champagne houses, Deutz and Moët & Chandon. In addition, Cloudy Bay is now largely owned by Veuve Clicquot-Ponsardin, although the famous house is not involved in the making of the company's sparkler, Pelorus.

ABOVE: tasting a recent vintage.

Making Wine

Grapes are quite capable of turning themselves into wine with no help from us whatever. The white bloom on the skin of ripe grapes is made of wild yeasts. Fracture the skin and the yeasts will set to work, eating the natural sugar and converting it to alcohol and carbon dioxide. This is fermentation, and controlling it is an important part of the winemaker's art. For a start, most winemakers prefer to use their own, laboratory-bred yeasts because of their greater predictability.

Fermentation can also be controlled by chilling the tanks. This slows the yeasts down, giving the winemaker more time to keep things in check. The technique is commonly used for white wines – reds are usually left to undergo a warm, tumultuous fermentation that gives added body and character.

When the grapes arrive from the vineyard, they are generally tipped into a crusher-destemmer to remove any stalks and leaves. White grapes are pressed and usually cold-settled to obtain purer juice which then goes into a fermentation tank. Red grapes are put straight into a fermentation tank or vat, skins and all. Some producers like to press the grapes as whole bunches, bypassing the crusher-destemmer. Others ferment their wines in oak barrels, rather than tanks or vats.

As red wines ferment, the skins float to the top of the tank or barrel and form a thick "cap". Most winemakers like to break this "cap" up, either by plunging a wooden paddle into it every few hours, or by pumping wine from the bottom of the container to the top. The aim is to extract every last nuance of colour and flavour from the grape skins.

After fermentation, most white wine is simply filtered and bottled, but with red wines and some whites there are other decisions to be made. The embryonic wine might be aged in oak barrels, either new or a year or two old, depending on how much new-oak character is wanted in the finished product. French barrels are the most popular in New Zealand, but American oak also has its proponents. Size is important: a *puncheon* holds 500 litres (110 gallons); a *barrique* only 225 (50 gallons). *Barriques* add more oak character because of the greater proportion of oak to wine.

And finally, it must be decided how long to leave the wine in oak. If new barrels have been used, they will add strong oak flavour initially, but soften in 18 months or so. Used barrels will add less oak character, but timing is still crucial.

Making a non-oaked white wine should be relatively simple, but here, too, there are decisions to be made. After fermentation, most white wine is bone dry. If the winemaker wants to make it sweeter, this can be done by the addition of a little unfermented grape juice. Alternatively, it can be sweetened by stopping the fermentation before the yeasts have converted all the sugar to alcohol, or by freezing the wine briefly to put the yeasts to sleep, then filtering it.

The most time-consuming wine to make is Méthode Champenoise or Méthode Traditionelle –

sparkling wine made in the style of Champagne. The process involves adding extra sugar and yeasts to bottles of still white wine, then sealing the bottle to contain the fermentation process. This second fermentation produces the bubbles – but also a sludge of dead yeast cells that must be removed. The bottles are rotated and gently shaken until they are upside down and all the sludge is resting against the bottle top. They are then taken to a brine tank, the neck is frozen and the bottle top removed. The plug of icy yeast flies out and the wine is perfectly clear, ready to be topped up, corked and wired.

There are cheaper alternatives, and indeed short cuts can be taken with almost any part of the winemaking process, but they are certain to show up. The best wine is made with care, patience and passion.

ABOVE RIGHT: vineyard in Hawke's Bay.

FARMING LIFE

*Although New Zealand was built on its farm produce, recent decades have
been tough for farmers – yet most of them wouldn't swap their jobs for the world*

It's early morning, high summer in the heart of the South Island. Daniel Jamieson, second-generation farmer, father of two and some-time recreational cricket player, has breakfast with his wife Colleen, then heads outdoors to start work on the land where he was born and raised. More than 600 dairy cows await him and his staff in a high-tech milking parlour not far from where the woolshed once stood.

Daniel checks the sky, makes a mental note to increase the flow of irrigation to parts of the farm, and remembers the heat, sweat and dust of summer shearing back when he used to be a sheep farmer. Four years ago he and Colleen were among the first to abandon tradition on the broad inland plains of North Canterbury. Now their dairy herd is one of many, each comprising several hundred cows, each grazing where sheep had been raised for nearly a century.

Thanks to irrigation schemes in the 1970s and 80s, which combined with fertile soils to facilitate grass growth in all but the depths of winter, the Jamiesons and others like them have quietly revolutionised farming in their community.

Fields of change

Such changes are sweeping the rural heartland of New Zealand. The rapid spread of dairy farming from traditional North Island regions like Waikato, Taranaki and Manawatu to former sheep farming strongholds in Canterbury, Otago and Southland has been one of the biggest, but is hardly an exception.

Thousands of acres of pine trees now cloak hills too steep to support profitable livestock farming, particularly in parts of the North Island. Horticulture, including apples, stone fruit and kiwi fruit, remains a mainstay in the Bay of Plenty, Gisborne, Hawke's Bay, Nelson and Otago. But new crops, particularly large-scale vegetable production, have made inroads into other fertile coastal areas. Grapes can now

be found flourishing on many hillsides. Olives, deer, ostriches, lavender and goats are all in commercial production.

Latest official reports estimate that nearly 25 percent of all farms in New Zealand have seen a change of land use in the past decade, and in particular the expansion of dairy farming and

forestry is predicted to continue for some time.

The humble sheep, it seems, is under siege. For decades a cornerstone of NZ agriculture, and indeed of the nation's export-driven economy, pastoral sheep production and its supporting industries have arguably borne the brunt of radical political and market changes.

Rural downturn

The loss of secure markets in the UK when Britain joined the European Common Market was the first blow. This was followed from 1984 by systematic dismantling of extensive farm subsidies which the government believed New Zealand could no longer afford. Sheep numbers,

PRECEDING PAGES: just a few of New Zealand's 47 million sheep. **LEFT:** logging contest. **ABOVE RIGHT:** the fastest shearers complete 300–350 sheep a day.

which had reached as much as 70 million under these support systems, plummeted and now continue to fall, at last count totalling 47 million. Profits, especially on less fertile land, took a severe beating, from which they have yet to recover. Debt escalated; land values dwindled and export meat processing plants closed throughout the country.

Those whose livelihood had been dependent on sheepmeat and wool were not alone in facing upheaval; New Zealand's rural industries are now among

to begin refrigerated shipment of frozen sheep carcases way back in 1882 has led to rapid advances in food processing technology and farm production systems, not to mention a whole new attitude down on the farm.

The sheer diversity of New Zealand's land-based exports, from powdered deer antler and fresh flowers to chilled gourmet meat cuts and hand-made boutique cheeses, reflects only part of the transformation that has taken place in recent years. Equally important though less

CHEESE PLEASE

More than 60 varieties of cheese are produced in New Zealand. Local types include aorangi, akronia and blue supreme.

the least subsidised in the OECD (Organisation for Economic Co-operation and Development).

New growth

The country's farming families have met these challenges head-on. Still responsible for producing over half New Zealand's merchandise exports, with dairying currently the biggest single export earner of any, they've scoured the world for fresh opportunities.

Traditional commodity sales to Europe may have withered. But sophisticated new products have found buyers elsewhere, most notably throughout Asia and in Australia. The same spirit of innovation that allowed New Zealand

apparent has been farmers' willingness to adapt to new market trends. For the thousands who remain committed to the nation's sheep industry, this has meant increasingly specialised production of specific types of meat and wool, many of which are now brand-marked. For others, it has meant branching out into different types of agriculture or horticulture altogether.

Environmental concerns

New Zealand's farmers have been quick to respond to the increasing worldwide consumer concern about chemical residues, animal welfare and food safety. Gifted with a sparse population, relatively clean air and water and a productive, temperate climate, the country's exports of organic products have shown tremendous growth, and strict animal welfare codes and quality assurance programmes have now been implemented in many of New Zealand's rural industries.

Underlying these recent refinements, the basic principle of New Zealand livestock production remains much the same as it was when the early settlers began farming sheep and cattle more than 100 years ago – namely, to convert grass into meat, wool and milk as efficiently as possible. Flocks and herds are farmed outdoors for 12 months of the year, and fed for most of

that time on fresh pasture with supplements like hay, grain or feed crops in winter.

Another key characteristic has also weathered the changes. Contrary to the doomsayers of the mid-1980s who predicted they would barely survive without subsidies, farms owned and operated by rural families have remained the backbone of New Zealand agriculture.

Admittedly, these properties now tend to be bigger than they used to be, with fewer staff. One or other of the spouses is likely to have a

PREVIOUS PAGE: prize stock at the Hereford Conference.
ABOVE: an up-and-coming young farmer at the annual Arrowtown Autumn Festival.

job off-farm to help supplement income; and the tradition of passing land down to the children is by no means as secure as it used to be.

New pressures

Domestic legislation protecting the environment has been overhauled in recent years. Local authorities are now empowered to police the use of natural resources in their regions to a degree previously unknown.

Meanwhile the cost of controlling endemic, highly destructive and non-native pests like possums and rabbits is increasingly transferred from the public purse to farmers' own chequebooks. Self-help has become the order of the day, not just with pests but also in relation to broader land-care issues such as widespread erosion, and sustainable land use.

Possession of the land itself is a source of contention in several regions, as many Maori tribes seek redress for grievances of the past, including the confiscation of large tracts of land.

The tortuous process of Government compensation for these losses has largely centred on cash settlements with some return of public land to Maori ownership. While today's farmers face little risk of being themselves dispossessed a century after European settlement, indigenous land claims have nonetheless heightened tensions in many small rural communities, especially in Taranaki and Northland.

Protecting the future

Beyond these domestic issues, and beyond its borders, insect pests and animal and plant diseases from other countries continue to pose enormous potential threats to New Zealand. Border control is among the strictest in the world, implemented with more than a little obsession as the country strives to protect its relative purity from tiny invaders which could torpedo multi-million dollar export markets.

The accidental importation of the Mediterranean fruit fly not so long ago cost horticultural producers dearly before an eradication campaign of near-military proportions was able to destroy all traces of the pest.

So it's hardly surprising that farmers like Daniel and Colleen Jamieson in Canterbury have much on their minds these days. But the interesting thing is that they, and thousands of others earning a livelihood from the land, wouldn't dream of doing anything else.

OUTDOOR ADVENTURES

New Zealanders have devised numerous imaginative ways to enjoy all that lovely countryside, from the ground, in the air, on the water, or just dangling upside down

When Edmund Hillary stood upon the summit of Everest in 1953 he encapsulated the spirit of a nation. Yet in many ways it's hardly surprising that a country that makes its living in the great outdoors should be in love with the great outdoors.

Mountaineering remains one of the country's most famous outdoor sports, with the Southern Alps offering challenges worthy of any climber. Among the peaks there are climbing huts, and even guiding services, but the ice is active, the rock often loose, and the weather notoriously fickle. Every year the mountains claim lives.

In winter, the mountains are a playground for skiers as well as climbers. At commercial fields, there are facilities familiar to skiers in Europe and North America, with restaurants and ski hire on site. Club fields offer a more rustic, but also a more personal approach to the sport.

Ski-mountaineering is practised too. The effort required is considerable, but so are the rewards – scintillating descents through criss-crossed crevasses and eerie ice cliffs, with high peaks crowding the sky. Helicopters and ski planes provide access to virgin terrain, with runs as long as in any skiers' dreams. Mountain winters also service skaters as small lakes freeze to form natural skating rinks.

Tramping

Peaks are the domain of the mountaineer, while valleys and passes are the domain of trampers and bushwalkers. There are marked tracks all around the country – some, like the Milford Track, world famous. While there are no poisonous snakes or spiders in New Zealand, the bush still has its dangers, which are mainly linked to the quickly changing weather. Thorough preparations should always be made before any trek.

A trans-alpine crossing in the South Island is the most dramatic tramp. From the east, in the rain shadow of the ranges, the mountains are

approached through wide and spacious shingle and tussock valleys. Over the Main Divide, however, the track drops suddenly into deep-cut gorges and dense forests. Sombre and mysterious in the rain, in sunlight these forests dance with shifting shades of green and yellow, always alive with the songs and swift movements of

birds. The trekker is immersed in the realm of beneficent Tane, the Maori god of forests.

Having evolved in isolation, many of Tane's plants and birds are unique to New Zealand and are the central attraction for many forest visitors. Prior to European settlement there were no browsing animals, but now thar, chamois, wild pigs and goats can all be found in New Zealand's forests and mountains.

Dangling in chasms

From New Zealand's mountains, swift rivers race down rapids and carve deep gorges ideal for river running. Canoeists shoot arrow-like through wild water; rubber-dinghy enthusiasts

PRECEDING PAGES: outward bound in the Marlborough Sounds. **LEFT:** vertical highs. **ABOVE RIGHT:** a rest on the Routeburn Track, Southern Alps.

crash down a turmoil of rocks and white waves. Commercial rafting now makes some of these thrills available to tourists.

Another sort of craft, a New Zealand invention, carries people up these rivers. The jet-boat is driven by a pump which sucks water in and shoots it astern in a deflectable plume. It is highly manoeuvrable and is ideal for shallow or rocky rivers, and rapids. White-water rafting and jet-boating are most developed around Queenstown, also the main centre for another New Zealand invention, bungee jumping, usually done from river gorge suspension bridges.

Fishing is the other major activity on the weather, changing rapidly from calm to chaos, adds a distinctive and dangerous note.

Power-boats are popular for family recreation and racing. Water-skiers and windsurfers have multiplied in recent years and some of the more popular stretches of water are close to becoming overcrowded. Surfing is also popular, especially on the wild beaches on Auckland's west coast, and on the east coast around Gisborne.

In pre-colonial times the sea was more than a recreation area – it was the realm of Tangoroa, god of the sea, and the vital source of *kai moana* (seafood). To this day it retains much of its cultural and spiritual significance for Maori, and

country's lakes and rivers. In past days eels and native fish were an important source of Maori food. Europeans brought brown and rainbow trout in the 19th century. They acclimatised well – frequently trout of 3 kg (7 lbs) or more are caught with rod and fly. During the season salmon run in many rivers. Fishermen on Lake Taupo enjoy a 90 percent chance of a catch.

Sailing is the premier sea sport, its profile enhanced when New Zealand won the America's Cup. It's estimated that one in four Auckland households own a boat, and every weekend thousands of yachts can be seen in the Hauraki Gulf, sailing for pleasure or competing in fiercefought races. The island climate's wayward some of its economic importance too – Maori predominate amongst those who fish and gather shellfish for food non-commercially. For them and for others, however, sea-fishing is also recreational. From wharves and sea walls and boats young and old hopefully hang hooks, others drag nets through rich waters of estuaries, or far out to sea to battle with deep-water fish.

Though much coastal water is murky there are some superb diving areas. Snorkelling is also popular. At the Poor Knights Islands, north of Auckland, cliffs plunge sheer beneath the sea for hundreds of metres. And in the fiords of south Westland the water is opaque on the surface but very clear below. Black coral is a rewarding sight, normally only found way down deep, but growing here in relatively low light conditions at moderate depths.

Sky high

Going up rather than under, New Zealanders take to the air for recreation as well. The most dramatic powered flights lift people from airstrip to mountain in moments. Gliders, and even hang-gliders, fly among the mountains too. Many mountain ranges rear at right-angles to strong northwest winds, creating

YACHTING TRIUMPH

One of the country's proudest moments came in 1995, when a New Zealand yacht, *Black Magic,* unexpectedly won the America's Cup.

it takes an overseas visitor, who is used to dense populations, crowded beaches and polluted rivers, to remind them of their good fortune.

When it comes to sport, there's nothing that is more appealing to New Zealanders than the volatile mixture of skill, running and occasional violence of rugby union and league.

The rugbies

Union has been the game of choice for New Zealanders for more than 100 years. Just why it took such a hold in New

towering wind waves which have lifted New Zealand glider pilots to world records.

Camping is virtually a national way of life during summer holidays. The densest concentrations are in well-appointed camping grounds at popular beaches, rivers and lakes.

Family camping holidays and tramping trips introduce many New Zealanders to outdoor life at an impressionable age, allowing them to grow up with the ability to gain deep pleasure from simple pursuits. They may take for granted the ease with which they can do so. Sometimes

Zealand is hard to pinpoint, although the game's camaraderie probably appealed, while men hacking a living from the bush might have found the physical rough and tumble of rugby light relief from their day-to-day work.

Rugby offers a place for all shapes and sizes, from minute halfbacks to giant forwards who wouldn't be out of place as linebackers in American football. At its best even the uninitiated can find the game thrilling.

For atmosphere the best rugby matches are internationals, usually played in New Zealand between June and August. The highly charged Super 12 series pits teams from Australia, South Africa and New Zealand against each other

LEFT: yacht race in Auckland Harbour. **ABOVE:** the joys of parapenting – a long, slow, scenic descent.

from March to May. Worth checking out too are Ranfurly Shield matches, provincial games on a challenge basis at the holder's home ground, played late in the season. Games between leading teams see normally stolid New Zealanders painting their faces, waving flags and scarves and screaming chants. But don't fear for your safety – New Zealand has never seen the sort of crowd violence that blights British soccer.

If there are no test matches on during a winter visit to New Zealand, consider watching a club match. On most club grounds there are clubrooms, and a newcomer showing mild interest will usually be welcomed in for a drink. League

rates behind union in terms of popularity, but its fortunes have risen with the entry of a New Zealand team, the Auckland Warriors, in the Australian club competition.

Cricket mad

New Zealand's main summer game is cricket. Bowlers hurl a leather-coated ball at speeds approaching 160 km/h (100 mph) at batsmen, who must hit it as hard and as often as possible. The teams play in coloured uniforms, with players' names across their backs, making the whole package entertaining and easy to follow.

One of the most exciting team spectator sports in New Zealand today is netball, which is the major sport for women.

Basketball here revolves around a national league, played through the winter. American imports have raised the level of local players and in some areas capacity crowds are common.

Golf for all

This is a huge sport in New Zealand, with an estimated 200,000 members of clubs, plus half as many again who enjoy a hack round the hundreds of public courses, which offer golf at a price unheard of in most of the world. Some say it's cheaper to fly from Tokyo to Auckland or Christchurch to play golf than to join a club in Japan. The main tournaments for spectators are in early summer, usually in December.

On the waterfront

The Auckland Anniversary regatta for yachts is held on the last Monday of every January, with more than 1,000 entries making it the biggest one-day yachting event in the world.

On Auckland Anniversary Day the harbour is almost covered in yachts, from little boys and girls in one-person P-class yachts to the majestic A-class keelers. The whole magnificent spectacle can probably best be viewed from Mt Victoria on North Head in the suburb of Devonport, or from ferry boats that cruise from the terminal in downtown Auckland.

On a Saturday in early March the waterfront drive in Auckland is covered for 11 km (7 miles) by more than 70,000 runners, joggers and shufflers in the annual Round-the-Bays run, one of the world's biggest fun-runs.

THE BIRTH OF BUNGEE

Bungee jumping was devised by Alan John Hackett, a New Zealander, who bungeed off the Eiffel Tower in 1986. The sport was inspired by the land divers of Pentecost Island, Vanuatu, in the Pacific, who for centuries have been leaping off specially constructed wooden towers 18 to 23 metres (60 to 77 ft high), with just a liana vine secured around each ankle, in order to ensure a bountiful yam harvest.

Since Hackett developed the practice to create a relatively safe sport, bungee jumping has become a worldwide craze. Yams everywhere should be thriving.

ABOVE: skiers at Mount Hutt.
RIGHT: taking the plunge, Kiwi style.

EXPLORING THE NATIONAL PARKS

Well-marked tracks with plenty of accommodation along the way make it a joy to explore New Zealand's great outdoors

People come from all over the world to tramp on New Zealand's famous tracks (long-distance footpaths), such as the Abel Tasman, along the north coast of the South Island; the Milford Track, which gets so crowded that booking ahead is necessary; and the Routeburn, in the south of the South Island. Yet there are some beautiful tracks where you can walk for hours without seeing a soul. An extra bonus is that there's often a hot spring around, just when you need to soothe those aching joints.

National parks offer much more than walking. Department of Conservation (DOC) offices, in all cities and in many towns, can provide information on wildlife, flora and fauna in the parks, and on walking the trails. Visitor Centres generally provide DOC leaflets and information, too.

UNIQUE WILDLIFE

New Zealand's wildlife developed in isolation from the rest of the world; the country's many flightless birds reflect the absence of predators. Many of its trees were equally defenceless, which is why possums, introduced from Australia to start a fur trade, are having such a destructive effect on the country's forests. In Australia the trees have evolved a built-in protection which stops them being stripped bare by the creatures. Not so in New Zealand. That's one reason why New Zealand often seems to be engaged in a running battle to preserve the natural ecological balance, but it also illustrates why this countryside is especially interesting and unique.

∇ **LAKE ROTOROA**
A fishing paradise, Lake Rotoroa is one of two glacial lakes which give Nelson Lakes National Park its name – the other one is Lake Rotoiti.

△ **SOUTHERN ALPS**
Mount Cook is the crowning glory of the magnificent Southern Alps range. The training ground for Everest conqueror Sir Edmund Hillary, it's a terrain that is not to be taken lightly. Heli-skiing and glacier skiing are popular here.

▷ **THE YAKAS TREE**
Waipoua Kauri Forest, Northland, is a protected nature reserve with trails that lead to the Yakas, the eighth-largest kauri in New Zealand. Trails also lead to Tane Mahuta, at 52 metres (170 ft) the country's tallest tree, and probably 1,200 years old.

SAFETY IN THE NATIONAL PARKS

◁ **GO WEST**
Lake Matheson with Mounts Tasman and Cook, Westland National Park. This park also contains the glaciers Fox and Franz Josef and has some great walks, like the Copland Track. Weather conditions here are very unpredictable.

△ **MOUNT NGAURUHOE**
The youngest of the three volcanoes in Tongariro National Park is a great tramping (hiking) location. The park is also renowned for the ski slopes on recently active Ruapeho, as well as wildlife, game and fishing.

△ **MOUNT TARANAKI**
Despite being one of New Zealand's wettest places, it's the country's most frequently climbed mountain and a popular winter skiing venue.

▷ **EMERALD LAKES**
Minerals give these mountain lakes their brilliant hues. The Tongariro Northern Circuit passes close by these and other brightly coloured lakes and volcanic formations.

A few simple precautions will help you enjoy some of the most beautiful scenery in the world. Never head off into the wilderness unprepared – always check with the local (DOC) office or Visitor Centre before you go tramping, as in some areas weather conditions can change very rapidly. Some DOC offices will also be able to advise you on the availability of accommodation (whether huts are still open), time and food supplies required, and even volcanic activity! You may get more out of some walks and climbs with the assistance of a guide (such as the one shown above) who knows the area well – guided group walks are available in some areas too.

Never set out on a long tramp without suitable clothing and footwear; if you haven't brought your own, there are plenty of shops where you can purchase or hire decent gear, and some hostels and hotels can supply clothes, gloves and hats. Always inform someone else where you're going before you depart.

For even a short walk, always take adequate footwear and clothing and bring a map, compass, torch, matches and first aid kit with you. Once you step off the main road, if you go off in the wrong direction it could become a longer walk than you'd planned.

NATURAL HISTORY

New Zealand has an exciting geological history and intriguing wildlife, from the lingering presence of the extinct moa to the tenuous hold of the symbolic kiwi

Of all the land masses on earth the islands of New Zealand take the prize for being the most isolated, surrounded on all sides by great expanses of ocean, and located thousands of miles away from Asia and the Americas, and a half a world away from Europe. But that has not always been the case.

The actual birth of a physically independent New Zealand occurred some 80 million years ago during the heyday of the dinosaurs. It was then, though over an extremely long period of time, that New Zealand split away from the prehistoric continent of Gondwana, as the Tasman Sea began to form. By 60 million years ago New Zealand had reached its present distance from Australia of more than 1,500 km (930 miles). But even by then the country's rocks had recorded an incredibly complex history.

In the beginning it is thought that a massive continent spanned the region where New Zealand was eventually going to appear. What is now the east of Australia was joined with another continent – and in one of the more interesting developments of geological investigation this has been suggested to have been North America. It was only when these two landmasses moved apart, over 500 million years ago, that an arc of volcanic islands was able to develop in between. These rocks, which are preserved in the mountains of Fiordland and the northwest of the South Island, record the start of New Zealand's history. In places they preserve fossils such as trilobites and brachiopods, the oldest signs of New Zealand's life.

Leaving Gondwana

For several hundred million years, New Zealand lay along a "convergent" edge of the supercontinent of Gondwana. Along this margin, oceanic crust, which is continually moving outwards from a mid-oceanic ridge, was pushed under the continent in a process known as plate tectonics.

LEFT: the great spotted kiwi in its habitat, South Island.
ABOVE RIGHT: the flightless kakapo is a nocturnal ground parrot.

Various types of rock and sediment occur from the sea floor and move along on the oceanic crust like a giant, though very slow, conveyor belt. Once they reach a convergent margin they get "plastered" on top of each other like layers of spread on a piece of toast. For many millions of years, New Zealand grew in this way, as a

rather chaotic collection of rock from various places was brought together.

Finally, a huge sliver of land broke away from Gondwana and headed out into the Pacific. Almost immediately it began to sink and the sea washed further and further inland. Mountains eroded to low hills and waves ate them away. The New Zealand of today is just the tiny emergent part of a huge drowned continent, "Tasmantis", which can be seen on charts of the sea floor, stretching all the way to New Caledonia in the north, and to Campbell Island in the south. In fact, by 30 million years ago New Zealand was so subdued and had sunk so much that there is very little evidence of any emergent land at all. Most of what is now New Zealand was a shallow undersea shelf rich in sea life.

It was only at the "last minute", geologically speaking, that compressive movements came to the rescue, pushing the country up, and back out of the sea. As these forces continued, hills grew to become jagged mountains, volcanoes erupted, and were then carved by water and ice to form the landscape of today.

New Zealand currently sits right on the boundary of two of the huge moving "plates"

NIGHT BIRD

The kiwi, New Zealand's national bird, got its name from the cry of the male. The nocturnal bird eats fruit, insects and worms.

Plate, while the Alps, from the base up, are on the Pacific Plate which is being thrust upwards.

The effect of the Alps is enormous. Besides creating alpine environments from a land that had for millions of years been flat, they present a major barrier to the westerly circulation flow. At this latitude only the Southern Alps and the southern tip of South America prevent free circulation of these moisture-laden winds. When the air currents are forced to rise over the mountains their moisture is dropped, causing the enormous

which cover the surface of the earth. In the south the Australian plate pushes under the Pacific one, while in the north the Pacific plate pushes the other way, under the Australian plate. In between, with little other option, the land rises and rises. The terrific wrenching forces that result can hardly help but produce a land of earthquakes and volcanoes.

The mighty Southern Alps in the South Island are almost entirely the result of the last 2 million years – a mere blink in geological time. They rose, and continue to rise by several centimetres a year. The plate boundary forming them is plain to see while travelling through Westland. The lowlands are on the Australian

rainfall (sometimes over 5,000 mm/200 inches in a year) now present on the West Coast.

Odd as it may sound, rainfall may actually be too much for rainforests, as the soil is rapidly leached of the nutrients they need and is able to offer a home only to stunted vegetation. This kind of extreme environment has ensured a minimum of human impact on the land. Much of the country remains in a near pristine state and any travellers who wish to experience a true "wilderness" are easily satisfied here.

On the other side of the Alps, a corresponding rainfall shadow was created. Only a few kilometers from the wettest parts of New Zealand, the annual rainfall can be as low as 300 mm

(12 inches). At the time that the Alps were growing, worldwide cooling became extreme and the Ice Age ensued. In reality this was a whole succession of cold periods, separated by warmer ones. In the colder intervals huge glaciers appeared in New Zealand and flowed down valleys. This period had an enormous effect on the present landscape – where young mountains and glaciers have combined, the scenery is some of the most spectacular on earth. In Fiordland, the rock walls of ancient glacial valleys drop vertically thousands of feet directly into the sea. On the other side of the Alps, the South Island lakes, like Wanaka and Wakatipu, are the

combine alpine weather with gentle topography, cross-country skiing has become popular.

Closely tied to the history of the Southern Alps are New Zealand's most precious materials. What the Maori call *pounamu* (greenstone) was formed from thin slivers of the exotic rock which exists deep below the earth's crust. Altered by heat and pressure during mountain-forming processes, these rocks were pushed to the surface in only a few isolated spots in the west of the South Island. Its difficulty to obtain, intrinsic beauty, and material properties in a culture where metal was unknown gave *pounamu* a value like gold had to the Europeans. Gold itself

direct result of glacial "bulldozing". Lying in the rainshadow, the sunny climate combines to make an ideal holiday environment. Swimming, water-skiing and fishing are the key activities.

Away from the Alps, one curious feature of much of the uplands is their flattened tops. These are fragments of the old land surface which has been broken and pushed up by the later mountain-building events. Much of the surface is probably a wave-cut platform, dating from the time when most, if not all, of New Zealand was below the waves. In regions that

weathered from quartz veins within "schist", the rock which forms most of the Alps. As the mountains grew, they eroded as well, and while the lighter and softer minerals of the schist washed away, gold, by virtue of its high density, became concentrated in the quieter nooks and crannies of river beds, providing a boom for another generation of settlers.

Not all of New Zealand's recent history has been one of uplift. In the north of the South Island, the Marlborough Sounds were produced by the drowning of an extensive river system. The sunny climate and the endless bays and islands make it another good place for boating and walking. In the North Island the major geo-

LEFT: land still in the making at White Island.
ABOVE: the tuatara, a prehistoric relic.

logical story is of volcanoes. In a complex situation a range of volcanic types is produced.

Auckland city is built amongst numerous small (extinct), perfectly formed volcanic cones. These were formed by gentle outpourings of lava and ash. As naturally defensive positions, most of them have since been terraced and palisaded by Maori to form "*pa*" (forts). In the Central Plateau a different form of lava produces a very dangerous, explosive type of volcano. About AD 130 one of the largest volcanic explosions in historical times formed Lake Taupo. This spread hot ash over a large part of the North Island, simultaneously annihilating

bats), as well as its complete lack of snakes. This used to be attributed to the timing of New Zealand's breaking-away from Gondwana. However, in light of recent discoveries, it is now believed that New Zealand did have a land fauna at one time: carnivorous and herbivorous dinosaurs, as well as the flying pterosaurs, were still living on New Zealand after it broke away from Gondwana. The only fossil evidence of land-based, four-footed animals since the dinosaurs is a single crocodile jawbone from near St Bathans, in Central Otago. Now, like snakes, crocodiles are a species which New Zealand lacks.

huge areas of forest and everything in them. There's never been a period in New Zealand's history where volcanism has been entirely absent and there is every reason to expect such behaviour will continue. In the long run these events are blessings in disguise. Volcanic rocks rejuvenate the landscape. They weather to form New Zealand's richest soils, a fact well-recognised by the dairy industry. The volcanoes of the Central Plateau form perfect ski-fields.

The dinosaurs

The most striking aspect of New Zealand's fauna is its absence of large four-footed land animals, in particular of mammals (other than

Mammals, too, may once have been part of a "native" fauna that developed before New Zealand broke from Australia. The present absence of large land animals – other than birds – is almost certainly a result of extinction over the last 80 million years. Of the very distinct New Zealand animals, such as the moa, kiwi and tuatara, (three-eyed centenarian lizards), we unfortunately have no ancient fossil record, and their means and date of arrival is contentious. Certainly the tuatara may have lived in New Zealand the whole time, although with the moas and kiwis there is room for argument. Both the moa and kiwi are now flightless, but it seems their ancestors could fly. They, like many other native birds, may well have flown to New Zealand only to become flightless later.

With nothing to prey on them, birds proliferated in New Zealand. They took over many niches which would elsewhere be occupied by mammals. Some, lacking the need, lost the ability to fly. Of New Zealand's numerous flightless birds, perhaps the most famous is the now extinct moa *(see page 117)*.

For much of the time New Zealand was a part of Gondwana, it lay in polar latitudes,

NEW ARRIVALS

There are at least 10,500 insect species in New Zealand, of which around 1,100 were introduced from other countries, generally inadvertently, by humans.

pine trees and tree ferns, and scattered around are long, straight petrified logs.

After New Zealand broke away it drifted towards the warmer equator and experienced a variety of climate changes. For instance, about 20 million years ago, a worldwide burst of warmth created what was probably the hottest period New Zealand has known. This was the only period when coral reefs grew around the coasts. Palm trees were once common throughout New Zealand, although now, the

that is, poleward of 66°S, the polar circle. The evidence of fossils indicates that there was no polar ice sheet, or even glaciers in the region. It certainly was not too cold for plant and animal life, but one inescapable fact of life at this latitude was the unusual light regime – permanent summer light, and the long, dark polar winters. At Curio Bay, near the southernmost point of the South Island, one of the best preserved "petrified forests" in the world is exposed on a tidal platform and dates from this early time. The lumps on the platform are actually stumps of

LEFT: kaka parrot on Kapati Island.
ABOVE: kea in the South Island.

southernmost limit of palm trees in the world lies part of the way down the South Island.

Some organisms didn't cope with the changes, and became extinct, while others managed to fly, swim, or simply got blown across the sea to New Zealand from elsewhere. The simple notion of New Zealand as an "ark" which drifted away and preserved ancient Gondwanan life is just not true – there may have been nearly complete replacement of the original biota. Nevertheless, over this time a biota evolved which was unique to New Zealand. Gum trees (*Eucalyptus*), wattles (*Acacia*) and she-oaks (*Casuarina*), which are all typical Australian plants, do not occur in the native vegetation of New Zealand (although fossil evidence proves they once did). Instead, New Zealand's native bush is dominated by tall, evergreen trees.

One of the most characteristic trees in New Zealand today is the southern beech (*Nothofagus*). This tree dominates large areas of forest, just as it proliferates in Tasmania, small patches of the Australian mainland, New Guinea, New Caledonia in the Pacific, and Patagonia in South America, and once did in Antarctica.

Man's first appearance

There is some debate as to when the ancestors of the Maori arrived. The more usual date of a

little over 1,000 years ago has been challenged by two recent hypotheses: that it was only about 900 years ago, or, on the basis of some carbon-dated rat bones, that it was much earlier than anyone has suspected. In any case, on a global scale, it was very recently and New Zealand was the last large landmass (Antarctica excepted) to be colonised. One immediate result of human settlement was an increase in fire frequency. Whether this was accidental or by design is academic – the result was the permanent removal of large areas of forest. The treeless landscape of Central Otago dates from around this time.

Another result was quick extinction of some of the bird life. Moas in any one area became

extinct within a few hundred years, no doubt due to "overkill" by humans. Rats and dogs were also introduced and took their toll on birdlife. Once the moas became scarce or disappeared altogether there was a corresponding and distinct change in human culture. Fish became more central in the diet and around the same time, cannibalism developed. One theory relates this early cannibalism amongst the Maori to a simple lack of animal protein.

The onslaught of Europeans from the late 18th century speeded up what the Polynesians had begun. A very large area of New Zealand's forest was milled, or simply burnt. Wholesale introduction of browsing mammals and farming have altered parts of the landscape to the point where today no native species remain. Possums, rabbits and deer browse plants so heavily they often kill them, and this destruction can take place on a huge scale. In very steep country which relies on forest to retain the soil, massive erosion has ensued. Introduced weasels, cats and rodents have wrought havoc on the native bird life, which never had to cope with these predators before.

No period has seen such a dramatic metamorphosis of the New Zealand landscape as the last few hundred years. The pace of change has been so rapid that many of New Zealand's large forest trees are old enough to have once had moas browsing around them, while many native birds have had little time to develop a fear of humans. This theme of constant change will no doubt continue. The challenge is to ensure that, despite inevitable alteration, the land and its biota remain distinctly "New Zealand."

New Zealanders are aware of this crisis. Tuataras, which have been around for 250 million years, are now being bred in captivity while sanctuaries are prepared for their safe return to the wild. Conservationists are also trying to restore lost nesting sites for birds and campaigning against further coastal development. A notable success has been the Penguin Place project set up to save the rare yellow-eyed penguin (of which only 5,000 survive in the wilds), which has seen numbers rise from 16 penguins in 1984 to 160 breeding pairs in 2000. Seals and the royal albatross have also been left to breed in healthy numbers on the Otago Peninsula (*see page 307*).

ABOVE LEFT: beech forest near "The Divide", Fiordland National Park.

The Moa

A children's song laments the loss of one of New Zealand's most unusual species of bird:

No moa, no moa, in all Aotearoa,
No moa, no moa,
They've gone and there aren't no moa.

The demise of the moa was a very big loss. The giant flightless bird weighed up to 250 kg (550 lbs) and stood up to 3 metres (10 ft) tall. A researcher surmised that it must have looked like "a forty gallon drum supported on knee-length gumboots".

The moa has become New Zealand's equivalent to Scotland's Loch Ness Monster. Moa sightings are claimed occasionally – a few years ago a pub owner near Arthur's Pass was adamant he'd photographed one running wild in the bush. The photo was less than conclusive, but has helped the moa loom almost as large in myth as it did in reality.

Bones and fossils have revealed that there were around 11 species of moa in New Zealand, from two distinct family groups. *Dinornis giganteus* was the largest moa, most commonly found on the lowland areas in the east of the South Island but rare in the North Island. *Dinornis novaezealandiae* was a mid-sized moa found on both islands, but rarest where its giant cousin roamed. *Dinornis struthoides* was the smallest of the big birds, and the most common overall. It roamed widely over both islands.

The second family, the Emeidae, contained the eight remaining moa species and were in general more heavily built, with a more squat shape.

Studies indicate that the diet of the moa was herbivorous, composed mainly of fruit and seeds of various trees, shrubs, leaves and twigs. Moa were also in the habit of swallowing stones, as they assisted the toothless moa in grinding down its food. The biggest moa could have up to 5 kg (10 lbs) of stones in its gizzard, some up to 10 cm (4 inches) long. Gizzard stones have provided scientists with good evidence of where the birds roamed, and can be viewed at museums around the country. They are found in clusters, often highly polished due to wear while grinding down food.

With few natural predators, save perhaps the giant eagle, the moa lived a peaceful, Garden of Eden-like existence in New Zealand for centuries –

ABOVE RIGHT: watch carefully – you might just spot a moa (along with Elvis and the yeti...).

until, that is, the arrival of man. To the earliest Polynesian settlers, the moa was a gift from the gods. It became an important food source in a land whose climate did not support many of their traditional crops. Archaeological digs have revealed sites around the country where moa meat was cooked in ovens in the ground. But the outsize bird was prized for much more than its flesh. Cloaks were made from moa feathers, ornaments from the bones, and the eggshells, after the egg was eaten, were used as containers for liquid.

Hunted with clubs and spears, the moa was easy prey. Its only refuge was the forest, but that too was soon under threat. Fire, maybe accidentally, pushed

back the forest, and with it the moa. The last moa is thought to have died around 500 years ago.

The Maori turned to the bountiful seas and developed their cropping skills to satisfy their hunger, so the big bird moved into the realm of lore. But it was never forgotten. In the 1860s, two gold prospectors claimed they saw an enormous bird "nine feet high" in a gully, and got locked up for their efforts. At the start of the 20th century, there was a sighting of a moa-like bird on the beach of Martins Bay in Fiordland. Add a sighting by a fisherman trawling for crayfish in Milford Sound to the Canterbury pub owner's recent claims and, who knows?

While the chances of a moa ever being found alive are remote, so too are parts of the remaining native forest. One day we may get a big surprise...

ANTARCTICA: A LAND FOR HEROES

Many travellers, like the brave explorers that blazed their trail, are succumbing to the lure of Antarctica, a continent with unusual beauty as well as unusual dangers

Antarctica is the coldest, windiest and most remote continent on Planet Earth, an environment utterly inimical to people. It has teased our curiosity for centuries and its short history is characterised by heroes. It was the last challenge explorers overcame before they turned their attention to the stars. Those who writer put it: "Nelson would be able to step off his column [in Trafalgar Square] into a boat ..."

But there are oases in Antarctica: the "dry valleys" opposite Ross Island near McMurdo Sound, as well as other ice-free areas, and some "hot-lakes" beneath the icecap. These oases are under intense study by scientists.

have been there report awesome encounters with the raw forces of the weather, but also times of ineffable, luminous peace and beauty.

Last wilderness

Technological advances have made Antarctic visits for tourists possible in the summer months from Christchurch. Antarctica is the last great wilderness, with close to 90 percent of the world's ice sprawling over an area larger than the United States, and packed up to an average height of 2,000 metres (6,550 ft). If all the ice melted, the continent would be about three-quarters of its present size and a lot less mountainous. World sea levels would rise. As one

Antarctica's exploration has close associations with New Zealand. The existence of a great southern continent had been mooted for hundreds of years before the Dutch explorer Abel Tasman was sent from Java in the Dutch East Indies to see if there was a sea passage eastwards across the southern ocean to South America. When he arrived off the west coast of New Zealand in 1642 he believed it might be the western edge of a continent that stretched across to South America. Accordingly, he called it Staten Landt, then the name for South America. A year later, when it was decided there was no huge landmass across the South Pacific, the name was changed to Zeelandia Nova.

The next European visitor to New Zealand, Captain James Cook, also showed an interest in a possible southern land mass. In one of the most daring voyages ever made, Cook sailed along 60 degrees latitude and then penetrated as far as 71 degrees 10 minutes south without sighting the legendary continent. He stayed south so long, his crew verged on mutiny.

The first known sighting came 50 years later, when the Russian navigator von Bellinghausen sailed completely round the world between 60 and 65

ICE MOUNTAINS

Antarctica's ice sheets are up to 4,775 metres (15,667 ft) thick – almost as high as Mont Blanc – and contain nearly 70 percent of the world's fresh water.

Adare, in January 1895. Exploration on the land began soon afterwards and, although New Zealand showed no enthusiasm for mounting its own expeditions, New Zealanders took part in the explorations by Englishmen Robert Falcon Scott and Ernest Shackleton between 1900 and 1917, and Australian Sir Douglas Mawson during the years before World War I. Scott, and all the men in his party which drove overland for the South Pole, died of exposure on their return journey, having learned on their arrival at the

degrees south, dipping to 69 degrees on two occasions, thus becoming the first man to see land inside the Antarctic Circle.

In 1840 James Clark Ross discovered that area of Antarctica south of New Zealand which has been within the country's sphere of interest throughout this century. In fact, New Zealander Alexander von Tunzelmann, the 17-year-old nephew of a pioneer settler and explorer of Central Otago, is believed to have been the first person to step ashore on Antarctica, at Cape

PRECEDING PAGES: natural ice-sculpture in Antarctica.
LEFT: Scott's expedition began in the *Discovery*.
ABOVE: tried and tested polar transport.

Pole that the Norwegians under Amundsen had beaten them to it.

In 1923, the territory south of latitude 60 degrees south and between longitudes 160 degrees east and 150 degrees west was claimed by the British government, placed under the administration of the Governor-General of New Zealand and named the "Ross Dependency".

Between 1929 and 1931 a British-Australian-New Zealand Antarctic Research Expedition focused interest on the continent, as did the exploration from the air by the United States Navy under Admiral Byrd. In 1933 the New Zealand Antarctic Society was formed, but it was not for another 15 years that the first New

Zealand onshore base was established on the continent, near Cape Adare.

The New Zealand Antarctic base was first set up in 1957, the International Geophysical Year, when Everest conqueror Sir Edmund Hillary led a group of five fellow countrymen on an overland dash by tractor to the South Pole. He was supposed to have acted solely as a support for Britain's transpolar expedition led by Sir Vivian Fuchs, laying down supply bases on the New Zealand side of Antarctica for Fuchs to use as he made the journey from the Pole across to the side of the Antarctic which lies below New Zealand. But Hillary and his small group made

such progress, and got so far ahead of schedule, that they decided to push for the Pole themselves, becoming the first to make it overland since Scott 45 years before.

Since 1958, parties from New Zealand have wintered over, exploring and trapping huge areas and intensively researching the geology of the region. New Zealand has always operated in the Antarctic in close association with the United States Navy, which has its own base at McMurdo Sound. In 1964, when fire destroyed most of the equipment at the combined NZ–US base at Cape Hallett, New Zealand erected a new base of her own, which is named Scott Base after Captain Scott, at McMurdo Sound.

Care of resources

Five years earlier, the Antarctic Treaty designed to "ensure the use of Antarctica for peaceful purposes only and the continuance of international harmony" had been signed by 12 nations – New Zealand, the United States, Australia, Britain, Belgium, Chile, France, Japan, Norway, South Africa, Russia and Argentina. Poland also became a signatory in 1977. All these Antarctic Treaty signatories have signed a convention since 1980 for the protection and proper exploitation of Antarctic marine living resources. This culminated in a Convention on the Regulation of Antarctic Mineral Resource Activities (CRAMRA) in Wellington in 1988. But the final fate of this Convention was placed in doubt the following year when France and Australia – both claimant nations to Antarctica – announced they would not ratify it. They want the area to become a wilderness park instead.

The economic exploitation of Antarctica began with the hunting of whales and seals in the sub-Antarctic islands and surrounding seas south of the Pacific Ocean in the late 18th century. The stocks were so depleted that there is little prospect of them ever recovering. Russian and Japanese scientists are investigating the krill, which are plentiful in the Antarctic waters.

There has also been much discussion about mineral resources on the Antarctic mainland and it is thought probable that mineral-bearing rocks of the sort prevalent in Australia and South Africa are common. There are known to be huge deposits of sub-bituminous coal and large deposits of low-grade iron ore. The CRAMRA agreement was an attempt to impose the strictest rules on any possible exploitation activities. The Antarctic Treaty partners are under pressure to consider a total protection regime.

Tourism interest in Antarctica remains strong. For many years, the Mount Erebus aviation disaster in the late 1970s discouraged sightseeing flights, especially when a subsequent inquiry revealed some distinctive dangers if pilots were not used to the Antarctic environment. Although there is renewed enthusiasm, access is still extremely difficult, and likely to stay that way for many years. If it becomes easier, protection of this special environment may have to include stringent controls on tourism.

ABOVE LEFT: the icy wastelands of central Antarctica.
RIGHT: tell-tale signs of the Antarctic experience.

PLACES

A detailed guide to the entire country, with principal sites cross-referenced to the maps

People aside – albeit friendly people worth knowing – it's places in New Zealand that nudge your sense of wonder, that make you take a quick breath with a sense that "Here and only here can I experience this." Milford Track with the Sound at its end, the pristine silver dazzle of the Southern Lakes, the bush-wrapped solitude of Lake Waikaremoana, the boiling surprises of the thermal regions ... they all have pulled superlatives from the mouths of even the most-travelled visitors.

Authors Rudyard Kipling, Anthony Trollope and Robert Louis Stevenson paid tribute to the loveliness of the landscape. James A. Michener wrote in *Return to Paradise* in 1951 that "New Zealand is probably the most beautiful place on earth" with "natural beauty difficult to believe". Thirty years later, in a magazine article entitled "The Memoirs of a Pacific Traveller", he listed Milford Sound as "The Most Stirring Sight" in the world.

The Maori story of the creation explains that land and human beings are all one, flesh and clay from the same source material. Maori emotional attachment to place is profound.

The first Europeans, 20,000 km (12,500 miles) from the tailored communities of Europe they still called home, tried at first to remake the face of the countryside into a Britain look-alike. They cut and burned the forest and sowed grass. But when they had the leisure to look around, they realised that packed into their small new country was a whole world of diverse and dramatic scenery.

The first place to attract world attention was Lake Rotomahana, with what were known as the Pink and White Terraces along its shore. The terraces were formed from silica deposits as water from boiling pools washed down the steep shore of the lake. Tourists could bathe in the cooler pools: "It is a spot," wrote Trollope, "for intense sensual enjoyment." The terraces were all brutally destroyed one night in 1886 when nearby Mount Tarawera exploded.

The North Island's spas and hot pools earned an early reputation for their curative powers. In 1901, the government hired an official balneologist and formed a tourist department, the first government-sponsored tourism promotion organisation in the world.

The thermal regions still draw enormous attention from travellers today. But nowadays, in a world packed with ever-increasing numbers of people in dense and clogged cities, it is mainly the unsullied, uncluttered landscape, the sense of space and timelessness, that attracts thousands of visitors who just like to ogle the scenery, and an ever-increasing number who want to walk in the wilderness. For them a tramp through New Zealand's outposts of scenic beauty becomes a sort of purification rite.

PRECEDING PAGES: pastures and peaks in perspective; a sea of sheep in the hills; memorable Milford Sound. **LEFT:** South Island splendour.

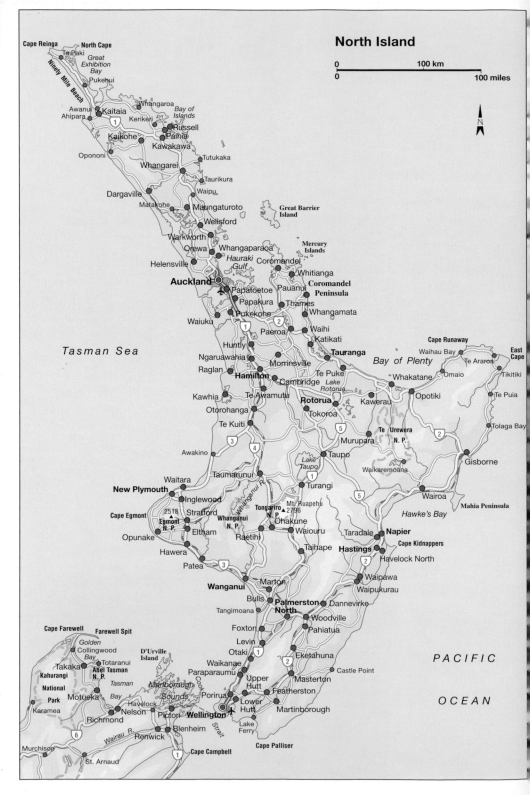

North Island

0   100 km
0   100 miles

N

Cape Reinga
North Cape
Te Paki
Great Exhibition Bay
Pukenui
Ninety Mile Beach
Whangaroa
Awanui
Ahipara
Kaitaia
Kerikeri
Bay of Islands
Russell
Paihia
Kaikohe
Kawakawa
Opononi
Whangarei
Tutukaka
Taurikura
Waipu
Dargaville
Matakohe
Maungaturoto
Wellsford
Great Barrier Island
Warkworth
Orewa
Whangaparaoa
Helensville
Hauraki Gulf
Mercury Islands
Coromandel
Whitianga
Auckland
Papatoetoe
Pauanui
Coromandel Peninsula
Papakura
Thames
Pukekohe
Whangamata
Waiuku
Paeroa
Waihi
Katikati
Huntly
Ngaruawahia
Tauranga
Morrinsville
Cape Runaway
Raglan
Hamilton
Cambridge
Waihau Bay
Te Puke
Lake Rotorua
Whakatane
Omaio
East Cape
Te Araroa
Tikitiki
Tasman Sea
Kawhia
Te Awamutu
Rotorua
Bay of Plenty
Kawerau
Opotiki
Te Puia
Otorohanga
Tokoroa
Te Urewera N. P.
Te Kuiti
Murupara
Tolaga Bay
Awakino
Taupo
Gisborne
Taumarunui
Lake Taupo
Waikaremoana
Waitara
Turangi
New Plymouth
Inglewood
Wairoa
Cape Egmont
2518
Stratford
Mt. Ruapehu 2796
Mahia Peninsula
Egmont N. P.
Whanganui N. P.
Tongariro N. P.
Ohakune
Hawke's Bay
Opunake
Eltham
Raetihi
Waiouru
Taradale
Napier
Hawera
Waioru
Cape Kidnappers
Patea
Taihape
Hastings
Havelock North
Marton
Waipawa
Wanganui
Waipukurau
Bulls
Palmerston North
Dannevirke
Tangimoana
Woodville
Cape Farewell
Farewell Spit
Foxton
Pahiatua
Golden Bay
Collingwood
D'Urville Island
Levin
Eketahuna
Takaka
Totaranui
Otaki
Kahurangi
Abel Tasman N. P.
Waikanae
Castle Point
Paraparaumu
Masterton
National
Tasman Bay
Upper Hutt
Park
Motueka
Marlborough Sounds
Porirua
Featherston
Martinborough
Karamea
Havelock
Lower Hutt
Wellington
Nelson
Richmond
Picton
Lake Ferry
Murchison
Blenheim
Renwick
Strait
Cape Palliser
St. Arnaud
Wairau R.
Cape Campbell

PACIFIC

OCEAN

NORTH ISLAND

New Zealand's hub, where high activity is a feature of business, leisure and even the earth itself

The North Island, according to Polynesian legend, is the fish pulled from the sea by Maui. What a catch. The more populous of the two main islands of New Zealand, the North Island will hook visitors too with its range of sights to see, and things to do.

Northland, the region that sits at the top of the island, has a strong Maori heritage and was also one of the first areas settled by Europeans. When the Bay of Islands townships of Paihia and Russell are visited it is easy to understand why. Activities here centre on the sea: sailing, big game fishing, pleasure cruising. There are also numerous sites of historical interest, from the house where the Treaty of Waitangi was signed, to the oldest stone building in the country.

The pace of life in the Far North is slow, but the same can't be said of its brash neighbour, Auckland. Auckland is home to more than a million of New Zealand's 3.9 million population. It is also the largest Polynesian city in the world and its wide range of shops, restaurants and activities make it truly cosmopolitan.

In common with the rest of New Zealand, it doesn't take much for a change of scene. An hour's drive and you are through fertile market gardening and dairy country and into the Waikato. The Waikato takes its name from New Zealand's longest waterway, the Waikato River, which winds its way through the region.

The gold rush was the magnet that drew the first European settlers to the Coromandel, and its beautiful beaches in secluded bays tempt modern day explorers to put down roots here. For sustenance the Bay of Plenty lives up to its name while the East Cape and its remoteness offers a special charm of its own.

Inland things heat up quite considerably. Here, hot mineral springs, boiling mud, geysers and volcanoes have led to Rotorua being aptly called a "thermal wonderland". The hot springs provide soothing relief from the exertions of the adventure activities on offer in the region. Further south at New Zealand's largest lake, Lake Taupo, fishing is the activity of choice for many.

The fertile grounds of Taranaki, Wanganui and Manawatu are some of the most intensely farmed regions in New Zealand, with the dairy industry to the fore. The numerous small towns that service local farms also offer friendly stop-over points to travellers.

Though situated at the bottom of the North Island, Wellington is at the centre of New Zealand life. It is the nation's capital and within its tightly packed, harbour-fringed inner city are the head offices of many of the country's major companies.

Our team of writers, with their in-depth knowledge and first-hand experience of each of these regions, will bait that hook so you, like Maui, can capture the essence of the North Island.

PRECEDING PAGES: Northland's Ninety Mile Beach.

AUCKLAND

Once New Zealand's capital, today it's a sprawling metropolis
of beaches and bays, high-rises and history, where
Polynesia and the old Pacific meet modern Asia and the West

Map,
page 140

T o Aucklanders it is the "City of Sails" or the "Queen City", the biggest and brightest metropolis in New Zealand. The city has a bigger population than the whole of the South Island, and everything they could possibly need can be found within the boundaries of the Auckland region. For such smug souls, the rest of the country does not exist.

To others living in New Zealand's wop-wops (provincial backcountry), and especially those in the capital city of Wellington, Auckland is "The Big Smoke" where people are preoccupied with the three b's: beaches, boats and barbecues. And who can blame them? They happen to be blessed with two beautiful harbours, scores of safe swimming beaches, a coastline dotted with secluded offshore islands, sophisticated city living and a climate made for outdoor leisure.

PRECEDING PAGES: yacht race in Auckland Harbour. **LEFT:** Auckland skyline and harbour. **BELOW:** Ponsonby's white-painted wooden buildings.

Water, water everywhere

Auckland's agreeable, aquatic lifestyle has largely been decreed by the city's geographical situation within the Hauraki Gulf. Apart from slender necks of land to the west and south, it's a metropolis surrounded by water and the locals love it. They paddle in it, swim in it, surf on it, sail on it, ski on it, dive in it and fish in it. Auckland is bounded by the Waitemata Harbour in the north and east, and by the Manukau Harbour to the south and west. Just outside Waitemata Harbour, Hauraki Gulf is one of the most favoured sailing playgrounds in the country.

Within an hour's drive of the city centre there are more than 100 mainland beaches and Auckland's "boat people" can seek further solitude in the hundreds of sandy bays nestled in 23 offshore islands in the gulf. To celebrate this natural, marine playground, Auckland has the greatest number of pleasure boats per capita of any coastal city in the world.

Fittingly, the sporting highlight of the year is the Auckland Anniversary Day Regatta, held annually towards the end of January, in which up to 1,000 sailboats, from 2-metre (6-ft) yachts to 30-metre (100-ft) keelers, compete on the Waitemata Harbour. Equally spectacular is the "Round-the-Bays" run held annually in March in which up to 80,000 joggers (one in 12 Aucklanders) run for fun over a 10.5-km (6.5-mile) course from Victoria Park along the waterfront to St Heliers Bay.

The Auckland isthmus was formed dynamically with the geologically recent eruption of 60 volcanoes, the oldest 50,000 years ago and the youngest – the bush-clad Rangitoto Island, only 8 km (5 miles) from downtown Auckland – blasted from the sea about 800 years ago. Just two centuries ago, Rangitoto's last blast buried a Maori settlement on the adjoining Motutapu Island.

The history of human habitation in the Auckland

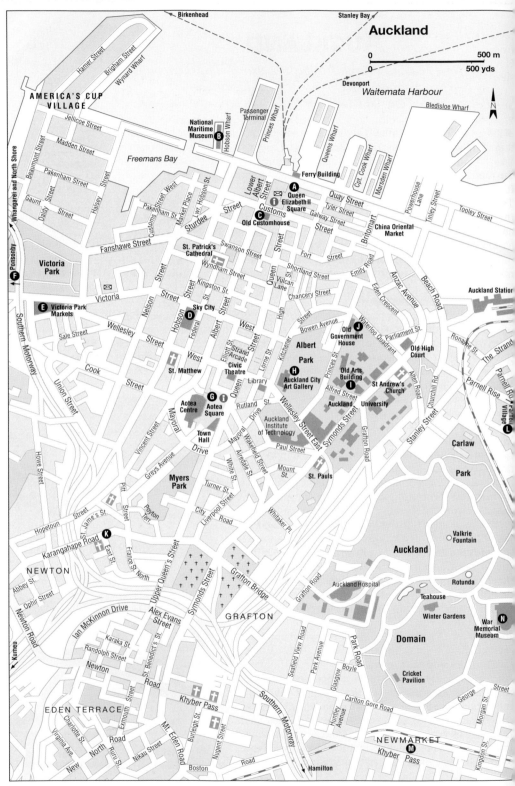

Auckland

region is no less turbulent. Ancestors of the Maori are believed to have arrived from eastern Polynesia around AD 800 and settled on the offshore islands of the Hauraki Gulf. Traditions of the Maori tribes tell of incessant warfare and bloodshed over the possession of such a salubrious region as the population expanded.

Auckland's waterways assumed strategic importance as canoe highways. At one time, every volcanic cone in Auckland was the site of a fortified *pa* or Maori village. Some vantage points like One Tree Hill and Mount Eden bear evidence of a system of terraces along which wooden palisades were erected; the *pa* on these hills may have boasted hundreds of warriors as little as 200 years ago.

Tamaki, battle of 100 lovers

It was the bloody inter-tribal conflicts that gave Auckland its early Maori name, Tamaki, the Maori word for *battle*. The isthmus was also called, rather charmingly, Tamaki makau rau (Battle of 100 lovers). This poetic description had absolutely nothing to do with love and romance but accurately portrayed Tamaki as a highly desirable region which was fought over by the several tribes.

The British settlement of Auckland began with the visit of the adventurous missionary Samuel Marsden, in 1820. Marsden, based in Sydney, Australia, was aboard the sailing ship *Coromandel*, which ventured into the Hauraki Gulf seeking masts and spars. While timber was being felled, the intrepid preacher covered about 900 km (550 miles) along rough tracks, by whaleboat and in canoes offered by the friendly Maori of Mokoia village, near the site of the present Auckland suburb of Panmure. Marsden, who crossed the Auckland isthmus on 9 and 10 November 1820, is credited with being the first European to do so.

The last recorded Maori battle in Auckland took place in 1827, when the Ngati Whatua tribe attacked the Ngapuhi tribe and seized control of the territory. The fighting reduced the Maori population such that, by 20 October 1840, the British found it much easier to win Auckland from the fierce Ngati Whatua. They purchased the area now comprising the heart of Auckland for 50 blankets, 20 trousers, 20 shirts and other assorted sundries plus £50 sterling cash, with another £6 paid the following year. Their prize: 1,200 hectares (3,000 acres) covering three bays from Freemans Bay to Parnell and inland to Mount Eden. Today, just one acre of downtown land in the city is worth at least NZ$12 million.

Plonked ignominiously on a traffic island at the entrance to King's Wharf, in downtown Auckland, is a piece of rock and a greening metal inscription marking Auckland's birth on 18 September 1840. The shabby memorial marks the spot where Auckland's founder and the first governor of New Zealand, Captain William Hobson, declared the settlement to be the capital.

Urban sprawl

A pioneer of the time described the settlement as consisting of "a few tents and huts and a sea of fern stretching as far as the eye could see". Today the eye ranges over a sea of suburbs. It's no accident that Auckland and Los Angeles have sister city status – both are gateways to their respective nations and both sprawl over huge areas. Auckland and its urban area occupy 1,016 sq km

Map, see opposite

TIP

New Zealand has an excellent public library system, which temporary residents can join for a small fee, for access to a huge range of books, magazines and audio-visual information about the country.

BELOW: Queen Street as it was.

ABOVE: Ponsonby Town Hall.

BELOW: smart glass-fronted buildings in downtown Auckland.

(392 sq miles) and are spread 80 km (50 miles) along the coast from Whanga-paraoa and Torbay in the north, to Papakura and Drury in the south.

Rapid economic change during the 1980s and 1990s has brought about the development of Auckland's inner city area, first with smart office blocks, and more recently with apartment blocks and townhouse complexes. The next most valuable real estate is to be found along the low hills around the bays that curve cosily around the central city area.

It was once joked that visitors arrived in Auckland and found it closed. But the liveliness of both city and suburbs has been enhanced by the extension of shopping hours from the severe opening restrictions that prevailed until the late 1980s. Now most shops, and all tourist retail outlets stay open till late on weekdays and through the weekends. New Zealand's second defence of the America's Cup has seen much development on Auckland's Viaduct Basin, including the construction of new marinas, the **America's Cup Village** and a massive apartment complex on **Princes Wharf**, complete with restaurants, bars, a hotel and boutique shops.

Auckland's suburban sprawl means it is not the easiest place for tourists to get around. Taxis are not cheap but there are bus services to almost anywhere in the region. Daily coach tours leave the city on sightseeing excursions ranging from three to eight hours long.

City walks

Auckland's "Golden Mile" is Queen Street, offering some of the best shopping in New Zealand. Souvenir shops are everywhere, while the main street is complemented by arcades and side-streets containing traders in antiques, rare books, second-hand jewellery, crafts and designer clothes. Pausing at the intersection of

Queen and Fort streets, it's hard to imagine that waves once lapped the shore at this spot. Little more than a century ago, Fort Street was the beach front, and Shortland Street in the next block was the main street of early Auckland. Queen Street in the 1840s was a bush-covered gully.

At the bottom of Queen Street, on the edge of the harbour, is **Queen Elizabeth II Square** Ⓐ, a favourite place for lunchtime office workers. A decorated fruit barrow, an ice-cream parlour and other snack stalls attract business in the square, where many people meet before crossing the street to the ferry building and embarking on cruises of the harbour and the Hauraki Gulf. Information on bus tours and attractions such as museums, art galleries, historic buildings, beaches and parks is readily available from the Auckland Visitor Centre.

A hundred metres or so from the square is the **National Maritime Museum** Ⓑ with a number of historic vessels berthed alongside. The museum and the adjacent Viaduct Basin are surrounded by busy taverns, restaurants and hotels, many of which were built for the end of the America's Cup race in April 2000.

Historic shops

Sitting majestically opposite the Downtown Complex on the corner of Customs Street and Albert Street is the **Old Customhouse** Ⓒ, which was the financial heart of Auckland for more than 80 years. Designed in French Renaissance style, the building was completed in 1889 and is one of the last remaining examples of monumental Victorian architecture to be found in the central business district.

The Customhouse cost $30,732 to erect but more than $3 million has been spent on its restoration. Open every day, it houses gift shops and restaurants. Between the Customhouse and the plush Stamford Plaza Hotel in Albert Street

Map, page 140

Bored with bungee jumping, high-adrenaline freaks have devised urban rap jumping, or abseiling face-forward down a sky-scraper. To see it, look at the Novotel Hotel, QEII Square around 11am or 2pm daily. To participate, visit the Hotel's Vertigo Bar.

BELOW: Auckland ferry building.

is a block of the most luxurious visitor apartments in Auckland. Towering above the bustle of downtown Auckland, is the **Sky City ⓓ** complex, hosting a casino, the Sky City Hotel and the cloud-piercing Sky Tower, currently the southern hemisphere's tallest structure.

Ten minutes' walk to the west is the **Victoria Park Market ⓔ**, located on the disused site of the city's former rubbish destructor. Completed in 1905, the brick buildings were opened by Mayor Arthur Myers, who was hauled to the top of the 40-metre (131-ft) chimney in a ship's bosun chair to lay the final brick. In a pioneer conservation move, heat from the old destructor was used to generate electricity. The site now offers seven-day buying at fruit, vegetable and craft shops or hawkers' barrows and food stalls.

West of Victoria Park Market and a 10-minute walk up the hill is **Ponsonby ⓕ**. With its abundance of restaurants, boutique shops and bars, this district has become one of the most sought after suburbs in Auckland to live in.

ABOVE: Old General Store, Auckland.

Movies and museums

Halfway up Queen Street is **Aotea Square**, dominated by the monolithic Auckland City Council administration building. The old Town Hall, built in 1911, forms the eastern boundary. On the western side of the square is the city's new cultural complex, the **Aotea Centre ⓖ**, built amid much controversy for $120 million. It has a 2,300 seat multi-purpose theatre, a convention centre, exhibition foyers and a restaurant. Just down the road is the opulent **Civic Theatre** (tel: 09-309 2677) which is mostly used for touring musicals and shows.

Central Queen Street is Auckland's cinema centre, housing a dozen movie theatres along with numerous fast food outlets. A block away in Lorne Street is

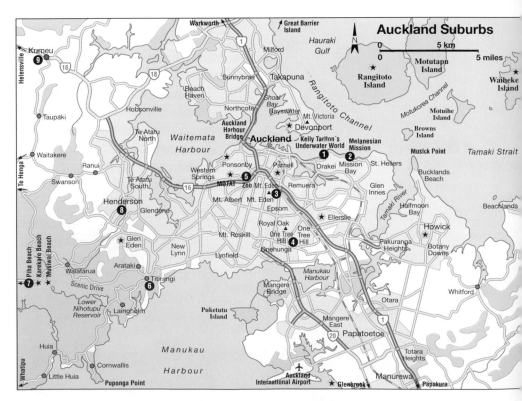

the public library's reading room, popular with homesick travellers and immigrants devouring newspaper pages from the foreign press. Not far away, in Wellesley Street East, is the **Auckland City Art Gallery** , which occupies a French Renaissance-style building opened in 1887. It has the biggest collection of New Zealand paintings in the country, including late 18th century works by John Webber and William Hodges, who travelled with Captain Cook.

Map, page 140

Griffins and muskets

Behind the Art Gallery is picturesque **Albert Park**, which was once the site of Albert Barracks, built in the 1840s to protect against attacks by Maori tribes. Remains of the barrack walls with musket holes can be seen in the grounds of Auckland University behind the main library on the eastern side of the park.

The intricate clock tower of the university's **Old Arts Building**, completed in 1926 in New Zealand Gothic style, was dubbed The Wedding Cake by locals because of its decorative pinnacles and original white-stone construction. In nearby Waterloo Quadrant, grinning griffins and gargoyles adorn the exterior walls of the castle-like Supreme Court, built in 1868. They were created by German engraver Anton Teutenberg. Also within the university confines, a stone's throw from the gargoyles, is the **Old Government House**, erected in 1856 and now used as a common room.

A few steps away is Parliament Street, another vestige of Auckland's former glory as New Zealand's capital. It was only pressure from the gold-rich South Island and vigorous new settlements further south in the North Island that resulted in the movement of the capital from Auckland to Wellington.

South along Symonds Street, in a cemetery opposite the Sheraton Hotel, is

The name of New Zealand's national Rugby team, the All Blacks, is thought to date from their 1905 tour of the United Kingdom, when they wore their new all-black togs and won all but one game.

BELOW: view across the harbour to Devonport.

the grave of Captain Hobson, who selected Auckland as the site of the nation's capital. Hobson chose Auckland because it was strategically placed between two main areas of Maori population (Northland and Waikato) and was centrally located for the main European settlements of the time (Russell and Wellington). He named the fledgling capital after the Earl of Auckland, George Eden, Viceroy of India who, as First Lord of the Admiralty, had given Hobson captaincy of the naval frigate HMS *Rattlesnake*.

Hobson is also remembered in landmarks like Mount Hobson, Hobson Bay and Hobsonville (15 km/9 miles northwest of the city). Hobsonville was the site he first selected for the capital but then rejected it in favour of the city's present location on the advice of his surveyor-general, Felton Mathew.

K-Road

Up at the top end of Queen Street, opposite Grafton Bridge – which was the biggest ferro-concrete span in the world on its completion in 1910 – is **Karangahape Road Ⓚ**, known to locals as "K-Road". Home to much of Auckland's sex industry and alternative fashion scene, the famous street is also the shopping place of the Pacific Island community of Samoans, Fijians, Tongans, Nuie and Cook Islanders. Shops display brilliantly coloured cloth, taro, yams, papaya, mangoes, green bananas, coconut products and other tropical foods.

Auckland is the world's biggest Polynesian city, with more than one-quarter of the Maori population and around 100,000 Pacific Islanders living in the urban area. The ethnic Chinese population is also fast growing, with many recent immigrants from Hong Kong and Taiwan.

Thanks to immigration, Auckland's restaurant cuisine now ranks for quality

and variety with the most cosmopolitan in the world, with specialities from Korea, Japan, India and Italy to name but a few. For inner-city visitors, the restaurant areas include Ponsonby Road, K-Road and along Tamaki Drive from Okahu Bay to St Heliers.

Touring the suburbs

East of the centre is historic Parnell, the city's first suburb, where pioneer homes, like Kinder House (1858) in Ayr Street, are open to the public. In Judge Street you'll find tiny St Stephen's Chapel (1857) with a pioneer cemetery, and the wooden Gothic Church of St Mary's (1888) is in Parnell Road.

Parnell Village ❶ on Parnell Road is a favourite shopping area with quaint Victorian-style shops, restaurants and boutiques. The Village is one of the successes of local millionaire property developer Les Harvey.

Four hundred metres (440 yards) to the south from the top of Parnell Rise is the busy shopping centre of **Newmarket ❶**. A number of major fashion chains opened stores in the shopping strip in the 1980s, triggering a boom that has run unabated since. Number 277 on Broadway is a major mall.

Overlooking Parnell, the city and harbour, in the rambling grounds of the Auckland Domain, is the **War Memorial Museum ❶**. The museum houses one of the finest displays of Maori and Polynesian culture in the world with exhibits of artefacts dating back to AD 1200. A highlight is the 30-metre (98-ft) war canoe, Te-Toki-A-Tapiri (The Axe of Tapiri), carved in 1836 from a single giant totara tree. The hall of New Zealand birds is another unique feature of the museum, incorporating skeletons and a reconstruction of Big Bird, the now extinct, 4-metre (13-ft) tall, flightless moa *(see page 117)*.

Map, page 140

BELOW: historic One Tree Hill – before the tree was cut down in 2002.

East from Parnell, along the Tamaki Drive seafront, are Judges Bay, Okahu Bay, Mission Bay, Kohimarama and St Heliers, luring weekend vendors and family fun-seekers with cafés, sandy beaches, and bicycle, yacht and windsurfer hire centres. **Kelly Tarlton's Antarctic Encounter and Underwater World ❶** is on the waterfront between Okahu Bay and Mission Bay. Dozens of varieties of fish and sharks can be viewed from the safety of a huge transparent tunnel. An Antarctic section features King and Gentoo penguins in their own world of snow and ice. At Mission Bay stands the **Melanesian Mission ❷** building, constructed in 1859 as a mission school, and now a museum of Melanesian artefacts.

High points

Just south of the city centre is the 196-metre (643-ft) extinct volcanic cone of **Mount Eden ❸**, Auckland's highest point, affording a dramatic 360-degree panorama of the region. In an old lava pit on the eastern side, Eden Gardens provides a dazzling display of more than 500 camellias, rhododendrons and azaleas amidst 1,000 trees and shrubs.

A short distance south again is the landmark cone of **One Tree Hill ❹** and the tomb of the "Father of Auckland", Sir John Logan Campbell. Sir John set up a tent as Auckland's first store at the bottom of Shortland Street on 21 December 1840, and was the city's most prominent businessman until his death in 1912 at the age of 95. With his partner, William Brown, he built **Acacia Cottage** in 1841. Now Auckland's oldest building, it is preserved in Cornwall Park at the base of One Tree Hill. In 1901, Sir John presented his 135-hectare (335-acre) farm, encompassing One Tree Hill, as a park for the people of Auckland. Although still called One Tree Hill, the lone pine tree that used to stand at the

ABOVE: Cricket at Eden Park.
BELOW: Victoria Park Market.

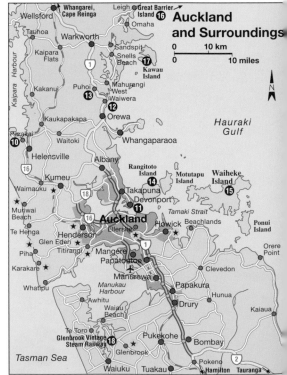

Auckland
and Surroundings

hill's summit is no longer there. In 2002, the tree had to be cut down after a Maori activist damaged the tree some years earlier.

Off the Western Motorway at Western Springs is **Motat** ❺ – the Museum of Transport and Technology – containing working displays of vintage vehicles, aircraft and machinery *(see page 330)*. Volunteer enthusiasts operate many exhibits on the weekends and displays include an aircraft built by New Zealander Richard Pearse which may have flown in March 1903, months before the Wright Brothers.

A brief ride in an old tram or a pleasant walk around the lake at Western Springs leads to Auckland Zoo, starring New Zealand's unique, flightless kiwi bird and the tuatara lizard, a "living fossil".

Heading west, a popular drive climbs over the forested Waitakere Ranges via **Titirangi** ❻. Tall kauri trees, giant ferns and nikau palms line the road to the rugged black-sand surfing beach of **Piha** ❼ and the kauri tree park at Swanson. Forest Hill Road provides an escape route from the trees, down into the grape-growing district of **Henderson** ❽ with its 30 vineyard wine-tasting bars.

About 50 km (30 miles) from Auckland through the wine-growing centres of **Kumeu** ❾, Huapai and Waimauku, is the thermal resort of **Parakai** ❿. Tired limbs can be soothed in hot mineral waters which bubble out of the earth into tiled pools before being pumped down exhilarating water chutes.

Over the bridge

Offering dramatic harbour views is **Auckland Harbour Bridge**, the city's best-known landmark. Built in 1959 as a four-lane span, its capacity was doubled 10 years later when Japanese engineers built two more lanes ("The Nippon Clip-ons") on each side. As far back as 1859 a bridge to connect the city with the North

Map, see pages 144 & 148

TIP

Auckland Observatory (tel: 09-624 1246) in One Tree Hill Domain, is open to the public from Wed to Sat evenings – if you're lucky you might get to see the Southern Cross and other constellations not visible in the Northern Hemisphere.

BELOW: Mansion House, Kawau Island.

Map, see page 148

ABOVE: café life.
BELOW: Maori rap artist.
RIGHT: Contrasting styles, downtown Auckland.

Shore was suggested, when it was estimated a pontoon structure would "be crossed daily by 110 people, 10 wagons, 20 horses, 10 cows, 12 sheep and 5 pigs". Today the bridge carries an average of 125,000 vehicles a day. For a bird's eye view of the city, try a two-hour guided climb over the Auckland Harbour Bridge.

Ferries offer a regular service through the day between downtown Auckland and **Devonport** ⓫ just across the harbour. Devonport has a charming, stylish shopping centre that attracts commuters who like to enjoy the quiet lifestyle, and tourists looking for a pleasant day in the sun. Its volcanic promontories of Mount Victoria and North Head give unobstructed views into downtown Auckland and across the harbour to the Eastern Bays. The two hills were honeycombed with fortified tunnels during a Russian invasion scare in the 1870s and were inhabited by Maori communities over a 700-year period through to 1863.

North from Devonport the coastline is an endless procession of sheltered coves and white-sand beaches stretching to the tip of the North Island. **Takapuna** offers good shopping and a popular beach overlooking Rangitoto Island.

Aquatic relaxation

Less than one hour's drive north of Auckland are the popular holiday resorts of **Orewa** and **Waiwera** ⓬. Waiwera means "hot water" and refers to thermal springs percolating up from volcanic layers onto a sandy beach in which the Maori dug holes and lay in pools of hot mineral waters. The Waiwera Hot Pools are a good deal more sophisticated today with a range of public and private pools of varying temperatures, barbecue facilities, picnic grounds and exhilarating steel water chutes called The Choobs. Just a few kilometres north is the **Puhoi Pub** ⓭, a veritable museum of the pioneers of that area, which was the country's earliest Bohemian settlement.

On a sparkling, calm day there is no substitute for a leisurely cruise to the offshore islands in the Hauraki Gulf. Cruise launches and ferries leave the wharves daily at the bottom of Queen Street to **Rangitoto Island** ⓮, Motuihe, Motutapu, Rakino and the holiday resort island of Pakatoa. A speedy catamaran service also links Auckland with **Waiheke Island** ⓯, only an hour away in the Hauraki Gulf but a thousand miles away in terms of pace and lifestyle.

A more in-depth look at the islands can be gained by a weekend cruise to **Great Barrier Island** ⓰, some 90 km (56 miles) northwest. Fullers Auckland (tel: 09-367 9111) offers a ferry service in January, February and Easter to Great Barrier Island, or else take one of the daily trips offered by **Subritzkyline Great Barrier** (tel 09-373 4036).

Leaving Auckland

Setting off for Northland, a diversion to Sandspit (at Warkworth) allows for a four-hour launch excursion to historic **Kawau Island** ⓱ – site of the restored Mansion House built by the controversial New Zealand Governor Sir George Grey, in 1862.

Departing from Auckland in the south, train buffs can leave the motorway at Drury and follow the signs from Waiuku Road to the **Glenbrook Vintage Steam Railway** ⓲, which operates on weekends.

HISTORIC NORTHLAND

Map, page 156

Northland's picturesque charm makes it an ideal holiday and retirement spot, while concealing a dramatic past of debauchery, excess, wars, rebellion, conquest and finally, settlement

Tribal warfare, bloody clashes between Maori and Pakeha, debauchery, insurrection, missionary zeal, a treaty of peace and promises – all are part of Northland's turbulent historical backdrop. But Northland has more to offer than the past. It is a place where you can relax and enjoy the sun, food, sights and distinctive way of life. It is famed for its scenery – its pastoral, productive south and the wilder, remoter and legendary far north. Northland is noted for its game fishing, unspoiled beaches, pleasant climate, thermal pools, kauri forests – and its friendliness.

The winterless Northland

This irregular peninsula juts upwards some 450 km (280 miles) north from Auckland to the rocky headlands of North Cape and Cape Reinga, the topmost tip of the land. It is labelled the winterless north after its mild, damp winters and warm and humid summers. A feature are the pohutukawa trees, which in early summer rim the coast and decorate the hinterland with their dark red blossoms.

For those wanting to explore the region freely, it is best to work from a base at Paihia, a Bay of Islands township on the far northeast coast. Air New Zealand Link offers daily flights to Whangarei, and Air New Zealand Link flies daily to both Kerikeri, on the northern coast of the Bay of Islands, and Kaitaia, further north again. Alternatively, it's a scenic three-and-a-half-hour drive up Highway One from Auckland.

PRECEDING PAGES: overlooking the Bay of Islands.
LEFT: Cape Reinga.
BELOW: kauri tree.

Bay of Islands

The route from Auckland begins across the Harbour Bridge, proceeds along the Hibiscus Coast with its beachfront resorts, then continues through the small farming towns of Warkworth and Wellsford and around Whangarei city, gateway to the north. Drivers leave the main highway at Kawakawa and snake down to the harbourside resort of **Paihia ❶**. This is the Bay of Islands, the cradle of New Zealand. Its irregular 800-km (500-mile) coastline, embracing 150 islands, is steeped in historical association with the country's early settlement.

Polynesian explorer Kupe is said to have visited here in the 10th century followed by another canoe voyager, Toi, 200 years later. Captain Cook discovered the harbour for Europeans in 1769. Impressed, he gave the sheltered waters of the bay their current name.

In the scattered group are eight larger islands and numerous islets. The biggest measures 22 hectares (54 acres). Many are uninhabited; two are privately owned; some are Maori reserves. About 4,000 people live permanently in the region, but in the summer holiday, from Christmas to late January, up to 50,000 people head north to camp, boat, swim, fish and relax. As most

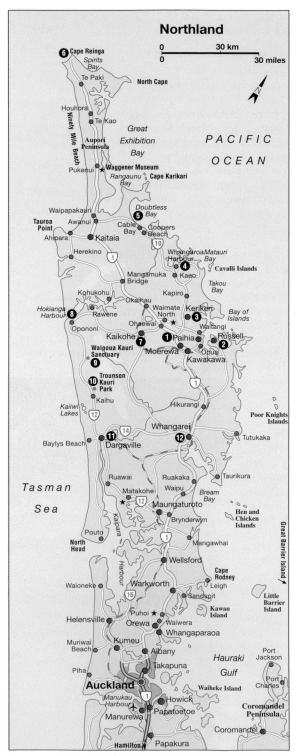

Northland

0   30 km
0   30 miles

6 Cape Reinga
Spirits Bay
Te Paki
North Cape
Houhora
Te Kao
Great Exhibition Bay
Ninety Mile Beach
Aupori Peninsula
Pukenui
Waggener Museum
Rangaunu Bay
Cape Karikari
PACIFIC OCEAN
Waipapakauri
Doubtless Bay **5**
Tauroa Point
Awanui
Cable Bay
Coopers Beach
Ahipara
Kaitaia **10**
Herekino
1
Whangaroa Matauri Bay
Harbour **4**
Mangamuka Bridge
Kaeo
Cavalli Islands
Takou Bay
Kohukohu
Kapiro
Okaihau
Hokianga Harbour **8**
Rawene
Waimate North
Kerikeri **3**
Bay of Islands
Ohaewai
Waitangi
Opononi
Kaikohe **7**
1 Paihia
Russell
Waipoua Kauri Sanctuary
Moerewa
Opua **2**
Kawakawa
9
Trounson **10** Kauri Park
Kaihu
Hikurangi
Kaiiwi Lakes **12**
Poor Knights Islands
14
Whangarei
Baylys Beach
11 Dargaville
12
Tutukaka
Tasman Sea
Ruawai
Ruakaka
Taurikura
Matakohe
Waipu
Bream Bay
12
Maungaturoto
Brynderwyn
Hen and Chicken Islands
Pouto
North Head
Mangawhai
Wellsford
Cape Rodney
Waioneke
Warkworth
Leigh
16
Sandspit
Little Barrier Island
Puhoi
Kawau Island
Helensville
Orewa
Waiwera
Whangaparaoa
Muriwai Beach
Kumeu
Albany
Takapuna
Hauraki Gulf
Port Jackson
Piha
Auckland
Manukau Harbour
Howick
Waiheke Island
Port Charles
Manurewa
Papatoetoe
Coromandel Peninsula
Coromandel
Hamilton
Papakura
Kaipara Harbour
Great Barrier Island

Northland visitors go to the bay, this period requires accommodation reservations well in advance.

Since the 1950s, the small township of Paihia has been revamped to meet the challenge of tourism. Modern motels have sprung up alongside a neat, expanded shopping centre. A variety of eating places and modest nightlife make it a worthy hub of Northland. The wharf, its focal point, caters for island cruises and fishing trips.

Paihia has marked its places of historical note with bronze plaques along the red-sand seafront. It has many firsts: New Zealand's oldest Norfolk pine stands here. A mission station was created on the town site in 1823. Missionaries built and launched the country's first ship, the *Herald*, here in 1826. From the first printing press, brought from England in 1834, came the first Bible in Maori. Colonial history is etched in the graveyard.

Kelly Tarlton's Shipwreck Museum is like a visit to Davy Jones's Locker. The beached bark houses an intriguing array of relics salvaged from wrecks around the New Zealand coast. Below decks, swinging lanterns, sailing-ship sound effects, and the smell of ropes and tar create a seagoing illusion.

The Treaty

The most significant act in New Zealand's early history took place on the lawn of the **Waitangi Treaty House**, about 2 km (1.4 miles) north of Paihia, over a one-way bridge that also leads to the Waitangi Reserve and a golf course.

In 1840, with Governor William Hobson signing on behalf of Queen Victoria, Maori chiefs and English gentlemen inked a pact to end Maori-Pakeha conflict, guarantee the Maori land rights, give them and the colonists Crown protection, and admit New Zealand to the British Empire.

At the time the Treaty of Waitangi was signed, the house was the home of James Busby, British Resident in New Zealand from 1832 to 1840. The gracious colonial dwelling, with its commanding views of the bay, later fell into disrepair, but has since been restored and today the Treaty House is a national museum. Visitors will be impressed by the splendour of an adjacent Maori meeting house and awed by a massive war canoe. Access is through an information-reception centre, which provides ample background plus an audiovisual on the Treaty signing.

Map, see opposite

Gone fishing

Deep-sea fishing for some of the world's biggest gamefish is a major lure at the Bay of Islands. The main fishing season is December through June when the huge marlin are running. Many world records for marlin, shark and tuna were set here. Yellowtail kingfish, running on till September, provide good sport on light rods. Snapper, one of New Zealand's favourite table fish, is plentiful.

Fighting fish up to 400 kg (880 pounds) are caught in the bay, and weigh-ins attract appreciative crowds. Competitions for line-fishing and surf-casting are frequently held; the foremost are in January. Despite the "seasons", fishing is a year-round sport here. Charter boats are available at Paihia or Russell for half- or full-day hire, and on a share basis.

A Maori legend tells how a wounded chief asked for penguin and on tasting the broth revived, and said, "Ka reka to korora", or "How sweet is the penguin".

Sin city

Runaway sailors, escaped convicts, lusty whalers, promiscuous women, brawling and drunkenness: **Russell ❷**, formerly Kororareka, has known them all.

Colonists first arrived in 1809, making it New Zealand's first white settlement. Today it's small, quiet and peaceful. There's an aura of stored history, of romance, of skeletons jangling in those Victorian cupboards. But things liven up at Christmas and New Year when celebrating boaties and other visitors get the place rocking again. This former (but short-lived) capital of New Zealand is

BELOW: Waitangi Treaty House.

linked by a regular launch service to Paihia and Waitangi. A vehicular ferry also serves the small peninsula from the deep-sea port of Opua south of the harbour.

In the early 1830s lust and lawlessness prevailed, with up to 30 grog shops operating on the tiny waterfront. Shocked early settlers responded by building Christ Church in 1835, which is now New Zealand's oldest church. Its bullet-holed walls are grim reminders of its siege in 1845.

Butcher shop in Rawene, Northland.

Maori Chief Hone Heke reluctantly signed the Treaty of Waitangi in 1840, then grew discontented over government land dealings. In 1845, he defiantly chopped down the British flagstaff, symbol of the new regime, on Maiki Hill behind Russell. Meanwhile, Chief Kawiti burned and sacked the town, sparing church property. A showdown came in 1846 near Kawakawa, at Kawiti's *pa* Ruapekapeka. A strong Redcoat force captured this formidable fortress somewhat unfairly on a Sunday when the converted Maori were busy worshipping their new Christian god. Heke was eventually pardoned and his men freed.

Pompallier House, a Catholic mission house, was spared in the fighting. It is now an elegant, refurbished tourist attraction. Russell's museum has a quarter-sized seagoing model of Cook's *Endeavour* and numerous colonial curios. Its Duke of Marlborough Hotel is a pub of great character.

Trips on the Bay

The true beauty of the islands in the bay can best be appreciated from the foredeck of one of the daily Cream Trips. These water tours out of Paihia and Russell retrace the voyages of bygone days when cream was regularly collected from island farms. Mail and provisions are still handled this way.

The Fullers launch cruise covers 96 km (60 miles). Passengers see the island

BELOW: sunset, Opononi Beach.

where Captain Cook first anchored on his 1769 voyage of discovery; the cove where French explorer Marion du Fresne, along with his 25 crew members, were slain by Maori in 1772; and bays where the earliest missionaries landed.

A catamaran offers a four-hour cruise and a three-hour scenic excursion to the Cape Brett lighthouse and Piercy Island and, weather permitting, passes through the famous Hole in the Rock. With its myriad of islands and clear waters, the Bay of Islands is a diver's paradise.

Sweet township

The "sweetest" place in Northland is **Kerikeri ❸**. Located 23 km (14 miles) north of Paihia by a pretty inlet, it is a township of unusual interest and character which has a rich backdrop of early Maori and European colonial history. Today, much of New Zealand's finest citrus and subtropical fruits are grown on Kerikeri's fertile land, including kiwi fruit.

The township and its immediate environs – with a population of more than 1,600 – has become a thriving centre for handicrafts and cottage industries. The climate and relaxed lifestyle have attracted many creative residents, along with wealthy retirees from other New Zealand centres.

Down at the inlet are two of New Zealand's oldest buildings. **Kemp House** is the oldest, built in 1822 of pit-sawn kauri and totara. It has since been fully restored. Next door is the **Old Stone Store**, which was constructed by missionaries in 1833 of thick stone to protect their wares from attack. It still serves as a shop, and has a museum upstairs. **Kororipa Pa** should not be overlooked. This was celebrated warrior Hongi Hika's forward army base between 1780 and 1828. Warriors were assembled here before launching raids on southern tribes as far south as Cook Strait.

Not far from Kerikeri is Waimate North, the first inland settlement for white people. Built in 1831–32, the two-storeyed kauri mission house in Waimate North was the home of Bishop George Augustus Selwyn, New Zealand's first bishop, in 1842.

Final shore

In Maori mythology, Cape Reinga is where the spirits of the dead depart on their homeward journey back to the ancestral land of Hawaiki. Coach tours now make their way up this legendary flight path, along the Aupori Peninsula to its northernmost point, and splash back down Ninety Mile Beach. Coaches leave Paihia daily at 7.30–8am, returning about 6pm.

The east-coast route traverses the worked-out gum fields north of Kerikeri, a relic of the huge kauri forests that once covered this region. The dead trees left pockets of gum in the soil, which early settlers found to be a valuable export for fine varnish. In fact, it triggered off a "gum rush". By the 1880s, more than 2,000 men were digging up a fortune there.

In **Whangaroa Harbour ❹**, a deep-sea fishing base, lies the wreck of the *Boyd*. The ship called in for kauri spars in 1809 and sent a party ashore. However, the party was murdered by the local Maori inhabitants, who donned the victims' clothes and rowed back to the vessel to massacre the rest of the crew and set fire to the

Map, page 156

TIP

If you have time, visit the Far North Regional Museum (*see page 331*), in Centennial Buildings, South Road, Kaitaia, just south of Ninety Mile Beach. Collections include Maori artefacts and a reconstructed Moa display.

BELOW: digging for kauri gum.

Map,
page 156

ABOVE: Flowers of the *pohutakawa* or "Christmas tree".
BELOW: Maori carved figure, Waitangi. **RIGHT:** Hokianga Harbour.

ship. This episode is said to have delayed Christian settlement in New Zealand for years.

Further on is **Doubtless Bay ⑤**, named by Cook, which has a string of superb, gently sloping sandy beaches. Coopers Beach, lined with pohutukawa trees, is just as attractive, as is Cable Bay with its golden sand and colourful shells.

At Awanui, the coach heads north, passing through Te Kao, the largest Maori settlement in the far north, to **Cape Reinga ⑥** with its distinctive lighthouse. At nearby Spirits Bay is the gnarled old pohutukawa from where Maori souls, homeward bound to Hawaiki, were said to take off. The whole district is rich in Maori folklore. Views from the cape are impressive, with the turbulent meeting line of the Pacific Ocean and Tasman Sea; the Three Kings Islands discovered by Abel Tasman in 1643; neighbouring capes and secluded beaches.

Ninety Mile Beach is actually 60 miles (96 km) long, and lined with dunes and hillocks of shell, reminders of bygone feasts. It is noted for its shellfish, particularly the succulent but protected toheroa. The route back to Paihia is via Kaitaia, New Zealand's northernmost town, and Mangamuka Scenic Reserve.

The west coast

An interesting west-coast route leads back to Auckland. **Kaikohe ⑦** has a hilltop monument to Chief Hone Heke (a descendant of the old renegade chief) who became a Member of Parliament. It has spectacular views of both coasts. Nearby are Ngawha Hot Mineral Springs, with tempting mercury-and-sulphur waters.

A prime destination is **Hokianga Harbour ⑧**, a long harbour with a score of ragged inlets that keep the place quiet, serene and rural. Kupe is said to have left from here in AD 900 to return to Hawaiki. The tiny seaside resort of Opononi at the harbour mouth briefly became world famous in the southern summer of 1955–56, when a young dolphin began frolicking with swimmers at the beach. When "Opo" died the nation mourned. She is remembered in a song and a monument.

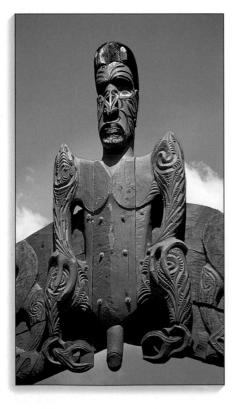

Fathers of the forest

The road then heads south through the **Waipoua Kauri Forest ⑨** with its 2,500 hectares (about 6,100 acres) of mature kauri trees, the largest pocket of kauri forest left in the land. Two giants, close to the unsealed road, tower above them all: Te Matua Ngahere ("Father of the Forest"), about 2,000 years old, and Tanemahuta ("Lord of the Forest"), 1,200 years old with a girth of 13.6 metres (44.6 ft). Further south at **Trounson Park ⑩** are more fine kauris, including one with four stems. **Dargaville ⑪**, 184 km (114 miles) from Auckland, was founded on the timber and kauri gum trade. Its museum has many fine gum samples and is built of clay bricks brought in from China as ship's ballast.

The highway turns east to **Whangarei ⑫**. This lightly industrialised city of 42,000 is a deep-sea port with a harbour, glassworks, cement plant and an oil refinery. There is plenty of accommodation. Mount Parahaki gives panoramic views of city and harbour. Major attractions are the Clapham Clock Collection (400 timepieces dating from the 17th century), safe swimming beaches and the deep-sea fishing base of Tutukaka.

WAIKATO

*Dairy production and agriculture flourish in these rich, fertile
lands south of Auckland, lands which also have a wealth of
historical and cultural artefacts and traditions*

**Map,
page 172**

Dawn birdsong in the central and western region of the North Island has an
unusual accompaniment – the chugalug-chugalug of electric milking
machines. Grass grows more quickly here through the year than anywhere
else in the world and the cows that crop it daily have brought prosperity to generations. Dairy herds free-graze on Waikato pastures along fertile river valleys.
The grass is fed by a mild, wet climate (rainfall averages 1,120 mm or 44 inches).
On the flats and rolling country, farm diversification has expanded the production of fruit and vegetables. The Waikato is also premium thoroughbred horse
breeding country, and dairy cattle studs abound.

A landscape flecked with blood

Much of the now-green pastures were the spoils of land wars between Maori
and Pakeha in the 1860s. The Waikato was once relatively highly populated by
Maori tribes and its land communally owned, according to ancestry. It was a
landscape of dense bush on the hills, peat swamp and kahikatea (white pine)
forests on flat land and the low hills of the Waikato and Waipa river systems.

PRECEDING PAGES:
ancient forest.
LEFT: Morokopa
Falls, Waikato.
BELOW: adventurous
parking.

The land wars changed everything; it took nearly 20 years for the British and
colonial forces to subdue Maori tribes who were intent on keeping what was
left of their land. What land was not confiscated by the
government was effectively taken through 1862 legislation which forced the traditional Maori group ownership to be individualised. Single owners were easy prey
for land agents and the way was opened for the gradual
development, during the 20th century, of the natural
wilderness into the intensively farmed land it is today.

Capital of the Waikato

Hamilton ❶, the country's fourth largest city, straddles
the Waikato River, 50 km (30 miles) inland in the heart
of farmland. Parklands and footpaths cover most of the
city's riverbanks, and these provide popular walking
and jogging routes for locals and visitors.

The central city's most notable riverbank amenity is
the **Waikato Museum of Art and History**. Its collections include treasured Tainui (the Waikato's Maori
tribe) artefacts. National and international touring exhibitions are a regular feature of the museum.

It was the Waikato River, long a vital Maori transport
and trading link to the coast, that first brought the Europeans to the area and led to the establishment of Hamilton in the 1860s. The first businesses grew up on the
riverbank and today the commercial hub of the city runs
parallel to it on the west bank. River cruises offer meals
and a different, more scenic view of the city.

The Waikato River is now a recreational asset for the
region but of primary importance are the eight power

Maori flag.

stations which harness the river's waters, to provide one-third of the nation's hydro-electric power. Behind each dam there are artificial lakes which are very popular spots for fishing, boating and rowing.

Racehorses and spas

The quiet, pretty town of **Cambridge ❷** sits on the Waikato river 24 km (15 miles) upstream from Hamilton. The town's charming Anglican church, tree-lined streets and village green give it a very English atmosphere.

To the east of the river are the Waikato towns of Morrinsville, Te Aroha and Matamata. **Morrinsville ❸** is itself a centre for the surrounding dairy land, with its own large processing factory (tours by arrangement). **Te Aroha ❹**, on the Waihou River farther east, was once a gold town and fashionable Victorian spa sitting at the foot of 952-metre (3,123-ft) bush-clad Mount Te Aroha. The world's only known hot soda-water fountain, the Mokena Geyser, is here.

Matamata ❺ is well-known for its thoroughbred racehorse stables. A three-storey blockhouse built by an early landowner, Josiah Clifton Firth, in 1881, stands as a reminder of the settlers' insecurity after the wars. It's now part of a reserve containing a museum. Several walking tracks lead into and over the nearby Kaimai-Mamaku forest park, one to the picturesque Wairere Falls. South of Matamata lie the pine forests and farmlands of Putaruru and Tokoroa.

Maori stronghold

BELOW: lush, green farmlands north of Te Kuiti.

Down the Waikato River from Hamilton is **Ngaruawahia ❻**, capital of the Maori King movement and an important Maori cultural centre. On the east river-bank in the town is the Turangawaewae Marae, its name meaning "a place to

Map, page 172

put one's feet". It contains traditionally carved meeting houses and a modern concert hall, and is only open to the public on special occasions. The Marae can be seen from the river bridge on the main road a little downstream. The famous **Waingaro Hot Springs** can be found 24 km (15 miles) west of Ngaruawahia.

Mount Taupiri, 6 km (4 miles) downstream, is the sacred burial ground of Waikato tribes. Nearby, the Waikato's waters are used to cool a massive coal-and-gas-fired power station at Huntly. Its two 150-metre (492-ft) chimneys tower over the town, which stands at the centre of New Zealand's largest coalfields.

Southwest of Hamilton is **Te Awamutu ❼**, which has been dubbed "the rose town" for its gardens and rose shows. One of the country's oldest and finest churches, St John's Anglican Church, stands in the main street, built in 1854. Another, St Paul's, built in 1856, lies to the east in Hairini.

Near Hairini is Orakau, scene of the final battle of the Waikato land wars in 1864 when Rewi Maniapoto and 300 Maori men, women and children fought for three days to defend a fortified *pa* against about 1,400 colonial soldiers. The Maori were defeated and retreated south to the King Country.

Caves

In the northern King Country are the famous **Waitomo Caves ❽** and glow-worm grottoes. Four caves are open to the public – Glowworm Cave, Ruakuri, Mangapu and Aranui. Take a boat ride to view the glow-worms, a speleological (cave) museum and a model Maori village or explore caves or go on bush walks. At Te Kuiti, 19 km (12 miles) further south, charismatic Maori leader Te Kooti Riki-rangi took refuge and built an impressively carved meeting house, later given to the local Maniapoto people as a gesture of thanks for their protection.

The full name of the Waikato River is Waikato-taniwa-rau, or "Flowing waters of a hundred river-monsters". The "river-monsters" were the mighty chieftains who lived along the Waikato.

BELOW: rainbow over Raglan, Manu Bay.

MAORI ART: FLAX AND FIGURES

The stone-age culture of the Maori developed extraordinary crafts using the simplest resources

When the Maori migrated to New Zealand from Polynesia, much of what they found was unfamiliar, but they soon learned to make the best use of the available resources. For example, they used stone adzes to make long, graceful canoes from giant kauri trees, or from totaras, whose wood was ideally suited to carving. They preserved their sculptures by painting them with a mixture of red clay and shark oil.

Practical objects and fine arts

Everyday items such as eating utensils, tools and weapons were obviously important to the Maori, but so were the fine arts, which were inextricably linked with the drama of Maori mythology. The *marae*, or traditional meeting-place, is still dominated by imposing wooden figures of important ancestors. A *tiki* is a good luck charm worn round the wrist and made from greenstone or bone, and a *hi-tiki* is worn round the neck. Traditionally, women wove flax leaves into mats and baskets, or turned the fibres into decorative clothing for special occasions.

Renaissance in traditional handicrafts

As the Maori have grown increasingly aware of their heritage, so traditional crafts have enjoyed a rebirth. The main place where young people learn to carve wood, bone and greenstone is the Maori Arts and Crafts Institute. Recently, there has been increased demand from New Zealanders of European origin for traditional Polynesian crafts. Greenstone carving in particular has become an extraordinarily intricate art, which has nothing in common with the mass-produced items for sale in souvenir shops.

▷ **TRAINING CENTRE**
The Maori Arts and Crafts Institute in Rotorua is where most traditional Maori woodcarvers are trained. Located in Whakarewarewa, it is open to visitors daily from 8am to 5pm.

▽ **TRADITIONAL WEAVING**
Flax leaves are softened in thermal springs before being woven into elegant dresses by Maori women. Maori men also wore cloaks made from flax and bordered with geometric patterns.

▷ **GRAPHIC STORYTELLING**
As the Maori had no written language, their myths and legends were passed on verbally from generation to generation. Here a grandmother skilfully creates string figures to illustrate her story of the Tongahiro and Ruapehu volcanoes, which are believed to personify temperamental nature gods.

◁ **BONE TIKI**
Centuries ago, these richly ornamented amulets were made from moa bones, using sharp stone tools. Now that the huge flightless birds have become extinct, tikis are made from the bones of other animals.

◁ FRIGHTENING FACE
Sculptures of monstrous skulls and grimacing faces are typical of Maori art, which had a strong spiritual dimension. Originally, such carvings would have been placed on the protecting palisades of a *pa* to frighten off attackers.

▽ RITUAL ADZE
Maoris used stone tools for woodcarving, but greenstone adzes, or *tokis*, like this one were too precious to use for that purpose. Ornate adzes were made to be carried in ceremonies by tribal chieftains and other high-ranking figures, to symbolise their status and authority.

▽ SPECIAL PROTECTION
Wooden figures of important ancestors were used to protect a tribe against the wrath of the gods and to intercede on the tribe's behalf.

COMMUNAL WAR CANOES

War canoes, ornately decorated with both sculpture and painting, were objects of great prestige in a Maori community. Most were painted red, with black and white detailing, and festooned with feathers. This magnificent 36.5-metre (120-ft) war canoe in Waitangi *(above)* was skilfully carved from the trunks of two huge kauri trees from the Puketi Forest. It took 27 months to build, and was launched in 1940 to mark the centenary of the Waitangi Treaty.

The streamlined hull is at no point more than 2 metres (6 ft 7 inches) wide, but the canoe was big enough for 200 warriors to sit without treading on one another's feet. Propelled by 80 paddles, the canoe reached an impressive speed in the sheltered waters of the Bay of Islands, and the seafaring skills of this Polynesian people were brought vividly to life for the spectators.

In their quest for a new homeland, the Maori crossed the vast and often turbulent Pacific in handbuilt boats; not slender war canoes like this one, but more stable outriggers with greater space for food and personal belongings. In 1985, a 21-metre (69-ft) replica of one of these traditional boats sailed from Rarotonga in the Cook Islands to New Zealand. The 5,000-km (3,100-mile) journey took just over five weeks, with the crew steering by the stars, moon and tides, just as the Maori had once done.

COROMANDEL AND THE BAY OF PLENTY

Map, page 172

A place where everyone can enjoy the great outdoors – camping, tramping, fishing, boating... the less energetic can enjoy lying in a hot pool or just soak up the scenery and the relaxed pace of life

The slogan "Coromandel: Mine Today, Gone Tomorrow!" reflects the strong feelings of its inhabitants that the Coromandel Peninsula's greatest asset is not mineral wealth but its natural attractions. The region once yielded abundant treasures, and early European settlers who flocked here were gold-seekers, gumdiggers and bushmen. Reminders of these earlier bonanzas abound, with colonial buildings, old gold-mine shafts and kauri relics.

Today people flock to the area for a less material and much more accessible treasure: the outdoors. "Outdoor" is the Coromandel's lodestone, offering opportunities for driving, diving, fishing, boating, swimming, camping, tramping, or fossicking for gemstones.

Gold fever territory

At the base of the peninsula, **Thames ❾** was officially declared a goldfield in August 1867. The ensuing gold rush swelled the town's population to 18,000 at its peak. In its heyday, Thames had more than 100 hotels. Today there are just four, the oldest (1868) being the Brian Boru on the corner of Pollen and Richmond streets. To appreciate the town's past, one should visit the Mineralogical Museum and adjacent School of Mines. Nearby, at the old gold mine and gold-stamper battery (well signposted at the northern end of Thames), members of the Hauraki Prospectors' Association will demonstrate the technology used to retrieve gold.

Kauaeranga Valley, also signposted in Thames, is the site of the Conservation Department's visitor and information centre, 10 km (6 miles) from Thames. The first kauri spars from here were taken in 1795, mainly for the Royal Navy; by 1830, kauri trees were being cut in greater numbers. This logging lasted for a century.

Late in the 1800s, huge kauri timber dams were built across creeks on the peninsula to bank up water and then float the logs to sea. About 300 such dams were built, more than 60 of them in the Kauaeranga Valley. Many are still there, slowly disintegrating. A working model of a kauri dam (made of pine, not of kauri) has been built near the information centre.

Today the Kauaeranga Valley is a favourite spot for camping and tramping. Along more than 50 km (30 miles) of tracks, visitors have plenty of access to the wilderness, with basic overnight hut accommodation.

Painters, potters and weavers

North of Thames, towards the town of Coromandel, up the west coast of the peninsula, with the Hauraki Gulf on the left, one soon experiences a winding road and

LEFT: farm meets beach on the Coromandel Peninsula. **BELOW:** kiwi fruit.

*Keep coming back to
the Coromandel.*

spectacularly changing views. The road hugs the coast for much of the way, passing bays where holiday homes huddle on the shore.

Tapu, 18.5 km (11 miles) north of Thames, is the junction for the Tapu-Coroglen road, a scenic route climbing to 448 metres (1,470 ft) above sea level. The road goes over the peninsula to the west coast but is rough and, in winter, dangerous. Most travellers to the east coast prefer to make the journey across at Kopu, just south of Thames.

Coromandel ❿ township, near the northern end of the peninsula, offers a quiet, alternative life for painters who farm, potters who garden, and weavers who rear their own sheep for wool. The town and peninsula were named after the Royal Navy ship HMS *Coromandel*, which called into the harbour there for spars early in the 19th century. The township was less peaceful when it became the site of New Zealand's first gold find by Charles Ring in 1852. More than 2,000 people dashed across the gulf from Auckland at the news, but on arrival they found that the gold was deeply embedded in quartz rock and expensive to extract. It wasn't until 15 years later that a gold-bearing reef rich enough to warrant expensive extraction machinery was discovered.

Coromandel has an air of the past about it and, even at the peak of the summer holiday season, the pace is slow and the lifestyle relaxed. Its history is recorded in institutions like the School of Mines with its collection of rock samples, mostly from the peninsula itself but some accumulated from around the world.

Mythical Turehu

Beyond Coromandel, 28 km (17 miles) north, is Colville, the last store before Cape Colville and the northernmost tip of the peninsula. Enthusiasts insist that

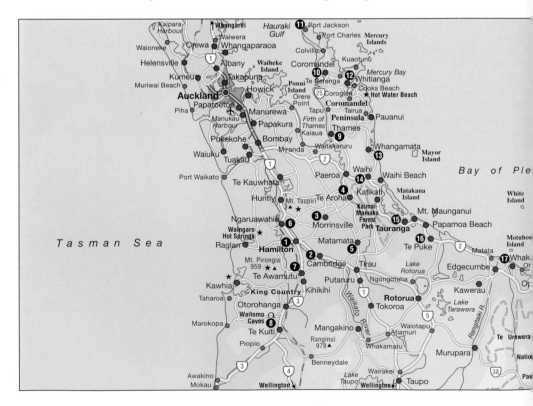

visitors cannot experience the full spirit of the peninsula unless they travel to the end of this road. En route, the road skirts the Moehau Range, whose 891-metre (2,923-ft) peak is the highest point on the peninsula. According to Maori legend, it is home of Turehu or Patupaiarehe, a short, fair-skinned being. But unlike the Himalayas' yeti or America's bigfoot, not so much as a footprint of the Turehu has ever been found. Today's visitors might, however, manage to see the small, rare, native frog *(Leiopeima archeyi).* A refugee from the remote past, it lives only on the Coromandel Peninsula.

The unspoilt beauty and isolation of **Port Jackson** ⓫ and Fletcher Bay draw people to enjoy some peace and solitude. Fletcher Bay, at the end of the road, is also the starting point for the Coromandel Walkway, a three-hour walk to **Stony Bay**. If you prefer less energetic pursuits, visit Stony Bay by taking the road just north of Colville, across the peninsula to Port Charles, and returning via Kennedy Bay on the east coast to Coromandel.

A gem of a town

Two roads lead from Coromandel to Whitianga, situated on the opposite coast of the peninsula. The first, longer and less developed, leads east to Whangapoua Harbour and Kuaotunu Beach. (Here, make a point of travelling the Black Jack Road, renowned as the most hair-raising route in the region.) Another 17 km (10.5 miles) southwest of Kuaotunu is Whitianga. The second route, 15 km (9.5 miles) shorter, climbs to 300 metres (984 ft) before descending to approach the town from the south, along the Whitianga Harbour edge.

Whitianga ⓬, opposite the present town, is said to have been occupied for more than 1,000 years by the descendants of the Polynesian explorer Kupe.

Map, see opposite

It is said that Maui's canoe still lies, petrified, on the summit of Mount Hikurangi, near the East Cape.

BELOW: timber craftsman and assistant.

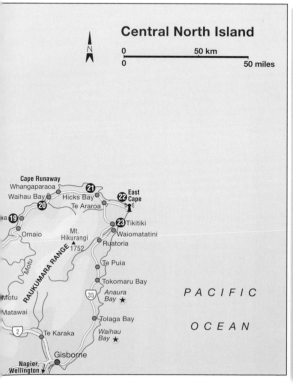

Kauri gum was shipped from Whitianga from 1844, peaking in 1899 with the shipment of 1,100 tonnes. Today's visitors enjoy fishing, swimming or rock-hunting. The latter draws those in search of the area's semi-precious gemstones, jasper, amethyst, quartz, chalcedony, agate and carnelian.

South of Whitianga lies Coroglen (formerly Gumtown). Eight km (5 miles) east is the access road to two essential stopping points. The first of these is **Cook's Bay**, also known as Mercury Bay, where Captain Cook first hoisted the British flag in New Zealand in November 1769 to claim the territory in the name of King George III. While here, he also observed the transit of Mercury; the occasion is marked by a cairn and plaque at the top of Shakespeare Cliffs.

Hot water

The second essential site on the peninsula is the unique **Hot Water Beach**, where thermal activity causes steam to rise from the sand in places and the visitor can dig a thermal hot pool on the beach, using "sand-castle" walls to keep the sea out or let it in to regulate the temperature. It is a great way to relax travel-weary bodies from the bumps and bends of the roads.

The new centre southward is Tairua, on the harbour of the same name. The area is dominated by 178-metre (584-ft) **Mount Paku**, whose summit offers views of nearby Shoe and Slipper islands. Across the harbour is the resort of Pauanui, billed as a Park by the Sea but described by some as almost too tidy to be true. **Whangamata Beach ⑬**, 40 km (25 miles) farther south, is a popular family holiday spot and the prime surfing beach of the peninsula.

The road winds inland from here. Thirty km (19 miles) south is **Waihi ⑭**, where a rich gold- and silver-bearing lode was discovered in 1878. Martha Hill

Take care when swimming at Hot Water Beach. It is notorious for rips and sudden changes in tides and has claimed many lives.

BELOW: rustic pub at Thames.

mine was the greatest source of these minerals. Shafts were sunk to a depth of more than 500 metres (1,600 ft); in 60-plus years, more than NZ$50 million worth of gold and silver was retrieved. Further gold is being won by an opencast mining venture which has laid bare the original mine shafts on Martha Hill.

The bullion trail led through the Karangahake Gorge to Paeroa, from where the ore was shipped to Auckland. A walkway through part of the gorge between Waikino and Karangahake has been developed.

The Kiwi Fruit Capital

A road through the Athenree Gorge south of Waihi leads to **Katikati**, promoted as "The Gateway to the Bay of Plenty". This is followed by the coastal city of **Tauranga** , which is both a tourist focal point and an important commercial centre, and served by a busy port at nearby Mount Maunganui. Flax-trading began here 150 years ago; missionaries arrived in 1838, and in 1864, during the New Zealand Wars, Tauranga was the site of fierce fighting during the battle of Gate Pa. That battlefield was the scene of heroic compassion when Heni Te Kirikamu heard mortally wounded British offices calling for water, and risked death during the battle to take water to his enemies.

The site of the original military camp, the Monmouth Redoubt and the mission cemetery holds not only the remains of the British troops killed at Gate Pa, but also the body of the defender of Gate Pa, Rawhiri Puhirake, killed during the subsequent battle of Te Ranga. Among the leading attractions in Tauranga are **Tauranga Historic Village** (on 17th Avenue), which explains the pioneer history of the area, and **The Elms** mission house in Mission Street, dating from 1847.

Across the harbour from Tauranga is the Mount Maunganui holiday resort. It is built around the 231-metre (758-ft) "Mount", affording views of Tauranga and the surrounding area. Visitors who are reluctant or lack the energy to climb the "Mount" can simply laze on the beach or swim in the saltwater pools near the foot of the hill.

The Bay of Plenty was named by Cook, and his description proved prophetic. Perhaps the greatest current evidence of plenitude is the phenomenal growth of the "furry" kiwi fruit, which has made the township of **Te Puke** the "Kiwi Fruit Capital of the World". Just beyond Te Puke is Kiwi Fruit Country, an orchard park, information centre and restaurant, with a "kiwi fruit train" to take visitors for trips around the park.

Te Puke is 28 km (17 miles) southeast of Tauranga. Its subtropical horticulture has brought prosperity. The kiwi fruit, originally known as the Chinese gooseberry, was introduced to New Zealand from China in 1906, and thrived best in the Bay of Plenty. In the 1970s and early 1980s, many farmers became millionaires from a harvest of only two or three hectares. High demand and high prices made Te Puke the wealthiest small town in the country. Acreage expanded swiftly through other New Zealand regions and gradually to other countries, until nowadays kiwi fruit is just another orchard crop.

Acting as a man

About 100 km (62 miles) from Tauranga and 85 km (53 miles) from the centre of Rotorua is **Whakatane** , at

Map, page 172

TIP

There's little New Zealanders haven't thought of doing with a kiwi fruit. Look out for kiwi fruit jam, honey and even chocolates – they make delicious souvenirs.

BELOW: rural idyll.

the mouth of the Whakatane River and the edge of the fertile Rangitaiki Plains. Until it was drained 70 years ago, the area was a 40,000-hectare (about 100,000-acre) tract of swampland.

Whakatane takes its name from the arrival of the Mataatua Canoe from Hawaiki at the local river mouth. Legend records that the men went ashore, leaving the women in the canoe, which then began to drift away. Though women were forbidden to touch paddles, the captain's daughter, Wairaka, seized one and shouted: "Kia whakatane au i ahau!" ("I will act as a man!"). Others followed her lead and the canoe was saved. A bronze statue of Wairaka now stands on a rock in the river mouth. Above the area known as The Heads is Kapu-te Rangi ("Ridge of the Heavens"), reputedly the oldest Maori *pa* site in New Zealand, established by the Polynesian explorer Toi.

White heat

Clearly visible from Whakatane is **White Island**, a privately owned active volcano 50 km (30 miles) from Whakatane. Scenic flights pass over the steaming island, which was mined for sulphur ore between 1885 and the mid-1930s. In 1914, 11 men lost their lives on the island during a violent eruption. Just over the hill, 7 km (about 4 miles) from Whakatane, is the popular Ohope Beach, described by former New Zealand Governor-General Lord Cobham as "the most beautiful beach in New Zealand".

The last centre of note between Whakatane and the eastern boundary of the Bay of Plenty at Cape Runaway is the rural centre of **Opotiki** ⓲. Here in 1865, missionary Rev. Carl Volkner was murdered by a Maori rebel leader, Kereopa, in a gruesome episode which saw Volkner's head cut off and placed on the

ABOVE: Hillwalkers enjoying the view at White Island.

BELOW: left-hand view of the beach at Te Kaha.

Map, page 172

church pulpit, and the communion chalice used to catch his blood. Eight km (5 miles) southwest of Opotiki is the Hikutaia Domain with some beautiful walks through a variety of native vegetation.

East Cape

From Opotiki there are two routes to the east coast: across or around. The route across follows State Highway 2, which runs through the spectacular Waioeka Gorge. The gorge narrows and becomes steeper before crossing into the green, rolling hills that line the descent into Gisborne.

The alternative route is to follow SH35 around East Cape. The road winds along the coast for 115 km (71 miles) to **Cape Runaway**. En route, it crosses the Motu River, which is known for its rafting and jet-boat rides, and then passes through the small settlements of **Te Kaha** ⓳, formerly a whaling center, and **Waihau Bay** ⓴, a popular camping area. Several beautiful bays are passed on the way to Whangaparaoa and Cape Runaway.

Rounding the cape, the next stop is **Hicks Bay** ㉑, followed 10 km (about 6 miles) on by **Te Araroa**. There's an information centre at Te Araroa, and a turn off to **East Cape** ㉒ and its lighthouse, the North Island's most easterly point. It is one of the first parts of the world to see the new day.

Heading south from Te Araroa, SH35 passes through **Tikitiki** ㉓, with its Anglican Church of Maori design. Just off the highway is Ruatoria, centre of the Ngati Porou tribe. **Te Puia**, 25 km (15 miles) further south is pleasant, with nearby hot springs, and a short drive on is **Tokomaru Bay** with its pretty cliff framed beach. This entire stretch of coast, down through Tolaga Bay and on to Gisborne, is popular with surfers and holidaymakers for its unhurried pace.

TIP

Paper fiends will enjoy a tour of Whakatane Board Mills, where cardboard has been produced since 1939. The Tasman Pulp and Paper Company, 32 km (20 miles) from Whakatane towards Rotorua, is also open to visitors.

BELOW: Marae Hako Bay.

ROTORUA AND THE VOLCANIC PLATEAU

Map, page 182

On the surface it's quiet and even genteel, but Rotorua's tranquillity is punctuated by intense hot and steamy thermal activity that has attracted tourists and healthseekers since Victorian times

O f his visit to Rotorua in 1934, playwright George Bernard Shaw declared: "I was pleased to get so close to Hades and be able to return." Shaw was not the first to draw an analogy between Rotorua and the devil's eternal dwelling of fire and brimstone. To pious Anglican pioneers the region must have had all the hallmarks of Dante's Inferno – a barren wasteland of stunted vegetation, cratered with scalding cauldrons, bubbling mud pools and roaring geysers hurling super-heated water into a sulphur-laden atmosphere.

Today Rotorua represents pleasure and not torment, and the unusual resort has become one of the two jewels of New Zealand tourism (along with Queenstown in the South Island) – a place of thermal wonders, lush forests, green pastures and crystal clear lakes abounding with fighting trout. No fewer than 10 lakes are now the playground of anglers, campers, swimmers, water-skiers, yachtsmen, pleasure boaters, trampers and hunters.

The Rotorua region is situated on a volcanic rift which stretches in a 200-km (124-mile) line from White Island off the coast of the Bay of Plenty to Lake Taupo and the volcanoes of the Tongariro National Park in the Central Plateau of the North Island. More than 60,000 people reside in the Rotorua urban area and close-by smaller towns, because tourism is not the only major industry centred in the region. Bordering on the city is Kaiangaroa, one of the world's largest man-made forests. Most of the exotic trees here are radiata pine, a renewable resource which is regularly cropped for pulp and paper. The region is also prolifically farmed.

Cultural hotspot

Rotorua was settled by descendants of voyagers from the legendary Maori homeland of Hawaiki. Among the arrivals in the Te Arawa canoe around AD 1350 was the discoverer of Lake Rotorua, named in Maori tradition as Ihenga, who travelled inland from the settlement of Maketu and came across a lake he called Rotoiti, "little lake". He journeyed on to see a much larger lake which he appropriately called Rotorua, the "second lake". The city still has the greatest concentration of Maori residents of any New Zealand centre. Much of its allure to tourists is derived from the fact that it is the national "hot spot" of Maori culture.

The first European to visit "the disturbed districts", in 1830, was a Danish sailor, Captain Phillip Tapsell, whose descendant was appointed Speaker to the House of Representatives in 1991.

During the mid-1880s the Arawa tribe remained loyal to the British Crown and, as a result, were subjected to

PRECEDING PAGES: Whakarewarewa. **LEFT:** Maori rooftop, Rotorua. **BELOW:** Champagne Pool, Waiotapu Thermal area, Rotorua.

raids by warring Maori tribes. When the fighting ceased, the government decided to turn Rotorua into a tourist and health-spa resort. An agreement was reached in November 1880 for land on which to build a town to be leased from the Maori owners. The town was administered by The Tourist and Health Resorts Department until 1923 when Rotorua finally achieved independent status.

Liquid assets

The majority of the town's biggest hotels and a large number of motels are located on or just off Fenton Street, running north-south across the city. It is only a short drive to the popular tourist attractions but some form of transport is essential. The Information Centre in Fenton Street will provide information on hire cars, coach excursions, trout fishing and sightseeing services.

East of the northern end of Fenton Street is a beautiful garden area dominated by the magnificent **Bath House**, built in 1908 as a sophisticated spa centre. The Bath House now houses an interesting local museum and art gallery.

To the right of Bath House are the **Polynesian Pools Ⓐ**. Here are contained a number of thermal pools, each with its own special mineral content and varying temperatures. The Priest Pool was named after a Father Mahoney, who pitched his tent alongside a hot spring on the site in 1878 and bathed in the warm water until he reportedly obtained complete relief for his rheumatism.

Rotorua's world-famous thermal waters and their alleged miraculous healing properties were central to the European development of the area. In 1874, former New Zealand Premier Sir William Fox urged the government to "secure the whole of the Lake Country as a sanatorium owing to the ascertained healing properties of the water". Bubbling with optimism, Sir William enthused that the

Relaxing at Rotorua.

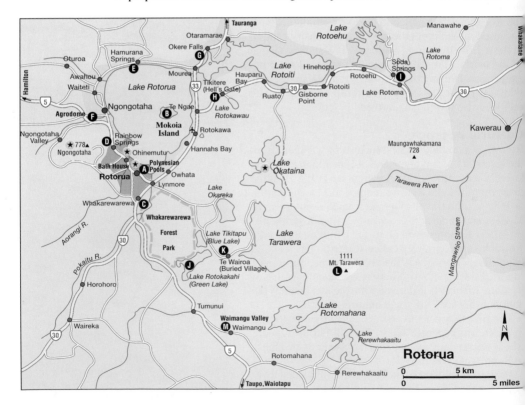

district "might be destined to be the sanatorium not only of the Australian colonies but of India and other portions of the globe".

The building of Rotorua's first sanatorium began in 1880 and, although the sulphurous waters of the baths are still regarded by some as useful in the treatment of arthritis and rheumatism, most people enjoy them as a pleasant form of relaxation. Fronting the pools is the Orchid Garden, two temperature-controlled glass houses filled with exotic blooms from around the world.

Legends of the pools

Further along the lakefront is the historic Maori village of Ohinemutu, once the main settlement on the lake. St Faith's Church, built in 1910, with its rich carvings, Maori Christ window and bust of Queen Victoria, was presented to the Maori people of Rotorua in appreciation of their loyalty to the Crown.

An adjacent 19th-century meeting house took 12 years to carve and is named after the captain of the Arawa canoe, Tama Te Kapua. It is said that Hine-te-Kakara, the daughter of Ihenga, Rotorua's Arawa discoverer, was murdered and her body thrown into a boiling mud pool where Ihenga set up a memorial stone, calling it Ohinemutu, or "the place where the young woman was killed".

At the lakeside, float-planes, helicopters, launches and the Lakeland Queen paddle steamer depart on sightseeing trips. Stop at **Mokoia Island** Ⓑ in the middle of Lake Rotorua, for a dip in Hinemoa's hot pool. Hinemoa is the legendary figure in a famous "Romeo and Juliet" style Maori love story. A young chieftain, Tutanekai, who lived on Mokoia Island, fell in love with the maiden Hinemoa, who lived in a village on the mainland. But their marriage was forbidden by family opposition. Hinemoa secretly planned to follow the sound of

Map, see opposite

Digging in Rotorua has to be a carefully controlled activity. Houses do not have basements, and graves have built-in vaults that sit above the ground.

BELOW: public gardens and the Bath House.

A steamy walk through Rotorua's boiling landscape.

Tutanekai's bone flute over the water during the night and join her lover. The plot was foiled when her people beached all the heavy canoes, so Hinemoa tied gourds to her body and swam across the chilling lake, following the sounds of Tutanekai's flute. She recovered from her ordeal by warming herself in the hot pool that bears her name, before being reunited with Tutanekai.

Mud and geysers

At the southern end of Fenton Street is the **Whakarewarewa**  thermal area, a must for tourists. On Geyser Flat is Pohutu ("splashing"), the greatest geyser in New Zealand, thundering to a height of more than 30 metres (about 100 feet). At the entrance to Whakarewarewa is a model Maori *pa* with a spacious meeting house, in which Maori concerts are performed in a realistic setting. Close to the top entrance is the Maori Arts and Crafts Institute where skilled Maori carvers and flax weavers can be observed at work. The intricately carved archway to the area depicts Hinemoa and Tutanekai embracing.

The bottom path leads past the Maori settlement where tribal people have, for generations, used the thermal waters for cooking, washing and heating.

In Tryon Street, colonial-style shops in the Little Village sell sheepskins, furs, handicrafts and souvenirs. A greenstone carver can be watched at work.

Departing via Froude Street, take a look at the Arikapakapa Golf Course, the only one in the world with boiling mud pool "traps" and hot pool "hazards".

BELOW: fire watcher at Rainbow Mountain.

Rainbow country

West from Rotorua on Highway 5, just 4 km (2.5 miles) from the city, are the fragrant delights of the Herb Garden. Visitors will find **Rainbow Springs**

Map, page 182

and Fairy Springs, containing natural pools crammed with thousands of brown, brook and rainbow trout among 12 hectares (30 acres) of native tree ferns and natural surroundings. Huge trout can be seen through an underwater viewing window and hand-fed along with species of New Zealand deer, native birds and "Captain Cooker" wild pigs, introduced by the famous explorer himself. Live kiwis peck around in a nocturnal house. Across the road is the Rainbow Springs farm show where sheepdogs can be seen at work.

Close by the springs is the Skyline-Skyrides terminus. Ride their gondolas midway up Mount Ngongotaha for a breathtaking view of the city, lake and surrounding countryside. The more adventurous can plunge downhill again in a high-speed luge cart. You can also drive to the top.

There are more trout springs at Paradise Valley, 11 km (7 miles) west of Rotorua, and **Hamurana Springs E** on the northern shore. To protect sports fisheries, it has been made illegal to buy or sell trout in New Zealand. But a trout dinner is an easy catch with fishing guides claiming a 97 percent daily "strike" rate. In fact, no trip to Rotorua-Taupo is complete without a fishing expedition on the lakes. Guides supply all tackle and will meet clients outside hotels, with trailer boats ready for action, or at the boat harbour.

Rainbow trout on most lakes around Rotorua and on Lake Taupo average 1.4 kg (3 pounds) but on Lake Tarawera, where they are tougher to catch, fish of 3.5 to 5.5 kg (8 to 12 pounds) are not uncommon. The icing on the cake after a day of fishing is having a hotel or restaurant chef prepare the catch – a service speciality which they are well used to providing.

Northwest of Rotorua, near Ngongotaha, is the spacious **Agrodome F** located in 142 hectares (350 acres) of pasture. Three times a day, 19 trained rams

TIP

DON'T step off the path! Accidents are rare but not unknown in this area.

BELOW: catch of the day, at Turangi near Lake Taupo.

are put through their paces for an hour in "sheep shows". It's an educational and entertaining performance, and visitors receive handfuls of freshly shorn wool.

Along Central Road, past Ngongotaha township, the Farm House hires out ponies and horses for riding over 245 hectares (600 acres) of bush-edged farmland. Carrying on clockwise around Lake Rotorua, the west-shore road continues to **Okere Falls** and Hinemoa Steps where, after a short walk through native forest and down a cliffside, the Kaituna River can be viewed thundering through a narrow chasm into the swirling pool below.

Crossing the Ohau Channel outlet into Lake Rotoiti, an eastbound turn on to Highway 30, towards Whakatane, takes visitors to the very door of **Hell's Gate** ⓗ. The Maori name, Tikitere, recalls the legend of Huritini, who threw herself into a boiling pool because her husband treated her with contempt. Tikitere is a contraction of Taku tiki i tere nei, "my daughter has floated away". The volcanic activity here covers 4 hectares (10 acres), highlighted by the Kakahi hot waterfall.

If you have some time to spare, take a drive farther down Highway 30 along the shores of Lakes Rotoiti, Rotoehu and Rotoma. With a diversion to the totally unspoiled Lake Okataina, it's well worthwhile.

For a dip with a difference, take a side-road between Lakes Rotoehu and Rotoma to **Soda Springs** ⓘ, where hot water percolates into a clear stream bed.

The eruption of Tarawera

Southeast of Rotorua, heading in the direction of the airport, is the turnoff to the forest-clad **Lake Tikitapu** (Blue Lake) and **Lake Rotokakahi** ⓙ (Green Lake), a favourite stomping ground for joggers and a retreat for those who enjoy walking

Tarawera Falls.

BELOW: silica terraces, Waiotapu.

or riding along the well-marked and graded trails through exotic pines and native bush. Horses and ponies are available for hire. On a fine day, the lakes reflect nicely contrasting blue and green colours, thus giving rise to their European names.

The road continues to Lake Tarawera via the buried village of **Te Wairoa** , destroyed on 10 June 1886 when an awesome eruption of Mount Tarawera blasted rock, lava and ash into the air over a 15,540-sq km (6,000-sq mile) area and buried the villages of Te Wairoa, Te Ariki and Moura, killing 147 Maori and six Europeans. The buried village contains items excavated from Te Wairoa including the *whare* (hut) of a *tohunga* (priest) who foretold the disaster and was unearthed alive four days after the eruption.

From Te Wairoa, before the eruption, many Victorian tourists were rowed across Lake Tarawera to the fabulous Pink and White Terraces – two huge silica formations which rose 250 metres (820 ft) from the shores of Lake Rotomahana and were billed as one of "the eight wonders of the world".

Mount Tarawera ("burnt spear") looms on the eastern shores of both lakes. Flights over the crater and the thermal areas depart from Rotorua Airport. A thrilling landing on the mountain's slopes allows close inspection of the 6-km long (4-mile), 250-metre (820-ft) deep chasm caused by the volcanic explosion.

Ghostly portents

Adding to Tarawera's mysterious aura is the verified account of a ghostly war canoe full of mourning, flax-robed Maori seen by two separate boatloads of tourists on Lake Tarawera on the misty morning of 31 May 1886. Returning to Te Wairoa, the tourists found the local Maori in a state of terror, for no such canoe existed in the region. Tuhuto, the *tohunga*, prophesied the apparition was

Waimangu Geyser was once the biggest in the world, reaching dizzy heights of 500 metres (1,640 ft). Now it has less force, and is dwarfed by New Zealand's biggest geyser, Pohutu, which regularly acheives heights of 20 to 30 metres (60–100 ft).

BELOW: hopeful angler at Taupo.

Wairakei Geothermal Power Station.

"an omen that all this region will be overwhelmed". On a chilly, moonlit night 11 days later, Mount Tarawera fulfilled his prophecy to the letter, blasting the Pink and White Terraces off the world tourist map forever.

Twenty km (12.5 miles) south of Rotorua, on Highway 5 going towards Taupo, is **Waimangu Valley M**. This unspoilt thermal area contains the Waimangu Cauldron, the world's largest boiling lake. An easy walk downhill from a tearoom leads past bubbling crater lakes, hot creeks and algae-covered silica terraces to the shores of Lake Rotomahana (a refuge of black swans), where a launch can be taken to the intensively active Steaming Cliffs and the site of the lost Pink and White Terraces.

Ten km (6 miles) south on Highway 5, a loop road leads to the **Waiotapu ❶** ("sacred waters") thermal area, home of the Lady Knox Geyser, which erupts daily at 10.15am (with the encouragement of a little soap). Other attractions include the bubbly Champagne Pool, tinted silica terraces and Bridal Veil Falls.

Trout galore

Taupo, an abbreviation of Taupo-nui-Tia ("the great shoulder cloak of Tia"), takes its name from the Arawa canoe explorer who discovered **Lake Taupo ❷**. The lake covers 608 sq km (235 sq miles) and was formed by volcanic explosions over thousands of years. It is now the most famous trout-fishing lake in the world, yielding in excess of 500 tons of rainbow trout annually. The rivers flowing into the lake are equally well stocked, so that fishermen frequently stand shoulder-to-shoulder at the mouth of the Waitahanui River, forming what has come to be known as the picket fence.

Arrangements for boat hires can be made at the picturesque boat harbour and

BELOW: Waimangu volcanic valley.

information centre, where a restored steamboat, *Ernest Kemp*, and a variety of other vessels depart regularly on lake excursions.

About 40 km (25 miles) north of Taupo and 70 km (44 miles) south of Rotorua is the active **Orakei-Korako ❸** thermal area. Maori chiefs painted themselves in mirror pools here, giving rise to the name, which means "place of adorning".

Special features are the jet-boat journey across Lake Ohakuri, the 40-metre (130-ft) Great Golden Fleece terrace, underground hot pools in Aladdin's Cave and a huge area of silica deposits which are pockmarked with hot springs.

Water power

Some 7 km (4 miles) north of Taupo, just below the junction of Highways 1 and 5, is **Wairakei ❹** with its dramatic geothermal power station. Super-heated water is drawn from the ground through a series of bores, enabling dry steam to be piped to electricity turbines in a nearby powerhouse. At the entrance to the field is an information office; a road to the left of the pipelines winds to a hilltop observation area. The international golf course at Wairakei is rated among the best in New Zealand.

A nearby loop road leads to the spectacular **Huka ("Foam") Falls**, where the full force of the newly born Waikato River hurtles from a narrow gorge over a 12-metre (40-ft) ledge. Lit by bright sunshine, the ice-cold water takes on a turquoise-blue colour before crashing into a foaming basin. The falls are best observed across the footbridge from the opposite side of the river.

A short distance along the loop road on the banks of the Waikato River is the famous Huka Fishing Lodge and a small replica pioneer village. Also between Wairakei and Taupo, on a gravel road, is the Craters of the Moon, a wild thermal

Map, pages 198–9

TIP

The Army Memorial Museum, on State Highway 1 south of Waiouru, houses military memorabilia and artefacts from the Maori Wars to the present day, and is open daily from 9am to 4.30pm.

BELOW: The Grand Chateau.

Map, pages 198–9

area. Visitors can gaze into a frightening abyss of furiously boiling mud and walk around a track to see steam rising from natural fumaroles in the hillside. Impressive scenic flights by floatplane from the lakefront or by fixed-winged aircraft and helicopters, leave the airport south of Taupo for the snow-capped volcanic summits of Tongariro National Park.

Three mountains

At the southern head of Lake Taupo is the breathtaking 7,600-sq km (2,930-sq mile) **Tongariro National Park ❺** containing the three active volcanic mountains of Tongariro (1,967 metres/6,453 ft), Ngauruhoe (2,287 metres/7,503 ft) and thirdly Ruapehu (2,797 metres/9,177 ft). The mountaintops were sacred to the Maori of the Ngati-Tuwharetoa tribe. In 1887, hereditary chief Te Heuheu Tukino made a gift of the summits to the federal government as New Zealand's first national park in order to protect them from exploitation.

The most scenic route from Taupo leaves Highway 1 at Turangi heading for Tokaanu, not far from the Tongariro Power Station, and winds up through bush-covered mountains and around the shore of Lake Rotoaira. The alternative route is to turn off the main highway at Rangipo on to Highway 47.

A brief diversion to **Tokaanu ❻**, 60 km (37 miles) from Taupo, reveals a small thermal area, the Domain Thermal Baths and the historic St Paul's 19th-century church. According to Maori legend, when the priest and explorer Nga-toro-i-rangi was in danger of freezing to death on the mountains his fervent prayers for assistance were answered by the fire demons of Hawaiki, who sent fire via White Island and Rotorua to burst out through the mountaintops. To appease the gods, Ngatoro cast his female slave into the Ngauruhoe volcano – called by the girl's name, Auruhoe, by the local Maori. Ngauruhoe with its typical volcanic cone is the most active of the three mountains. A major eruption in 1954–5 continued intermittently for nine months.

Ruapehu ("exploding hole") is a perpetually snow-capped, multiple volcano with a flattened summit stretching 3 km (1.8 miles) and incorporating acidic, bubbling Crater Lake and six small glaciers. Ruapehu has blown out clouds of steam and ash a number of times in the past 100 years, raining dust over a 90-km (56-mile) radius in 1945, and closing the nearby Whakapapa and Turoa skifields as recently as 1996. On Christmas Eve, 1953, 151 people died in a tragic train disaster when a *lahar*, or violent discharge of water, roared down the Whangaehu River from Crater Lake. The torrent slammed into a railway bridge at Tangiwai, 35 km (22 miles) away, sweeping it into the night. Minutes later, a Wellington-Auckland express train and five carriages careened down the track, plunging to its doom in the raging river below.

Mount Ruapehu is the major ski area of the North Island. Adventure tour operators offer white-water rafting down the Tongariro and Rangitikei rivers.

Tongariro is the lowest of the three mountains, with a series of small craters and the Ketetahi hot springs on the northern slopes. Rangers at the national park headquarters near The Grand Chateau can give full information on walking tracks and accommodation huts.

BELOW: white-water rafting, Rangitaiki River. **RIGHT:** distant Mount Ngauruhoe (left) and Ruapehu.

THE WATERS OF ROTORUA

This strange, steamy landscape of bubbling springs and mud pools, saturated in Maori lore and history, has been attracting tourists for over a century

Rotorua has been a top tourist resort for decades. A century ago genteel folk came to the spa from all over the world to promenade and take the waters. So it's a little surprising to learn that the town has been described as "Stink-ville" and "Rotten Egg Town". All becomes clear when you take your first breath of the sulphur-laden mist. You soon forget the sulphuric odour as you explore the surreal steamy surroundings. Every geyser, every spring, it seems, has a curious name with a story attached, like the Lobster Pool in Kuirau Park, so named because of the shade its acidic waters tinted fair European skins. And a concentrically ringed mud pool, charmingly named "Gramophone Record Pool".

LUNAR REBIRTH

One of these stories relates to the moon. Rotorua's healing waters have been described as "Wai-ora-a-Tane" (Living water of Tane), where according to Maori legend the dying moon bathes each month, in the great mythical lake of Aewa. Here, she receives the gift of life to sustain her in her journey through the heavens.

It's very important to obey the signposts and keep to the paths in this region, where the earth is a bit less stable than most of us are used to. The thermal pools may look tempting, but some of them are boiling hot. If your vision gets blocked with the steam, be sure to take a rest until it clears – don't stagger on blindly.

▷ **WAIOTAPU**
The name means "sacred waters", and Waiotapu is often justly billed as a "thermal wonderland". Star attractions are the Artist's Palette (shown here), Lady Knox Geyser and Champagne Pool, the Waiotapu Terraces and Bridal Veil Falls – plus boiling mud pools galore. The Rainbow Crater is an underground thermal spring grotto which was formed by a violent hydrothermal explosion about 850 years ago.

◁ **CHAMPAGNE POOL**

Dinner parties and concerts are sometimes held in the misty, ethereal atmosphere of the Champagne Pool at Waiotapu Thermal Area, just a few kilometres south of Rotorua. The pool is actually quite blue and steamy, and doesn't really look like champagne at all, but if a handful of sand is thrown into it, the water fizzes enthusiastically, just like a large glass of bubbly.

▽ **LADY KNOX GEYSER**

It's definitely not a good idea to peer into the throat of a geyser, even if it is guaranteed to go off just once a day promptly at 10.15am. Geysers tend to be rather unpredictable – Lady Knox Geyser's efficient timekeeping is kept to the minute with regular helpings of soap, as well as a few rags to help the pressure build up.

CROQUET AT THE BATH HOUSE

How very English! Splendid buildings like this one, the town's most frequently photographed edifice and superb backdrop to a croquet match, gives Rotorua its genteel charm.

Now known as Tudor Towers, the elegant building which graces Government Gardens was originally constructed as a bath house in 1908, complete with ancient sculptures in the foyer. To the left and right of the entrance foyer, double doors led to men's and women's bath houses, where treatment could be obtained for rheumatism. The baths had facilities for Aix massage, steam baths and mud baths.

The building is no longer a bath house – if you want a dip in a thermal pool, the Polynesian spa, built in 1886 and the site of Rotorua's first building and bath house, is open daily.

Today, Tudor Towers houses the Rotorua Museum of Art and History (open daily 10am–5pm, *see page 349*), with a number of collections tracing the development of painting and printmaking in New Zealand, as well as contemporary paintings. There is also a kauri gum collection and a wildlife display, plus exhibitions about the Te Arawa Maori people who first settled the area. A video on the 1886 Mount Tarawera eruption shows how the magnificent Pink and White Terraces, formed of silica deposits, were destroyed.

WHAKAREWAREWA

...is famous thermal area's full name is Whakarewarewa-...nga-o-te-a-Wahiao, which ...eans, "the uprising of a war ...rty of Wahiao". New ...aland's highest geyser, ...hutu, bursts forth several ...nes a day for up to 40 ...inutes at a time, reaching ...ights of 20 to 30 metres ...0–100 ft). The nearby ...ince of Wales Feathers ...yser generally goes off just ...fore Pohutu.

POVERTY BAY AND HAWKE'S BAY

Map, pages 198–9

Hawke's Bay and its neighbour, inappropriately named Poverty Bay, have a wealth of agriculture, bountiful vineyards, history, interesting architecture – and New Zealand's most easterly city

There are several reasons why Gisborne and the area around it are special to New Zealanders. Situated on 178 degrees longitude, Gisborne is noted for being the first city in the world to greet the rising sun each day. That has given rise to the name the Sunrise Coast. It is also a historic coast. Young Nick's Head, a promontory across the bay from the city of Gisborne, was the first siting of the country for British explorer Captain James Cook and the crew of his ship *Endeavour* in 1769. High on Kaiti Hill, overlooking Gisborne and the sprawling countryside beyond, is a memorial to Captain Cook, and below, at the mouth of the Turanganui River, is the spot where a landing party from the *Endeavour* first set foot on New Zealand soil on 9 October 1769.

Not exactly poor

Cook erred badly, however, in calling the region Poverty Bay because "it did not afford a single article we wanted, except a little firewood". Poverty Bay retains the name grudgingly. It is now sheep and cattle country and rich in citrus and kiwi fruit orchards, vineyards, vegetable gardens and a variety of food crops which all support a large processing industry. Its wines – particularly Chardonnay and Gewürtztraminer – are among the best in the country and should be tried on a visit to one of the many vineyards open to the public.

PRECEDING PAGES: grazing on Gisborne's green pastures. **LEFT:** Lake Waikaremoana. **BELOW:** Pania, maiden of Napier.

Poverty Bay offers spectacular coastal vistas of white sands and sparkling blue summer waters, accompanied by the scarlet blossom of the pohutukawa, often known as the New Zealand Christmas tree because it is at its best and brightest in late December. Some of this colour rubs off on **Gisborne ❼** (with an urban area population of 33,000), a city of sun and water, parks, bridges and beaches. Water sports are a recreational way of life to people whose main commercial street is only a few metres away from a long, curving white sandy beach. Gisborne is also called the "City of Bridges" and is situated on the banks of the Taruheru and Waimata rivers and Waikenai Creek, all joining to form the Turanganui River. On Stout Street in the town centre, the city's museum and arts centre, **Tairawhiti Museum**, recounts the region's history. Near the main museum building is the maritime museum, made up from parts of the steamship *Star of Canada*, which was wrecked on Kaiti Beach in 1912.

Gisborne lingers over its association with Cook. But the area's historic wealth pre-dates his visit. Maori landholdings – some of them leased to Europeans – are extensive. Meeting houses are numerous and can be seen at many of the Maori settlements along the coast.

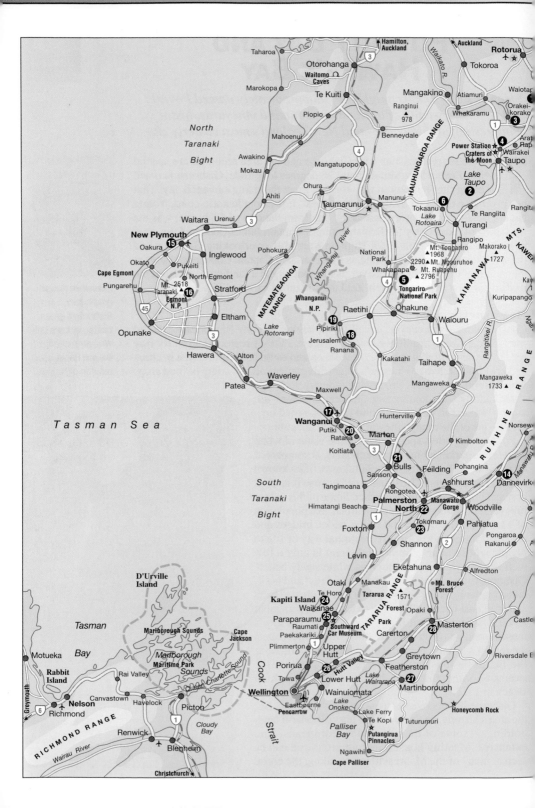

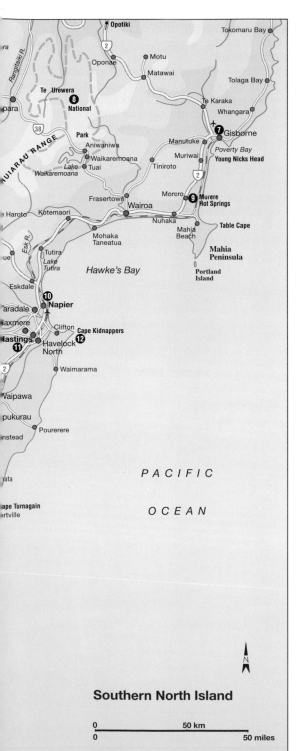

Southern North Island

0   50 km

0   50 miles

traditional style, and the unorthodox painting of patterned foliage, birds and mythical human figures. One of the largest meeting houses in the country is Poho-o-Rawiri (the Bosom of Rawiri), at the base of Kaiti Hill. Built in 1925, it did not use the traditional ridge-pole structure because of its size. However, it still contains some impressive *tututuku* (woven reed) panels and impressive carvings. Almost every one of the numerous Maori settlements that lie along the coast has its treasured meeting house.

While Poverty Bay is tranquil today, there were many tribal battles in the past. One of the most interesting stories concerns a prophet called Te Kooti, who in the last century led a prolonged rebellion against settlers. He was exiled to the Chatham Islands, hundreds of kilometres off the east coast of the North Island, along with dozens of other Maori arrested in the 1860s, but that wasn't to be the end of him. He masterminded a daring escape back to the mainland and founded a religious movement which still exists, called Ringatu. The government sent an army in pursuit but Te Kooti proved a formidable enemy in the wild bush of the Urewera Range, striking back with guerrilla attacks that kept him free and the government harassed. He was eventually pardoned in his old age and allowed to live with his followers in the far away King Country.

Many of Te Kooti's old haunts have been preserved in the **Te Urewera National Park ❽**, 212,000 hectares (500,000 acres) of rugged mountains, forests and lakes, much of it still inaccessible to all but the toughest trampers. The park's highlight is unquestionably Lake Waikaremoana ("Lake of the Rippling Waters"), rich in trout and with bush thick to the water's edge on all but the eastern side, where it is hemmed in by steep cliffs. Chalet, motel and motor camp accommodation is available at Waikaremoana, and there are tramping huts throughout the park.

Quake disaster

Poverty Bay runs southward to Wairoa and the Mahia Peninsula where it merges into the Hawke's Bay region. Sitting on into the Hawke's Bay region. Sitting on the neck of the peninsula separating the two bays is **Morere ❾**, an attractive, small town that is worth visiting for its hot springs, or for bush walks in the surrounding native forest. The town sits on the edge of the Wharerata State Forest.

With similar land use to Gisborne, Hawke's Bay is centred on the twin cities of Napier and Hastings, which may be close but are strongly independent and even competitive. Napier is a seafront city with a population of 55,100, and Hastings, 20 km (12 miles) away, is an agricultural marketing centre of 59,432. The cities are bounded to the east by the Pacific Ocean (although Hastings is a little inland) and to their west plains sweep away to the Kaweka and Ruahine ranges, rugged areas for hunters and trampers.

Hawke's Bay shares with Gisborne the memory of New Zealand's worst earthquake tragedy, on 3 February 1931. Buildings crumpled under the impact of a 7.9 Richter Scale quake. What the shock did not destroy in Napier and Hastings, fire finished off. The death toll of 258 included a number of people killed by falling parapets. Napier was closest to the epicentre and heroic deeds were performed by rescuers and by naval personnel from a sloop, HMS *Veronica*, which happened to be in harbour.

New towns

It was a time of economic depression, but a sympathetic government and a sympathetic world came to Hawke's Bay's post-quake aid with funds for a massive relief and rebuilding campaign. The opportunity was taken to widen streets and a strict earthquake-proof building code was enforced. Along the seafront today is a colonnade named after the naval sloop. It could be said that the whole of

Art Deco, Napier.

BELOW: Napier after the terrible 1931 earthquake.

Napier today is a kind of memorial to the earthquake. Much of its inland suburban area, stretching out to the once-independent borough of Taradale in the southwest, is built on the 4,000 hectares (10,000 acres) of former marshland the earthquake pushed up.

Art Deco

A more distinctive inheritance is the inner city's increasingly famous Art Deco architecture which was chosen by the architects to reflect both the era and the attitude of the new city. The collection of Art Deco buildings in the inner city, with bold lines, elaborate motifs and pretty pastel colours, is recognised internationally as extraordinary. Recognition of the quality of the architecture – and its popularity – has come only in the past few years but has come with a vengeance. Building owners are encouraged to restore and preserve the façades; and a trust has been set up to promote and protect this valued feature of the city's heritage. Civic leaders have done their bit too, developing the main street in a sympathetic fashion. The **Hawke's Bay Museum** in the central city details events surrounding the earthquake and the city's rebuilding.

Just as no mention of Napier would be complete without including Art Deco, neither would it be complete if the city's Marine Parade was ignored. A large recreational collection of gardens, sculptures, fountains, earthquake memorials and varied visitor attractions, the seaside is dominated by towering rows of Norfolk pines. Marine Parade includes the statue of Pania, a maiden of local legend; and it has long boasted Marineland, New Zealand's only marine park with performing dolphins, along with an adjacent aquarium.

Hulking above the city centre is Napier Hill, home to many residents. Before

Map, pages 198–9

The famous statue of Pania on Marine Parade commemorates the Maori legend of a young chief who fell in love with a beautiful sea maiden, Pania, but later lost her and their child to the sea.

BELOW: Napier today.

Sunset at Napier Marina.

the earthquake it was almost an island and was the earliest developed area of the city by Europeans. Evidence of this remains in some of the fine Victorian and Edwardian homes and in the maze of twisting, narrow streets, designed before motor cars were anticipated. On the north side of the hill, next to the bustling port, is another historic area, Ahuriri, the cradle of Napier and the site of the very first European settlement in the area. A scenic road winds up Bluff Hill to a lookout for views over the city, harbour and the bay.

Fruitful city

Architectural treasures from the post-earthquake period dot **Hastings ⑪**, too, in the Art Deco and Spanish Mission style. Despite their closeness, Hastings is rather a different city from Napier, laid out in a flat and formal fashion, surrounded by a rich alluvial plain which hosts a huge range of horticultural crops.

A chief attraction of Hastings is **Splash Planet**, a family-orientated fun park with such amusements as a life-sized pirate ship, a castle, water slides, and many more escapes from reality. But Hastings' main role is, as it is proudly called by locals, "The Fruit Bowl of New Zealand". A Mediterranean-type climate, pure water from an underground aquifer, and innovative growers have made this one of the most important apple-growing regions in the world. Apricots, peaches, nectarines, plums, kiwi fruit, pears, berries and cherries also grow profusely here and are on offer from roadside stalls during the harvesting season, along with tomatoes, sweet corn, asparagus and peas. Most of the produce is processed for export at large food processing factories on the edge of the city.

Despite the horticultural bounty, the twin cities rely heavily on farming, which has generated the region's historic wealth. Only pine forests are challenging the

BELOW: Waipiro Bay, north of Gisborne.

supremacy of sheep and cattle in the rolling hinterland. The pastoral farms are the legacy of Victorian settlers who laid claim to huge tracts of Hawke's Bay, and made their fortunes from wool and, later, sheep-meat, beef and hides.

Hastings has a **Scenic Drive**, a signposted tour of its suburbs, parks and major visitor attractions. Among these is Oak Avenue, a magnificent 1.5 kilometre (about 1 mile) stretch of road planted in oaks and other huge deciduous trees by a nostalgic 19th-century landowner and carefully tended by his successors.

A short distance across the plain from Hastings is "The Village", as the pretty, genteel town of **Havelock North** is known locally. It sits in the shadow of Te Mata Peak, a limestone mountain with a summit accessible by car. From the top you can enjoy the sweeping views or, if you are daring enough, you may go hang-gliding or paragliding from the steep cliff on one side.

Wine and gannets

Hastings and Napier may enjoy distinctive identities (and may even indulge in parochialism to go with it) but they share some significant attractions – the Cape Kidnappers gannet colony, for example, and the local wine industry. **Cape Kidnappers** ⓬ is a 20- to 30-minute drive from either city, followed by a ride along the beach in one of the tractor-towed trailer vehicles to what is thought to be the largest mainland gannet colony in the world. The Cape's name harks back to an incident in which local Maori attempted to abduct a Tahitian youth from the serving staff of Captain Cook's *Endeavour* while it lay at anchor nearby.

About two dozen wineries are established around Napier and Hastings. Hawke's Bay is the oldest of the country's wine-growing regions and sees itself as the finest. Certainly it enjoys ever-increasing recognition for the quality of its Chardonnays, Sauvignon Blancs and Cabernet Sauvignons. Most wineries are open to visitors.

South of Hastings, pastoral farming is the reason for the existence of another set of Hawke's Bay twin towns, Waipukurau and Waipawa. But near **Waipukurau** ⓭ is a hill with one of the longest names of any place in the world: Taumatawhakatangihangakoauauotamatea-pokaiwhenuakitanatahu.

The 57 letters translate into "The hill where the great husband of heaven, Tamatea, caused plaintive music from his nose flute to ascend to his beloved".

Maori have roots in Hawke's Bay marked today by the many *marae* (meeting grounds) in the region. And in 1872, Te Aute College was founded just south of Hastings to educate the sons of chiefs. It is still a force in Maori education.

Further south again, another culture has left its mark. Last century, hardy Norwegian and Danish settlers cleared the rainforest in southern Hawke's Bay, which was so dense it had discouraged all others. They established such towns as Norsewood and **Dannevirke** ⓮ ("Dane's Work"). Norsewood, although a tiny town, has a well-known woollen mill producing a range of knitted goods bearing the settlement's name. Dannevirke, which likes to promote its historic links with Scandinavia, is a farm service town and a convenient staging post on the busy highway between Manawatu to the south and Hawke's Bay to the north.

Map, pages 198–9

Napier's official "sister city" is, oddly enough, the Chatham Islands, tiny specks in the sea about 770 km (480 miles) east of Christchurch. Due to its proximity to the Dateline, Pitt Island in The Chathams was the world's first inhabited landmass to greet the millennium in 2000.

BELOW: gannet at Cape Kidnappers.

MANAWATU, TARANAKI AND WANGANUI

These predominantly rural regions encompass scenic splendour peppered with quiet, pleasant townships and crowned with the majestic peak of volcanic Taranaki, Mount Egmont

Map, pages 198–9

The 169-km (105-mile) Te Kuiti to New Plymouth road leads the southbound traveller through rugged farmed hill country, the Awakino River gorge and beautiful coast with cliffs and placid sandy bays. After a climb up the road over Mount Messenger, Taranaki – Mount Egmont – is in full view on a clear day. The road passes by a striking memorial to the famous Polynesian anthropologist Sir Peter Buck just north of Urenui, his birthplace, and Motunui, a synthetic petrol plant with the world's largest gas-to-gasoline plant.

Near New Plymouth, Taranaki's capital, the land flattens to fertile dairy plains which encircle the dormant volcano of Mount Taranaki, a near-perfect cone 2,518 metres (8,261 ft) high. Southwest of the city are the well-heads and processing-plant towers of the Kapuni natural gas field.

Heritage trail

With Mount Taranaki as its backdrop, the town of **New Plymouth** ⓯ spreads down the coast. Its location, soils and climate were immediately attractive to European settlers in the 1840s. Early missionaries and settlers found a Maori population depleted by inter-tribal wars, yet land troubles between the natives and newcomers still beset the settlement. War broke out in 1860 and eventually placed New Plymouth under virtual siege.

LEFT: verdant landscape northeast of Wanganui. **BELOW:** colonial house, Pipiriki, Wanganui.

The city has several historical buildings, including St Mary's Church, the oldest stone church in New Zealand, Richmond Cottage, home of three of the first settler families, and Hurworth Cottage, built in 1855 and home of four-times New Zealand premier Sir Harry Atkinson. The **Govett-Brewster Art Gallery** in Queen Street has one of the best collections of contemporary art in New Zealand. But New Plymouth is best known for its beautiful parks. At Pukekura Park, wasteland has been transformed into lovely lakes, gardens, a fernery, fountains and a waterfall, lit by night. From September to November, a 360-hectare (890-acre) park, 29 km (18 miles) from New Plymouth, provides one of the world's best displays of flowering rhododendron and azalea bushes in a native bush setting. The Pukeiti Rhododendron Trust is also a bird sanctuary, nestling between the Kaitake and Pouakai ranges. A loop road to the park passes the Pouakai Wildlife Reserve.

Winter skiers and summer climbers enjoy **Egmont National Park** ⓰, with more than 300 km (190 miles) of bush walks. Climbing to Taranaki's summit is not difficult, but weather conditions can change rapidly. State Highway 3 from New Plymouth passes through the agricultural towns of Stratford, Hawera and Patea

on the way to **Wanganui** ⑰, a city most famous for its river. The Whanganui is New Zealand's longest navigable river, much loved by canoeists and jet-boaters. In the superb **Wanganui Regional Museum** is a store of Maori artefacts, a war canoe, Te Mata-o-Hoturoa, and a remarkable collection of Lindauer paintings.

Before further exploring Wanganui, take the lift up the Memorial Tower on Durie Hill. The elevator climbs 66 metres (216 ft) inside the hill. But the 176 tower steps are worth the trouble on a fine day, when you'll be rewarded with a magnificent view of the city and river – and may even spot the South Island.

Virginia Lake is a popular stop by day and night, when a fountain plays in colour. Spend some time in Putiki Church, and Sarjeant Gallery, where you can see the Denton Collection of 19th- and 20th-century photography. Children love the Kowhai Children's Playpark and Riverlands Family Park. Restored heritage buildings, gaslights and wrought iron establish an old-world feel.

Chief attractions west on Highway 3 from the city are the **Bason Botanical Reserve** and **Bushy Park** scenic reserve, both easily reached with short detours. Highway 4 north, through the Paraparas, is justly noted for its beauty. To the east of Wanganui and north of Palmerston North, the Rangitikei River – excellent in its upper reaches for white-water rafting – links with Highway 1 near Managaweka. Enquire there or in Wanganui or Palmerston North about rafting.

The road to Jerusalem

One highlight of any visit to the Wanganui area is the 79-km (49-mile) River Road. A bus tour (booked through the Visitor Information Centre in Wanganui) will give you the chance to sample a slice of remote New Zealand life, as the driver delivers mail, bread and milk to the small settlements along the banks of

ABOVE: sign for a café situated in an old plane.

BELOW: down on the Whanganui.

the Whanganui River. As you approach **Jerusalem** (Hiruharama to the Maori), you will understand why Roman Catholic missionaries established themselves at this bend in the river, and why poet James Baxter chose the serenity of this site for a commune in the early 1970s (it disintegrated after Baxter's death in 1972). There is a small charge to view his grave.

Top of the route is **Pipiriki** ⑲, a popular base for tramping and once the site of the stylish Pipiriki House hotel, which burned down in 1959. There are many listed walks; Mangapurua, north of Pipiriki, enjoys increased fame.

The valley was settled after World War I by returning soldiers. The Depression and farming difficulties forced them out by 1942. An eerie reminder of their presence is the Bridge to Nowhere, an abandoned concrete bridge.

Historic homestead

Highway 3 proceeds southeast from Wanganui to Palmerston North, 70 km (43 miles) away. If you have time, visit **Ratana** ⑳, a small township named after a famous Maori prophet and faith healer. A temple was built there in 1927.

The largest township en route to Palmerston North is **Bulls** ㉑. Further your agricultural education by branching off here towards the coast to Flock House, an agricultural training institute. The house was built in 1895; it was purchased in 1923 by the New Zealand Sheepgrowers, an organisation which ran a scheme to train the sons of British seamen's widows as farmers. Between Bulls and Sanson is the Royal New Zealand Air Force Base (RNZAF) at Ohakea, home to the No 75 Squadron of the RNZAF. The base also trains all of the RNZAF's pilots.

Approaching Palmerston North is Mount Stewart, with fine views of the rich Manawatu pastures. A memorial near the road commemorates early settlers. It's

Map, pages 198–9

Taranaki is the Maori name for the volcano that Captain Cook named Mount Egmont. After decades of dispute over the name, in 1986 the New Zealand Government ruled that both names would be official.

BELOW: Jerusalem, Whanganui River.

a short hop from here to the historic homestead and gardens at Mount Lees Reserve. **Palmerston North ㉒** itself is the flourishing centre of agricultural Manawatu, and its square is the city's focal point. Named in Maori Te Marae o Hine or "Courtyard of the Daughter of Peace", it commemorates a chieftainess named Te Rongorito who sought an end to inter-tribal warfare during the early days of European settlement. The nearby Civic Centre, extending back on to former railway land, is also the site for Te Manawa, a theatre, a convention centre, a new museum and science centre and Manawatu Art Gallery.

Over the past few years, Palmerston North has developed remarkably. There has been a boom in small wine bars and cafés, and a seven-cinema multiplex has been so successful that Palmerston North people are now officially the most regular cinema attenders in New Zealand. The historic Regent Theatre, formerly mainly used as a picture palace, is restored as the city's main auditorium.

Education and research

Roads radiate outwards. Fitzherbert Avenue leads to the city's other major focal point, the Manawatu River. It is a matter of contention that the river is crossed by only one bridge, used by thousands of cars and bicycles each day en route to Massey University and a number of science research stations. Also over the bridge is the International Pacific College, and New Zealand's largest army base at Linton. Given the number of educational institutions in Palmerston North, it's not surprising that it calls itself the Knowledge Centre of New Zealand.

On the city side of the Manawatu River, the pride of Palmerston North is the **Esplanade**, a reserve catering for light recreation. Children can enjoy the playground, and adults can join them on the miniature railway. The Lido swimming

BELOW: farmer and friend.

complex (including an indoor pool) adjoins the motor camp. Don't miss the Rose Garden, which has a proud record for developing new varieties.

A walkway girdles Palmerston North and native bush reserves are close by. The city is frequently the venue for national sports tournaments, partly because of its central location, but mostly because of its first-rate sports facilities, including a 4,000-seat stadium which is used for rock concerts and netball tests, and cricket, rugby, hockey and rugby league are all played under lights.

Exploring Manawatu

A short drive south of Palmerston North on Highway 57 is **Tokomaru** ㉓ and its Steam Engine Museum. Visitors can picnic and swim here at Horseshoe Bend. Highway 56 heads west to beaches at Himatangi and Foxton. They may not be the best in New Zealand, but they are well-patronised.

Feilding, 20 minutes north on Highway 54, is a large town which boasts two squares, a motor-racing track and racecourse, and a stock sale on Friday mornings. The region is perhaps the best place for a stud-farm tour, which is certainly a worthwhile experience in Manawatu.

But perhaps the most dramatic route in or out of Palmerston North and the Manawatu region is via the rugged **Manawatu Gorge**. SH3 first passes through the growing country town of Ashhurst. Travellers can detour here to Pohangina and Totara Reserve, an area of virgin native bush favoured locally for picnics. The road then narrows, and clinging to the southern side of the Manawatu Gorge it links the region to Hawke's Bay. Drive with care here. On the opposite bank of the river is the Hastings and Napier railway line, opened in 1891. But try not to be distracted by it: this road demands attention.

Map, pages 198–9

Palmerston North is New Zealand's second most populous inland city.

BELOW: enjoying the national sport.

WELLINGTON

New Zealand's attractive capital city is colourful, approachable and undaunting for the first-time visitor, and offers much to see and do – with many tempting refreshment stops

Map, page 214

Tawhiri-ma-tea, the Polynesian god of wind and storm, fought many fierce battles with his earthbound brother gods in Wellington and the Wairarapa. No wonder the Cook Strait, the stretch of water separating this end of the North Island from the South Island, had an early start as one of the most treacherous dozen miles of open water in the world, and as a result its citizens have a spectacular and somewhat nervy existence.

The glass capital

The early Maori saw the North Island as a great fish, rich with food for their Polynesian families. Today the mouth of the fish is as pretty a capital city as any in the world. Wellington's great blue bowl of harbour is only mildly scarred by port reclamations and a clutch of high-rise offices set below green hills dotted with white wooden houses. The favourite romantic image of the locals is the best-selling print of New Zealand Company draughtsman Charles Heaphy, depicting the first sailing ships at anchor in this fledgling Victorian colony. If you are up high enough, you will see that things have not changed that much.

It's quite a different matter at street level. In the second half of the 1970s the city was shaken by man-made quakes, as a downtown area of quaint Victorian wedding-cake two- and three-storey premises were demolished on the grounds of earthquake risk. The skyscrapers of steel and glass that replaced them look equally vulnerable, so much so that locals have dubbed this part of town "Glass City".

Wellington is often compared to San Francisco, and accurately so for it, too, has its share of "painted ladies", old wooden houses done up in rainbow colours. Like San Francisco, Wellington has a cable-car (funicular railway) zooming out of its city belly to a fine view of the harbour, beside an ivy-clad red-brick university building recently refurbished to earthquake standards.

After a decade of demolition, Wellington has begun to tart up the few old buildings left, like the university, the red-brick monastery that stands on the opposite promontory, some of the downtown relics like the baroque St James Theatre and the Government Buildings, which made use of native woods in the masonry style of European architecture and claims to have the world's largest wooden floor area.

In between the remnants of Wellington's Victoriana, colourful and adventurous buildings and malls and a craze for cafés selling many kinds of coffee have brightened up the city. Nowhere is this more apparent than in the generous pink and beige piazza of **Civic Square Ⓐ**. There is the trendy steel colander of the new town hall, the trendily painted plaster puddings of the fortress-like municipal chambers and the rectangular Old Town Hall,

PRECEDING PAGES: Wellington awakes. **LEFT:** juxtaposition of old and new architecture, Wellington. **BELOW:** Civic Square complex.

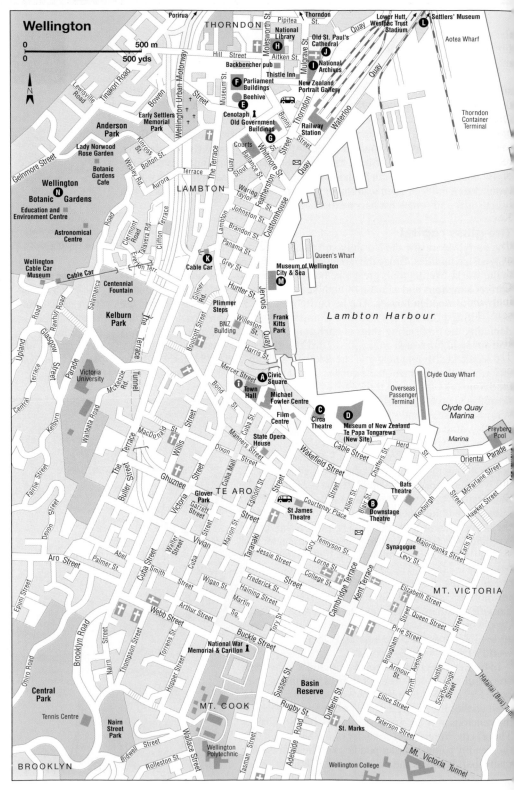

Wellington

0 ———————— 500 m
0 ———————— 500 yds

N

THORNDON

PORIRUA
Pipitea
Thorndon St.

National Library H
Aitken St.
Molesworth St.
Hill Street
Backbencher pub

Old St. Paul's Cathedral J
National Archives I
Thistle Inn
Mulgrave St.

Museum St.

F Parliament Buildings
E Beehive
New Zealand Portrait Gallery

Lower Hutt, Westpac Trust Stadium
Settlers' Museum L

Aotea Wharf

Bowen
Wellington Urban Motorway

Early Settlers Memorial Park
Anderson Park

Cenotaph
Old Government Buildings G

Bunny
Thorndon
Waterloo
Quay

Thorndon Container Terminal

Lady Norwood Rose Garden
Kinross St.
Bolton St.

Courts
Whitmore St.
Railway Station

Botanic Gardens Cafe
Wesley Rd.
Aurora
Terrace
The Terrace

Balance St.
Stout St.
Customhouse Quay

Wellington Botanic N Gardens

Education and Environment Centre

LAMBTON

Waring Taylor
Johnston St.
Brandon St.
Panama St.

Queen's Wharf

Astronomical Centre

Clermont Road
Talavera Rd.
Clifton Terrace

Grey St.
Cable Car K

Lambton
Jervois

Museum of Wellington City & Sea M

Wellington Cable Car Museum
Cable Car

Everton Terr.
Gilmer Rd.

Hunter St.

Lambton Harbour

Centennial Fountain

Plimmer Steps
Willeston St.
BNZ Building

Frank Kitts Park

Kelburn Park
The Terrace
Boulcott Street

Harris St.

Clyde Quay Wharf

Glasgow Street
Rawhiti Road
Salamanca Road
Upland Road

Victoria University

Mercer Street

Quay

Overseas Passenger Terminal

Clyde Quay Marina

McKenzie Rd.
Tunnel
Bond
Cuba St.

Civic Square A
Town Hall i

Michael Fowler Centre
Film Centre
State Opera House

Cable Street

Clyde Quay Wharf
Herd St.
Marina
Freyberg Pool

Central Terrace
Kelburn Parade
Waiteata Road

The Terrace
Buller Street
Willis Street
Victoria

MacDonald St.

Manners Street
Dixon Street

Circa Theatre C
Museum of New Zealand Te Papa Tongarewa (New Site) D

Wakefield Street
Charters St.

Oriental Parade

Bats Theatre

Ghuznee Street

Glover Park
Garrett Street

TE ARO
Cuba Mall
Egmont St.

Courtenay Place
Allen St.
Blair St.

Downstage Theatre B

McFarlane Street
Roxburgh St.
Hawker Street
Earls St.

Fairlie Terrace
Devon Street

Vivian Street

St James Theatre

Tennyson St.

Synagogue
Levy St.

Majoribanks Street

MT. VICTORIA

Aro Street
Epuni Street
Abel
Palmer St.

Walter Street
Cuba Smith Street
Wigan St.

Jessie Street
Marion St.
Taranaki

Tory
Lorne St.
College St.

Cambridge Terrace
Kent Terrace

Elizabeth Street
Queen Street
Pirie Street

Frederick St.
Haining Street

Brougham St.

Webb Street
Arthur Street
Martin Sq.

Tory St.

Brooklyn Road
Thompson Street
Torrens Street
Hopper Street

Buckle Street
Sussex St.

Armour St.
Porritt Avenue
Austin
Scarborough Street

National War Memorial & Carillon

Basin Reserve

Dufferin St.
Rugby St.

Ellice Street

Central Park

Tennis Centre

Nairn Street Park

MT. COOK

Wallace Street
Bidwell Street
Tasman St.

Adelaide Road

St. Marks
Paterson Street

Ohiro Road

Wellington Polytechnic

Rolleston St.

BROOKLYN

Wellington College

MT. VICTORIA
Hataitai (Bus) Tun.

Mt. Victoria Tunnel

the old square library refurbished as the avant-garde **City Gallery** and the new library alongside. Within, the new library is like an industrial plant of exposed metal; outside, its gorgeous plaster curve is decorated with metal palms.

The Old Town Hall was saved after testimonials from visiting conductors, such as the late Leonard Bernstein, rated it one of the best symphonic halls in the world, a fitting venue for the home-base of the New Zealand Symphony Orchestra. Every second year the old and new town halls are the focus of the New Zealand Festival, with a fringe festival all around, reinforcing Wellington's status as the capital of the performing arts in New Zealand. The nearby refurbished State Opera House and St James Theatre have been involved in hundreds of festival performances. Highlights of successive festivals have included two opera productions with international casts, with Donald McIntyre returning to his home country to take the lead in *Die Meistersinger von Nürnberg* and Ken Russell's *Madame Butterfly*.

Nearby is the skew-whiff concrete, iron and wood pyramid of **Downstage Ⓑ**, the country's first professional theatre, established in 1964. Out on the old wharf area, the new building with the wedding-cake façade was retained from the demolished Westport Chambers for the city's other professional theatre, **Circa Ⓒ**. The Circa building is a perfect example of the born-again look for the original port area. Bats Theatre in nearby Kent Terrace is a small venue that presents diverse and challenging theatre.

Recent upheaval

The buildings left behind after port operations moved north to a new container complex are a major part of Wellington's reinvention of itself following the political restructuring of the public service under the successive market-driven, privatising governments of the 1980s. Reducing public servants from 88,000 to 36,000 in five years undercut Wellington's economy and forced the city to redefine itself.

The physically confined capital has gone about the job with gusto. Arches lead from the civic centre across the main road to the old wharf area that was Wellington's first development. Here a lagoon has been carved out beside the rehousing of the two traditional rowing clubs of the city. The ambitious new $280 million **Museum of New Zealand – Te Papa Tongarewa Ⓓ** is regarded as one of the finest in the country and houses some of the finest *taonga* (treasures) of New Zealand.

It features a range of exhibits and presents uniquely New Zealand experiences from the Te Marae, a living contemporary *marae*, to the Bush City, a recreated habitat island representing New Zealand's great outdoors. There are also discovery and state-of-the-art-time travel and virtual reality centres, cafés, the Icon Restaurant, a souvenir shop and a bar. Visitors to Wellington should spend at least one full day at this landmark museum.

Despite the move of its port operations a mile or so to the north, Wellington continues to rate as the busiest of the country's 13 main ports. This is largely due to the all-weather sailing of the Cook Strait rail ferries and foreign fishing vessels calling here for registration and provisioning. The movement across this wild strait is

Map, see opposite

BELOW: detail of the Opera Bar in Courtenay Place.

increasing as the government-encouraged winds of competition see faster ferries enter the field. The established ferries are part of the privatised NZ Rail, owned by an American company. The government department employed 20,000; the privatised rail is a quarter of that size.

Buzzing around the Beehive

Politicians and top public officials and business folk buzz around the capital's unique circular Cabinet offices, known as **The Beehive E**. A large amount of the administrative and financial clout of the country is at work within these few hundred acres of largely reclaimed land.

Built in the late 1970s, the copper-domed Beehive is a soft contrast with the square marble angles of the adjacent **Parliament Buildings F** (1922) and the Gothic turrets of the General Assembly Library (1897). The parliamentary chambers have recently had a face-lift. On the flat below the drive are the **Government Buildings G** (1876) on Lambton Quay, where the tides lapped in 1840.

To one side of the Beehive is the historic red-brick Turnbull House, tucked below the pristine skyscraper Number One The Terrace, office for the Treasury, with the Reserve Bank across the road. On the other side of the Beehive and Parliament is the new St Paul's Cathedral and the **National Library H**, within which is the Alexander Turnbull Library with its remarkable collection of New Zealand and Pacific history. One street behind that is the **National Archives I**, beside the mellow pohutukawa trees that surround **Old St Paul's J** (1866), an impressive little colonial Gothic former cathedral made entirely of wood, even down to the nails. This is the jewel in a city of 30 churches, many of them built in the same wooden adaptation of the soaring stone Gothic style that is a unique

Metal palm tree,
Civic Square,
Wellington.

BELOW LEFT: the famous Beehive.
BELOW RIGHT: new development.

colonial feature. After work most government officials travel a few miles into the foothills or along the harbour motorway directly on the earthquake fault line to the Hutt Valley and the Eastern Bays.

Map, page 214

New homelands

The **Hutt Valley** was largely a kahikatea swamp, with thick native forests that plunged to the water's edge, making these areas uninhabitable for the Maori in pre-Colonial times. The great earthquakes of 1848 and 1855 raised the land about 1.5 metres (5 ft), enough to persuade the Pakeha it was safer to build in wood – especially after a proprietor was killed in his collapsed hotel. Reclamation of the sea was the answer to the space problem. Over the last 150 years, hundreds of acres of land have been reclaimed, half as much again as the original plan for the colony.

For safety reasons, the Maori preferred to live on an island that was linked by a subsequent earthquake to the rest of Wellington. Today this suburban peninsula is called Miramar, Spanish for "behold the sea", and the sandy strip linking it to the city is now the airport that modern travellers flying into the capital love to hate. The runway's too short to cater for larger international aircraft, and winds often make landing a breathtaking experience, while the airport's suburban neighbours complain about the noise of aircraft at night.

Hundreds of years before Cook, the great Polynesian explorer Kupe landed on the land now known as Miramar and cultivated crops there, and that is where the tribe of his son Tara settled. There was such an abundance of fish and birds and sunny north-facing slopes to cultivate the delicate kumara or sweet potato, that Tara's tribe was willing to share the area with migrating groups. Occasional

BELOW: Wellington's Civic Square complex.

marauders were repelled by fortifications which were developed around the headlands. For more than 600 years there was a relatively peaceful occupation of Te Whanganui a Tara, the Great Harbour of Tara.

The Pakeha musket ended that. In 1819 Te Rauparaha and other warrior chiefs led a savage assault on the local tribes, wiping out people who stood there unable to comprehend why they were falling. The new occupiers had enemies on all sides and thus welcomed the arrival of the white tribe in 1839.

The white tribe brought with them the potato, which was easier to cultivate than the kumara. The Hutt Valley was particularly fertile – Charles Heaphy measured 2.5 meters (8 ft) in compost. The Maori gardeners of the Hutt Valley arguably kept the settlers alive in the first few years with two potato crops a year from the productive soil. The settlers were often contemptuous of the Maori and indifferent to requests that cultivation, living and burial grounds be protected. This is still apparent in the viewing platform on Mount Victoria overlooking the harbour, which was built on top of an ancient burial ground. The summit is 196 metres (643 ft), up a good road. Another viewpoint is at **Kelburn**, above the magnificent Botanical Gardens, reached by **Wellington Cable Car** (funicular railway) ⓚ 120 metres (400 ft) from Lambton Quay.

Wakefield's settlement

The citizens of Wellington have shown scant respect for their Pakeha founding father Edward Gibbon Wakefield. There is no memorial to Wakefield in Wellington other than his gravesite, partly due to lingering disapproval over a prison term he served for allegedly abducting an heiress; she was willing, but her father was not, and he brought a successful court case against the young Wakefield. It

Looking out over New Zealand's capital city.

BELOW: cable car to Kelburn

Map, page 214

was in Newgate Prison that Wakefield witnessed first-hand the miserable lot of England's poor and devised a scheme to attract investment from the well-off in projects that offered a chance to those with nothing. John Stuart Mill, the great libertarian thinker, was among admirers of the plan.

In practice it was a mess. Idealists were thin on the ground, speculators as thick as shovels in a gold rush. Wakefield's brother, William, was in charge of acquiring land for the new emigrants, but he had only four months to do so. His quick deals with the Maori included buying Wellington for 100 muskets, 100 blankets, 60 red nightcaps, a dozen umbrellas and such goods as nails and axes.

Wakefield claimed to have bought for £9,000 the "head of the fish and much of its body", a total of about 8 million hectares (20 million acres). He failed to understand the Maori concept of communal ownership, whereby all shared the land but the Maori reserved the areas they lived in, cultivated and used for burial. Some of the misunderstandings may have come about from the pidgin Maori and pidgin English of translator Dicky Barrett. Barrett is also known for setting up the first pub in Wellington, later hiring it out for government offices.

The early settlers had little to thank Wakefield for when they were dumped on a beach at the swampy bottom of the Hutt Valley. After their tents flooded, the settlement moved to the narrow but dry site of the present city. The abandoned area is called Petone, meaning the End of the Sand, which eventually developed into a vigorous working-class town of heavy and light industry. The flat shoreline is becoming a popular recreational area, the workers' cottages are being gentrified and the **Settlers' Museum** commemorates the early struggles.

Wakefield's part in the struggles of these early settlers may explain why the title "Father of Wellington" was conferred on a merchant settler who displayed

TIP

If you're batty over cricket, don't miss the National Cricket Museum in the old Basin Reserve Grandstand. Open daily.

BELOW: Lambton Quay in 1903.

less idealism. John Plimmer complained that a place represented to him as "a veritable Eden" had proved "a wild and stern reality". Plimmer in fact had little cause for complaint – he had converted a shipwreck, the fallout from a bad day, into a flourishing trading enterprise on the beach. Like many of his fellow entrepreneurs, he added his own wharf, eventually becoming one of the solid citizens of the town, and his wreck ended up as the boardroom chair in the country's leading trading bank, the Bank of New Zealand. The **Plimmer's Ark Gallery** on Queens Wharf contains the excavated remains of the 150-year-old sailing ship, *Inconstant*, later known as Plimmer's Ark.

Lambton Quay was the beachfront where Plimmer and fellow traders set up shops, its narrowness prompting reclamations ever since. The enforced shift across the harbour to the narrow Wellington foreshore ensured a continuous struggle to turn back the tide. The result today is that Lambton Quay has moved back several blocks from the harbour.

Wellington's wharves

The streets between the skyscrapers are narrow and windswept with few parks, but Wellingtonians are never more than a stone's throw from the Botanic Gardens or the wharves. The wharves are among the few in the world open to the public, and politicians and civil servants are among the lunchtime joggers who zip past puzzled Russian and Korean fishing crews. New restaurants in converted stores offer haute fish cuisine, but if you're not hungry you can still see what the sea has to offer, at the **Museum of Wellington City and Sea** Ⓜ. The museum houses a captivating collection of maritime memorabilia.

At the southern end, the Overseas Passenger Terminal occasionally hosts cruise

BELOW: Wellington Harbour.

Map,
page 214

ships, and there is a popular restaurant. Part of the new development on the city side is a marina, matching the established one on the other side, the graceful Royal Port Nicholson Yacht Club with its popular clubrooms. Beside that is the Freyberg indoor swimming pool on the edge of the city beach of Oriental Bay, created by the dumping of sand ballast from ships. A line of mature Norfolk pines makes this an attractive promenade, leading up to the steep slopes of Mount Victoria. This suburb that faces the setting sun is frequently called a mini-Riviera. Where Maori once cultivated kumara, Pakeha now cultivate suntans.

Across the bay in the shadow of the hill is the country's oldest suburb of Thorndon, where the little wooden workers' and soldiers' cottages have been gentrified into "painted ladies". Historic walks head from here and downtown up into the luxuriant **Botanic Gardens** and the formal glory of the Lady Norwood Rose Garden and tearooms. The gardens are ideal for a stroll, and in the summer months, the blooms are especially spectacular. A motorway has bifurcated this old suburb and ripped out the heart of the settlers' cemetery before coming to a full-stop in the middle of town, against a brick wall of environmental opposition.

From the late 1960s, citizens of gentrified Thorndon cut their conservation teeth on opposition to the motorway and saved some of the threatened suburb. Even more successful were residents on the other side of the city, in the raffish community of the Aro Valley below the university. Students and old-timers successfully repelled council plans to demolish their wooden cottages in favour of concrete. From Aro Valley, head southeast through Mt Cook towards the **Basin Reserve** cricket ground, which was a lake before an earthquake drained it.

Behind the basin is the suburb of **Newtown**, its narrow streets teeming with new migrants from the Pacific, Asia and Europe. At the local school, you can

TIP

The Carter Observatory in the Botanic Gardens is open to the public Monday to Friday for enlightening talks and demonstrations about the southern sky at night.

BELOW: Wellington's colourful suburbs.

hear 20 different languages spoken, while shops that look like the clapboard façades of a Hollywood Wild West set sell exotic foods from a dozen lands. Nearby is Island Bay, which is losing the Italian fishermen from Stromboli and Sorrento who gave it its nickname of Little Italy, when there were 50 fishing craft in the bay. Now there are about 10, some still with names like *Michelangelo* and *San Marino*. A few rugged bays around this southern coast, on foot or by four-wheel-drive, you come to the famous Red Rocks, supposedly stained by the blood from Kupe's cut hand, and the seal colony.

The Italians of Island Bay have been joined by settlers from Gujurat province around Bombay, and many of the small shops are Indian-owned. Here, you can find a Presbyterian church holding services in Niuean, a magnificent Greek Orthodox temple, a Serbian Orthodox wooden church and chapel and Polish clubrooms, all evidence of Wellington's days as the first port of call for migrants.

Valley of the Hutt

In the last half-century it has been traditional for families to follow the New Zealand trend to move from city to suburbs, to new settlements principally in the Hutt Valley and over the hills in the Porirua basin. At weekends many still go well beyond, northwest to cottages or *baches* (holiday homes) on the Kapiti coast, or to Paremata for underwater and on-water sports in rather less blustery conditions than the capital's harbour.

Further up the Gold Coast, as this warmer clime is known, it is possible to arrange trips out to the unspoiled native bird sanctuary of **Kapiti Island** ㉔, which was the capital of the warrior chief Te Rauparaha who ruled the Wellington region when the Pakeha arrived. One of the many good beaches in the area

MLC Building.

BELOW: farming lands of the Wairarapa.

is at **Paraparaumu** ㉕, where there are water slides and watersports facilities. A few miles further up the Gold Coast you can enjoy locally made gourmet cheeses, watch the sheep shearing and milking of cows at Lindale and visit the vintage car collection in the Southward Car Museum.

This blander environment is also shared by the **Hutt Valley** ㉖, the cities of Lower Hutt and Upper Hutt and their satellite suburbs. On the flat lands near the flood-prone Hutt River are television and film studio facilities. Most of the time the river is peaceful enough for trout fishing, kayaking and jet-boating. Further up the valley at Silver Stream is a hillside steam train excursion.

Heading south, there are small communities tucked into the steep eastern bays. **Eastbourne** is worth a visit, either by water ferry or a drive around the bays, for its craft shops and quiet contrast to the glass towers. House prices are always high, and the image of Katherine Mansfield gentility lingers on. A hill road away is another valley city, **Wainuiomata**, famous for its rugby league club, gateway to the serious tramping country of Rimutaka Forest Park. At the Hutt base of the hill is the collection of government science research institutes and the petrol storage wharf complex, leading to exclusive bushy bays.

It is an easy hike around this coast to view the country's first lighthouse at **Pencarrow**. Once the rugged coastline beyond was the preferred pathway for sheep herders who set up the country's first sheep stations on the Wairarapa acres. The Maori canoed the settlers across the lake and sold them the land.

Productive hinterland

Wellington's central position ensures that it continues to handle almost a third of the country's 60 million annual gross shipping tonnage. Almost half of this is produced in the adjacent farming lands of the Wairarapa. It takes an hour or so to drive over the 305 metres (1,000 ft) of the Rimutaka mountains, although cars sometimes need chains to negotiate the road in winter. Once a fell engine hauled people and goods up the mountain's almost vertical incline, leaving behind a relic that is unique in the world.

The vast plain north of Lake Wairarapa hosts towns of marked contrast to the rowdy capital. Greytown is associated with a former Governor, while Featherston played a grim part in history as a former prisoner-of-war camp for Japanese. The prisoners threatened a break-out and were massacred by nervous guards. Now these are places to buy adzed as well as second-hand furniture, while **Martinborough** ㉗ has burst onto the map as a producer of boutique white wines. In fact, a good way to experience the area is to join one of the vineyard tours that leave from Wellington.

The large town of **Masterton** ㉘ at the northern end still caters to the traditional sheep image of the area with the hosting of the Golden Shears competition every year. In the duck shooting season the population rises as dramatically as the lake levels after heavy rain. The hills and the rivers around are popular with trampers, canoeists, rafters, botanists, conservationists, hunters, and those who just like to get away from the almost 400,000 people crowded into the much smaller space the other side of the Rimutakas.

Map, pages 198–9

Twelve thousand people visit the birthplace of Katherine Mansfield, at 25 Tinakori Road, Wellington, every year. The house is open daily to the public.

BELOW: exterior of Old St Paul's Cathedral.

South Island

0   100 km

0   100 miles

N

Tasman Sea

Cape Farewell   Farewell Spit   D'Urville Island

Cape Jackson

Golden Collingwood *Bay*   Totaranui

Takaka   Abel Tasman N. P.

Marlborough Sounds

Cook Strait

Kahurangi

Motueka   *Tasman Bay*

Havelock   Picton

Wellington

Richmond   **Nelson**   Blenheim

National

Karamea   Park   Renwick

Wairau R.   Cape Campbell

Murchison   St. Arnaud

Westport   *Lake Rotoroa*   *Lake Rotoiti*

Cape Foulwind   Nelson Lakes N. P.

INLAND KAIKOURA RANGE

Reefton

Paparoa N. P.   Punakaiki   Lewis Pass   Hanmer Springs   **Kaikoura**

1

6   7

Greymouth   *Hurunui R.*   Cheviot

Hokitika   Waipara

Ross   Arthur's Pass N. P.   924   Rangiora   Kaiapoi

Arthur's Pass   Darfield   **Christchurch**

Lake Coleridge   Lyttelton

S   O   U   T   H   E   R   N

Akaroa

Franz Josef Glacier   Methven   Banks Peninsula

Fox Glacier   Mt. Cook N. P.   3754   Mt. Cook

Westland N. P.   *Rangitata R.*   *Canterbury Plains*   Ashburton

Haast R.   Mt. Cook   *Lake Tekapo*   Geraldine

Haast   *Lake Pukaki*   Fairlie   Temuka

A   L   P   S

Canterbury   *Bight*

Twizel   Timaru

Mount Aspiring N. P.   *Lake Ohau*   8   *Lake Benmore*   Waimate

Mt. Aspiring   3030   Omarama   *Waitaki R.*   971   Kurow

Lake Wanaka   6   Lindis Pass   Oamaru

Treble Cone   2088   *Lake Hawea*

Milford Sound   Milford Sound   **Wanaka**   Ranfurly

Glenorchy   Cromwell   Omakau

Fiordland   Alexandra   Palmerston

Queenstown   Port Chalmers

National   *Lake Wakatipu*   *Clutha R.*   Roxburgh   Mosgiel   Otago Peninsula

Te Anau Downs

Doubtful Sound   *Lake Te Anau*   Te Anau   Mossburn   Lawrence   **Dunedin**

Park

Manapouri   Riversdale   Milton

Lake Manapouri   Lumsden

Dusky Sound   6   Winton   Gore   1   Balclutha

Clifden   Catlins Forest Park   Owaka

Tuatapere   **Invercargill**

Riverton

Bluff   Waipapa Point

Foveaux Strait

D   980   Oban

Mt. Anglem

Stewart Island   Mt. Allen   750

Southwest Cape

PACIFIC

OCEAN

SOUTH ISLAND

*An island of unparalleled scenic variety, where you can sit on
a beach and look at nearby snow-capped mountains*

If variety is the spice of life then the South Island could equally be
called the Spice Island. Towering, snow-capped peaks preside over
flat, broad sun-parched plains. In dense, almost impenetrable rainforests, spectacular waterfalls wash into deep fjords, and then there is
the rich farmland and inhospitable inland basins; glaciers of immense
grandeur and lakes of serene beauty. Variety is the catch-cry of the
South Island: the boat from which Maui fished the North Island out
of the sea, according to the ancient Polynesian legend, seems to have
captured much of nature's bounty.

The two main points of entry are Christchurch, the very English
"garden city" of New Zealand, or Picton in the picturesque Marlborough Sounds. From there our writers, each with an intimate
knowledge of their region, will let you in on their secrets to unlock
what the land has to offer. In Marlborough, a region of secluded bays,
there are also plains that soak up some of the highest sunshine hours
in the whole country, much to the pleasure of grape growers who turn
out vintage after vintage of fine wine.

Hit the West Coast and things start to get wild; beaches pounded by
the Tasman meet with the immensity of the Southern Alps while
spilling out in between are seams rich in coal and once rich in gold.
The West Coast is a region that's taken time out from the glory days
of the gold rush era, but is now beginning to reinvent itself as a tourist
destination where the real treasure is its raw natural beauty. Through
the winding mountain passes the landscape opens up to one of wide
braided rivers and high country sheep farms. Hot mineral springs
seep from the ground where the great giant moa once roamed.

Christchurch adds its touch of colour with parks and gardens,
pedestrian malls and cafés all lining the meandering Avon River.
Queenstown is the jewel in the tourist crown, combining a setting of
unparalleled beauty with a range of adventure activities guaranteed to
get the adrenaline pumping. East and on the coast is Dunedin, a university city where the influence of the early Scottish settlers is plain
to see. Not half an hour's drive from the city centre you can watch
albatross nesting on cliff faces.

Southland forms the base of the Island, a region of rich farmland
where the people shine, perhaps in place of the sun. The Bluff oyster,
a national culinary treasure, is dredged from the seabed of Foveaux
Strait. And if all the above is not enough, there is Fiordland. Hardly
an afterthought, Fiordland is the area of the renowned Milford Track,
Milford Sound, Mitre Peak and Doubtful Sound.

Stewart Island is the anchor of the South Island. Just as well it has
one, or someone seeking paradise might run off with it.

PRECEDING PAGES: Southern Alps; the South Island's wild coast.

CHRISTCHURCH

A city that has always prided itself on its Englishness, and true to fine old British tradition, among the pleasantly cultivated gardens and elegant edifices you can generally find the odd eccentric

Map, page 234

C hristchurch likes to boast its traditional pleasures – punting on the Avon River, riding a tram through the inner-city streets, taking coffee al fresco in the old university precinct. Such pastimes say much about the way Christchurch loves to see itself, as peculiarly English.

Yet of all New Zealand's main centres, Christchurch was the first to adopt some rather more aggressive tactics to entice tourists. So now it's possible to take an aerial gondola up the Port Hills, the city's volcanic backdrop. Or shop in one of the many multi-lingual souvenir shops that dot the inner city. Or gamble in a casino. Or ride a hot-air balloon over the city and plains at dawn. Or fly in a helicopter to sample the French charms of Akaroa, out on Banks Peninsula.

But first, the city itself. You can start at the centre, and it is easy to find – Cathedral Square is smack in the middle. There, a lofty neo-Gothic Church of England cathedral presides. From its base a grid of streets spreads across the plains. The central streets assume the names of English bishoprics – minor ones, because by the time the city was planned in the early 1850s, the best names had already been taken for other communities of the Canterbury province.

At the limits of the city centre run four broad avenues. They enclose a square mile that echoes the City of London. Within their bounds are tidy, tree-lined parks with names such as Cranmer and Latimer, and woe betide any city planner who even thinks about roading that may encroach on these precious parks, as past administrators have learnt.

Winding serpentine through the city is the Avon River. Locals like to believe the stream got its name from the river in Shakespeare's Stratford. In fact, the tag came from a tiny Scottish stream that burbled past the home of one of the city's pioneering families. Along with the Port Hills to the southeast, the Avon is the city's greatest natural asset. Its grassy banks are wide and well-planted in trees. In a recent break with tradition, city horticulturalists have allowed the return of native grasses. The willows along one stretch allegedly grew from slips brought from Napoleon's grave on St Helena, but Christchurch is full of stories like that.

PRECEDING PAGES: giant chess board, Cathedral Square. **LEFT:** town crier. **BELOW:** Captain Scott memorial.

Forever England

To the west of the Four Avenues is the massive **Hagley Park**, set aside as a barrier between city and farm. It is filled with playing fields, botanic gardens and broad open spaces modelled, Christchurch boasts, on the style of classic English landscape gardening.

Christchurch did not happen by accident. A city does not become more English than England without putting its mind to it. It was a planned Anglican settlement, masterminded largely by a young English Tory with the delightfully apt name of John Robert Godley. Repelled

*Morris dancers,
Cathedral Square.*

by the egalitarianism and industrialisation of the 19th-century, Godley aspired to a medieval notion of a harmoniously blended church and state, presided over by a benevolent gentry. He founded the Canterbury Association, with no fewer than two archbishops, seven bishops, 14 peers, four baronets and 16 Members of Parliament as backers. The idea was to raise money and find settlers for the new, perfect little corner of England in the South Pacific.

Only the best sort of migrant needed apply. To qualify for an assisted passage to the other side of the world, a migrant had to furnish a certificate from his vicar vouching that "the applicant is sober, industrious and honest", and that "he and all his family are amongst the most respectable in the parish".

From such ideals came the Canterbury Pilgrims. Their first four ships – Christchurch's *Mayflower* – berthed at the neighbouring port of Lyttelton in 1850. By 1855, a total of 3,549 migrants had made the journey.

Inevitably, things went wrong. Dreams of an ecclesiastical utopia crumbled under the harsh realities of colonial life. The Canterbury Association foundered. It was as difficult to revitalise Anglicanism in the New World as it was anywhere else. Christchurch's growth from the mid-1850s became less ordered, less ideal.

Yet dreams endure. To be of First Four Ships stock still brings some cachet, even today. You can find the names of those first official migrants engraved on plaques in a corner of Cathedral Square.

A city of Godley-ness

Christchurch holds its traditions dear. It has also recognised that its charms have more tangible values: Japanese newlyweds come to Christchurch to have their marriage vows blessed in the cute Gothic charm of churches like St Barnabas

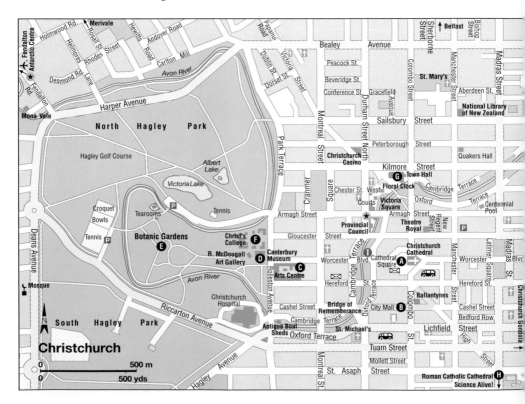

Christchurch

in the leafy, blue-chip real-estate suburb of Fendalton. And there are gardens – acres and acres of them – both public and private. Somebody at one time called Christchurch the "Garden City" and the citizens have been living up to it ever since. Gardening is the biggest leisure time activity, and makes for some extremely pleasant drives and walks. Come to Christchurch – especially in late summer – and you will truly see a city that knows how to garden.

You will also find a city whose interests go much deeper than pretty park-like surroundings. Christchurch is not without its share of interesting characters and interesting stories. An instance: in the 1950s the city was rocked by a scandal that became known as the Parker-Hulme murder. Two teenage girls of good standing successfully plotted to murder the mother of one of the girls. The case shocked the city to its respectable foundations and for a generation it was spoken of in tones of hushed distaste. The story was revived in a stage-play and an award-winning film, by director Peter Jackson, called *Heavenly Creatures*. You can visit the environs where the dreadful deed was done, Victoria Park, in the high-toned suburb of Cashmere on the slopes of the Port Hills, but as yet no enterprising entrepreneur has erected plaques to guide you to the spot. You'll have to ask locals. But be wary. The response could still be frosty.

Map, see opposite

Christchurch has revived its old system of trams, which operate daily in the city centre from 8am till 11pm.

Speaker's corner

Take a walk round the city centre and you will see a few of the city's interesting sites and characters. Start, naturally, from **Cathedral Square Ⓐ**. It was paved as a pedestrian precinct for the 1974 Commonwealth Games, when the city embarked on a beautification programme. Now it is the subject of a new remodelling programme. The square is officially countenanced, Hyde Park-style, as

BELOW: punting through the city centre.

*The Wizard,
Cathedral Square.*

BELOW: Council
Chambers.

a public speaking area. Lunchtime on a sunny weekday is best. Star performer is The Wizard. An immigrant from Australia in the early 1970s, he has been haranguing bemused crowds ever since. Dressed in black robes or sackcloth, he delivers an impassioned line on everything from Queen and Country through feminism to his view of the causes of global warming. No one quite knows whether to take The Wizard seriously or not, but he has been granted more or less official status as the city's mascot.

During summer, the square is alive with festivals of fun and food. There are all sorts of stalls selling art and crafts and ethnic foods. Lunchtime concerts run through December and January. Sadly, the square takes on a more sinister tone after dark, when it is not advisable to walk there alone.

City centre stroll

The **Cathedral** itself is worth a visit. Construction began in 1864 and it is one of the Southern Hemisphere's finest neo-Gothic churches. Climb the steps up the tower past the belfry for a breathless view of the city.

Directly behind it are the offices of *The Press*, the newspaper of record for the Canterbury establishment, while west across the Square is the newly opened Southern Encounter complex – a walk-through, hands-on style aquarium. South down Colombo Street you will find Ballantynes, on the corner of the **City Mall B**, a pedestrian precinct. Ballantynes is the establishment department store, Christchurch's Harrods or Marshall Field's. The assistants dress in black and are notoriously helpful. Very other-worldly.

A walk down the City Mall, going towards the Avon River and the Bridge of Remembrance, takes in some of Christchurch's best shopping territory. Across

he bridge and north along Cambridge Terrace is the city's old library, a small
architectural gem. Like many others, the building has been carefully restored
and now houses offices and a bank.

Map,
page 234

Dreaming spires

If you walk north along the Avon, you will come to the recently renamed
Worcester Boulevard, route of the freshly restored traditional trams that ply the
inner city. Turn right across the river to find the city's information centre. Turn
left down the boulevard and you will come to the **Christchurch Arts Centre**
G. A mass of dreaming spires, turrets and cloisters, this was once the site of the
University of Canterbury. When the university moved out to more spacious
grounds in the suburbs, the site was dedicated to arts and crafts studios, theatres,
restaurants and apartments, all nestled within the granite Gothic shells. The centre is home to the Court Theatre, a professional theatre company which has been
long established as one of New Zealand's best.

This is the heart of old Christchurch. Directly over Rolleston Avenue is the
Canterbury Museum D. The building is almost as noteworthy as the exhibits.
Behind the museum is the municipal art gallery. The McDougall Gallery offers a
collection of early and contemporary New Zealand art.

Beyond, the **Botanic Gardens E** are a truly splendid celebration of the city's
gardening heritage, from English herbaceous borders to native sections and
glasshouses of subtropical and desert specimens. They are enclosed within a
loop of the Avon River, as it winds through Hagley Park.

Immediately north along Rolleston Avenue is **Christ's College F**, a very
Anglican, very proper English public school for boys. The buildings, old and

TIP

Built in 1843, Dean's
Cottage is the oldest
building in Canterbury
and is now a private
museum.

BELOW: Dean's
Cottage.

new, are marvellous. Head back to town down Armagh Street and you'll pass Cranmer Square. On the far side is the old Christchurch Normal School. Like half of Christchurch's notable buildings, it is mock Gothic and was long ago deserted by educationalists; vandals and squatters had their way with the old folly for years. But a developer took over the buildings and transformed them into luxury apartments. The buildings also house one of the city's best restaurants.

Further down Armagh Street are the old Provincial Council buildings, once the home of local government, fine examples of more modest architecture than some of the city's landmarks.

Architectural triumphs

Beyond is the recently remodelled Victoria Square. Last century it was the city's marketplace. Now it is a wonderful expanse of green anchored by the **Town Hall ⑤**. The Town Hall was opened in 1972 after the city had dithered for 122 years about a civic centre, and it remains the pride of modern Christchurch. It is still one of the architectural triumphs of its time, and has been echoed around the country. Designed by local architects Warren and Mahoney, it is restrained and elegant, with an auditorium, concert chamber, conference rooms, banquet hall and restaurant overlooking the Avon and square.

The Town Hall has been linked recently to one of the city's new architectural features, the Parkroyal Hotel, and via an overhead walkway to a new convention centre for the city. Just another block away on Victoria Street stands the country's first casino with its distinctive stylised roulette-wheel façade.

ABOVE: Juggler in the Arts Centre Market. **BELOW:** Victoria Square.

If you're interested in ecclesiastical architecture, the city's other cathedral is worth seeking out. The Roman Catholic **Cathedral of the Blessed Sacrament ⑪** is a High Renaissance Romanesque basilica, built early this century, in a somewhat tacky part of town. George Bernard Shaw visited the city soon after the building opened and praised Christchurch's "splendid cathedral". The pride of local Anglicans turned to chagrin when they realised that he was not referring to Christchurch Cathedral, but to the Catholic basilica.

In the same part of the city, the old railway station has been converted into a hands-on science centre, attached to a multiplex cinema centre.

Hagley Park is the best jogging circuit enjoyed by hundreds of officer workers every lunchtime. Then there is cycling, the perfect mode of transport for flat Christchurch. Hordes of school pupils and workers take to the streets on two wheels. Visitors can hire bikes, but beware of motorists. If bashful, stick to Hagley Park or streets with cycle lanes. For a less strenuous way of getting about you can boat on the Avon, and catch an altogether new perspective on the city.

The suburbs

Out of the city centre you can tour countless streets of fine homes, going northwest towards Fendalton and Merivale, or south up to the Port Hills.

Christchurch's real estate is fiercely class-conscious, along lines that are somewhat inexplicable. Fendalton and Merivale are easily recognised, with their fine trees and secluded gardens, as havens of the wealthy. Yet cross the wrong street and values plummet. Merivale's mall is one of the city's best shopping regions, with stores and restaurants that rival the inner city.

The **Port Hills** are the only area with a clear geographical advantage over the rest of the city. The hills' elevation lifts them above the winter smog. The Summit Road, along the tops of the hills, gives spectacular views of the city, the plains and the Southern Alps and, on the other side, the port of Lyttelton and the hills of Banks Peninsula. There are extensive walking tracks over the Port Hills and peninsula beyond. They range from one- or two-hour strolls to ambitious hikes, with shelters to rest in. Ask at an information centre for details. The hills can be tackled by a high-tech gondola that has become one of the city's big attractions. A restaurant, bar and souvenir shops have been installed for diversions after the ride. The hardier can hire mountain bikes at the summit for an alternative route down, or an exploration of the hills.

There are many gardens up here. One of the most notable is the **Garden of Gethsemane**, a private garden-cum-commercial nursery that has many unusual specimens. Its little avenues and tiny trellised chapel are worth a visit.

It's worth taking a drive or bus to **Lyttelton** ❶, the sleepy-looking port over the hill from Christchurch, with its stack of charming cottages that cling to the slopes. You can return through a road tunnel or drive over the hill to the seaside suburbs of Ferrymead, Redcliffs and Sumner. The **Transport Museum** ❷ at Ferrymead is a big attraction for train buffs, colonial enthusiasts and the like. Sumner has the air of an artists' retreat. It's also slightly bohemian and gets extra busy at weekends, when families come to frolic in the sands.

On the other side of the city, the airport has an interesting **Antarctic Centre** ❸, which celebrates Christchurch's history as the stepping-off point for ice-

Map, page 240

TIP

A courtesy bus runs to the Port Hills Gondola from the Visitor Centre in Worcester Boulevard.

BELOW: Roman Catholic Cathedral.

bound expeditions. It's well worth a visit. Nearby is **Orana Park**, a safari-style zoo with an ever-increasing range of animals roaming around on "African plains" and specially created islands. Cars can enter the lion enclosure.

If talk of Antarctic expeditions and wild animals seems a bit rugged, the rest of the family can take more refined pleasures at the many wineries that have dotted the rural outskirts of Christchurch, since Canterbury became one of New Zealand's boutique wine-growing regions.

To the northeast is **Queen Elizabeth II Park ❹**. Its stadium and swimming sports complex was built for the 1974 Commonwealth Games. City ratepayers didn't want to be landed with a white elephant, so it's been turned into an all-round family attraction, with water slides, a maze, go-karts and other diversions.

Peninsula excursion

If you have time before you head south to the mountains and lakes, you might want a change from the city lights. Banks Peninsula, over the Port Hills, is the best destination for a short trip.

It is the scene of one of two blunders made by Captain James Cook when he circumnavigated New Zealand in the 18th century. He mapped the peninsula as an island. He would have been right if he had come several millennia earlier. The extinct volcanoes which formed the peninsula were once separated from the mainland. (Cook's other gaffe was Stewart Island, at the southern tip of the South Island, which he linked to the mainland.)

The once bush-covered hills of Banks Peninsula were long ago logged for timber. There are still some pocket remnants of bush, and plenty of delightful valleys and bays. Sheltered microclimates support many horticultural products

International Antarctic Centre.

BELOW: Botanic Gardens.

and plants that cannot be cultivated anywhere else this far south, including kiwi fruit. There are also some keen growers of exotic nuts and herbs in the area.

To experience the real charm of Canterbury, seek out Diamond Harbour, Okains Bay, Okuti Valley and Port Levy. They are fertile, inviting and unspoiled. In many other parts of the world they would be bristling with condominiums.

French settlement

But the real gem of the peninsula is **Akaroa ❺**, about 80 km (50 miles) from Christchurch. This little settlement began its European life in 1838 when a French whaler landed. For a short while it flourished as a French settlement, and 63 migrants set out from France on the *Comte de Paris* to create a South Seas outpost. But they arrived in 1840 to find the Union Jack flying.

Piqued and pipped at the colonial post, the French settlers nevertheless stayed. They planted poplars from Normandy, named streets and grew grapes, but they were outnumbered by the English.

The dream lingers on though, and of late it has been brushed up for visitors. Little streets wind up the hill from the harbour front, with names such as Rue Lavaud and Rue Jolie. A charming colonial style predominates, and has been protected by town planning rules. Of most note is the **Langlois-Eteveneaux House**, now fitted out as a display with an attached colonial museum.

Many Christchurch people own holiday houses, or baches, in Akaroa or nearby. The town can become crowded in January and February. There are many bars, restaurants and cafés. Because of the isolation, restaurants tend to be pricey. Fresh catches of fish can be bought from the wharf.

Akaroa Harbour, on the south coast of Banks Peninsula, is on the doorstep of

Map, see opposite

TIP

A courtesy bus runs from the visitor centre to the Air Force Museum, where displays include Antarctic aircraft. The Museum is situated south of the city at the former Wigram Air Force Base.

BELOW: Lyttelton Harbour.

Map, page 240

The Banks Peninsula.

BELOW: museum in Langlois-Eteveneaux House. **RIGHT:** wildlife, Akaroa Harbour.

the habitat of the rare Hector's dolphin. There are regular sea cruises to catch glimpses of the dolphin and other features of the region.

Churches are among Akaroa's notable features. The Roman Catholic church of St Patrick is the oldest in anything like original form. It was built in 1864 and was in fact the third in town to serve Akaroa's French and Irish – hence the name – Catholics. It is a charming and cluttered little building with a noteworthy Bavarian window on the east wall.

St Peter's Anglican church was built in 1863, and generously enlarged about 15 years later. It is a more austere building in the Protestant style. Most distinctive of all is the tiny Kaik, a Maori church some 6 km (4 miles) south of the township along the foreshore. It is a remnant of a once strong Maori presence around Akaroa Harbour, in a haunting and evocative setting.

In the town of Akaroa, a climb through the domain, called the Garden of Tane, is worthwhile on its own count, and will take you to the spectacularly sited graveyard. Its graves must have the best views in the country and they make up a rich record of the region's history. The Old French Cemetery however, on the other side of town, is a disappointment. It was the resting place of Akaroa's earliest Europeans and after a hot slog up the hill it affords a good view of the harbour. But a benevolent government tidied the place up in 1925, in the process destroying most of the headstones for a mediocre memorial.

Further afield

Turning inland from the peninsula, Christchurch has a huge hinterland. Its province, Canterbury, runs from the Southern Alps to the sea, and stretches hundreds of miles from north to south. A popular traditional day trip is **Hanmer Springs** to the north, with its spa, horse riding and mountain walks. Hanmer is home to the old Queen Mary Hospital, built as a convalescence centre for returning war veterans and subsequently a rehabilitation centre for recovering alcoholics. Its setting, hidden in a valley off the beaten track, gave rise to an unofficial slogan: "1,200 feet above worry level." It is still there, in a somewhat reduced state, but the visitors taking the waters are likely to be tourists or Cantabrians visiting their holiday homes.

A very comfortable and nostalgic way to see both the Canterbury Plains and the Southern Alps is the popular TransAlpine Express. The train pulls out of Christchurch, heads across the plains and up into the mountains at Arthur's Pass, an especially appealing trip in winter when the mountains are covered in snow. The return ride takes a day. It's popular, so book ahead.

The plains you will cross are New Zealand's biggest, richest cropping area, though they are prone to summer droughts, which is why local farmers have battled for years for legal rights to take irrigation water from local rivers such as the Rakaia. Visitors here are more likely to be interested in the rivers' salmon and trout content. On the outskirts of Christchurch is Lincoln University, about 20 km (12 miles) south of the city. It is at the centre of an agricultural campus that is at the forefront of New Zealand's farming practices. A telephone call beforehand can arrange a guided tour.

CANTERBURY

A province whose flat coastal and inland plains are bordered with mountain ranges of breathtaking beauty – there can be no finer place to be – when the wind's in the right direction

Canterbury is a marriage of mountain and sea, linked by snow-fed rivers that cut braided courses across the plain. The Southern Alps, Pacific Ocean and two rivers (the Conway in the north and Waitaki in the south) form the boundaries of this eastern province. The popular view of Canterbury is a patchwork plain where lambs frolic under a nor'west sky. This Canterbury does exist.

The plain, 180 km (110 miles) long and an average of 40 km (25 miles) wide, is New Zealand's largest area of flat land. Canterbury lamb, bred for meat and wool, is regarded as the country's best. The Canterbury nor'wester is a notorious wind, a true föhn with its warm, dry, blustery weather whipping up dust from riverbeds and furrowed farmlands, blamed for the moodiness of Cantabrians.

The province also encompasses New Zealand's highest mountains and widest rivers, alongside pastoral and forested hills, fine beaches, extinct volcanoes and the sheltered bays of Banks Peninsula. Settlement is diverse, from cities to high-country sheep stations where genteel English traditions are vigorously upheld.

Plain fascination

The Canterbury plains are merely the corridor to its special characteristic – sky, earth and sea, yet conveniently close to civilisation. From any point in the province one is never more than a couple of hours from mountains, lakes, beaches, plains, rivers, cities and airports. The openness of the landscape and the ever-changing climate inspire an awareness of the environment. The traveller soon learns that southerly wind invariably brings rain and a quick drop in temperature; a nor'wester, dry heat and rising rivers from its high-country rainstorms; an easterly, a chill breeze to Christchurch and along the coast.

One-and-a-half centuries of European settlement have tamed the flat land. The treeless landscape that appeared so desolate to Canterbury's pilgrims is today a pastoral scene like no other: a patchwork of cropped fields dotted with sheep, divided by shelter belts of pines and macrocarpas, and sewn through with long straight roads that would have gladdened the hearts of the Romans. From the air the view has a certain fascination. Patterned on the multi-coloured quilt of crops and pastures are vein-like shadows of ancient streams, while the existing rivers gleam silver as they flow. Towns, small and large, sprawl elegantly along the roads like aphids clinging to sap-rich stems. From the ground the plains are less imposing. Travelling lengthwise in Canterbury is a monotonous journey, especially on the main highway between Christchurch and the province's second city, **Timaru ❶**. Canterbury's finest scenery is inland, along the foothills and valleys of the Southern Alps.

Map, pages 248–9

Auckland
North Island
Wellington
Christchurch
South Island

PRECEDING PAGES: Church of the Good Shepherd, Lake Tekapo.
LEFT: Arthur's Pass, Mount Rolleston.
BELOW: lone sheep.

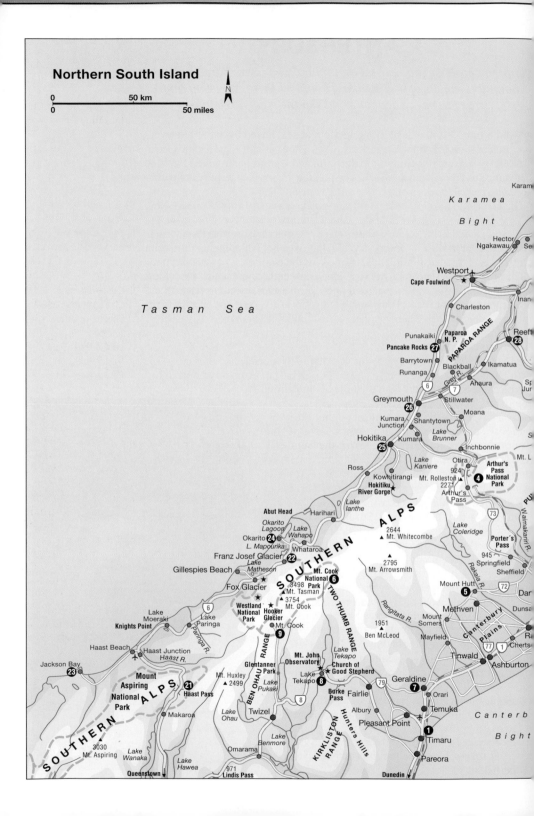

Northern South Island

0   50 km

0   50 miles

N

Karamea

K a r a m e a

B i g h t

Karam

Hector
Ngakawau   Se

Westport ★
Cape Foulwind

Inan

Charleston

T a s m a n   S e a

Punakaiki   **Paparoa**
     N. P.

Pancake Rocks 27

Reeft

28

Barrytown

Blackball

Ikamatua

PAPAROA RANGE

Runanga

Grey R.

6

Ahaura

Sp
Jun

7

Greymouth

26

Stillwater

Moana

Kumara
Junction

Shantytown

*Lake
Brunner*

Hokitika

Kumara

S

25

Inchbonnie

*Lake
Kaniere*

Otira

Mt. L

Ross

924

**Arthur's
Pass
National
Park**

Kowhitirangi

Mt. Rolleston

**Hokitiku
River Gorge**

2271

★

4

Arthur's
Pass

PU

Abut Head

Harihari

*Lake
Ianthe*

73

Warmakarni R.

*Okarito
Lagoon*

*Lake
Coleridge*

**Porter´s
Pass**

Okarito
L. Mapourika

24

*Lake
Wahapo*

2644
▲ Mt. Whitecombe

945

Springfield

S O U T H E R N

Whataroa

Franz Josef Glacier

22

*Lake
Matheson*

2795
▲ Mt. Arrowsmith

Sheffield

Gillespies Beach

A L P S

Mount Hutt

Dar

Fox Glacier

Mt. Cook
National
Park

6

72

3498
▲ Mt. Tasman

★

5

Lake
Moeraki

6

3754
Mt. Cook

**Westland
National
Park**

**Hooker
Glacier**

TWO THUMB RANGE

Methven

Dunsa

Rangitata R.

Knights Point

*Lake
Paringa*

★ Mt. Cook

9

Mount
Somers

1951
Ben McLeod

Canterbury

Plains

Haast Beach

Paringa R.

Mayfield

Ra

77

Chert

1

Jackson Bay

Haast Junction

Haast R.

Tinwald

Ashburton

23

**Mount
Aspiring**

21

BEN OHAU RANGE

**Glentanner
Park**

Mt. Huxley
▲ 2499

**Mt. John
Observatory**

*Lake
Tekapo*

**Church of
Good Shepherd**

★

79

Geraldine

Orari

**National
Park**

Haast Pass

*Lake
Pukaki*

*Lake
Tekapo*

8

7

Temuka

S O U T H E R N

A L P S

Makaroa

*Lake
Ohau*

Twizel

8

Burke
Pass

Fairlie

Hunters Hills

Albury

Pleasant Point

1

Timaru

Canterb

3030
Mt. Aspiring

*Lake
Wanaka*

*Lake
Benmore*

KIRKLISTON RANGE

Bight

Omarama

Pareora

Queenstown

971
Lindis Pass

*Lake
Hawea*

Dunedin

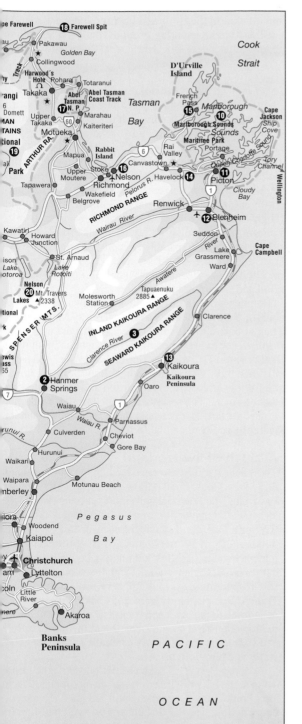

Three main roads provide easy access to passes to the mountains beyond which lies Westland. Northernmost is the Lewis Pass, and its rewarding short detour to the tiny spa resort of Hanmer Springs; central is spectacular Arthur's Pass and the surrounding national park of the same name; southernmost is Burke Pass, which leads to Mackenzie Country and the magnificent panorama of glacial lakes and alps of the Mount Cook region.

Getting healthy at Hanmer

Bypassed by conventional tourist traffic, **Hanmer Springs ❷** survives as one of New Zealand's quietest resorts. This little village, an easy 136-km (84-mile) drive north of Christchurch, nestles in a sheltered, forested valley. Its hot mineral pools are set in a garden of giant conifers. Few experiences are more pleasurable than relaxing in these open-air pools on a winter's night, watching the snowflakes dissolve silently in the steam.

A European settler stumbled upon the springs in 1859; they were harnessed by the government in 1883. Since then their recuperative powers have been used to help rehabilitate wounded soldiers, the pyschiatrically disturbed and, in more recent years, alcoholics. Originally maintained by the Queen Mary Hospital, the recently modernised pool complex is now controlled by the Hurunui District Council. The landscaped rock gardens include several plunge pools, communal pools of varying (indicated) temperatures, a freshwater swimming pool, children's pool and a warm running stream. Several easy, well-defined paths meander through more species of exotic trees than on any other plantation in New Zealand. This was the first exotic forest established by the government in the South Island; some of it was planted more than 90 years ago.

More demanding walks to the summits of Conical Hill and Mount Isobel provide magnificent panoramas. The Mount Isobel track, which passes 200 different kinds of sub-alpine flowering plants and ferns, is a naturalist's delight.

Hanmer's 18-hole golf course is one of the highest in New Zealand, while fishing, hunting, jet-boating, skiing and horse-trekking are also available. Although Hanmer provides accommodation in the form of a licensed hotel and a good selection of motels, guest houses, and camping grounds, the main street has retained the low-key, subdued atmosphere of a typical rural township.

Rugged beauty

Alpine flora, Arthur's Pass.

From Hanmer, the road over Jack's Pass to the isolated **Clarence Valley ❸** is worth exploring for its rugged tussocked beauty, especially upstream. A word of warning, though: the road, which was originally built to install and maintain the high-voltage transmission lines from the hydro schemes of Otago to Blenheim, Nelson and beyond, is an unsealed, often steep track, and is suitable only in good weather. It is not a through road and it ends in locked gates at the Acheron River bridge (downstream from Jack's Pass) and at the Rainbow Station over the Main Divide. Hanmer, therefore, remains very much a "dead-end" town. Travellers have little choice but to backtrack 13 km (8 miles) to the Waipara-Reefton road (Highway 7).

Westwards this road climbs up the Waisu Valley to Lewis Pass. This all-weather route (opened in 1939) offers a comparatively gentle, picturesque crossing to the West Coast at an altitude of 865 metres (2,838 ft) through beech-covered mountains. The highway descends to Maruia Springs and then on to the Rahu Saddle, Reefton and Greymouth.

BELOW: Oahu B Power Station.

Southwards from the "Hanmer turn-off", as it is locally known, Highway 7 runs through the rolling hills of North Canterbury to join Highway 1 at Waipara. While here, sample the fare at one of the several vineyards that are earning a good reputation for their wines. The road then continues through the small rural settlements of Culverden, Hurunui and Waikari. An old historic pub is now Hurunui's chief claim to fame, thankfully saved from demolition and frequented by local farmers. The road then passes through Waikari's limestone landscape, where the keen-eyed can detect naturally sculpted animal forms.

A touch of Switzerland

The quickest route between Christchurch and Westland is the West Coast Road (Highway 73) through Arthur's Pass. This, the South Island's most central pass, boasts New Zealand's version of a Swiss village. Although **Arthur's Pass ❹** township, nestling in the heart of the Southern Alps 154 km (96 miles) west of Christchurch, may lack green pastures and tinkling cowbells, it does have a chalet-style restaurant and, in keeping with any self-respecting Swiss village, a railway station. The TransAlpine passenger train stops here twice daily on its journey to the coast and back. There is also an information centre run by the Department of Conservation and staff there can offer advice on the numerous good walks and climbs in the area.

Arthur's Pass marks the eastern portal of the Otira Tunnel, the only rail link through the mountains. The 8 km (5 mile) tunnel, completed in 1923 after 15 years of construction, was the first electrified stretch of line in what was then the British Empire – a necessary advance to save passengers from being choked to death by the steam locomotive's sulphurous smoke. Today the rail link between the West Coast and Canterbury remains a vital one. As an extra bonus, it is without a doubt the most scenic railway in New Zealand.

Arthur's Pass is also the headquarters of the national park of the same name. Its close proximity to Christchurch and its many comparatively civilised tracks make the 100,000-hectare (247,000-acre) park one of the best utilised in the country. Mount Rolleston, 2,271 metres (7,451 ft), dominates the region, in which there are 30 peaks over 1,800 metres (about 6,000 ft). Motels and a youth hostel provide accommodation.

The 924-metre (3,032-ft) pass is named after Arthur Dudley Dobson, who rediscovered the former Maori route in 1864. It marks the boundary between Canterbury and Westland, a boundary often reinforced by distinctive weather patterns. During a nor'wester, travellers leave a dry and warm day on the Canterbury side of the pass to descend into heavy rain in the West Coast's Otira Gorge. Conversely, during a southerly or easterly, West Coast-bound travellers leave the rain and cold behind in Canterbury for a landscape bathed in sunshine.

Storms are often as intense as they are sudden, dropping as much as 250 mm (10 inches) of rain in 24 hours. The annual rainfall here is 3,000 mm (about 120 inches). Bad weather in winter often forces the closure of the highway, which in the Otira Gorge is very steep with a series of hairpin bends requiring special care in wet weather and in winter. The road is not suitable for caravans. (Indeed, in bad weather, the Automobile Association often advises travellers to take the longer but easier and safer Lewis Pass route to Westland.)

A common sight in this vicinity is the kea, the native parrot. This unique mountain species has criminal tendencies that surpass those of any thieving

TIP

One way to get really stunning views of Canterbury is to drift over it sipping champagne in a hot-air balloon, gazing at the Southern Alps. Hot-air balloon safaris run from Methven.

BELOW: Rakaia River.

magpie, as the pioneer explorer Julius von Haast discovered when a vandalistic kea tumbled his valuable collection of native plants down a ravine. Careless visitors will discover this same cheeky tendency today if they leave any food or shiny belongings unattended – be warned.

Arthur's Pass is actually not the highest point on the West Coast road. That distinction belongs to **Porter's Pass**, 88 km (55 miles) west of Christchurch, which traverses the foothills at 945 metres (3,100 ft). Porter's Pass is a popular winter destination for day-trippers from Christchurch who enjoy tobogganing and ice-skating at Lake Lyndon and skiing on the many skifields in the vicinity such as the commercial field at Porter Heights and the club fields at Craigieburn, Broken River and Mount Cheesman.

Canterbury's most popular and best developed skifield is **Mount Hutt ❺**, 100 km (62 miles) west of Christchurch and serviced by the small town of Methven, 11 km (7 miles) away, which provides accommodation to suit all budgets.

Rooftop of New Zealand

The monarch of New Zealand's national parks is the **Aoraki Mount Cook National Park ❻**, where the highest peaks in the land soar above the crest of the Southern Alps. Supreme is Mount Cook itself, which until 1991 was 3,764 metres (12,349 ft) high. However, the famous mountain lost about 10 metres (around 34 ft) from its summit in that year, in a massive landslide. The re-surveyed official height is now 3,754 metres (12,316 ft) which, in spite of its diminished stature, retains its standing as New Zealand's highest mountain.

The Mount Cook alpine region was the training ground for Sir Edmund Hillary, the first person in the world to scale Mount Everest. The narrow park

extends only 80 km (50 miles) along the alpine spine, yet it contains 140 peaks over 2,134 metres (7,000 ft) as well as five of New Zealand's largest glaciers.

The Mount Cook Line, a subsidiary of Air New Zealand, runs daily air services to the park, only 35 minutes' flying time from either Christchurch or Queenstown. If the weather at the Mount Cook airstrip is too bad for flying, the airline uses the Pukaki airstrip near Twizel, and then carries its passengers by road.

Paradoxically, although Mount Cook is almost directly due west from Christchurch, the journey by road is a circuitous distance of 330 km (205 miles). Getting there, however, is half the fun.

The main route follows Highway 1 south for 121 km (75 miles), marching easily across plain and braided river alike, casually belying the mighty challenges this journey once posed for Maori and pioneer. The wide rivers proved major obstacles to travel and settlement in the 1850s and difficult river crossings caused numerous drownings in Canterbury. Throughout New Zealand 1,115 people lost their lives in river accidents between 1840 and 1870 and it was suggested in Parliament that drowning be classified a natural death! Nowadays motorists speed over the Rakaia, Ashburton and Rangitata rivers without a thought for the hazards that once confronted travellers.

Immediately past the Rangitata River the road to the Mackenzie Country (Highway 79) branches westwards from the main highway. It leads to the foothills and the tiny town of **Geraldine** ❼ which snuggles into them, offering detours to an historic pioneer homestead in the Orari Gorge and excellent picnic and fishing spots in the nearby Waihi and Te Moana gorges.

Mackenzie Country

The road to Fairlie, a country town with an historical museum, passes a Clydesdale stud farm and Barkers, the only elderberry wine cellars in New Zealand. Try their famous and aptly named mulled wine, Mountain Thunder. The gentle, green countryside is left behind at Fairlie as the road, now Highway 8, rises with deceptive ease to Burke Pass. At this gap through the foothills a different world stretches beyond – the great tussocked basin known as the Mackenzie Country, named after a Scottish shepherd who in 1855 tried to hide stolen sheep in this isolated high-country area.

Long and straight stretches of road take you eventually to Twizel, a town built to provide accommodation to workers on the region's major dam projects, and thought likely to become a ghost-town when the projects were completed. The town, however, has defied pundits, and is enjoying a mini boom. The Department of Conservation runs an information centre on the outskirts of town, where you can learn about the region's wildlife, including the rare black stilt. There are little more than 60 black stilt left in the wild now, and a breeding site for the birds can be visited just a few kilometres further down the main highway.

Winding across the stark-bronzed landscape the road first reaches **Lake Tekapo** ❽, a lovely turquoise glacial lake reflecting the surrounding mountains. By the lake's edge the simple stone Church of the Good Shepherd stands in harmony with its surroundings. Nearby, the

Map, pages 248–9

Beautiful Lake Tekapo, about 710 metres (2,330 feet) above sea level, gets its name from the Maori words Taka, meaning sleeping mat, and Po, meaning night. The lake's gorgeous turquoise colour is caused by "rock flour", finely ground rock particles suspended in glacial meltwater.

BELOW: look out for the thieving kea.

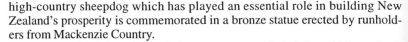

Map, pages 248–9

Mount Cook.

BELOW: Mackenzie Highland Show. **RIGHT:** Tasman Glacier, Mount Cook.

high-country sheepdog which has played an essential role in building New Zealand's prosperity is commemorated in a bronze statue erected by runholders from Mackenzie Country.

A major aerial sightseeing and charter company, Air Safaris and Mount Cook Scenic Flights, based at the lakeside town of Tekapo, operates scenic alpine helicopter and fixed wing flights. From Tekapo the road south continues across the tussocked quilt of the Mackenzie Basin. Winter sports are popular here, with skiing at Round Hill and ice-skating on the lake. In summer, fishing and boating take over.

The road passes Irishman Creek, the sheep station where Sir William Hamilton developed the propellerless jet boat to travel up, as well as down the shallow rivers of the lonely backcountry. Nearby is the Mount John Observatory, open to visitors. It was previously used to help track United States satellites and is well-placed to take advantage of the pristine Mackenzie Country atmosphere.

For much of the way, the road follows the course of the man-made canal that drains Tekapo's turquoise waters to the first of the Waitaki hydroelectric scheme's powerhouses on the northern shore of Lake Pukaki. Lake Pukaki today is twice the size it was in 1979, when its waters were allowed to flow unimpeded to Lake Benmore. Concrete dams now hold Pukaki in check, forcing it to rise to a new level for controlled use in hydro electric generation. The dams have flooded forever the once convoluted maze of streams of the broad river that flows into it from the Tasman and Hooker glaciers.

Travellers on the new highway that skirts the southern slopes of the Pukaki valley to **Mount Cook village ❾** might catch glimpses of the old road undulating above and disappearing into the surface of the lake far below. But that road's death by drowning drew little sympathy from those who really knew it well, the travellers who rode its unsealed corrugations and choked in its dust. The new highway, sealed with an easy gradient, has halved the driving time to the lodge with the million dollar views, The Hermitage.

The village lies within the Mount Cook National Park and the development of accommodation, therefore, has been limited. Nevertheless, in addition to The Hermitage hotel, there are also self-contained A-frame chalets, the Glencoe Lodge, a camping ground and a well-equipped youth hostel.

Well-defined tracks lead from the village up to the surrounding valleys. These eventually become "climbs" that are not for novices and should only be tackled with the right equipment, and these only after consultation with the Park Board rangers. Easier mountain ascents are provided by ski-equipped scenic aircraft which land on the high snowfields. Skiing is available throughout most of the year, the most exciting run being the descent of the 29-km (18-mile) Tasman Glacier.

The spectacular views of Mount Cook, especially when the last rays of the midsummer sun strike its blushing peak in late twilight, form the highlight of many a traveller's exploration of Canterbury. The mountain, named Aorangi (Cloud Piercer) by the Maori, frequently hides shyly in a cloak of cloud, depriving sightseers of its face. But come rain or shine, this alpine region is ever-masterful, ever dramatic, and a corner of Canterbury where people are dwarfed into insignificance.

NELSON AND MARLBOROUGH

The South Island's northern tip is a magnet for wildlife and offers rest, relaxation and a slow pace, which many travellers will welcome after a bumpy journey across the Cook Strait

Map, pages 248–9

Nelson and Marlborough see themselves as a glittering sun-belt around the midriff of a country which boasts about its climate from top to toe. This metaphoric belt is elastic to cope with the great summer tourist influx. Nelson City's usual 43,000 population is said to double at Christmas and New Year, and at beach resorts like Kaiteriteri, numbers jump from several to several thousand. Visitors pour into hotels, motels and motor camps in cars full of children, towing caravans or boats or with tents strapped to roof-racks.

The approach to Nelson and Marlborough can be by road from the south, by scheduled air services from Air New Zealand Link or the locally-based Origin Pacific Airlines into Nelson or Blenheim airports or, perhaps most dramatically, by the frequent ferry services across Cook Strait from Wellington.

Straight through the Strait

Cook Strait is a natural wind funnel for the Roaring Forties and it can be one of the most unpleasant short stretches of water on earth on a bad day. But the moment you enter the **Marlborough Sounds ⑩** through the narrow entrance of Tory Channel, you enter a different world, a world of myriad inlets and bays with hills plunging steeply into the sea. There used to be a whaling station at the entrance to Tory Channel, the last one in New Zealand when it closed in 1964, ending more than 50 years of pursuit of the migratory humpback whale by the Perano family. This channel has been the sole highway for the Peranos, and for most owners of the many holiday homes and farm properties of the Marlborough Sounds, for the better part of a century. Only a few enjoy the luxury of road access, with boats the main mode of transport and communication: the doctor does his rounds by launch; the mail is delivered by launch.

The hour-long journey down Tory Channel and Queen Charlotte Sound aboard the big rail ferries gives only a glimpse of all the glorious scenery in this region. The shores are dotted with isolated houses, many offering holiday accommodation.

The most famous of all Pacific explorers, Captain James Cook, spent something like 100 days in and around Ship Cove during his travels, and it is easy to see why. He first hoisted the British flag in New Zealand there on 15 January 1770, and a monument has been erected near the entrance to Queen Charlotte Sound, to commemorate Cook's visits.

The commercial centre for almost all activity in the Sounds is the town of **Picton ⑪** in one of the bays near the head of Queen Charlotte Sound. Picton is the start (or finish) of the South Island section of Highway 1 and of the main trunk railway. It is the terminal for the Cook Strait ferries and the base for the assorted launches,

PRECEDING PAGES: Marlborough vineyards. **LEFT:** whale watching. **BELOW:** Motueka sand flats.

*Looking across
Marlborough Sounds
from Picton.*

water taxis and charter boats on which locals and visitors rely for transport. There is also a float plane providing scenic flights, as well as a short-cut to accommodation in adjacent Kenepuru Sound. It is a mere 10 minutes' journey by float plane against a minimum of two hours by car and two days by boat.

An old trading scow, the *Echo*, is drawn up on the beach on one side of Picton Bay. The *Echo* was one of the last of New Zealand's old trading scows to remain in service, though ironically these flat-bottomed sailing craft were designed for shallow river harbours rather than the deep waters of the sounds.

A shipping relic of far greater antiquity lies across the bay. The teak-hulled *Edwin Fox* is the only remaining East Indiaman, or ship of the British East India Company, in the world. It came to New Zealand as a 19th-century immigrant ship and ended its working life as a storage hulk for meat-freezing works, which operated at Picton.

Wine and whales

Thirty km (19 miles) south of Picton, **Blenheim ⑫** is the administrative centre of sparsely populated Marlborough. Sitting on the Wairau Plain, it is a pleasant if unspectacular farm service town which has, since the establishment of the Montana vineyards close by, in the late 1960s, become one of New Zealand's most important wine-producing areas. Many wineries have opened retail and food outlets here, and vineyard tours and an annual wine and food festival have become important attractions of the region.

BELOW: vines near Blenheim.

Grapes, apples, cherries, sheep – all these take advantage of the Marlborough sunshine to grow and grow fat. But nothing needs the province's hot, dry days of summer more than the salt works at Lake Grassmere, where the sea water is

Map, pages 248–9

ponded in shallow lagoons and then allowed to evaporate until nothing is left of it but blinding white salt crystals.

In marked contrast to the sounds, the coastline in the southern part of the province is exposed and rocky. Near the small town of Kaikoura, in the west, the sea and the mountains meet head-on, leaving merely a narrow beach past which the road and railway must squeeze.

Kaikoura ⓭ nestles at the base of a small peninsula which provides shelter for the fishing boats based here. The crayfish or rock lobster which they pursue on this rocky coast is sold fresh from numerous roadside stalls. More important now to Kaikoura's economy are the visitors who come to see the whales which congregate close to the shore. Whale watching trips can be taken by sea or air, but if you're lucky you might even spot them from the shore. Whale watching has provided a big boost for the town and it's now a worthy stopover point in any journey to Christchurch. While there, take a walk to the seal colony.

Kaikoura is Maori for "to eat crayfish".

Inland from Kaikoura, two parallel mountain ranges thrust skywards, to reach their acme in the peak of Tapuaenuku, towering 2,885 metres (9,465 ft) above sea level. Beyond that again is the Awatere Valley and Molesworth, which is New Zealand's largest sheep and cattle station.

The Wairau and Awatere valleys have been described as "the cradle of South Island pastoralism". But they were also places where some of the most destructive overgrazing of the country's erosion-prone high country took place, until a derelict Molesworth was finally taken over by the government in the 1930s. Since then, much of its 182,000 hectares (450,000 acres) has been painfully rehabilitated and the station now runs 10,000 head of cattle. Visitors can take safari tours of the area by four-wheel-drive vehicle, going from Nelson through Molesworth to the North Canterbury resort of Hanmer Springs.

BELOW: Graham Valley, Nelson.

Mussels and gold

The road from Blenheim to Nelson takes you down the attractive Kaituna Valley to **Havelock** ⓮, a fishing and holiday settlement at the head of Pelorus Sound. Havelock is like a smaller Picton, without the bustle of the inter-island ferries, but with the same feeling that all the important business of the town is waterborne. Pelorus and Kenepuru sounds are key to New Zealand's expanding aquaculture industry, their uncrowded and sheltered waters being used for growing salmon in sea cages and green-lipped mussels on buoyed rope lines. Scallops and Pacific oysters are also grown.

Just beyond Havelock is **Canvastown**, named after the tent town which popped up mushroom-like when gold was discovered on the Wakamarina River in the 1860s. It was a short-lived rush, with most of the diggers going on to Otago. Canvastown remembers its brief heyday with a memorial of old mining tools and equipment set in concrete. Visitors can hire pans and still get a "show" of gold on the Wakamarina.

Rai Valley provides a rest stop for buses travelling the 115 km (72 miles) between Blenheim and Nelson. A road turning off here leads to **French Pass** ⓯ at the outermost edge of the sounds. This is a narrow, reef-strewn waterway between the mainland and D'Urville Island, which was named after 19th-century French explorer

Dumont d'Urville who discovered the pass in 1827 and piloted through in an extraordinary feat of seamanship.

A city apart

Nelson ⓰ is a city apart from the rest of New Zealand. It has never been linked with the country's railway network, although recent air services to Wellington have helped to alleviate its past feeling of isolation. The acquisition of the city status (by royal charter in 1858 as the seat of an Anglican bishop), 16 years after the New Zealand Company landed the first settlers in the district, sets Nelson apart from new and bigger cities.

The city owes more than city status to its bishop. Andrew Suter, Bishop of Nelson from 1867 to 1891, bequeathed what is considered to be the country's finest collection of early colonial watercolours to the people of Nelson. The **Suter Gallery** on Bridge Street, in which they are housed, is one of the centres of cultural life in the city along with the School of Music and the Theatre Royal, the oldest theatre building in the country.

Churches (of all denominations) also contribute to the architectural style of a district which retains much from colonial days, including the pioneer homestead Broadgreen. Some of the prettiest churches are found in the settlements of the Waimea Plain – at Richmond, Waimea West and Wakefield, where the parish church of St John's was built in 1846, making it New Zealand's second oldest church and the oldest in the South Island.

Nelson's image has been built on its sandy beaches and extensive apple orchards as well as its thriving arts and cultural community. It is home to the world-famous World of Wearable Art Awards. Nelson also contributes a large

Wine bar in a converted warehouse, Nelson.

BELOW: Colonial lounge, Broadgreen.

part of the nation's production of nashi pears, kiwi fruit and berryfruit and the whole of the national crop of hops. Vineyards in Nelson are increasing in number, particularly in Waimea and the Moutere Hills.

Forestry and fishing are other big local industries. The handicraft revival of the 1960s saw Nelson develop as an important pottery centre, largely because of the good local clay. Potteries still abound but weaving, silver working, glass blowing and other crafts are also well represented. Enquire at the Nelson Visitor Centre for information about both vineyard and crafts tours.

Golden Bay alternatives

The availability of relatively cheap smallholdings and seasonal work has made Nelson province, like Coromandel, something of a magnet for people seeking alternative lifestyles. House trucks abound and the valleys of the Motueka River and Golden Bay have attracted many people with ideas about holistic living.

If Nelson feels isolated from the rest of New Zealand, Golden Bay is isolated even from Nelson. A single road over the steep marble and limestone Takaka Hill is the only way in for anything but birds, fish, or people with stout boots. All people and produce go this way, whether it be heavy trucks or holiday traffic heading for Pohara Beach or the **Abel Tasman National Park** .

A memorial to Abel Tasman, the 17th-century Dutchman who discovered this island for Europe, stands at Tarakohe on the road to the park which bears his name. It was here that the first rather inauspicious encounter between Europeans and the Maori took place in December 1642, when Tasman anchored his ships *Heemskerck* and *Zeehaen* only to have one of his longboats attacked. He lost four of his men, named the area "Massacre Bay" and then made no further

Map, pages 248–9

TIP

The Marlborough Wine and Food Festival is held on the second Saturday in February every year.

BELOW: Graham Valley communal living.

Map, pages 248–9

Marlborough fisherman.

attempt to land in New Zealand, thereby leaving the Maori in ignorance of the questionable delights of European civilisation for another 130 years.

The modern name of Golden Bay derives from the beautiful colour of the sand which fringes the granite-edged coastline. This coast is enjoyed especially by the many people who walk the coastal track from Totaranui to Marahau. The full walk takes three or four days but the less energetic can take coastal launch services from Kaiteriteri or Tarakohe to several bays along the way. Kayak trips around the bays are also popular.

Just 5 km (about 3 miles) west of Takaka is Pupu Springs, where a short walking track leads to pools of some of the clearest fresh water in the world.

Farewell Spit ⓲, at the western tip of Golden Bay, is a naturalist's delight. The 25-km (15-mile) long spit of sand curves round the bay like a scimitar, growing each year as millions of cubic metres of new sand are added by the current, which sweeps up the West Coast and then dumps its load upon meeting the conflicting tides of Cook Strait. The spit is classed as a wetland of international importance and is managed by the government with strict limits on access. However, four-wheel-drive sightseeing trips leave Collingwood regularly for the lighthouse near the spit's end. Departure time depends on the tide.

Trout and trampers

BELOW AND RIGHT: Different perspectives of Kaikoura's mountain backdrop.

South of Golden Bay, even four-wheel drive-vehicles are of no use. This is the area set aside for **Kahurangi National Park** ⓳, which is the country's second largest national park. Many people come here to tramp in the forest or to enjoy the popular Heaphy Track. This is a tramp of four to five days which starts a little way south of Collingwood and heads up through the mountains, then down the West Coast to Karamea. Overnight accommodation along the way is available, for a small charge, in Department of Conservation huts.

Although Nelson itself enjoys a generally dry climate, vast deluges quite often occur in the western mountain ranges of Golden Bay, the water seeping through the soft limestone to create the underground network of caves and rivers that attract expeditions of pot-holers from the other side of the world. Thus began Harwood's Hole on Takaka Hill which is more than 200 metres (650 ft) deep and was regarded for many years as New Zealand's deepest cave. A walk of 400 metres (440 yd) from the end of a road up the Riwaka Valley, on the Nelson side of Takaka Hill, will take you to the first visible part of the Riwaka River where it emerges in full spate from its invisible source inside the hill.

There are other oases, too, for people of softer feet and softer muscles. A restored 1920s fishing lodge on the shores of Lake Rotoroa, 90 km (56 miles) south of the city in the **Nelson Lakes National Park** ⓴, boasts "blue-chip" fishing water within a short walk of the front door, and 26 top-class fishing rivers within an hour's drive. St Arnaud village on the shores of the nearby Lake Rotoiti also offers comfortable accommodation and (for winter visitors) two ski fields nearby.

It also offers another route down the Wairau Valley and back to Blenheim, if you don't want to go on through the mountains to Christchurch or the West Coast.

THE WEST COAST

Wild and rugged, the West Coast's inhospitable terrain makes many of its beauty spots hard to reach, but if you persevere you'll be well rewarded with untamed nature at its best

Map, pages 248–9

ollywood has immortalised the Wild West of North America's heritage but no such fame has attached itself to the equally deserving Wild West Coast of New Zealand's South Island, where the coast and its coasters have a past as rip-roaring as that of the American West. In the gold rush days of the 1860s men lit their cigars with £5 notes and dozens of towns with populations of thousands mushroomed around the promise of buried riches.

The hard-drinking, hard-fighting and hardworking men and women of those bygone days have left behind little more than a legend. The entire population of the 500-km (310-mile) coast is now less than it was in 1867 when it peaked at 40,000 – 13 percent of New Zealand's total population. Today West Coasters number 30,000 – less than one percent of the country's 3.3 million people – and the land itself relentlessly reclaims sites where towns such as Charleston (with 12,000 souls and 80 grog shops) once boomed.

PRECEDING PAGES: miners, Sullivan Coal mine. **LEFT:** fertile fields, Westland National Park. **BELOW:** Fox Glacier.

An independent character

The Coasters who remain have developed a strong identity, with a reputation for being down-to-earth, rugged, independent and hospitable. On the West Coast, the liquor licensing laws have been flouted with impunity for years. But the West Coasters' chief "enemy" nowadays is not central government, but a conservation lobby that wants to preserve intact the native forests and birdlife. Many locals, struggling to scratch a living from coal-mining and timber-milling angrily oppose the conservationist concerns of those who live elsewhere.

The West Coast has never seduced its inhabitants with an easy life. It was settled late by the Maori, from about AD 1400, but even then only sparsely. The main interest of the Maori was in the much-coveted greenstone at Arahura, carried out of the region with difficulty, first though a route north to Nelson and later across alpine passes in the Main Divide to Canterbury.

Early explorers

Neither of the two great discoverers, Abel Tasman and James Cook, were enamoured with what they saw when sailing past the West Coast in 1642 and 1769 respectively. "An inhospitable shore" was Captain Cook's description. "One long solitude with a forbidding sky and impenetrable forest" was the view, about 50 years later, of an officer in a French expedition.

So forbidding was the West Coast that European exploration did not begin in earnest until 1846. And the opinion of one of those first explorers, Thomas Brunner ("The very worst country I have seen in New Zealand") served to discourage others. His distaste resulted from the great hardships suffered during his

Franz Josef Glacier.

550-day journey through the region. It was only in 1860 that the authorities responded positively to reports of glaciers in the south and of routes through the Alps to Canterbury: the central government bought the entire West Coast from the Maori for 300 gold sovereigns. Appropriately, European settlers then made determined attempts to find gold. By 1865 the rush was in full swing.

To the modern visitor, the West Coast appears more inviting, a long narrow strip of vigorous beauty, bounded on the east by the Alps and pounded on the west by the Tasman Sea. Glaciers, the largest anywhere in the temperate zones, grind their way down canyon-like valleys from about 3,000 metres (10,000 ft) to a mere 300 metres (1,000 ft) above sea level. Fern-fringed lakes mirror the mighty mountains and dense natural forests. Rivers cascade through boulder-strewn valleys to the sea. Rain falls frequently, waterfalls burst in great torrents. This is the wettest inhabited area in all New Zealand. When the rain is exhausted and the cloud rolls back from the mountaintops, the air fills with birdsong and – the sole flaw in this Eden – sandflies with their itch for human blood.

A raw savagery pervades the West Coast today. Days of disappointment and hardship are given mute testimony in the tumbledown weatherboard farmhouses and moss-covered fences. Everywhere the sense of decline, not seedy but sad, is tangible. New Zealand's past is frozen here, an unheralded bonus for the traveller in this naturally primeval and emotionally raw retreat.

Travelling up the coast

The opening in 1965 of the **Haast Pass** ㉑ has enabled travellers to trace almost the entire length of the coast as part of a round-trip through the South Island. This pass, linking Westland with the Southern Lakes of Central Otago, is also the

BELOW: West Coast fury on the rocks.

most dramatic of the passes, providing a contrast between the dry, tussocked Otago landscape and the lush vegetation to the west.

Most famous of the West Coast's attractions are the Fox Glacier and **Franz Josef Glacier** ㉒, about 120 km (75 miles) north of Haast. Both glaciers began a spectacular advance in 1982. Such has been the progress of Franz Josef Glacier that its sparkling white ice can be seen again for the first time in 40 years from the altar window of St James Anglican Church, which sits hidden in a superb setting of native bush near the centre of Franz Josef township. Fox Glacier's advance has been less rushed, but it still extends 600 metres (1,969 ft) further down the valley than its position two decades ago.

Both glaciers are located about 25 km (15 miles) apart, in the **Westland National Park**, with its 88,000 hectares (217,000 acres) of alpine peaks, snowfields, forests, lakes and rivers. The main highway which traverses the park's western edge passes close to both glaciers.

Narrow bush-clad roads provide easy access to good vantage points for those visitors who want to view the southernmost Fox Glacier and the more picturesque Franz Josef Glacier from a reasonably close vantage point. Helicopter and skiplane flights over both glaciers provide remarkable views of the greenish-blue tints and the infinite crevasses. Guided walks are available.

Two small townships, each with a range of accommodation on offer, cater competitively for the needs of visitors to the glaciers. Department of Conservation offices in both towns also provide detailed information about the numerous walks available. These include the difficult but rewarding climb over the Copland Pass in the Main Divide to the Hermitage at Mount Cook. In fact, the park provides some 110 km (68 miles) of walking tracks through a sanctuary of

Map, pages 248–9

The first European to explore Franz Josef Glacier was the Austrian Julius Haast, in 1865, who named it after the Austrian emperor.

BELOW: the Old West at Glenmore Station.

varied native forest and birdlife, all dominated by the peaks of Cook, Tasman and La Perouse. This trio is beautifully mirrored in Lake Matheson, one of the park's three calm lakes formed by the glacial dramas of 10,000 years ago.

Whitebait and white herons

The region south of the national park has a stunning coastline. Far to the south of Haast township is an especially lonely terrain, crossed by a secondary road leading to the fishing village of **Jackson Bay ㉓**, where it comes to an end. This small community swells during the spring, when whitebaiters descend en masse to the nearby river mouth, an annual occurrence which is repeated beside swift-flowing rivers all along the coast. Fishing is a major preoccupation in this southern part of Westland. Haast in particular offers good surf and river fishing while 45 km (28 miles) north at the quiet holiday spot of Lake Pargina, anglers are enticed by the prospect of brown trout and quinnat salmon.

Lake Matheson with Mount Tasman and Mount Cook.

A short detour west of Fox Glacier township is Gillespie's Beach, noted for its miners' cemetery and seal colony. Some 60 km (37 miles) further north on the main road, another detour leads to **Okarito Lagoon ㉔**, famous as the only breeding ground of the rare white heron. Okarito once boomed with 31 hotels; now only a few holiday cottages remain. Northwards, the main highway to Ross passes the idyllic Lake Ianthe. Ross was once a flourishing goldfield, producing the largest nugget (2,970 grammes/105 ounces) recorded on the coast. Relics of its once proud history can be viewed in a small museum.

BELOW: dandelions, Westland National Park.

Hokitika ㉕, formerly the "Wonder City of the Southern Hemisphere" with "streets of gold" and a thriving seaport with 100 grog shops, is 30 km (19 miles) north of Ross. Hokitika is now, not surprisingly, a rather quiet town, although it is served by the West Coast's main airfield and its many tourist attractions include an historical museum, greenstone factories, a gold mine, gold panning and a glowworm dell. Lake Kaniere and the Hokitika Gorge are worthwhile side trips.

Twenty-three kilometres (14 miles) north of the town, at Kumara Junction, the highway is intersected by the Arthur's Pass Highway which links Westland and Canterbury. A few kilometres east of the junction this intersecting road enters the old gold-mining town of Kumara, from where a scenic detour of Lake Brunner, the largest lake on the West Coast, winds its way through dense native forest.

Gold and pancakes

Towards Greymouth, about 10 km (6 miles) north of Kumara Junction, is Shantytown, a reproduction of an early gold town offering sluicing and a railway ride to old Chinese workings. At **Greymouth ㉖**, the other trans-alpine route from Canterbury connects with Highway 6. The largest town on the coast (population 3,000), Greymouth owes its commanding position to its seaport and its proximity to timber mills and coal mines.

Beyond Greymouth, the Coast Road to Westport hugs the coastline which, 43 km (27 miles) north at Punakaiki, takes on the extraordinary appearance of a pile of petrified pancakes. The **Pancake Rocks ㉗** and their blowholes consist of eroded limestone. Reached by a short, scenic walk from the main road, the rocks are best visited when there is an incoming tide, when the brisk westerly wind causes the tempestuous sea to surge explosively and dramatically through the chasms.

Thirty-two km (20 miles) north is Charleston, the once-booming centre of the Buller district, with old gold workings nearby. At a junction 21 km (13 miles) farther to the north, the coastal road becomes Highway 67, leading to nearby Westport and beyond to the West Coast's northernmost town of Karamea, 88 km (55 miles) away. The road also provides access to two acclaimed walks – the Wangapeka Track, which traces the Little Wanganui River, and the 70-km (43-mile) Heaphy Track, a four-to-six-day tramp to Karamea and Golden Bay.

Five km (3 miles) south of Westport, Highway 6 turns inland to follow one of the South Island's most beautiful rivers, the Buller, through its lower and upper gorges for 84 km (52 miles) to Murchison. At this point the West Coast is left behind and the road continues to Nelson and Blenheim.

Branching south

The West Coast section of this road, however, extends two branches southward, Highways 69 and 65, to connect with the Lewis Pass Highway. Highway 69, which turns off at the Inangahua Junction halfway between Westport and Murchison, traverses one of the most mineralised districts of New Zealand. Thirty-four km (21 miles) south, it enters **Reefton** ㉘, named for its famous quartz reefs. This region was abundant in gold and coal, and the story of their extraction is told in the town's School of Mines and the Black's Point Museum.

The other route (Highway 65) to the Lewis Pass from Murchison joins up with the main Lewis Pass Highway at Springs Junction, 72 km (45 miles) south.

Map, pages 248–9

TIP

If you like seafood, and you're in the West Coast in spring, make sure you sample that scrumptious New Zealand speciality, whitebait fritters. Packed with small but nutritious worm-like creatures with eyes, they're not for the faint-hearted.

BELOW: Pancake Rocks, Punakaiki.

QUEENSTOWN AND OTAGO

Map, page 278

Located in an area of spectacular natural beauty, it's easy to understand why Queenstown is unashamedly a tourist town, with a huge range of leisure activities on offer, and great shopping

At the hub of Central Otago is the jewel in New Zealand's tourism crown. It has become such a popular destination for overseas visitors that some New Zealanders complain that they can't get a look in. In less than 30 years, Queenstown ❶ has grown from a sleepy lakeside town into a sophisticated all-year tourist resort, a sort of Antipodean Saint Moritz. Queenstown has been nurtured on tourism and while other towns have struggled to survive in a sluggish economy, Queenstown has flourished. Within a radius of only a few kilometres, the ingenuity and mechanical wizardry of New Zealanders have combined with the stunning landscape to provide an unrivalled range of adventure activities.

Landscape burnished in gold

Central Otago possesses a regional personality quite distinct from other parts of the country. Some of the Southern Alps' most impressive peaks dominate its western flank, towering over deep glacier-gouged lakes. Yet its enduring impact lies with more subtlety in the strange landscape chiselled and shaved from Central Otago's plateau of mica schist rock. In the dry continental climate of the inland plateau, the pure atmosphere aids the play of light, evoking nuances few other landscapes permit. The overwhelming impression is of a stark, simple landscape burnished in glowing browns tinged with white, gold, ochre and sienna. The effect has attracted generations of landscape painters to the area.

Yet scenery alone is not enough to lure people into staking out a patch of earth in what in the past has been an arid and often inhospitable region. Over nine centuries of sketchy human habitation, Central Otago's bait has been successively moa, jade, grazing land, gold, hydroelectric power and now tourism.

Hunters of moa and greenstone

The first humans to set foot in the region were Maori moa-hunters who pushed inland around the 12th century AD. Central Otago could not offer lasting refuge to the magnificent endangered moa. As fire ravaged native bush and forest, the moa and other birds disappeared forever. Some of New Zealand's best moa remains have been found in the banks of the Clutha River as it winds through the plateau on its 322-km (200-mile) journey to the Pacific.

Towards the end of the 15th century, the moa-hunters were conquered by the Ngati-Mamoe tribe, moving down from the north. This group, defeated in turn two centuries later by another invading Maori tribe, supposedly fled into the forest of Fiordland and thereafter they disappeared into the mists of legend.

The victors, the Ngati-Tahu, then took control of the supply of the Maori's most precious stone – the New

PRECEDING PAGES: spectacular Central Otago. **LEFT:** jet-boating on the Shotover, Central Otago. **BELOW:** landscape west of Queenstown.

Chinese camp at Arrowtown, Otago.

Grenstone was often used to make tikis, *Polynesian amulets in the shape of a human figure, believed to be endowed with* mana *or power.*

Zealand jade known variously as pounamu, nephrite or greenstone. Hard, durable and workable, it was in demand for adzes, chisels and weapons. So desirable was the jade, in fact, that the Maori made epic expeditions through Central Otago and the alpine divide to bring it out from the West Coast, the only place it was found, via the head of Lake Wakatipu to the east coast. It was then "processed" and exported to northern tribes. Today, the same jade is a major feature in New Zealand's jewellery and souvenir industries.

Despite the lucrative trade route, the Maori population of Central Otago was never large. The extremes of temperature (the severest in New Zealand) were too harsh for the descendants of Polynesian voyagers from the tropical Pacific. In 1836, the last few remaining Maori settlements disappeared entirely when a war party from the North Island attacked on its way south.

Gold in Gabriel's Gully

For about 10 years trespassing man was absent and Central Otago was left to nature, as if gathering strength for the sudden stampede of people and merino sheep that would soon disturb the deep peace.

The European era began in 1847 when a surveyor blazed a trail for pioneers in quest of land to establish large sheep runs. By 1861 the new settlers were squatting on most of the potential grazing land, battling ravages wrought by winter snows, spring floods, summer droughts, fires, wild dogs, rats, rabbits and keas.

These pioneers, predominantly of Scottish origin, were just settling in when in 1861, the first major discovery of gold "shining like the stars in Orion on a dark frosty night" was made in a gully along the Tuapeka River by Gabriel Read, a prospector with experience of the California gold rush of 1849. Central Otago's

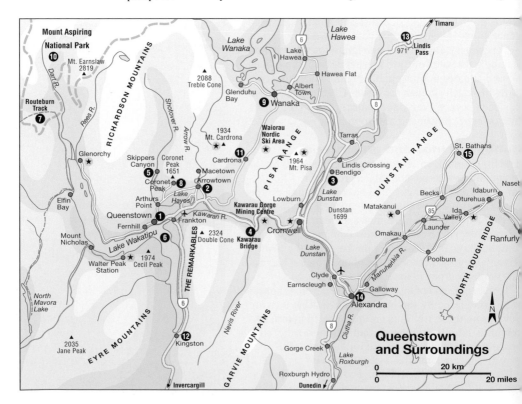

gold boom had begun. In just four months, 3,000 men were swarming over the 5-km (3-mile) valley, probing and sifting each centimetre for glowing alluvial gold. A year on, the population of the Tuapeka goldfield was 11,500, double that of the fast-emptying provisional capital, Dunedin. Otago's income trebled in 12 months, while the number of ship arrivals quadrupled, many of the 200 vessels bringing miners from Australia's gold fields in Victoria.

In Gabriel's Gully, all miners, regardless of social rank, wore identical blue shirts and moleskin trousers. A feeling of egalitarianism, echoed by a newspaper's praise of "the free and careless bluffness which is a great relief from the reserve and formality that prevail among all classes in the Old Country" (England), was reflected in a song:

On the diggings we're all on a level you know
The poor out here ain't oppressed by the rich
But dressed in blue shirts,
You can't tell which is which.

Richest river in the world

The search for gold soon spread beyond Gabriel's Gully and as prospectors moved inland to the then inhospitable hinterland of Central, new fields were discovered in quick succession in other valleys – the Clutha at the foot of the Dunstan Range, the Cardrona, Shotover, Arrow and Kawarau. In 1862 the Shotover, then yielding as much as 155 grammes (5 ounces) of gold by the shovelful, was known as the richest river in the world. In one afternoon two Maori men going to the rescue of their near-drowned dog recovered no less than 11 kg

Map, see opposite

BELOW: Lake Wakatipu promenade, Queenstown.

(388 ounces) of gold. But if gold was plentiful, "tucker" was scarce. Flour and tea, augmented perhaps by poached sheep, was all that kept many a miner alive.

Arrowtown ❷, 20 km (12 miles) from Queenstown, is the most picturesque and best preserved gold-mining settlement in Central and arguably the prettiest small town in New Zealand. Its lead and stone beauty has endured as if to compensate for the comparatively scant evidence of the estimated 80 goldfields that mushroomed, then wilted, in Central over one hectic decade.

Barmaid bride

BUNGY

Ghost towns are scattered throughout the region, shadows of the calico, sod and corrugated-iron settlements that seemed "ugly" to visiting English novelist Anthony Trollope in 1872. Two such towns, Macetown and Carrona, haunt the hills above Arrowtown. **Bendigo ❸**, near the Clutha River 25 km (15 miles) north of Cromwell (off Highway 8), is a dream ghost town, especially when the wind whistles through the tumbledown stone cottages at the bleak crossroads. A concentrated effort is required to visualise Bendigo's saloon on a Saturday night during the 1860s when "a hideous maniacal yelling…entirely overpowered and drowned every sound within a radius of a mile or so."

Behind the imagined bar, picture Mary Ann, probably the most successful novice barmaid in New Zealand's history. After being jilted on her wedding day, she fled Cromwell, the scene of her humiliation, to begin work the same day at the Bendigo saloon. In just two hours flat, the bar was drunk dry by miners eager to see the bartender bride in all her nuptial finery.

BELOW: Masonic Hall, Arrowtown.

Several tiny gold-rush towns, with substance was well as atmosphere, have refused to die so easily. The original gold-rush settlement – then Tuapeka, now Lawrence – still survives with a strongly Victorian flavour, a nearby monument in Gabriel's Gully marking the site of Gabriel Read's discovery. Pockets of old gold towns are stitched into the ranges, gullies, gorges and valleys elsewhere in Central. Some of these towns, particularly in Queenstown's rugged hinterland, attract specialised four-wheel-drive tours.

Today the river valleys are clear of the calico cities that sprouted during the 1860s and the dredges that savagely exhausted leftover traces of gold during the early 1900s. Few prospectors remain. Gold-fossicking is almost solely the preserve of tourists for whom it is a popular, but not (at least not admittedly) very profitable pastime.

White-water adventures

Swift-flowing rivers near Queenstown also set the scene for white-water rafting and jet-boating adventures. The latter is New Zealand's home-grown style of running rivers, upstream as well as down. Propellerless power boats speed over rapid shallows barely ankle-deep.

These nifty craft are thrust along by their jet-stream as water, drawn in through an intake in the bottom of the hull, is pumped out at high pressure through a nozzle at the rear. The typical jet-boat can skim over shallows no more than 10 cm (4 inches) deep, and can execute sudden 180-degree turns within a single boat length.

The best-known of the dozen or so commercial options, Shotover Jet, takes passengers on a thrilling ride, swerving up and down the Shotover River a hair's breadth from jagged cliffs. It is without a doubt the world's most exciting jet-boat ride. Another, the Heli-Jet, offers a triple-thrill ride in helicopter, jet-boat and white-water raft.

Other commercial water adventures on Queenstown's lakes and rivers include canoeing, yachting, windsurfing, parasailing, water-skiing and hobie-cat sailing, as well as hydrofoil and jet-bike rides. Bungee jumping from several different sites has also become a popular activity: a short but spectacular jump has recently opened at the top of the Skyline gondola overlooking Queenstown; a longer jump is offered off the historic **Kawarau Bridge** ❹ 20 km (12 miles) north; and one of the highest bungee jumps in the world is offered at the end of a dramatic four-wheel-drive ride up **Skippers Canyon** ❺.

But traditional and sedate activities are available too – trout fishing in lonely rivers and streams, or an excursion in the ageing steamship *Earnslaw*, a grand old lady which has graced the waters of **Lake Wakatipu** ❻ since 1912.

Hollow of the giant

Perhaps the most haunting body of water in Central Otago, Lake Wakatipu has captured man's imagination with its strange serpentine shape, rhythmic "breathing" and constant coldness. According to Maori legend, the lake is the "Hollow of the Giant" (Whakatipua), formed when an evil sleeping giant was set on fire by a brave youth, thus melting the snow and ice of the surrounding mountains to fill the 80-km (50-mile) long, double-dog-legged hollow.

In fact, the major lakes of Wakatipu, Wanaka and Hawea were all gouged by glaciers, and the peculiar rise and fall of Wakatipu every five minutes is not the effect of a giant's heartbeat, as legend dictates, but of a natural oscillation caused

Map, page 278

TIP

Arrowtown's Lake District Museum (*see page 349*) is a mine of information about the gold rush, with gold and mineral specimens, miners' tools, relics of the Chinese miners, plus colonial era memorabilia and a collection of horse-drawn vehicles.

BELOW: Lake Hayes.

by variations in atmospheric pressure. But regardless of the origin of all three lakes, their appearance is indisputably handsome. "I do not know that lake scenery can be finer than this," enthused Trollope in 1872.

By foot, water or air

A thorough exploration of this magnificent region of snow-peaked mountains, virgin forest, uninhabited valleys and moody lakes is possible only for the traveller who takes to the air, the water, the open road and the narrow walking track.

Of all the many tracks in the Wakatipu Basin, the most rewarding is certainly the **Routeburn Track** ❼. Trailing through splendidly isolated country at the head of Lake Wakatipu to the Upper Hollyford Valley, this four-day trek is one of New Zealand's best, but requires a greater degree of experience and fitness than the famed Milford Track in neighbouring Fiordland.

Passenger launches on Lake Wakatipu take visitors to otherwise inaccessible sheep stations for a taste of high-country farm life and food, pioneering days, and trout fishing. In the fishing season (1 October–31 July) jet-boat, helicopter or four-wheel-drive excursions are available to remote pristine waters.

Some of the world's finest scenic flights operate from Queenstown, over lakes, alps and fiords. Subject to demand and weather, a number of flightseeing trips operate daily. Helicopter Line operates helicopter flights.

The largest skifields in the South Island are Coronet Peak, The Remarkables, Treble Cone and Cardrona. Coronet Peak, only 18 km (11 miles) by sealed road from Queenstown, has a ski season that extends from July to September. In the summer, sightseers can take chairlifts to the summit (1,645 metres/5,397 ft) for a spectacular view, while thrill-seekers can enjoy a rapid descent in a Cresta Run

Huge fruit sculptures, Cromwell.

company's second major ski field is The Remarkables, the rugged range that forms the famous spectacular backdrop to Queenstown. Cross-country and downhill trips are available at Browns Basin, Cardrona and Mount Pisa.

Queenstown has a wide variety of accommodation, restaurants, après-ski entertainment and shops displaying quality handcrafted New Zealand articles such as suede and leather goods, sheepskin and woollen products, local pottery, woodcarving and attractive greenstone jewellery.

Motoring the backcountry

Central Otago's network of roads is among the most interesting and challenging in New Zealand. Most roads are sealed, but extra skill and caution are needed on narrower roads, particularly in winter. Rental-car companies advise their customers that if they drive on certain specified roads – through Skippers Canyon, for instance – they do so at their own risk.

An especially attractive circuit is the 50-km (31-mile) round-trip between Queenstown and Arrowtown, taking the "back" road past **Coronet Peak ❽** and the Millbrook Resort, with its Bob Charles designed golf course, and returning via mirror-like Lake Hayes. New Zealand's own distinctive architectural styles are visible in the thoughtfully designed farmlet dwellings where craftspeople, artists, and retired folk enjoy a gentle way of life.

New Zealand's Matterhorn

Northeast of Queenstown, Highway 6 follows the upper Clutha River to its source at **Wanaka ❾**, a more modest resort which is gaining new importance (with two ski fields and a natural ice-skating rink) since the opening of the Haast

Queenstown is small, but packed with things to do, including a scenic gondola, a motor museum with vintage vehicles, a kiwi and birdlife park, Underwater World (where you can see under the lake behind glass), ski and snowboard hire – and two radio stations just for tourists!

BELOW: excellent skiing in Central Otago.

Map, page 278

Old-style driving, Arrowtown.

BELOW: Otago land shapes.
RIGHT: foxgloves in bloom.

Pass in 1965. This trans-alpine route, the lowest over the Main Divide, links Central Otago with the glacier-renowned region of the West Coast. It also crosses **Mount Aspiring National Park ⑩**, a 161-km (100-mile) long alpine reserve dominated by New Zealand's Matterhorn, Mount Aspiring, at 3,030 metres (9,941 ft). The park and the lonely valleys extending into Lake Wanaka present unrivalled opportunities for hiking, tramping and fishing in unspoilt wilderness.

An alternative shortcut between Queenstown and Wanaka is the Crown Range road through the **Cardrona Valley ⑪**. The highest in New Zealand, this route is not suitable for caravans; it is closed in winter, and even in good weather, it merely reduces the distance to be covered, not the travelling time.

Directly south of Queenstown, Highway 6 skirts Lake Wakatipu to **Kingston ⑫** – base for a vintage steam train, the *Kingston Flyer* – and continues south to Invercargill and the south coast. Midway, before Lumsden, it is intersected by Highway 94, a well-trodden scenic route which branches west out of Central Otago to Southland's Lake Te Anau, the Eglinton Valley and Milford Sound.

One of New Zealand's best-kept secrets is the **Lindis Pass ⑬** (Highway 8) which links northern Central Otago with Mount Cook and the Mackenzie Country and winds through some of the most evocative hill country in New Zealand.

Worthwhile routes

The southern extension of Highway 8 is the main artery to the heart of Central Otago. It runs parallel with the Clutha River, past the former gold towns of Roxburgh, Alexandra, Clyde and Cromwell. These prospering towns are still vital today through their connection with Otago's lifeblood: that same mighty Clutha. The river that once surrendered gold has since, through irrigation, transformed parched land into fertile country famous for its stoned fruit. Now it is a major generator for electricity. A dam at Roxburgh, built in 1956, has formed a 32-km (20-mile) long lake between the town and Alexandra. In 1993 a bigger dam was built close to where the Clutha River leaves the Cromwell Gorge near Clyde. The water behind has expanded through the gorge to a massive lake beyond, drowning the old town of Cromwell and much of the lower Clutha Valley.

Arrowtown holds an annual festival, and **Alexandra ⑭** distinguishes itself by its colourful, blossom-parade tribute to spring. In winter, ice-skating and curling take place on natural ice on the Manorburn Dam.

Gold town side trip

North of Alexandra, Highway 85 goes east through the Manuherikia Valley to the Otago coast, offering a worthwhile side trip to **St Bathans ⑮**, an old gold town, and another to Naseby, a quaint hamlet on a hillside at an altitude of 600 metres (about 2,000 ft). A little-known, good-weather road climbs Dansey's Pass to the town of Duntroon and the Waitaki River flats.

Central Otago is an intense experience, whatever the time of year. In autumn, poplars planted by the settlers glow gold. In winter, nature adorns the work of people, transforming power lines into glistening lace-like threads of white across a frosty fairyland. In summer, the bronzed limbs of the hills sear the imagination.

THRILL-SEEKERS' PARADISE

There's no end to the variety of adventure sports in New Zealand. Just as your heartbeat slows to normal speed, a new crazy activity comes along

How and why New Zealanders first thought of jumping off bridges, speeding down shallow rivers, or rolling down hills inside inflatable balls is a mystery. What is certain is that they have introduced new adrenaline-pumping sports to the world, and they do it safely. Every week thousands of visitors experience the heady euphoric feeling of an adrenaline rush.

New Zealanders seem to be addicted to adrenaline. It's the best legal drug you can get, but like any drug you have to get more of it in different forms. So adventure addicts now consider bungee jumping "boring" – rap jumping is currently their way to get a high. Another favourite thrill is jet-boat rides down river gorges, travelling at breakneak speeds perilously close to the rocky banks *(above)*.

TALKING UP THE RISKS

The industry is now strongly regulated and the operators highly trained. They've all been to the same charm school and so delight in making any activity seem more dangerous than it really is. They reason that the higher you think the risk is, the higher the adrenaline rush when you "miraculously" survive the experience.

Should you ask your partner for a parachute jump how long he's been doing tandem jumps, he'll tell you that today is his first time with a paying customer. Stand on a bridge and ask how many jumps a bungee rope does before it's retired, and you'll be told "100, and yours is the 99th".

Such tricks are simple but extremely effective. In fact, the adventure sports industry in New Zealand has a remarkably good safety record.

Nobody has ever satisfactorily explained why New Zealanders are so successful at dreaming up new adventure activities – from cave-rafting to parapenting. It must be a combination of the beautiful outdoors and their isolation from the rest of the world. They have to get their kicks at home and they'll try anything once. If it works, they'll develop it for their visitors' fun and enjoyment.

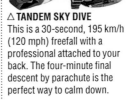

△ **TANDEM SKY DIVE**
This is a 30-second, 195 km/h (120 mph) freefall with a professional attached to your back. The four-minute final descent by parachute is the perfect way to calm down.

▽ **RAP JUMPING**
Face-forward abseiling was invented by the SAS. It allows you to safely see the city from a new angle.

ZORBING YOUR WAY DOWN THE HILL

Zorbing is the epitome of New Zealanders' love of the bizarre. An NZ Air Force pilot described zorbing as "the same sensation as spinning loops and barrel rolls and then crashing to the ground in a jet. Only in a zorb it doesn't hurt." Lesser mortals say it's like "being inside a tumble drier".

The zorb is actually two spheres, one suspended inside the inflated outer one. The view from inside is a tumbling blur of blue sky and green grass which eventually seem to blend into one as you bounce and fall and roll down a hillside. Aficionados throw a bucket of water in first just to remove any chance that they can cling to the sides. There are also plans to take it onto the country's fast-flowing rivers and over waterfalls.

Like many adventure sports, it's almost as much fun to watch as to participate. It starts with mirth as a vacuum cleaner working in reverse is used to pump up the zorb, and finishes with laughter as the dizzy participant tries to climb out of the sphere.

Zorbing is probably the safest of all the adventure sports. Like all of them there is no logical reason to do it. New Zealand's first and foremost adventure sports- man was Sir Edmund Hillary, who probably climbed Everest in 1953 for the same reason as today's adrenaline seekers: because it's there.

△ **AEROBATICS**
The plane looks tiny and the pilot looks crazy. They don't even give you a sick bag, although you can tell the pilot to stop. Loops and rolls, upside-down flying, inverted turns and more all conspire to twist your stomach into unbelievable shapes. Miles better than any fun-fair ride – just remember not to have a meal first.

TANDEM HANG-GLIDING
his is probably one of the fer activities, even though e aluminium and fabric wing oks fragile. If you're lucky, ou can fly yourself during the e minutes aloft.

▽ **GLACIER WALKING**
Walking on what appears to be a living, moving, creaking, mountain of ice is awe-inspiring. You'll be roped up to your guide in case you slip and fall down a crevasse.

△ **HELI-BUNGEE**
To jump out of a helicopter attached to a rubber band is the ultimate dinner party story – but is (perhaps temporarily) banned by the CAA.

SOUTHLAND

It's at the end of the world – almost – and its staggeringly beautiful scenery could convince you that you were indeed stepping on to another plane. Some even say that Southland doesn't exist at all...

Map,
pages
292–3

Speak to the historical purist and you will learn that Southland does not exist. Officially, there is no such province. Question him further and you will find contradiction in his answers.

When Southland's early settlers demanded provincial government in 1861, they forgot the canny nature of their Scottish background and in nine heady years developed town, country, rail, road and other signs of civilisation to such extent that the provincial government was declared bankrupt and their province was legally and administratively fixed to their neighbour, Otago, in 1870.

Yet despite this, the future of the province was assured, albeit unofficially, because the 150,000 people who proudly call themselves Southlanders to this day have scant regard for the historical purist's arguments about their legitimacy. They live in New Zealand's southernmost land district – Murihiku, the last joint of the tail, as the Maori called it.

Their "province" takes in about 28,000 sq km (some 11,000 sq miles); its boundary starts just above the breathtaking hills and valleys of Milford Sound on the West Coast, skirts the southern shores of Lake Wakatipu bordering Central Otago, and meanders its way through some of the lushest, most productive land in New Zealand to join the southeast coast near an unspoiled area called Catlins.

Southland is a province of contrast. Signs of Maori settlement go back as far as the 12th century around the southern coast, and since those days of rapid development in the 1860s, its people have developed a land of unlimited potential for agricultural purposes and regained the conservative reputation for which their largely Scottish forebears were known. Yet there is a grittiness in the Southland character. It manifests itself in an agrarian excellence that would not have otherwise been achieved had conservatism dominated.

Contrast continues in the land itself. On the West Coast, deep fiords lap against towering mountains and snow-capped peaks reach skywards amidst a myriad of vast bush-clad valleys in an area that is called, not surprisingly, Fiordland. Inland stretch the two massive plains on which the province's prosperity has grown to depend, surrounding the commercial heart of the city of Invercargill, and eventually reaching the southern and southeastern coasts.

Tuataras and aluminium

The 57,000 people who live in **Invercargill ❶** reside close to an estuary once plied by steamers and sailing ships. The city's Scottish heritage is well-reflected in its street names, and its original town planners were generous in the amount of space devoted to main thoroughfares and parks. Today, Queens Park provides a wide range of recreational pursuits for the visitor, from

PRECEDING PAGES: ancient forest of Fiordland. **LEFT:** Milford Track. **BELOW:** Sutherland Falls, Fiordland National Park.

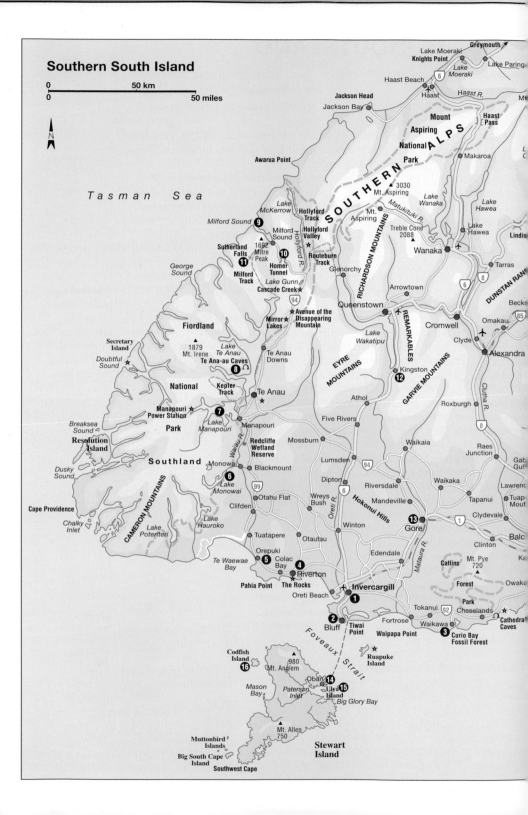

Southern South Island

0 ————————— 50 km

0 ————————— 50 miles

N

Tasman Sea

Greymouth
Lake Moeraki
Knights Point
Lake Paring
Haast Beach
Lake Moeraki
Haast
Haast R.
Jackson Head
Jackson Bay

Mount
Aspiring
National
Park

SOUTHERN ALPS

Makaroa
Haast Pass

▲ 3030
Mt. Aspiring
Lake Wanaka
Lake Hawea
Awarua Point
Lake McKerrow
Hollyford Track
Mt. Aspiring
Matukituki R.
Lindis
Lake Hawea
Milford Sound ⑨
Milford Sound
Hollyford Valley
Hollyford R.
Treble Cone 2088
Wanaka
Tarras
George Sound
Sutherland Falls
1692 ▲ Mitre Peak
⑪
Milford Track
⑩
Homer Tunnel
Routeburn Track
Glenorchy
DUNSTAN RANGE
Lake Gunn
Cascade Creek ★
RICHARDSON MOUNTAINS
Arrowtown
Omakau
★ Avenue of the Disappearing Mountain
Queenstown
Cromwell
Clyde
85
Fiordland
Mirror ★ Lakes
Lake Wakatipu
REMARKABLES
Alexandra
Secretary Island
1879 ▲ Mt. Irene
Lake Te Anau
Te Ana-au Caves
Te Anau Downs
EYRE MOUNTAINS
Kingston ⑫
GARVIE MOUNTAINS
Clutha R.
Doubtful Sound
⑧
National
Kepler Track
Te Anau
Athol
Roxburgh
Manapouri Power Station ★
⑦
Lake Manapouri
Manapouri
Five Rivers
8
Breaksea Sound
Park
Waiau R.
Redcliffe Wetland Reserve
Mossburn
Waikaia
Raes Junction
Resolution Island
Monowai
Blackmount
Lumsden
94
Riversdale
Waikaka
Lawrenc
Dusky Sound
Southland
⑥
Lake Monowai
99
Dipton
6
Mandeville
Tapanui
Tuap Mout
Otahu Flat
Hokonui Hills
Clydevale
Balc
Cape Providence
Lake Poteriteri
Clifden
Wreys Bush
Oreti R.
Winton
Clinton
Chalky Inlet
CAMERON MOUNTAINS
Lake Hauroko
Tuatapere
Otautau
⑬
Gore
Mt. Pye 720 ▲
Ka
Orepuki
Edendale
Catlins
Owaka
Te Waewae Bay
⑤ Colac Bay
④
Riverton
Mataura R.
Forest
Pahia Point
The Rocks
Invercargill
Tokanui
Park
Chaselands
Oreti Beach
①
92
Cathedral Caves
②
Bluff
Tiwai Point
Fortrose
Waikawa
Foveaux Strait
Waipapa Point
③
Curio Bay
Fossil Forest
Codfish Island
⑯
980 ▲ Mt. Anglem
Ruapuke Island
Mason Bay
Oban ⑭
Paterson Inlet
Ulva ⑮
Island
Big Glory Bay
Muttonbird Islands
Mt. Allen 750 ▲
Stewart Island
Big South Cape Island
Southwest Cape

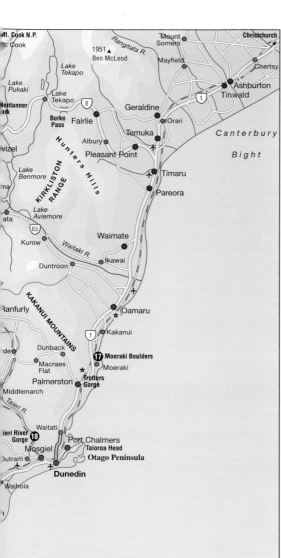

Mt. Cook N.P.
Mt. Cook
Lake Pukaki
Lake Tekapo
Mentanner Park
vizel
Lake Benmore
na
ata
Ranfurly
de
Middlemarch
Waihola
Lake Tekapo
Burke Pass
Fairlie
Albury
Pleasant Point
Lake Aviemore
Kurow
Duntroon
Dunback
Macraes Flat
Palmerston
Waitati
Mosgiel
Dutram
Dunedin
Rangitata R.
1951 ▲
Ben McLeod
Geraldine
Temuka
Waimate
Ikawai
Oamaru
Kakanui

Moeraki Boulders
Moeraki
Trotters Gorge

ieri River Gorge
Port Chalmers
Taioroa Head
Otago Peninsula

Mount Somers
Mayfield
Christchurch
Chertsy
Ashburton
Tinwald
Orari
Timaru
Pareora

Canterbury

Bight

PACFIC

OCEAN

sunken rose gardens and statuary created by Sir Charles Wheeler to a golf course and swimming pool.

The southernmost city in the Commonwealth, and the eleventh largest in New Zealand, Invercargill was the first to have within its pyramid-shaped museum a "tuatarium" where visitors can watch lizards (tuatara) whose forebears survived the Stone Age roaming at leisure in a large, natural sanctuary. Combined with the **Southland Centennial Museum** is the city's art gallery and observatory.

Just 10 km (6 miles) south of the city centre is Oreti Beach, a long stretch of sand popular amongst the hardy locals for swimming, yachting and water-skiing. The beach is also famous for the succulent toheroa, a rare shellfish that grows up to 15 cm (6 inches) in length.

End of the road

Invercargill is also the stepping off point for Southland. Twenty-seven km (17 miles) south is **Bluff ❷** and the journey to this port town emphasises Southland's agricultural development. A massive fertiliser works, processing phosphate rock imported from various foreign lands, underpins the fact that Southland's soils need constant nourishment. Deer farms along both sides of the road are evidence of the fast-developing new pastoral industry. Thirty years ago, deer were found only in the bush; today they are raised on farms by the thousands and their velvet, in particular, is keenly sought.

There is no mistaking Bluff as a port town. The air is dashed with salt; large vessels tie up at a massive man-made island within the inland harbour (cleverly created so that tidal flows were not disturbed); and workers toil around the clock. Aluminium-clad, snake-like machines, their tails buried in a large building and their heads in ships' holds, disgorge hundreds of thousands of carcases of frozen lamb and mutton for worldwide markets.

Across the harbour, look out for three buildings 600 metres (2,000 feet) long, surrounded by other massive structures and dominated by a huge chimney stack

*Doubtful Sound,
Fiordland National
Park.*

137 metres (450 ft) high. These make up the Tiwai Point aluminium smelter, which produces 244,000 tons of aluminium a year. Tucked away on the lonely Tiwai peninsula, where almost non-stop winds disperse effluent, the smelter, which recently underwent a $400 million upgrade, is the major industrial employer in the south. Power is provided by the Lake Manapouri hydroelectric power station in the Fiordland National Park.

Yet Bluff is famous also for something that just lies there, waiting to be picked up. Beneath the Foveaux Strait, a 35-km (22-mile) stretch of water that separates Stewart Island from the mainland, lie beds of oysters. In past years these beds have been stricken by disease but steps have been taken to help them recover. The resource is being carefully managed, and it is hoped that the numbers harvested will soon return to levels of the past. Tales have it that many visiting football teams in Southland have been taken to Bluff before their matches and have left the province beaten but craving for more of the delicious molluscs.

For New Zealand, Bluff is the end of the road. From Bluff, the visitor gazes out to sea, taking in Dog Island and its lighthouse, Stewart Island, then the great emptiness of the Great South Basin, beyond which lie only a few sub-Antarctic islands and the vast expanse of Antarctica. A signpost has been erected at Stirling Point nearby, stating the distance to London, New York and other faraway places. This is as close as many will ever get to the bottom of the world.

Fish and fiords

BELOW: majestic
Milford Sound.

Southeast of Invercargill lies the small fishing port of Waikawa, reached by comfortable road through rolling countryside which not long ago was scrub- and bush-covered. Vast areas of bush remain in Southland, well-managed and

controlled. At the end of the road, 5 km (3 miles) from Waikawa, are the remains of a petrified forest buried millions of years ago at a place called **Curio Bay ❸**. This freeze-frame of time has caught every grain of timber in the fossilised stumps; boulders which have broken open through some unknown force show patterns of leaves and twigs. Waikawa is on the Southern Scenic Route, a major tourism highlight in the south which stretches from Balclutha in South Otago, along the southern coast, past Waikawa, and eventually ends in Te Anau.

No dedicated angler could make the journey southeast without stopping at an unremarkable bridge. It crosses the Mataura River and it is among the very best brown trout fisheries anywhere. Nearly 500 km (300 miles) of fishing waters stretch along Southland's three main fishing rivers – the Mataura, the Oreti and the Aparima – which cut the province in three.

There are at least eight smaller rivers (the Wyndham, Mimihau, Hedgehope, Makarewa, Lora, Otapiri, Dunsdale and Waimatuku) and numerous streams well-stocked with brown trout. The angler who goes home empty-handed must have been holding his rod at the wrong end.

Tussock country

Flat as it is, there are very few days in Invercargill when residents cannot raise their eye to the mountains tens of kilometres away, bordering Fiordland. For those in a hurry, this vast natural area can be reached in less than two hours, travelling across the central Southland plains via Winton and Dipton, over the Josephville Hill and through Lumsden, until rolling tussock country indicates that you are in land of an altogether tougher nature. This journey, through prime country bearing several million head of stock, aptly shows how Southland has

Map, pages 292–3

TIP

Coach tours take visitors down a 2-km (one-and-a-quarter mile) spiral tunnel into the machine hall of the Manapouri Power Station.

BELOW: Takitimu Mountains, east of Fiordland National Park.

grown on agricultural production, the most significant change recently being the conversion of many sheep farms to dairy units. This has manifested itself in the building of a huge $50 million milk powder plant at Edendale in Eastern Southland, with promise of further expansion to come.

The historic town of **Riverton** ❹ nestles by the sea, 38 km (24 miles) from Invercargill. Sealers and whalers made Riverton their home in 1836 and Southland's first European settlement still bears signs of those times. Preservation is a way of life here; recently, the New Zealand Historic Place Trust offered a whaler's cottage for sale for the sum of just $1, so long as the owner promised to preserve it according to the trust's specifications.

The takahe, one of New Zealand's rarest birds.

Wonderful highs and lows

Jet-boat operators offer exciting rides on the Wairaurahiri River. Ten km (6 miles) further is **Colac Bay**, another historic area. It was once a Maori settlement, and then a town with a population of 6,000 during the gold-rush days of the 1890s. Now it is a popular holiday spot for Southlanders. Near Colac Bay is the town of **Orepuki** ❺, where history merges with the present: what once was a courthouse is now a sheep-shearing shed. Note how the southerly wind has turned the macrocarpa trees away from the shore.

Thundering surf follows the traveller between Orepuki and Tuatapere along a fine ocean view. Looming darkly across Te Waewae Bay, where Hector's Dolphins and southern right whales can sometimes be seen, are bush-clad mountains, the first signs of what is to come. From the timber town of Tuatapere, where fishing and deer-hunting stories are as common as logs from the town's mills, the road heads north, close to the recreational mecca of **Lake Monowai** ❻.

BELOW: Pastoral tranquillity near Te Anau.

Southeast of Lake Monowai is the town of Clifden which is notable for two nearby attractions; the Clifden Suspension Bridge (built in 1902) and the spooky Clifden caves. The caves can be explored without a guide but make sure you have at least two torches and follow all the signposted instructions. To get there travel 17 km (10 miles) from Tuatapere and turn left towards Eastern Bush.

For the adventurous, a 30-km (18-mile) unsealed road leads to Lake Hauroko, the deepest lake in New Zealand. The lake is set amongst dense bush and steep slopes. A good example of Maori cave burial was discovered in 1660 on a tapu (sacred) island in the middle of the lake. Continuing north from Clifden the road leads through Blackmount and then the Redcliff Wetland Reserve, where lucky bird-watchers might sight the predatory bush falcon in action.

Beyond the wetlands is **Lake Manapouri** ❼, and standing majestically ahead of that are the mountains and lakes of Fiordland.

A lost tribe

With an area of 1,209,485 hectares (nearly 3 million acres), Fiordland is New Zealand's largest national park and a World Heritage Park. That first glimpse across Lake Manapouri, to sheer mountains and remote deep valleys on the other side of the lake, gives the observer some understanding of why some of the ancient Maori legends – such as that of the mythical lost tribe of Te Anau – never lose their romantic hold in this wild region.

Fiordland is a land of firsts. Captain James Cook discovered Dusky Sound, largest of the fiords, in 1770. He returned three years later and established New Zealand's first brewery. Of course, he also established some other important things while refitting his ship, such as a workshop and a smithy. In 1792, New

Map, pages 292–3

TIP

Bring your waterproofs and wellies, especially if visiting Milford Sound or Track – in this area the rainfall is measured in metres.

BELOW: deer sale.

Zealand's first residential home was built in the Sound for whalers and the following year the New Zealand shipbuilding industry was born in Dusky Sound, when a 65-tonne vessel was floated.

Today, fishermen still manoeuvre small boats along the jagged coast where once sealers and whalers eked out an existence. Most of these isolated sounds can be reached only by sea or air, or by the hardiest of trampers.

But there are two glorious opportunities to experience the mountains, the sea and the bush together. One is by taking a launch across Lake Manapouri to its West Arm. Ponder man's folly, for once planning to raise this lake by 27 metres (90 ft) for hydroelectric purposes. Conservation eventually prevailed, although a massive power station, 200 metres (650 ft) under the mountains at West Arm, was built to supply power for the Tiwai Point aluminium smelter; and the lake level can now be controlled.

Mackay Falls, Milford Track.

BELOW: reflection at Mirror Lakes, between Te Anau and Milford Sound.

But a necessary part of the construction was the building of a road from West Arm across the Wilmot Pass, through rainforest, to the Hall Arm of Doubtful Sound in an area known as Deep Cove. Water from Lake Manapouri is discharged into the sea by a 10-km (6-mile) tailrace tunnel under the mountains. In spite of this development, it remains virgin country. Bottlenose and dusky dolphins can be seen frolicking in the deep blue waters. Divers can view black coral, which grows at an unusually shallow depth due to the darker fresh water that pours into the cove from the power station.

Headquarters of this vast wilderness is the developing tourist town of Te Anau, where hotels, motels and lodges mingle alongside Lake Te Anau with the homes of its 3,000 residents. The valley floors behind the town are the scene of perhaps the biggest land projects in New Zealand, with scores of new farms being developed. A highlight of this area is the **Te Ana-au Caves ❽** on Lake Te Anau which, although believed to have been known to early Maori explorers, were only rediscovered in 1948, by a local explorer, Lawson Burrows. A trip to the caves takes between two and three hours and can be booked at Fiordland Travel in Te Anau. A walkway and two short punt rides take people to the heart of the caves system, which also features whirlpools, magical waterfalls and a glow-worm grotto. The Department of Conservation runs the **Te Anau Wildlife Centre**, just outside the town. There you can see the rare takahe, amongst other native birds.

Eighth wonder

The second, most spectacular way to the sea through Fiordland is by road to **Milford Sound ❾**, world-renowned and described by Rudyard Kipling as "the eighth wonder of the world". Authors and artists have struggled to put into words the beauty that unfolds as the road follows Lake Te Anau for 30 km (19 miles), enters dense forests, and then passes through such features as the "Avenue of the Disappearing Mountain" where the eyes are not to be believed. Forests, river flats and small lakes pass by as the journey through the mountains progresses, until the road drops towards the forested upper Hollyford Valley at Marian Camp.

From there, the road splits in two directions. One arm ventures into the no-exit Hollyford with its Murray

Gunn Camp, a well-established camp run by one of Fiordland's most interesting characters. The main highway proceeds west from here, steeply up the mountain towards the eastern portal of the **Homer Tunnel** . Named after the man who discovered the Homer Saddle between the Hollyford and Cleddau valleys in 1899, this 1 km-long tunnel was completed in 1940 after five years of construction. It was not until 1953, however, that it was widened sufficiently for road traffic. Avalanches claimed the lives of three men, and in 1983, a road overseer was killed near the area. Homer can be Fiordland at its roughest.

The most beautiful Sound

From the Milford side, the road drops 690 metres (2,264 ft) in 10 km (6 miles) between sheer mountain faces to emerge into the Cleddau Valley with its awe-inspiring chasm. Eventually it reaches the head of Milford Sound, where fine accommodation awaits to remind the traveller of life's contrasts. In the foyer of the Milford Sound Hotel you will find a small photographic display, relating some of the history of the region. Behind the hotel is the grave of Donald Sutherland (1843–1919), "the hermit of Milford", who ran the first accommodation place at Milford. He gave his name to the **Sutherland Falls** .

Boats from the southernmost end of Milford Sound regularly carry visitors 16 km (10 miles) on excursions to the open sea. They are very popular and should be booked in advance. The sound is dominated by the unforgettable Mitre Peak – a 1,692-metre (5,551-ft) pinnacle of rock – and several landmarks, notably the Bowen Falls (162 metres or 531 ft).

If you have more time and energy you may consider a sea-kayak trip, details of which can be found at the Te Anau Information Centre. Milford tends to buzz

At 670 metres (2233 feet) high, the Wilmot Pass is the steepest road in New Zealand, winding through beech forests with more than 500 varieties of moss and lichen coating the rocks from which the road was carved.

BELOW: "Twelve Second Drop", Staircase Valley, MacKinnon Pass.

Map, pages 292–3

Peaks of perfection.

BELOW: Sterling Falls, Milford Sound.

with day-trippers, but remains remarkably empty at either end of the day. It also buzzes with sandflies, so insect repellent should be liberally applied.

Milford Sound is also accessible on foot. A launch takes walkers from Te Anau to Glade House at the head of the lake. From there, through some of the most majestic scenery nature can devise, walkers take three days to reach the Sound via the Milford Track. Meals and accommodation are provided at huts.

Fiordland boasts other world-renowned treks, including the **Routeburn Track** and the spectacular **Kepler Track** which meanders along mountain tops and through valleys across the lake from Te Anau. Red deer shooting is encouraged in specified areas. The park's native bird life – including the flightless takahe, thought to be extinct until rediscovered in 1948 – is strictly protected. From the park headquarters in Te Anau, numerous delightful bush walks can be recommended; similar hikes for the less energetic criss-cross the Manapouri area. Launch trips and scenic flights give new perspectives.

Fiordland is to Southland, and to New Zealand, what the Mona Lisa is to the Louvre – an incomparable highlight. Those departing Southland travel north towards Queenstown via **Kingston ⑫**, where a vintage steam train, the *Kingston Flyer*, chugs to and fro between Fairlight and Kingston.

Alternatively, motorists proceed northeast toward Dunedin via the Mataura Valley; Southland's second largest town, **Gore ⑬**, which annually hosts a national Country and Western music festival; and the rich countryside of Eastern Southland. In the background stand the Hokonui Hills, which divide the two main plains of the province. In those hills, illicit whisky stills once produced a potent brew. You may see a wisp of smoke, for there are those who claim the long arm of the law has not reached all the moonshiners.

Tracks

Seeking the great New Zealand outdoor experience can be as simple as a walk in the park. The Department of Conservation administers walking tracks throughout national parks that stretch almost the entire length of the country, and it is often these tracks that lead to New Zealand's very best scenery.

Perhaps the most famous is the Milford Track in Fiordland. It leads from an inland lake through a deep river valley and over an alpine pass to finish four days later by a fiord.

The track follows the Clinton River from the head of Lake Te Anau up to the Mintaro Hut. From there it crosses the scenic MacKinnon Pass and descends to the Quintin Hut. Packs can be left here while walkers make a worthwhile return journey to Sutherland Falls, the highest waterfall in New Zealand. From the Quintin Hut the track leads out through rainforest to Milford Sound.

Because of its popularity you must book ahead if you want to walk the Milford Track. A permit can be obtained from the national park headquarters in Te Anau. The track can be completed either as part of a guided walk, costing around $1,400, or independently as a "freedom walker" at around $200. It attracts people of all ages but a reasonable standard of fitness is required and all-weather clothing is essential.

Only slightly less well known, but equally spectacular, is the three-day Routeburn Track that links the Fiordland National Park with the Mount Aspiring National Park. This track was part of an early Maori route to find greenstone (jade). It leads from the main divide on the Te Anau–Milford Highway over Key Summit to Lake Howden before dropping into the Mackenzie Basin. From there it crosses the Harris Saddle into the Routeburn Valley. The highlight is the view from Key Summit.

A very different experience is offered by the Abel Tasman National Park Coastal Track. This three- to four- day track passes through bush and dips down into beaches of golden sand. The exceptional beauty of the track has made it immensely popular in recent years

and it can be difficult getting hut accommodation, so bring a tent. The track operates on a "Great Walks" pass system which costs $6 per night whether you stay in the huts or camp. If the tide is in you occasionally have to divert around the inlets: check in the local paper for details. Bring repellent for sandflies.

The Heaphy Track, from Collingwood to Karamea, takes four–six days. Most of it is within the boundary of Kahurangi National Park. From Brown Hut the track rises through beech forest to Perry Saddle. One highlight is the view from the summit of Mount Perry (a two-hour return walk from Perry Saddle Hut). The track then winds through the open spaces of the Gouland Downs and on to the Mackay Hut. Nikau palm trees are a feature of the next section through to the Heaphy Hut. Heavy bush offers shade over the final section of the track, which drops down along the beach in parts. This is the most beautiful part of the walk, but be prepared for sandflies.

Detailed information on these and other tracks can be obtained from offices of the Department of Conservation.

RIGHT: MacKinnon Pass in the mist.

STEWART ISLAND

A paradise for numerous species of wildlife, this island can be harsh at times for the human species, yet that remote, evocative bleakness brings its own special magic

A beautiful, peaceful island on the southern fringe of the world lies across Foveaux Strait, 20 minutes by air from Invercargill and 45 minutes by catamaran from Bluff. According to Polynesian legend Stewart Island was the anchor of Maui's boat (the South Island) when he pulled the great fish (the North Island) from the sea. Lapped by both the Pacific and Antarctic oceans, Stewart Island rests easily as New Zealand's anchor.

The island's first European discoverer was Captain Cook, who initially mapped it as a peninsula when he sailed by its southern coast in 1770. The settlers who followed left a wealth of history now gone – sawmills, tin mines and whaling stations. Today, most of the 450 Stewart Islanders depend upon the industry of their forebears. Their small fishing boats venture into often-stormy waters around the rocky coast for blue cod, more lucrative crayfish and other marine species. Their main base, **Oban ⑭** in Halfmoon Bay, is on the north end of this triangular, 172,000-hectare (425,000-acre) island, but the land itself extends about 65 km (40 miles) north to south and 40 km (25 miles) east to west.

Small islands, even quieter than Stewart Island itself, dot the coastline, many of them home to succulent young muttonbirds (titi). They breed on the islands after a round-the-world migration, and have been a source of food, oil and feather down for the Maori for several centuries. Maori were granted exclusive rights to harvest the birds in 1864, and once a year this tradition is continued.

BELOW: Paterson Inlet, Stewart Island.

Harsh contentment

Many newcomers arrive on Stewart Island in search of tranquillity. But the island's harsh life is dominated by the weather and the sea. Those who choose to live here must be hardy and determined. Yet they live on a bush-clad island whose beauty breeds contentment. No wonder the Maori called it Rakiura, "heavenly glow". Peace is paramount. Here, road vehicles are subservient to pedestrians, and roads total a mere 20 km (12 miles). There is no chance of life in the fast lane.

Both the island's airstrip and its port are close to Oban, where most residents live. The Visitor Information Centre is just a few minutes walk from the wharf, for detailed information on the island's many walks.

The small **Rakiura Museum** recounts the history of the island, with seafaring relics and tools from the tin-mining days, as well as samples of the island's wildlife. There is also a collection of adzes and other items that were traded between early whalers and local Maori.

Stewart Island has accommodation to suit all budgets, in response to growing tourist demand, and now boasts its own electricity scheme, but its way of life remains easy-going. Native bush and fern and moss-carpeted glades teem with native bird life. In spring, tui

Map, pages 292–3

and bellbirds call out through the forest. In summer, the curious weka and the tomtit are here, while in winter, the fantail hovers about. Always, there is the swish of the wood pigeon as it flies from tree to tree. The island is a bird-watcher's paradise.

Over the hill from Halfmoon Bay is the large Paterson Inlet, which juts deep into the island's hinterland. Tracks and small roads take the walker to many of its beauty spots; launch trips are also available. A highlight is a trip to **Ulva Island ⓰** in the inlet's centre. From Ulva Island a pioneer postmaster would raise a flag to signal to other islands that the mail had arrived. With an absence of predators, bird life once again thrives and you may see weka, kakariki and kereru (native pigeon). The birds make their home amongst a moss-covered forest floor and stands of native trees. Further inside are the remains of an old sawmill and whaling station. In Big Glory Bay a salmon farm has been established. Boats will take visitors to the salmon farm with a stopover at Ulva Island along the way. You can also get to the island by water taxi from the main wharf.

For the fitter visitor, longer tracks meander around much of the island, to take in exotically named haunts like Port William, Christmas Village and Yankee River. Off Stewart Island's western coast is **Codfish Island ⓰**, once a European settlement whose harshness of life eventually proved overwhelming; today it is a protected sanctuary for birds, which include the rare and endangered kakapo. Sea-fishing trips can be made, and most parts of Stewart Island are a deer hunter's dream. The white-tailed deer in particular is highly sought.

With daylight saving time in summer it is often light on Stewart Island until 10pm. At that time, on a clear night, it is worth standing on Observation Rock above Paterson Inlet to see why the Maori name for Stewart Island is so apt.

The Department of Conservation is currently making strenuous efforts to save the kakapo from extinction, with a breeding programme on the mainland producing chicks for Codfish Island.

BELOW: Stewart Islander.

DUNEDIN

Map, page 309

Behind the solid, sombre façade of a city built by Scots and leavened in gold rush wealth lies a lively university town splendidly placed to take advantage of surroundings rich in natural treasures

Dunedin reclines, all-embracing, at the head of a bay, a green-belted city of slate and tin-roofed houses, of spires, chimneys and churches, of glorious Victorian and Edwardian buildings, of culture, of learning. In the opinion of its 100,000 friendly citizens this is as it should be, for here is a way of life, a peace and a tranquillity that few cities can match. Growth is slowly on the move again, with the city secure in its present, sanguine about its future.

The best first view is from the haven of Otago Harbour, the 20-km (12-mile) long, shallow-bottomed fiord where container ships and coastal traders now ply in place of Maori war canoes, whaling ships and three-masters. It is a view that inspired early Dunedin poet Thomas Bracken to write:

Go, trav'ler, unto others boast of Venice and of Rome,
Of saintly Mark's majestic pile, and Peter's lofty dome;
Of Naples and her trellised bowers, of Rhineland far away
These may be grand, but give to me Dunedin from the Bay.

Around the road-fringed harbourside sprout green hills; among them are the 300-metre (1,000-ft) dead volcano of Harbour Cone on the steep and skinny Otago Peninsula, and the curiously cloud-carpeted cap of 680-metre (2,231-ft) Mount Cargill. Wood and brick houses, some holiday homes (known as cribs here; *baches* in the north), beribbon the harbour perimeter, some with bushy foliage, others the more basic homes of fishermen, wharf workers and commuters.

LEFT: Moeraki Boulders. **BELOW:** Dunedin Town Hall and Cathedral.

A peninsula drive

To fully appreciate the bay and its views of the city, take the "low road" and return via the "high". The 64-km (40-mile) round trip can take anything from 90 minutes to a full day. Much of Dunedin's history is illustrated here. The narrow, winding road calls for careful driving, built as part of it was by convict labour for horse and buggy traffic. (The prisoners were housed in an old hulk that was dragged slowly along the seafront.)

Soon you will see **Glenfalloch ❶**, 11 lovely hectares (27 acres) of woodland gardens; an ideal refreshment stop. At **Portobello ❷**, visit the local museum, then head left to the Portobello Marine laboratory. In aquariums and "touch" tanks you'll be able to see – and fondle – everything marine from a 6-metre (20-ft) shark to a small shrimp, plus sea horses, octopuses and penguins.

At **Otakou ❸**, the Maori church and meeting house appear to be carved, but are actually cast in concrete. In the cemetery behind are buried three great Maori chiefs of last century – the warlike Taiaroa, Ngatata (a northern chief said to have "welcomed the Pakeha to Cook

*On Penguin Beach,
you may spot an
oystercatcher (above)
as well as the
delightful penguins.
You may also see
southern fur seals
and spotted shags.*

BELOW: stained-
glass window in
Dunedin Railway
Station.

Strait") and Karetai, induced by the missionaries to abandon cannibalism and take up the Bible. The marae here is sacred to local Maori and is still the most historic Maori site in Otago. (The name "Otago", in fact, is a European corruption of "Otakou"). There's a Maori museum here, but to assure that it is open you must call in advance (tel: 478-0352).

Just north lie remains of the whaling industry founded in Otago Harbour in 1831, 17 years before European settlement. The old factory is clearly visible and marked by a plaque. Another plaque across the road commemorates the first Christian service held in Otago Harbour, by Bishop Pompalier, in 1840.

Albatrosses and a castle

As you crest the hill past Otakou and look towards lofty **Taiaroa Head ❹**, the tip of the peninsula, glance up. Those huge sea birds resting lazily on the wind are the world's largest birds of flight, rare Royal Albatrosses. Incredibly graceful, they swoop, turn and soar with barely a flick of their 3-metre (10-ft) wings. Up to 20 pairs circle the globe, at speeds of up to 110 km/h (70 mph), returning to roost here, pair-mating for life and producing a chick every two years.

The Trust Bank Royal Albatross Centre, opened in 1989 by Princess Anne, has viewing galleries and display areas. Escorted groups observe most of the spring-summer breeding cycle and pre-flight peregrinations of the fledglings. To visit, contact the Albatross Centre or the Dunedin Visitor Centre. Take in (for free) the antics of a southern fur seal colony at Pilot Beach.

At Taiaroa Head you can visit the unusual Armstrong Disappearing Gun, which was built in 1886 at the height of a "Russian scare". The 15-cm (6-inch) cannon is hidden in the bowels of the earth, rising to fire, then sinking again for

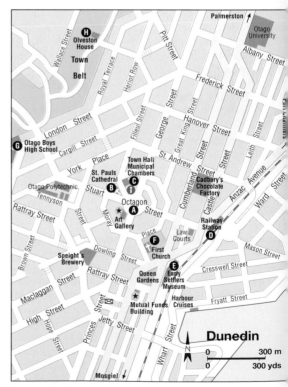

reloading. One mile to the east, along a farm road, is **Penguin Place ❺**. Here, rare Chaplinesque yellow-eyed penguins strut in the surf. Contact Dunedin Visitor Centre for viewing instructions and guided tours.

One has to return along the Taiaroa Head access road to Portobello to gain the "high road" back to the city. Up there is **Larnach Castle ❻**, a century-old baronial manor that is New Zealand's only castle. It took 14 years to build (from 1871) as the home of the Hon. William J.M. Larnach, financier and later Minister of the Crown. An English workman spent 12 years carving the ceilings, along with two Italian craftsmen. The materials were imported from Europe. The castle fell into disrepair but has now been fully restored and most of its 43 rooms, including accommodation, are open to the public. The "high road" that leads back to suburbia has commanding views of the harbour.

The MV *Monarch* provides a regular tourist service from the inner harbour basin at Dunedin down the harbour to Taiaroa Head.

A proud history

While Dunedin is still a very proud city, it was once also the most populous and richest in all New Zealand. In the 1860s, with the discovery of gold in the Otago hinterland and a rush that rivalled California's, Dunedin rapidly became the financial centre of the country. Immigrants flocked from around the world, head offices of national companies sprang up, industry and civic enterprise flourished. Here was the country's first university, medical school, finest educational institutions, first electric trams, then the first cable-car system in the world outside the United States, the country's first woollen mills, and daily newspaper.

Even centuries before that, the coast of Otago was more densely settled than

Map, page 309

If you're coming to see the albatross, check that they're going to be at home. Sept: adults arrive. Oct: courting and mating. Nov: eggs are laid. Feb: chicks hatch. Sept: chicks fly the nest.

BELOW: watching the surf roll in, Tunnel Beach, Dunedin.

any part of the North Island. The moa-hunters lived here, often nomadic Maori groups who thrived on fish, waterfowl and the moa, the giant flightless bird that resembled a huge emu and was easy prey. At the height of the moa-hunter occupation, probably the 11th and 12th centuries, there may have been up to 8,000 Maori living in the estuaries and river mouths of Otago. As the moa retreated, the Maori followed them inland. Their fires destroyed much of the thick native bush, leaving behind the bare tussock country which today covers most of the inland hills from behind Dunedin almost to the foothills of the Southern Alps.

When Captain Cook sailed past Otago in 1770, he missed the harbour entrance, while noting the long white beaches now called St Kilda and St Clair. "A land green and woody but without any sign of inhabitants," he logged. There were Maori there, of course, but in small numbers in nomadic communities.

Fewer than 30 years later, sealers and whalers were in the Otago region. Soon, Europeans were quite familiar along the coastline, if not always popular with the locals. In 1813, four sailors were killed and eaten by Maori; in 1817, at what is still called Murdering Beach, just north of the harbour entrance, three sealers offended natives and were killed. In retribution, their captain, James Kelly, led a massacre of what some reports say was as many as 70 Maori.

Religious fervour on the other side of the world led to Dunedin's European colonisation. Disruption in the Presbyterian Church of Scotland gave birth to the idea of a new settlement in the colony of New Zealand where "piety, rectitude and industry" could flourish. Free Kirk advocates Captain William Cargill, a veteran of the Peninsula War, and the Rev. Thomas Burns, nephew of poet Robbie, were the leaders. The ships *John Wickliffe* and *Philip Laing* landed 300 Scots in March and April 1848 to a site already chosen by the London-based

Dunedin Railway Station.

BELOW LEFT:
albatross from the colony at Taiaroa Head. **BELOW RIGHT:**
Larnach Castle.

Map, page 306

New Zealand Company and purchased – for £2,400 – from the local Maori. Its first name was New Edinburgh; soon it became Dunedin (Edin on the Hill).

A taste of the Wild West

Once gold was discovered inland, there was no holding Dunedin back. In two years, the population of Otago rocketed from 12,000 to 60,000 – 35,000 of them immigrant gold-seekers. Dunedin was the arrival point for the miners, the service centre for the goldfields and the bank for the gold. With all this new prosperity came saloons, gambling dens, brothels, dubious dance halls. Pubs there were aplenty, breweries too. Dunedin to this day has retained a high reputation for its well-patronised licensed premises.

For a quarter of a century, Dunedin boomed. And where Dunedin went, the rest of New Zealand followed, until the gold ran out. Gradually, commercial and climatic attractions in the north led to the decline of the southern cities and provinces. For the last few decades, Dunedin has fought the inevitable drift north. Its greatly expanded university – now with more than 17,000 students and a reputation as the friendliest and most social in the country – together with the College of Education for training schoolteachers and the Otago Polytechnic, pour 20,000 youngsters into the Dunedin community, consolidating Dunedin's place as the leading city of learning in New Zealand.

In Dunedin's gold rush days one local bishop set tongues wagging when it was learned that a building he owned was used by a bevy of irreverent young ladies. It was eventually accepted that no fault lay with the man of the cloth.

Tartan town

Dunedin is known as New Zealand's Scottish city and its Victorian city. A giant statue of Scottish poet Robbie Burns sits in the town centre, fittingly with the bard's back to the Anglican St Paul's Cathedral, and facing what was formerly

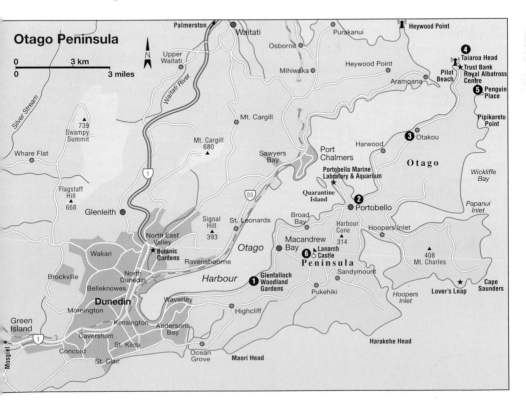

Otago Peninsula

0 ___ 3 km
0 ___ 3 miles

N

a corner pub. Here, too is the country's only kilt manufacturer, its sole whisky distillery, lots of highland pipe bands and regularly celebrated Burns' Nights.

But Dunedin folk are a little weary of continual references to the "Edinburgh of the South" and "Victorian City"; there are equally fine examples of Edwardian and later-style buildings that qualify the city as the most interesting and diverse architecturally in the country. The range is delightful, from full-fashioned ornate Victoriana through Edwardian splendour to impressive Art Deco and modern concrete-and-glass structures that have won national awards.

Dunedin Town Hall.

Buildings of distinction

Start in the **Octagon Ⓐ**, which links Princes and George streets in the centre. Tall, leafy trees and grass plots make this a popular lunch spot. Immediately west is the Dunedin Public Art Gallery, with a large collection of 18th and 19th century English watercolours. Just north of the gallery is **St Paul's Cathedral Ⓑ**, with Gothic pillars rising 40 metres (130 ft) and supporting the only stone-vaulted nave roof in New Zealand. The four-manual organ has 3,500 pipes. The "new" sanctuary and chancel, consecrated in 1971, won a national design award.

Next door to St Paul's are the century-old **Municipal Chambers Ⓒ**, which were designed by the noted colonial architect R.W. Lawson, and behind it the 2,280-seat Town Hall, which was until recently the largest in the country. The Municipal Chambers have been replaced by the adjacent Civic Centre as local government offices, although the modern, stepped design of the Centre has drawn criticism for its contrast with the Victorian Chambers.

BELOW: Otago University.

The city's Visitor Centre, as well as conference facilities, are housed in the Municipal Chambers, whose imposing clock tower and spire were re-erected in

1989 amid an overall greening and spring-cleaning of the city centre. Moving east, down Lower Stuart Street, look out for classic old buildings such as the Allied Press newspaper offices, the Law Courts and the Police Station, which are excellent examples of art in stone.

Then comes the **Dunedin Railway Station D**, which is perhaps the finest stone structure in the country. It earned designer George Troup, a knighthood and the nickname "Gingerbread George". Of Flemish Renaissance style, it has a 37-metre (120-ft) high square tower, three huge clock faces and a covered carriageway projecting from the arched colonnade.

In the main foyer is a majolica mosaic-tiled floor with nine central panels showing a small English "Puffing Billy". The original floor consisted of 725,760 half-inch Royal Doulton porcelain squares. Other ornamentation in the station is in original Doulton china and church-like stained glass. Only two passenger trains a day now use this gingerbread house.

On the right track

Maybe it's not surprising that Dunedin has such a remarkable railway station, as the city has a fascination with trains. *Josephine*, one of the country's first steam engines (a double-boiler, double-facing Fairlie) is in a glass case on public display beside the **Otago Early Settlers Museum E**, with *JA1274*, the last Dunedin-made steam locomotive to haul the main trunk-line trains. A train enthusiasts' group operates all manner of machines along a private line between St Clair and St Kilda beaches. The Otago Excursion Train Trust has renovated vintage carriages and rolling stock and operates a private-hire train.

Special excursion trains run north and sometimes south on the main trunk line

Map, page 306

TIP

You don't need to have children to enjoy a tour of Cadbury's Chocolate Factory on Cumberland Street (to find it, follow your nose). It's a slightly unreal atmosphere of tumbling chocolate eggs and giant choccie bunnies, with all the chocolate you can eat. Booking ahead is essential.

BELOW: Dunedin from Mount Cargill.

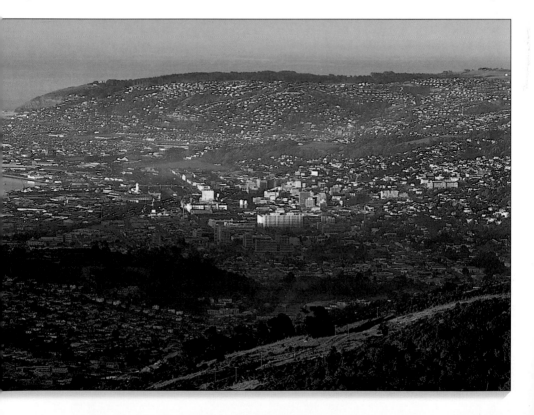

from the town. Tourist trains enter Otago's hinterland through the rugged and spectacularly bridged Taieri Gorge. Coach connections from the terminus at Middlemarch in Central Otago take onward tourists straight to Queenstown.

City highlights

The country's first skyscraper, the Mutual Funds Building (1910), stands near the station close to the original centre of Dunedin, the Stock Exchange area. Land reclamation has since pushed back the harbour edge with a proliferation of fine old office buildings, but movement of the city centre north has forced many into use as storage areas and some into demolition.

A gargoyled "bride's-cake" monument in the Stock Exchange area pays homage to founder Captain Cargill. It once sat atop men's underground toilets until public opprobrium led to the conveniences being closed.

First Church ❻, in Moray Place, was the founders' tribute to their Father in 1867. Its spire soars 55 metres (180 ft) heavenwards. The church, another Lawson design, is arguably the most historical building in the city.

Some of the banks and other churches in the central city area inspire praise, as does the Lawson-designed **Otago Boys High School ❼** tower block, dominant above the city. It is situated just below the Town Belt, a 200-hectare (500-acre), 8-km (5-mile) long green swath that separates city from suburbs.

A walk through the Town Belt offers some of the best views of a city and harbour in New Zealand. Hear the tui and the bellbird; observe, too, the many wooded reserves and sports fields, fine golf courses, cotula-turfed bowling greens, huge heated swimming pools and fine swimming and surfing beaches.

Olveston ❽, "the jewel in Dunedin's crown", lies within the Town Belt. A

Yellow-eyed penguin, Otago Peninsula.

BELOW: Otago Early Settlers Museum.

Jacobean-style manor of double brick and oak, it was built in 1904 to the design of celebrated English architect Sir Ernest George for a local businessman, David Theomin. It was bequeathed to the city in 1966. The 35-room house is rated the best example in New Zealand of the grand style of Edwardian living.

In the north of the city are the (almost) combined campuses of the University of Otago, Otago Polytechnic and Dunedin College of Education. Dominating the Gothic rockpiles of the university, beside the grass-banked water of the Leith, is the main clock tower. Just west is the fascinating **Otago Museum**, with Pacific Island and Maori artefacts, maritime relics and colonial era collections.

Venture forth

Dunedin visitors should not restrict themselves to the city. Beyond the outskirts lie fascinating sights of natural and historic beauty. Eighty km (50 miles) north are the queer **Moeraki Boulders** ⓱, huge round stones that lie "like devil's marbles" on the seashore. The food baskets of a wrecked canoe in Maori legend, they were formed on the seashore 60 million years ago by the gradual accumulation of lime salts around a small centre. Several tons in weight and up to 4.3 metres (14 ft) in circumference, they gradually take shape from the bank behind the beach as the soft mudstone is weathered by the sea.

Just west of Dunedin, in the **Taieri River Gorge** ⓲, jet-boat and white-water raft tours tumble more adventurous tourists between virgin bush-edged cliffs. For the less energetically inclined, there are plenty of trout to catch.

Both north and south of Dunedin are coastlines of immense natural beauty and quality of lifestyle, peopled by relatively few and as yet undiscovered by the tourist hordes. Inland, to Central Otago, lies another world again.

Map, pages 292–3

The Otago Museum has a sorry collection of stuffed kakapos from the early colonial era, with interesting clippings explaining how they came to be stuffed, throwing light on the bird's current near-extinction.

BELOW: seal on Penguin Beach. **OVERLEAF:** on foot into the Southern Alps.

INSIGHT GUIDES

Travel Tips

Insight FlexiMaps

Maps in Insight Guides are tailored to complement the text. But when you're on the road you sometimes need the big picture that only a large-scale map can provide. This new range of durable Insight Fleximaps has been designed to meet just that need.

Detailed, clear cartography
makes the comprehensive route and city maps easy to follow, highlights all the major tourist sites and provides valuable motoring information plus a full index.

Informative and easy to use
with additional text and photographs covering a destination's top 10 essential sites, plus useful addresses, facts about the destination and handy tips on getting around.

Laminated finish
allows you to mark your route on the map using a non-permanent marker pen, and wipe it off. It makes the maps more durable and easier to fold than traditional maps.

The world's most popular destinations
are covered by the 125 titles in the series – and new destinations are being added all the time. They include Alaska, Amsterdam, Bangkok, Barbados, Beijing, Brussels, Dallas/Fort Worth, Florence, Hong Kong, Ireland, Madrid, New York, Orlando, Peru, Prague, Rio, Rome, San Francisco, Sydney, Thailand, Turkey, Venice, and Vienna.

INSIGHT GUIDES
The world's largest collection of visual travel guides

CONTENTS

Getting Acquainted

The Place

Situation: Located in the Southern Hemisphere in the middle of the Pacific Ocean, New Zealand is approximately 2,250 km (1,398 miles) east of Australia.

Area: 268,680 sq. km (103,788 sq. miles)

Capital: Wellington (pop. 345,000) – Wellington is the political, banking and financial centre of New Zealand. The Parliament Building known as "the Beehive" is one of the city's top attractions. The National Archives, National Library and Old Government Buildings (the second largest wooden building in the world) are also located in Wellington. Wellington is also known as the arts capital of New Zealand.

Population: 3.9 million

Language: English/Maori

Religion: Predominantly Christian (81 percent)

Currency: New Zealand dollar

Weights & measures: Metric

Telephone Codes: International dialling code: 64

Electricity: New Zealand's AC

Early Start to the Day

Travellers from the Western Hemisphere moving west into New Zealand lose a full day crossing the International Dateline, and regain a full day returning eastwards from New Zealand. Because the country is so advanced in time, being close to the International Dateline, it is one of the very first nations to welcome each day (preceded only by Fiji, Kiribati and some of the other small Pacific islands).

electricity supply operates at 230/240 volts which is the same as Australia. Most hotels and motels proved 110-volt, 20-watt AC sockets for electric razors only. An adaptor is necessary to operate all other electrical equipment. It's important to note that power outlets only accept flat 3 or 2 pin plugs, depending on whether an earth connection is fitted.

Time Zone: There is only one time zone throughout most of the country – 12 hours in advance of Greenwich Mean Time (GMT).

From early October until late March, time is advanced by one hour to give extended daytime throughout summer.

Time in the remote Chatham Islands, 800 km (500 miles) east of Christchurch, is 45 minutes ahead of that in the rest of the country.

Geography

New Zealand has three main islands – the North Island, the South Island and Stewart Island – running roughly from north to south over 1,600 km (994 miles), between 34°S and 47°S. The two main islands, North and South Islands, are separated by a 22 km- (14 mile-) wide body of water, called the Cook Strait.

New Zealand's spectacular landscape includes vast mountain chains, steaming volcanoes, sweeping coastlines, indented fiords and lush rainforests.

In the South Island, the Southern Alps run from north to south, and in the southwest reach the sea in the deeply indented coast of Fiordland. The highest point is Mount Cook, now standing at 3,754 metres (12,315 ft) – a major rock slide reduced the height of the mountain in December 1991 by 10 metres (33 ft). The Canterbury Plains lie to the east of the mountains.

The North Island is mainly hilly with isolated mountains, including volcanoes – two of which are active. Lowlands on North Island are largely restricted to coastal areas and the Waikato Valley.

Land Mass

New Zealand's combined total land area of 268,680 sq m (103,788 sq miles) is approximately 36 times less than the US. It is similar in size to Colorado and somewhere in between the size of Japan and the United Kingdom.

The principal rivers are the Waikato, Clutha, Waihou, Rangitikei, Mokau, Wanganui and Manawatu.

Climate

New Zealand's climate is reverse to that of the Northern Hemisphere. Which means New Zealanders get to experience a warm Christmas in the sun while June and July are some of the coldest months.

The climate is generally temperate with rainfall spread fairly evenly throughout the year, although the weather is very changeable. The summer and autumn seasons from December to May are the most settled and the best for holidaying. New Zealanders traditionally take their main family holiday break at Christmas through January, so visitors are advised to make sure of advance bookings for accommodation and domestic transport over this period because of the pressure on travel and tourist facilities.

The north of New Zealand is generally subtropical and the south, temperate. You can check on weather conditions in New Zealand by accessing the New Zealand weather service's internet site: www.metservice.co.nz.

Winds can be strong at any time on the Cook Strait, between the two main islands, but summer days are generally warm and pleasant in the

National Symbols

The national plant of New Zealand is the Pohutukawa and the national bird is the flightless Kiwi.

Temperature Ranges

Winter (June–August) and summer (December–February/March) temperature ranges are as follows:
Auckland: 8–15°C (48–59°F) in winter; 14–23°C (57–74°F) in summer.
Wellington: 6–13°C (43–55°F) in winter; 12–20°C (53–69°F) in summer.
Christchurch: 2–11°C (33–52°F) in winter; 10–22°C (50–73°F) in summer.
Queenstown: -1–10°C (30–50°F) in winter; 19–22°C (66–73°F) in summer.
Dunedin: 4–12°C (39–53°F) in winter; 9–19°C (48–66°F) in summer.

majority of the regions. Winters can be cold in the central and southern North Island and coastal districts of the South Island, and can be severe in central regions of the South Island.

Economy

The majority of New Zealand's export earnings come from tourism and agriculture, in particular from meat, wool and dairy products, food processing, and steel and iron.

Forestry is now an expanding business and supports an important pulp and paper industry. Apart from coal, lignite, natural gas and gold, the country has few natural resources, although its considerable hydroelectric power potential has been exploited to produce plentiful cheap electricity – an important basis of New Zealand's manufacturing industry. Natural gas – from the Kapuni Field on the North Island and the Maui Field off the Taranaki coast – is converted to liquid fuel for use both in the domestic and foreign markets.

New Zealand has an increasingly strong competitive advantage in food processing, technology, telecommunications, plastics, textiles, plantation forest products,

electronics, climbing equipment and apparel. In recent years, there has also been a great interest in the production of specialised lifestyle products such as yachts.

Major trading partners are Japan, Australia and the USA.

Despite the country's small domestic market and its remoteness from the world's major industrial powers, New Zealand enjoys a high standard of living.

Government

New Zealand has a centralised democracy with a Western-style economy. The 120-member House of Representatives is elected by universal adult suffrage (under a system of "mixed member" proportional representation) for three years. There are four constituencies specifically for those Maori who choose to vote on a separate roll. Half of the remainder of the house is decided according to the proportion of each party's support in a special "party" vote on election day. The rest of the members of parliament represent constituencies.

The Governor General – the representative of the British Queen as sovereign of New Zealand – appoints a Prime Minister who commands a majority in the House. The Prime Minister, in turn, appoints a Cabinet, which is responsible to the House.

For local government purposes, New Zealand is divided into cities and districts. The Chatham Islands, a separate district, are not included in any region. Tokelau is an autonomous island territory, which is legally part of the Dominion of New Zealand.

The main political parties are the Labour Party, the (conservative) National Party, the Alliance Party, ACT and the New Zealand First Party.

Planning the Trip

What to Bring

Travel as lightly as possible because there are plenty of bargains to be found in New Zealand. Travellers to New Zealand can pretty much buy anything they need from spectacles and prescription medicines to clothing and shoes. Remember to stock up on plenty of sunscreen and insect repellent in the summer months.

Clothing

New Zealanders are regarded as fairly casual dressers although you will need to bring something dressy if you plan to go to any arts events, fancy restaurants or clubbing. Some nightclubs and bars do not allow shorts or trainers.

For summer visits, you are advised to bring sweaters or wind-breakers for the cooler evenings or brisk days, especially if you are planning to travel to regions in the South Island.

Medium-thick clothing with a raincoat or umbrella is adequate for most regions most of the year, but in midwinter in the tourist areas of Rotorua, Taupo and Queenstown, winter clothing and shoes are essential. The South Island is generally much more colder than the North.

New Zealand is noted for the brilliance of its light. This can lead to severe sunburn on days when the temperature may be deceptively low. It is important to wear sunscreen lotions, a hat, sunglasses and protective clothing.

Visas & Passports

All visitors to New Zealand require passports which must be valid for at least three months beyond the date you intend leaving the country.

Visa requirements differ, depending on nationality, purpose of visit and length of stay. Visitors must produce an onward or return ticket and sufficient funds to support themselves during their stay. Check with the New Zealand diplomatic or consular office in your country.

Customs

New Zealand has three levels of control at all points of entry into the country: immigration, customs and agriculture. Everyone arriving in New Zealand must complete an arrival card that will be handed out on the aircraft. Present this to an immigration official with your passport, and, if required, a valid visa.

The following classes of people are prohibited by law from entering, either as tourists or immigrants, regardless of country of origin:
● Those suffering from tuberculosis, syphilis, leprosy, or any mental disorders.
● Those convicted of an offence which drew a sentence of imprisonment of over one year.
● Those who have previously been deported from New Zealand.

A traveller, over the age of 17, may import 200 cigarettes or 250 grams of tobacco; 4.5 litres of wine or beer and one bottle of spirits. Excess quantities are subject to customs charges.

Strict laws prevent the entry of drugs, weapons, illicit material, wildlife products, firearms and quarantine items.

FARM REGULATIONS

Because New Zealand relies heavily on agricultural and horticultural trade with the rest of the world, it has stringent regulations governing the import of animals, and the import of vegetable and animal

matter. Visitors planning to bring in any material of this sort should make inquiries at the New Zealand Government offices overseas before proceeding. Live animals legally brought into the country must undergo strict quarantine periods.

Health

Only limited medical treatment is available free to visitors so health insurance is recommended. To be eligible for the same health care benefits as New Zealand residents, you must have been or intend to remain in New Zealand for two years or more. If you are studying in New Zealand for less than two years, you are responsible for any health costs you may incur. In New Zealand there are two types of hospitals: public and private. In most cases, you pay for private or public hospital care.

Most tap water in New Zealand is safe to drink. But where possible drink boiled or bottled water and never drink untreated water from lakes and streams.

There are no snakes or dangerous wild animals in New Zealand, although a bite from the Red-backed Katipo spider requires medical treatment. Sandflies and mosquitos are prevalent in some areas – bring insect repellent.

Currency

The New Zealand dollar (NZ$), divided into 100 cents, is the unit of currency. Currency conversion facilities are available at Auckland, Wellington and Christchurch international airports as well as most banks and bureaux de change in the larger cities and resorts.

There is no restriction on the amount of domestic or foreign currency (or traveller's cheques in New Zealand dollars) a visitor may bring into or take out of New Zealand. In international financial markets, the New Zealand dollar is frequently called "the kiwi" as the dollar coin features a kiwi bird on one side.

Credit Cards

Credit cards, including Visa, American Express, Diners Club and MasterCard, are widely accepted throughout New Zealand. If your credit card is encoded with a pin, you may be able to withdraw cash from automatic teller machines (ATMs) situated at banks and shopping centres throughout the country.

Goods & Services Tax

A Goods and Services Tax (GST) is applied to the cost of all goods and services and is generally included in all prices. GST is not included in duty-free prices or where the goods are posted by a retailer to an international visitor's home address. GST is also not included in international airfares purchased in New Zealand.

Overseas Tourism Offices

There is an official and award-winning New Zealand Tourism web site at www.purenz.com.

Alternatively, contact one of the following offices:

London: New Zealand Tourism Board, New Zealand House, 80 Haymarket, London SW1Y 4TQ, tel: 207 930 1662/info line: 9069 101 010 (calls charged at premium rate).

New York: New Zealand Tourism Board, 780 3rd Avenue, Suite 1904, New York, NY10017-2024, tel: 212 832 8482.

Los Angeles: New Zealand Tourism Board, 501 Santa Monica Boulevard, Suite 300, Santa Monica, CA 90401, tel: 310 395 7480.

Sydney: New Zealand Tourism Board, Level 8, 35 Pitt Street, P.O. Box R1546 Royal Exchange, Sydney NSW2000, tel: 2 9247 5222.

Germany: Rossmarkt 11 60311 Frankfurt am Main, Germany, tel: 69 97 12 11.

Overseas Missions

There is a New Zealand Diplomatic Post finder at www.nzembassy.com which details all New Zealand embassies and consulates around the world. Here are a few of them.

Canberra
New Zealand High Commission, Commonwealth Avenue, Canberra ACT 2600, Australia, tel: 02 6270 4211; e-mail: nzhccba@austarmetro.com.au

France
New Zealand Embassy, 7 ter, rue Leonard de Vinci, 75116 Paris, France, tel: 01 4500 2411; e-mail: nzembassy.paris@wanadoo.fr

Germany
New Zealand Embassy, Atrium Building, Friedrichstrasse 60, 10117 Berlin, Germany, tel: 030 206 2110; e-mail: nzemb@t-online.de

London
New Zealand High Commission, New Zealand House, 80 Haymarket, London SW1Y 4TQ, United Kingdom, tel: 020 7930 8422; www.newzealandhc.org.uk

New York
New Zealand Mission, One UN Plaza, 25th floor New York, NY 10017, tel: 212 826 1960; www.un.int/newzealand/

Singapore
New Zealand High Commission, 391A Orchard Road, #15-06/10, Ngee Ann City, Singapore 238873, tel: 65 6235 9966; www.nz-high-com.org.sg

Sydney
New Zealand Consulate-General, Level 10, 55 Hunter Street, Sydney, NSW 2000, Australia, tel: 02 8356 2000; e-mail: nzcqsydney@bigpond.com.au

Washington DC
New Zealand Embassy, 37 Observatory Circle, Washington DC 20008, USA, tel: 202 328 4800; www.nzemb.org

Public Holidays

January New Year's Day (1st) and next working day; provincial anniversaries: Wellington (22nd), Northland and Auckland (29th)
February Waitangi Day (6th); provincial anniversaries: Nelson Day (1st)
March Provincial anniversaries: Otago (23rd), Taranaki (31st)
Good Friday and Easter Monday
April ANZAC Day (25th)
June Queen's Birthday (usually the first Monday)
October Labour Day (usually the last Monday)
November Provincial anniversaries: Marlborough and Hawke's Bay (1st)
December Provincial anniversaries: Westland (1st), Canterbury (16th); South Canterbury (16th, but observed in late September); Christmas (25th, 26th, and next working day)
   Note Provincial anniversaries are usually observed on the Monday closest to the actual date.

Getting There
BY AIR

More than 99 percent of the 1.9 million tourists who visit New Zealand each year arrive by air.

International Airports
The main gateway is the Auckland International Airport at Mangere, 24 km (15 miles) south-west of downtown **Auckland**. Bus, shuttle and taxi transfers are available.
   There is also an international airport in **Hamilton** although this tends to service only New Zealand and Australian flights.
   The airport at **Wellington**, the capital city, has restricted access for most wide-bodied aircraft types because of the runway length.
   There is a good international airport at Harewood, close to **Christchurch**, the main South Island city, and many international airlines are now scheduling flights there.
   New Zealand has direct air links with the Pacific Islands, all the major Australian cities, many of the Southeast Asian destinations, and cities in North America and Europe. Passengers arriving on long-haul flights should allow themselves a couple of rest days on arrival.

Departure Tax

A tax of NZ$22–25 must be paid when you leave New Zealand. Please note that this tax is not included in your ticket price.

BY SEA

A few cruise ships visit New Zealand but there are no regular passenger ship visits to the country. Most cruises in the South Pacific originate in Sydney, so cruise operators generally fly their passengers to and from New Zealand. However, P&O Line, Sitmar, Royal Viking, and some other cruise lines travel to New Zealand, mostly from November to April. Some cargo vessels also take small groups of passengers.

Practical Tips

Business Hours

Shops are open for business 9am–5.30pm (Mon–Fri), and usually stay open one night of the week until 9pm. Hours on Saturday are usually from 10am until the early afternoon. Main cities and the larger tourist areas have extended opening hours, with many shops open seven days a week.

Banks are open 9.30am–4.30pm (Mon–Fri), and ATMs are plentiful.

Bars, pubs and taverns are open 11am–late (Mon–Sat). Nightclubs usually open their doors 7.30–8pm and close between 4–6am.

All banks, post offices, government and private offices and most shops close on public holidays. Most nightclubs and bars also close at midnight the night before each public holiday.

Tipping

Tipping is becoming more widespread in New Zealand although it is still regarded as a foreign custom. In the more major centres, tipping is encouraged. You should tip 5–10 percent of your restaurant bill if you feel the service was worthy. Service charges are not added to hotel or restaurant accounts.

Media

PRINT

In New Zealand English is the most widely used language and Maori, the indigenous language. There is a high level of literacy in New Zealand: most communities have a decent library, and sales of books, magazines and newspapers on a

per capita basis are unparalleled anywhere in the world. One in four people in Greater Auckland buys the New Zealand Herald, the morning daily. Most large towns have their own newspaper, and community newspapers abound.

International newspapers can be found in the larger bookstores and outlets at New Zealand's international airports.

TV & RADIO

Two television channels are administered by a nominally independent government corporation: Television One and TV2. Two more channels, TV3 and TV4, are run by a privately owned company. National and International news and current affairs programmes are usually carried on TV3 and Television One. There are also several local television stations. Most hotels and motels subscribe to the Sky satellite service for international sports and news links.

New Zealand has a variety of AM- and FM-band radio stations across the country, satisfying a wide variety of tastes.

Postal Services

Post offices are generally open 9am–5pm (Mon–Fri). Some are also open Saturday mornings until midday. In many areas, postal services and stamps are also available from stores and other outlets. Post offices sell stamps, magazines and a range of stationary. NZ Post also offers a courier service within New Zealand.

Communications

Most public call-phones accept cards purchased from bookstalls and newsagents with a minimum value of NZ$2. Some public call-phones also accept credit cards. Calls made from public telephones to the local area (free call zone) cost NZ50¢. When calling another area within New Zealand, dial 0

Telephone Area Codes

Northland: 09
Auckland: 09
Waikato: 07
Bay of Plenty: 07
Gisborne: 06
Hawke's Bay: 06
Taranaki: 06
Wairarapa: 06
Wellington: 04
Nelson: 03
West Coast and Buller: 03
Christchurch: 03
Timaru/Oamaru: 03
Otago: 03
Southland: 03

before the city code. Some businesses have free 0800 numbers while 0900 numbers are usually charged per minute to the caller. Such numbers can only be dialled within New Zealand.

New Zealand phone numbers appear in the White Pages (alphabetical listings) and the Yellow Pages (business category listings).

E-mail and Internet: There are a number of internet cafés throughout New Zealand that provide access to internet and e-mail. Many hotels and motels also have modem connections. You will need a RJ45 type plug to be able to connect your laptop into a computer socket in New Zealand and an adaptor with a flat two- or three-point power plug to connect to the power supply.

Mobile phones: Check with your phone company before leaving home about international mobile roam facilities available in New Zealand. Mobile phones can also be hired on arrival in New Zealand (outlets are available at international airports).

Local Tourist Offices

New Zealand is well served in terms of visitor information. In the city of Auckland, a team of "Ambassadors" wander the streets, waiting to answer your every query. In addition to this, you will find desks offering information and booking services at most airports and at more than 60 other prime locations around the country. A good start point is the general website of **Tourism New Zealand**: www.purenz.com.

Regional Listings

For specific contact details of local tourism offices, see relevant regional listings on pages 335–373.

Local Missions

If you need help with such matters as legal advice or a stolen passport while in New Zealand, most countries have diplomatic representations in New Zealand. You'll find most foreign embassies are located in Wellington. Below are some of the bigger ones.
Australia: Australian High Commission, 72-78 Hobson Street, Thorndon, Wellington, tel: 04 473 6411.
France: French Embassy, 32-42 Manners Street, Wellington, tel: 04 384 5042/43.
Great Britain: British High Commission, 44 Hill Street, Thorndon, Wellington, tel: 04 924 2888.
United States: United States Embassy, 29 Fitzherbert Terrace, Thorndon, Wellington, tel: 04 462 6000.

Disabled Travellers

Every new building or major reconstruction in New Zealand is required, by law, to provide "reasonable and adequate" access for people with disabilities. Most facilities have wheelchair access but it pays to check when booking.

A thorough guide for disabled travellers *Accessible New Zealand*, can be ordered online www.travelaxess.co/nzguide.htm or call tel: 07 839 6545. This book has information on the terrain of each city and town, shopping and parking, location of accessible

toilets, restaurants and a range of transport.

Tour companies such as Accessible Tours provide holiday packages for individuals and groups. Most transport operators can cater for people with special needs but most urban transport buses are not equipped to cater for the disabled.

Parking concessions are available for people with disabilities and temporary display cards can be issued for the length of the visitor's stay.

For more information about travelling for the disabled in New Zealand, contact:
Accessible Kiwi Tours, P.O. Box 550, Opotiki, New Zealand, tel: 07 315 6988; www.tours-nz.com; e-mail: info@tours-nz.com

Gay Travellers

There are plenty of facilities in New Zealand catering for the gay, lesbian and bisexual traveller. There is a range of diverse activities for this segment of travellers in the main cities of Auckland, Wellington, Christchurch and Queenstown. The best organisations to contact for further information about accommodation, events, nightlife, travel and transport are:
Gay Tourism New Zealand: P.O. Box 11-462, Wellington 6001, tel: 04 917 9176; e-mail: info@gaytourismnewzealand.com
New Zealand Gay & Lesbian Tourism Association: Private Bag MBE P255, Auckland, tel: 09 374 2161; e-mail: info@nzglta.org.nz
Gaytravel New Zealand: www.gaytravel.co.nz

Travelling with Children

New Zealand is a great place to visit with children. There are a range of activities for the whole family to enjoy. Most hotels have reliable babysitters, kids' clubs and programmes. For more information about planning family holidays in New Zealand, contact:
Familystophere.com: P.O. Box 12087, Wellington 6038, tel: 04

971 0646; www.familystophere.com; e-mail: info@familystophere.com

Personal Security

New Zealand is considered to be one of the safest countries in the world for travellers. New Zealand suffers only isolated incidences of serious crime. However, petty crime is a problem. Take precautions to secure and conceal your valuables at all times, and never leave them in a car.

To report a crime, contact your nearest police station.

New Zealand police generally do not carry weapons. You should find them approachable and helpful.

Medical Services

For non-emergencies, full instructions for obtaining assistance are printed in the front of telephone directories. Hotels and motels normally have individual arrangements with duty doctors for guests' attention, and they can also assist you in finding a dentist.

New Zealand's medical and hospital facilities, both public and private, provide a high standard of treatment and care. It is important to note that medical services are not free to visitors, except treatment for injuries in an accident *(also see page 318)*.

Health and Beauty

PHARMACIES

Pharmacies or chemists are generally open 9am–5.30pm weekdays. Some also open on Saturday mornings and for one late night a week. Most major cities also have Urgent Dispensaries for emergencies, which remain open overnight and through the weekends.

Emergencies

In an emergency dial 111 for ambulance, police or fire service. Emergency calls are free from public call boxes.

HAIRDRESSERS

Hairdressers and barbers are located in most New Zealand cities and towns. Many have late nights and are open on Saturday. It's a good idea to book first although smaller hair salons and barbers will take customers straight off the street. Check the Yellow Pages for your nearest hair salon.

HEALTH SPAS

The spa industry is an industry that fits well with New Zealand's clean, green image.

Since the 1800's early New Zealand settlers have been soaking in the country's mineral waters, while local Maori have been doing so for far longer. Waiwera, north of Auckland was the site of New Zealand's first natural spa.

It wasn't until the last part of the 19th century that the spa industry in New Zealand began in earnest.

Today there are numerous natural spas and thermal resorts in New Zealand. These include the Polynesian Spa in Rotorua, the Taupo Hot Springs Health Spa in the central North Island and Hamner Springs Thermal Resort in the South Island, to name a few.

BEAUTY THERAPY AND DAY SPAS

Beauty therapy clinics offering sunbeds, day spas, manicures, pedicures, massage, body-wraps, waxing, skin care and make-up artistry are dotted throughout New Zealand. Prices range from NZ$50 for a forty minute massage to NZ$500 for a full-day and complete beauty spa experience. Check the Yellow Pages for your nearest beauty salon or day spa.

GYMNASIUMS

Most cities and towns have gymnasiums and offer casual rates to visitors. The most popular are Les Mills which has a wide range of facilities and aerobics sessions (Combat, Pump, Body Balance, Step), and the YMCA, which isn't as flash as Les Mills but still has all the necessary equipment and trained gym instructors.

Photography

Most New Zealanders don't mind being photographed but it's best to ask before shooting. Professional photographic labs and camera centres are dotted throughout the country. You can also drop your film in at local pharmacies to be processed. New Zealand has access to the latest film processing and development technology, camera and video gear and some stores will even rent you equipment. There are also plenty of camera repair services throughout New Zealand. Check the Yellow Pages or search the internet for the camera store nearest you. A roll of 36-shot Kodak print film costs around NZ$12.

Language

English is the common language of New Zealand. However, as New Zealand is a multicultural society, you may hear other languages spoken including Te Reo Maori, the official language of New Zealand. A vast majority of New Zealand place names are of Maori origin. There are also television and radio stations devoted entirely to the Maori language.

Useful Maori Phrases

Kia ora – hello
Kia ora tatou – hello everyone
Tena koe – greetings to you (said to one person)
Tena koutou – greetings to you all
Haere mai – welcome
Haere ra – farewell
Ka kite ano – until I see you again (bye)

Useful Websites

www.purenz.com – All you ever wanted to know about New Zealand and more. This award-winning website was set up by Tourism New Zealand.
www.holiday.co.nz – A New Zealand travel guide and vacation planner that features a comprehensive range of holiday options from motorcycle tours to accommodation. There is a German translation of the website available.
www.aotearoa.co.nz – A site dedicated to promoting New Zealand and Pacific arts and crafts. Order bone carvings, glass art, wood carvings and designer jewellery online.
www.nzedge.com – A comprehensive and eclectic site that explores the lives and achievements of New Zealanders living overseas and connects them on a global scale. The site contains a unique online shopping guide, news stories, a section dedicated to New Zealand "heroes", image galleries, speeches, web links and a global register.
www.stuff.co.nz – Stuff covers New Zealand news nationally and internationally. It has a strong regional focus and draws its content from a number of newspapers in the INL stable. INL is New Zealand's leading media group.
www.nzmusic.com – The diversity of the Pacific sound is at your fingertips in this progressive and fascinating site. It contains a catalogue of Kiwi artists, bios, music, news, an extensive gig guide and a section dedicated to forums.
www.allblacks.com – The official site of the New Zealand Rugby Football Union and the All Blacks. You can't come to New Zealand without doing a wee bit of reading up on the country's most beloved sport.
www.nzaa.co.nz – The website for New Zealand's leading motoring organisation. On this site you will find everything from driver information to accommodation and travel guides.

Getting Around

By Air

Air New Zealand and **Qantas New Zealand** are the main domestic carriers. There are also a number of smaller regional carriers like the no-frills **Freedom Air**, whose subsdiary **Freedom Air International** flies passengers direct to Hamilton from Australia's Gold Coast. **Origin Pacific Airways**, based in Nelson in the South Island, also has regular flights around the country.

Helicopters are readily available in main cities and in the main tourist resort areas.

Although domestic flights can be expensive, there are plenty of deals around for flying in off-peak times, internet and advance booking or for booking ahead from overseas. Flights can be booked online through internet sites, through travel agents or accredited agents. **Air New Zealand**, Sales and Reservations, tel: 0800 737 000 (reservations) or 0800 737 767 (travel centres) – New Zealand only; www.airnz.co.nz

Qantas New Zealand, 191 Queen Street, Auckland, tel: 09 357 8700, fax: 09 358 0304; www.qantas.co.nz. For reservations, contact, tel: 09 357 8900.

Freedom Air, tel: 0800 600 500 (New Zealand only); www.freedomair.com

Origin Pacific Airways, tel: 0800 302 302 (New Zealand only); www.originpacific.co.nz

By Sea

The North and South Islands are linked by modern ferries operated by **Interisland Line**. The ferries sail between Wellington and Picton and carry passengers, vehicles and freight. There are frequent daily crossings in both directions, though it is important to book vehicle space in advance during summer holiday periods. The journey time varies from 135 minutes (*The Lynx*) to 3 hours (*The Interislander*).

There are a wide range of facilities and entertainment on board *The Interislander* including a bar, lounges and a café. Tickets can be purchased for ferry services through any NZ Post outlets, travel agents, visitor information centres and other agencies.

The Interislander and The Lynx, tel: 04 498 3302 or 0800 802 802 (New Zealand only); www.interislandline.co.nz

By Rail

Tranz Rail has six long-distance train services covering both North and South islands. The trains are comfortably outfitted and a dining car onboard serves sells light meals, sandwiches and beverages. These train services, operated by **Tranz Scenic**, cut across some of the most spectacular scenery in the world. A commentary is given onboard some services.

Overlander: Southbound from Auckland to Wellington and vice versa. Connects with the *Lynx* and *Interislander* ferries for the sea crossing over Cook Strait to Picton in the South Island.

Northerner: Overnight journey from Wellington and vice versa.

Geyserland Connection: From Auckland to Hamilton on the Overlander train, where a connecting Tranz Scenic coach continues on to Rotorua.

Capital Connection: Links Palmerstown North with Wellington (and vice versa) on weekdays only.

Tranz Coastal: Along the coast from Picton to Christchurch and vice versa. Connects with the *Lynx* and *Interislander* ferries for the sea crossing over Cook Strait to Wellington in the North Island.

Tranz Alpine: From Christchurch in the east to Greymouth on the west, and vice versa.

Have Pass Will Travel

If you're not planning to drive in New Zealand, consider buying travel passes which allow a combination of bus, train, ferry and plane travel. Tranz Rail's "Best of New Zealand Pass" is one such deal; the other is "New Zealand Travel Pass". Both give substantial discounts over what you would have to pay if you booked trips individually.

Best Pass: Tranz Rail, tel: 04 498 3303, 0800 692 378 (New Zealand only); e-mail: bestpass@tranzrail.co.nz; www.bestpass.co.nz.

Travel Pass: New Zealand Travel Pass Ltd, tel: 03 961 5245, 0800 339 966 (New Zealand only); e-mail: res@travelpass.co.nz; www.travelpass.co.nz.

Passes can be bought direct or at visitor information centres and travel agents locally.

Tickets can be purchased from any Tranz Rail accredited agency, travel agents and visitor information centres.

Tranz Scenic, tel: 04 498 3303 or 0800 802 802 (New Zealand only); www.tranzscenic.co.nz; e-mail: passengerservices@tranzrail.co.nz

Auckland and Wellington both have a commuter train system linking outer suburbs to the central city.

Tranzmetro, www.tranzmetro.co.nz

By Bus

City transport: Major cities all have extensive local bus services for getting you out and about economically. Check with information offices (see local telephone directory) in each town for details of how they operate. Have coins ready, as you usually pay on boarding. Bus passes are also available and are sometimes sold at dairies and local convenience stores.

Inter-city coaches: There is an excellent inter-city coach network throughout the country using modern and comfortable coaches, some with toilets. It is wise to reserve seats in advance, especially during summer months.

The major bus operators are **Intercity Coachlines** and **Newmans**. Travel and information centres throughout New Zealand can book bus tickets and multi-day passes for visitors. Services on main bus routes are frequent but slow. In addition, several smaller bus and shuttle companies operate regional and inter-city coach services. Check with local visitor information centres for contacts.

Intercity Coachlines:
www.intercitycoach.co.nz
Auckland, tel: 09 913 6100
Wellington, tel: 04 472 5111
Christchurch, tel: 03 379 9020

Newmans:
www.newmanscoach.co.nz
Auckland, tel: 09 913 6200
Rotorua, tel: 07 348 0999
Wellington, tel: 04 499 3261
Christchurch, tel: 03 374 6149

Taxis

All cities and most towns have 24-hour taxicab services. Chauffeur-driven cars are also readily available, as are hire cars offering a wide range of vehicle types.

By Car

With New Zealand host to so much natural beauty, driving offers one of the best ways to see the country.
Road conditions: Multi-lane motorways are few – they generally only provide immediate access to and through major cities. Instead, single-lane highways are the norm. While traffic is generally light by European standards, the winding and narrow nature of some stretches of road means you can only go as fast as the slowest truck, so do not under-estimate driving times. Main road surfaces are good and conditions are usually comfortable, the main

problem being wet road surfaces after heavy rains. Roads are generally well signposted.
Petrol: Unleaded 91 and 96 octane petrol is sold, along with diesel, at most service stations. Compressed natural gas and liquid petroleum gas are also offered as alternative fuels.
Motoring Associations: A comprehensive range of services for motorists is available from the Automobile Association, and reciprocal membership arrangements may be available for those holding membership of foreign motoring organisations.
Automobile Association, Head Office, 99 Albert Street, Auckland City, tel: 09 3774660;
www.nzaa.co.nz
Documentation: You can legally drive in New Zealand for up to 12 months if you have either a current driver's licence from your home country or an International Driving Permit (IDP).

Steep Streets

Dunedin in the South Island has the steepest street in the world. Baldwin Street has a 38 percent grade and motorists are advised not to attempt to drive up it.

CAR HIRE

Hirers of cars must be 21 years or over and hold a current New Zealand or international driver's licence. Check with your local motoring organisation before departure if in doubt. Third-party insurance is compulsory although most hire companies will insist on full insurance cover before hiring out their vehicles.

You would be wise to book in advance. Major international hire firms such as Avis, Hertz and Budget offer good deals for pre-booking. If you have not pre-booked, tourist information desks at most airports can direct you to other operators to fit your budget.

The approximate cost per day for car rental of a mid-sized car is

NZ$80–$110 with competitive rates negotiable for longer hires.

Car Hire Companies
Avis:
Auckland: tel: 09 379 2650;
Wellington: tel: 04 801 8108;
Christchurch: tel: 03 379 6133;
Queenstown: tel: 03 442 7280;
Dunedin: tel: 03 486 2780;
www.avis.com

Ace Rental Cars:
Auckland: tel: 0800 502 277;
Wellington: tel: 0800 535 500;
Christchurch: tel: 0800 202 029;
Queenstown: tel: 0800 002 203;
www.acerentalcars.co.nz

Budget:
Nationwide: tel: 0800 652227;
Auckland: tel: 09 375 2220;
Wellington: tel: 04 802 4548;
Christchurch: tel: 03 366 0072;
www.budget.co.nz

Hertz:
Auckland: tel: 09 367 6350;
Wellington: tel: 04 384 3809;
Christchurch: tel: 03 366 0549;
Queenstown: tel: 03 442 4106;
Dunedin: tel: 03 477 7385;
www.hertz.com

Kiwi Car Rentals:
Christchurch: tel: 03 377 0201;
0800 549 4227;
www.carrentals.co.nz

National Car Rentals:
Nationwide: tel: 03 366 5574 or
0800 800 115;
www.nationalcar.co.nz

Rules of the Road

Drive on the left side of the road and give way to traffic on the right. Also, if you are turning left, give way to right-turning oncoming traffic. The wearing of seat belts by the driver and passengers is compulsory.

The legal speed limit on open roads is 100 kmh/(60 mph), while the speed limit in built-up areas is usually 50 km/h (30 mph) – but watch for signposts. New Zealand's signs use internationally recognised driving symbols.

Where to Stay

Accommodation

HOTELS & MOTELS

International-standard hotels are available in all large cities, in many provincial cities, and in all resort areas frequented by tourists. In smaller cities and towns, smaller hotels are the norm.

Motels are prolific throughout the country and are almost always clean and comfortable, with facilities ideal for family holidays. Many offer kitchen facilities and often full kitchens and dining tables to make it possible to have meals in the units. At some motels, a cooked breakfast is available, and the units are serviced daily.

The New Zealand tourism industry uses Qualmark as a classification and grading system to help you find the best accommodation and shopping. There are five levels of grading from one star (minimum) to five stars (best available). Participation in the Qualmark system is voluntary so if a motel or hotel doesn't have a grading, the location of the accommodation and the tariff will usually give a reliable indication. The price bands listed in this guide are for two people sharing a double room; expect to pay surcharges for additional occupants and peak season.

Travel agents are good sources of information and will be able to

Regional Listings

For specific recommendations on Where to Stay, look up the regional listings on pages 335–373.

give details of concessions generally available for children. (A guide is: children under two years of age, free; two to four, quarter of tariff; five to nine, half tariff; 10 years and over, full tariff.) Goods and Services Tax (GST) of 12.5 percent is added to most bills *(see page 318).*

International hotel chains that operate in New Zealand include Flag, Ibis, Quality, Rydges and Novotel in the main centres and resort areas. Room rates range from NZ$200 to NZ$500 per night.

FARM, HOMESTAYS AND BED & BREAKFASTS (B&B)

More New Zealanders are opening their homes to thousands of visitors each year, whether in the form of a B&B, Homestay, Farmstay, Barnstay or Vineyardstay. There are a large number of B&B properties in New Zealand cities, towns and rural locations, ranging from historic and heritage buildings to boutique B&Bs, guesthouses and inns.

For farmstays, visitors may share the homestead with the farmer and his family, or, in many cases, may have the use of a cottage on the farm. This is one of the fastest growing forms of holiday in New Zealand over the past decade and is an excellent way for visitors to see the real New Zealand which has been dependent on pastoral farming since the earliest colonial days. Farming families are usually excellent hosts. Farmstays are also the best way to get to meet local people and experience New Zealand stories. Depending on the farm, you may get the chance to share home-cooked meals with your hosts, join in milking the farm animals, sheep shearing, lambing, kiwifruit harvesting and other farm activities.

If you are on a limited budget, free, working farm stays are a cheap way of getting to know the countryside and the people. Over 180 farms offer free

accommodation, meals and friendly hospitality in exchange for four hours of light work a day, doing tasks such as gardening, chopping firewood and feeding the animals. It is also possible to work flexible hours so that you have time to explore the area. Contact regional visitor information centres for detailed listings or check websites below under "Homestay Contacts".

Homestay Contacts

New Zealand Farm stays and Home stays:
www.nzhomestay.co.nz
Homestay Ltd, P.O. Box 25, 115 Auckland, tel: 09 411 9166.
Rural Holidays New Zealand, P.O. Box 2155, Christchurch, tel: 03 355 6218;
www.ruralhols.co.nz
Rural Tours NZ, P.O. Box 228, Cambridge, North Island, tel: 07 827 8055, fax: 07 827 7154; www.ruraltours.co.nz;
e-mail: info@ruraltourism.co.nz
Bed & Breakfast Collection, P.O. Box 31-250, Auckland, New Zealand, tel: 09 478 7149;
www.bedandbreakfast.collection. co.nz

HOSTELS

The Youth Hostel Association offers an extensive chain of hostels to members throughout New Zealand. Details of their location and membership of the organisation can be obtained from the **Youth Hostel Association of New Zealand**, P.O. Box 436, Christchurch, New Zealand, tel: 03 379 9970 or Freephone: 0800 279 299 (New Zealand only); www.yha.org.nz

---

MOTOR CAMPS

Most motor camps (caravan parks with tent sites as well) offer communal washing, cooking and toilet facilities. The camper is required to supply his own trailer or tent, but camps in larger towns and in the cities have cabins available.

Motor Camps

For more information about motor camps and holiday parks in New Zealand, contact: **Automobile Association**, Head Office, 99 Albert St, Auckland City, tel: 09 3774660; www.nzaa.co.nz
Top 10 Holiday Parks, P.O. Box 959, Christchurch 8015, New Zealand, tel: 03 377 9900 or Freephone: 0800 TOP TEN (New Zealand only); www.topparks.co.nz

Motor camps are licensed under the Camping Ground Regulation (1936) and are all graded by the Automobile Association. It is a good idea to check with the Association on current standards within the camps.

In summer, you would be well advised to book ahead, as New Zealanders are inveterate campers.

What to Eat

General

An abundance, variety and quality of fresh meat and garden produce fill the New Zealand larder with riches on which a world class cuisine has been built.

New Zealand's market gardens are perhaps only rivalled by those of California. Vegetables such as asparagus, globe artichokes and silver beet (swiss chard) – luxuries in some countries – are abundant here, as are pumpkins and kumara, the waxiest and most succulent of the world's sweet potatoes. Kiwifruit, apples, tamarillos, strawberries, passionfruit, pears and boysenberries are shipped all over the globe, but it's also well worth trying less famous fruits such as pepinos, babacos and prince melons.

The seas surrounding New Zealand are the source of at least 50 commercially viable varieties of fish and shellfish – try the crayfish, mussels, paua (abalone) and whitebait.

New Zealand lamb is perfection: dishes particularly worthy of note are crown roast lamb and lamb spare ribs. The beef is excellent too and game is plentiful.

For dishes that have a unique New Zealand style, look out for lamb, pork and venison, kumara (sweet potato), paua (abalone), kiwifruit and tamarillo, feijoa and pavlova – the country's national dessert.

What to Drink

Wine: New Zealand wines win awards all over the world and are well worth trying. The coutry's cool maritime climate and its summer rains produce light, elegant, fruity white wines – and, in recent years, some very fine red wines. See Food and Wine pages 89–93 for more details of New Zealand's wines.
Beer: New Zealanders, with Australians, are among the biggest beer drinkers in the world: many of New Zealand's beers – Steinlager, Speights, Tui, DB Draught, Monteiths – rank with the great beers of Denmark and Germany.

Most nightspots, restaurants and cafés serve liquor seven days a week and you can buy alcohol from liquor outlets and supermarkets (beer and wine only) every day of the week.

Regional Listings

For specific recommendations on Where to Eat, look up the regional listings on pages 335–373.

Where To Eat

There are hundreds of good restaurants in the cities of Auckland, Wellington, Christchurch and Dunedin, and many places in between.

Resort towns also have good quality restaurants and many of them specialise in ethnic meals, most notably Japanese, Vietnamese, Indonesian, Chinese, Indian, Italian and Thai. BYO means "Bring Your Own" bottle, and indicates that a restaurant is licensed for the consumption, though not the sale, of alcohol. At BYO restaurants you are likely to be charged a small "corkage" fee for supplying glasses and a corkscrew.

Culture

General

New Zealand's nightlife options can vary considerably, depending on the size of the place you are visiting. In small towns, you will find little more than a humble pub. Pubs are a great New Zealand social institution and you will seldom find yourself short of conversation or an opinion. In recent years, many city pubs have become more sophisticated, with 'boutique' beer brewed on the premises, brasserie-style food and more fashionable furnishings.

The main cities have a variety of cosmopolitan dance clubs with a predominantly young clientele, as well as late night bars. In Auckland and Wellington, and to a growing extent Christchurch, activity in the bars doesn't peak until after midnight. Auckland and Wellington are busy most nights of the week, while it is a little quieter in Christchurch until Thursday, Friday and Saturday nights. Queenstown reaches a critical mass at times, such as during the winter festival, when the parties don't seem to stop.

New Zealand's culture comprises a blend of cultural influences, including Maori and Pacific Island, European and Asian. New Zealand performers, film-makers, writers, designers and musicians have made their mark overseas with their own unique style and talent.
Museums and Galleries: New Zealand has a vibrant contemporary art scene and most towns have museums and art galleries. Keep an eye out for works by some of the country's top artists including Ralph Hotere, Colin McCahon, Michael Parekowhai and Robyn Kahukiwa. The Dunedin Public Art Gallery is the country's oldest viewing room.

Regional Listings

For specific recommendations on nightlife and entertainment, look up the regional listings on pages 335–373.

Classical Music and Ballet: The country has three professional symphony orchestras including the New Zealand Symphony Orchestra and its own professional ballet company, the Royal New Zealand Ballet. There are a number of contemporary dance companies throughout the country including Black Grace Dance Company (Auckland) and Footnote Dance Company (Wellington).
Contemporary Music: The music scene varies from rappers and DJs to jazz musicians and opera singers. It has produced some world-class performers from Kiri Te Kanawa to Neil Finn (Crowded House) and Pauly Feumana (OMC). Other Kiwi performers making a name for themselves include Pacifier, Bic Runga and Stellar.
Theatre: Theatre is a thriving industry and New Zealand boasts a number of theatre companies including Taki Rua in Wellington and the Auckland Theatre Company. There are venues for live theatre in most towns and cities and strong repertory theatre companies throughout the country.
Festivals: Festivals are plentiful and there are arts festivals in most major New Zealand towns from Dunedin in the South to the Bay of Islands in the North. *(See pages 328–330 for listings.)*
Film: Movies such as Peter Jackson's *Lord of the Rings*, Lee Tamahori's *Once Were Warriors* and the hit cult television series, *Xena, Warrior Princess* have established the country's film-makers as some of the best in the world.
Listings: To find out what cultural event is showing in a town nearest you, check the entertainment pages of the local newspaper or go to: www.artscalendar.co.nz. Other useful sources of information are: the monthly magazine *Theatre News*; *NZ Musician* (modern music); *Music in New Zealand* (classical); *Rip it Up*; *Real Groove* (pop/rock) and *Pulp*, all available at major newsagents or in libraries.

Most major events can be booked through the national ticketing agency, **Ticketek**. There are over 200 Ticketek outlets in New Zealand. Contact: Auckland, tel: 09-307 5000; Wellington, tel: 04-384 3840; Christchurch, tel: 03-377 8899. www.ticketek.com.

Maori Culture

The Maori people were the first to arrive in New Zealand and are the indigenous people of this country or the Tangata Whenua (people of the land). The Maori make up more than 15 percent of the population and most Maori live in the North Island. Maori language (*te reo*) is spoken throughout New Zealand and the vast majority of place names are of Maori origin. As Maori are a tribal Polynesian people, they have a unique protocol which should be observed on a *marae* (religious site). There are many tourist operators in New Zealand, particularly in Rotorua and Tauranga, who can organise *marae* visits. The important things to remember when visiting a *marae* are to take off your shoes before entering a meeting house and greeting your hosts with a "hongi" – a traditional Maori welcome where you press noses to signify friendship. Visitors to *marae* are often welcomed with a *powhiri* (formal welcome) and a *wero* (challenge). Many places in New Zealand have significant historical and spiritual value and are sacred to Maori. Visitors are urged to recognise the cultural significance of these places and treat them with respect.

If you would like more information about Maori culture, visit the following websites: www.culture.co.nz or www.maori.com.

Festivals

January

Auckland
Anniversary Regatta – Annual sailing regatta that celebrates Auckland's birthday (one-day event).
Auckland Cup – One of the biggest days in New Zealand for thoroughbred horse-racing. Held on New Year's Day (one-day event).
Heineken Tennis Open – International men's ATP tennis tour that precedes the Australian Open (week-long event).
New Zealand Golf Open – New Zealand's official golf championship. An open event that features players from throughout Australasia (three-day event).

Christchurch
World Buskers Festival – Some of the world's best street acts converge on Christchurch (10-day event).

Wellington
Summercity – A series of small festivals around the city supported by the local council (two-month event).

February

Auckland
Devonport Wine and Food Festival – A food and wine festival that is one of the highlights of the Auckland summer calendar (two-day event).

Blenheim
Marlborough Wine and Food Festival – Gourmet cuisine, local wine, workshops and music make up this extremely popular festival (one-day event).

Canterbury
Coast to Coast – Longest running multisport event in the world. National and international participants run, kayak and cycle 238 km/148 miles from the West Coast to Sumner Bay (two-day event).

Hamilton
Hamilton Gardens Summer Festival – A celebration of opera, theatre, concerts and performing arts in a garden setting.

Wanganui
Masters Games – The largest multisport event in New Zealand (one-week event).

March

Auckland
Pasifika Festival – The biggest one-day Pacific Island Festival celebrating the Pacific Island culture with food, arts and crafts, music, theatre, comedy and arts.

Taupo
Ironman New Zealand – The longest endurance triathlon in New Zealand. One of six qualifying races for the Ironman Triathlon World Championships (one-day event).

Tauranga
National Jazz Festival – Tauranga's bars and nightclubs come alive with the sounds of jazz during this weekend festival.

Wairarapa
Golden Shears – The world's premiere shearing and woolhandling championships (four-day event).

Wellington
New Zealand Arts Festival – Even numbered years only – New Zealand's premiere arts festival featuring national and international acts (four-week event).

April

Auckland
Royal Easter Show – Livestock competitions, arts and crafts awards, wine awards and one of the largest equestrian shows in the southern hemisphere (one-week event).
Waiheke Island Wine Festival – A new event for wine lovers that showcases the island's vineyards. Located on Waiheke Island in the Hauraki Gulf (two-day event).

May

Auckland
International Laugh Festival – New Zealand's international comedy festival showcases the best up and coming local, national and international comedians (two-week event).

Manawatu
Manawatu Jazz Festival – Live jazz festival at various venues throughout Palmerston North (one-week event).

Rotorua
Rotorua Tagged Trout Competition – Rotorua's premier fishing competition with a NZ$50,000 trout just waiting to be hooked (two-day event).

June

Rotorua
International Rally of Rotorua – FIA Pacific Rally championships in the forest roads of Rotorua (two-day event).

Waikato
Festival of New Zealand Theatre – A biennial national festival of Kiwi theatre held in Hamilton (three-week event).
National Agricultural Field Days – One of the largest agricultural shows in the world held at Mystery Creek (three-day event).

July

Christchurch
International Jazz Festival – Top national and international musicians in a feast of music and wine (one-week event).

Queenstown
Queenstown Winter Festival – One of the southern hemisphere's

biggest and brightest winter parties in downtown Queenstown. The events range from the zany and hilarious to serious mountain competition (two-week event).

Wanaka
World Heli-challenge – The annual gathering of the world's leading snowboarders and skiers in the world's premiere helicopter-accessed free ski and free-ride competition. The two-week event ends with the Wanaka Big Air (free-style ski and snowboard championships).

Wellington
International Film Festival – Three weeks of movie-lovers madness, the festival showcases the year's best cinematic offerings from New Zealand and overseas.

August

Christchurch
Christchurch Winter Carnival – The week-long winter carnival celebrates the great features of Christchurch and Canterbury with featured events, skiing and snowboarding championships, winter "extreme" games and a celebrity charity ball and dinner.

September

Hastings
Hastings Blossom Festival – A celebration of spring. Hawke's Bay is one of the country's leading producing apple exporters and Hastings is known as the fruit bowl of New Zealand. Highlights include a parade and national acts, celebrity artist performances, concerts and other events.

Nelson
Nelson Arts Festival – A showcase of artists from throughout New Zealand in a blend of cabaret, music, theatre, sculpture, comedy and art. A yearly event that lasts two weeks and takes over the South Island city.
Nelson Wearable Arts – A fashion extravaganza of weird and

wonderful designs by national and international designers, craftspeople and artists. Tickets are snapped up quickly for this acclaimed event (three-day event).

Rotorua
Rotorua Trout Festival – A festival that marks the opening of the Rotorua Lakes. Anglers, kept at bay since June, are out in full force (one-day event).

Wellington
Wellington Fashion Festival – The capital kicks off Spring in style with fashion shows and in store promotions (one-week event).

October

Auckland
New Zealand Fashion Week – A showcase of some of the best of New Zealand fashion involving a series of catwalk shows and a trade exhibition (one-week event).

Gisborne
Gisborne Wine and Food Festival – The festival brings together a range of Gisborne wines and the culinary expertise of top New Zealand chefs using Gisborne products (one-day event).

Hawke's Bay
Hawke's Bay Show – One of Hawke's Bay's biggest events, attracting 60,000 each year. Plenty of attractions, competitions and entertainment (two-day event).

Taranaki
Taranaki Rhododendron Festival – This regional garden festival features over 60 private gardens open to the public during the 10-day blooming period for rhododendrons (one-week event).

Tauranga
Tauranga Arts Festival – Street theatre, dance, literature and other performing arts in this biennial event which is staged throughout the region (10-day event).

Wellington
Wellington International Jazz Festival – One of the country's largest jazz festivals representing many different kinds of music from New Orleans, swing and fusion to experimental jazz (three-week event).

November

Auckland
Ellerslie Flower Show – The largest floral exhibition in the southern hemisphere (five-day event).

Christchurch
New Zealand Royal Show – The country's biggest A&P show (agriculture and pastoral) with a programme for all ages (two-day event).

Martinborough
Toast Martinborough – A wine, food and music festival that promotes the quality wine region of Martinborough. A hugely popular festival so get tickets early (one-day event).

December

Auckland
ASB Bank Classic – Leading women tennis players battle it out in this annual tournament. The event features top international and national players (one-week event).

Nelson
Nelson Jazz Festival – Variety of local and national jazz bands saturate Nelson in a week-long festival.

Taranaki
Festival of Lights – New Plymouth's Pukekura park is lit up by lights at night. A festival is held to mark the occasion. The festival lasts one day but the lights stay on for several weeks.

Wellington
Summercity – A series of small festivals around the city supported by the local council (two-month event).

Shopping

SHEEPSKIN

With more than 45 million sheep in New Zealand, it comes as no surprise that among the country's major shopping attractions are its sheepskin and woollen products. You are unlikely to find cheaper sheepskin clothing anywhere in the world, and the colour and variety of sheepskins make them ideal gifts or souvenirs. Many shops stock a huge range of coats and jackets made from sheepskin, possum, deerskin, leather and suede. Car seat covers are popular as are sheepskin floor rugs.

Regional Listings

For specific recommendations on Shopping, look up the regional listings on pages 335–373.

WOOLLENS

New Zealand is one of the world's major wool producers, and experienced manufacturers take the raw material right through to quality finished products. Handknitted, chunky sweaters from naturally-dyed wool or mohair are ideal if you are heading back to a northern winter. Innovative wall hangings created from home-spun yarns make another worthwhile purchase.

WOODCARVINGS

The time-honoured skills involved in Maori carvings have been passed down from one generation to the other. Carvings usually tell stories

from mythology and often represent a special relationship with the spirits of the land. Maori carvings of both wood and bone can command high prices.

GREENSTONE

New Zealand jade, more commonly referred to as greenstone, is a distinctive Kiwi product. The jade, found only on the West Coast of the South Island, is worked into jewellery, figurines, ornaments and Maori tikis. Factories in the West Coast towns of Greymouth and Hokitika allow visitors to see the jade being worked.

JEWELLERY

Jewellery made from greenstone and the iridescent paua shell (abalone) have been treasured by Maori for centuries. Today, you can buy such ornaments and unique contemporary jewellery from specialised stores throughout New Zealand.

HANDICRAFTS

There has been an explosion of handicrafts in recent years – sold by local craftsmen and craftswomen and by local shops catering specifically to tourists. Pottery is perhaps the most widely available craft product, though patchwork, quilting, canework, wood-carving, Kauri woodware, wooden toys, bark pictures, paintings, glassware and leather goods are among the enormous range of crafts available at the major tourist centres.

HIGH-FASHION CLOTHING

New Zealand designers such as World, Karen Walker and Zambesi are making their mark on the international catwalk. Boutique stores in the main cities stock these award-winning New Zealand labels as well as a range of international designs.

Most shops are open from 9am–5.30pm, (Mon–Fri); and 9am–4pm on Saturday and Sunday. Late night shopping (until 9pm) usually occurs on a Thursday or Friday night in cities and major towns depending on which part of the country you are in.

SPORTS & OUTDOOR EQUIPMENT

New Zealanders love the great outdoors so it should come as little surprise that they have developed a wide range of hard-wearing clothing and equipment to match tough environmental demands.

Warm and rugged farm-wear like Swandri bush shirts and jackets are popular purchases, while mountaineering equipment, camping gear and backpacks set world standards. Some items have even become fashion success stories, like the Canterbury range of rugby and yachting jerseys.

FOOD

Savour the taste of New Zealand back home with its natural produce. Processed items like local jams, chutney, pates, smoked beef and honey do not need documentation, and make excellent gifts as they are attractively packaged.

WINES

Wines are a real New Zealand success story. The country's young wines, with their fresh and exciting flavours, are jumping up and demanding attention in the international market. White varietal wines such as Sauvignon Blanc and Chardonnay are consistently well grown in New Zealand. Call in at local wineries or talk to people in bottle-stores or restaurants. They will be happy to guide you in the right direction if you wish to pick up a bottle or two.

Outdoor Activities

General

New Zealanders love the outdoors and there are plenty of places to cycle, walk, swim, ski, bungy jump, fish, play golf or go rafting. Because the country has a low population density and spectacular scenery, there is an outdoor activity to enjoy at nearly every back door.

Summer Sports

CYCLING

New Zealand's windy, rainy weather can sometimes take the pleasure out of cycling, as can the hilly terrain and narrow winding roads crowded with badly driven recreational vehicles. Cycle touring nevertheless offers huge rewards, and some organised tours include a bus to carry your luggage. Mountain bikes are available for rent. Some of the best places for cycling are on South Island, in areas such as **Wanaka, Glenorchy, Queenstown** and the **Fiordland**. Highlights include abandoned gold-diggers' villages such as Macetown, breathtaking ravines in the Nevis Valley, and the roads leading up to the ski resorts, which offer superb lakeland views. One book providing detailed route descriptions is *Classic New Zealand Mountain-Bike Rides* which has over 400 rides researched from Cape Reinga to Scott Base. You can order the book online: www.kennett.co.nz/books/

SURFING

New Zealand is surrounded by coastline, from gentle sloping beaches to rocky cliff access. There are excellent surfing conditions throughout the country from **Raglan** in the North Island to **Dunedin** in the South. Water temperatures vary and the best waves are usually found in the winter months. A wetsuit is required most of the year round, although surfers can get by with a rash shirt in the North during the summer months (Dec–Mar). You'll find clean, barreling waves in the **East Coast** and heavier sets, sometimes as big as 3 metres (10 feet), in the **West Coast**.

For daily weather and surf conditions, up-to-date access to satellite images, surf cams and photographs of some of New Zealand's top surfing spots and information about contests, surf travel and surf stores around the country, check out: www.surf.co.nz or tel: **Wavetrack Surf Report**: 0900-99 777 (New Zealand only) (calls are at premium rates).

WINDSURFING

Windsurfing is a popular sport in New Zealand thanks to the miles of coastlines, harbours and lakes in the country. Wavesailing conditions similar to Hawaii can be found in the North Island province of **Taranaki**. Those who prefer lakes will find plenty of opportunities at **Lake Taupo**, the largest in the country. or on the alpine lakes of the **South Island**.

New Zealand is an ideal place for windsurfing because windless days are few and far between. Other good windsurfing destinations include **Orewa Beach** (north of Auckland), **Piha Beach** (northwest of Auckland), **New Plymouth** and **Makatana Island** near Tauranga, and **Gisborne**. In the South Island, the wind and waves are particularly good at **Kaikoura, Whites Bay** (Blenheim), **Pegasus** and **Sumner** bays near Christchurch, and the bays around **Dunedin** and **Cape**

Regional Listings

For specific recommendations on Outdoor Activities, look up the regional listings on pages 353–373.

Foulwind (Westport). For more information check out: www.winzurf.co.nz.

BUNGEE JUMPING

World-famous in New Zealand, this exhilarating experience of throwing oneself off a high platform with a large rubber-band attached to the ankles, was developed in the 1980s by Kiwi adventurers A.J Hackett and Henry Van Asch.

Today, there are four official A.J Hackett bungy jump sites including the world's first 43-metre (47-yard) site at Kawarau Bridge near **Queenstown**.

Bungy jumps are also offered by other operators throughout New Zealand.

SKYDIVING

If jumping from a ledge with a rubber band tied to your leg is too passé for you – how about jumping from a plane? Tandem skydiving has made this thrill accessible to all. Attached to an experienced skydiver by a special harness, there is little you need to do except follow the instructions and keep control of your fear. The bonus with this thrill is the stunning views offered by the plane ride as you circle up above the drop zone. Operators are found throughout the country but especially in **Queenstown** and **Wanaka**.

PARAPENTING/HANG GLIDING

You can do away with the plane ride altogether if you like by trying parapenting. The approach here is to unfurl a canopy that lifts you from the ground as you take off down a hill. Once airborne you gain height and drift lazily around the sky. Again it can be done in tandem with an experienced operator.

In hang gliding, you are strapped to a giant kite (together with the pilot of course!) and literally run off a mountain.

CLIMBING

Rock climbing has experienced a phenomenal growth in New Zealand. There are now lots of indoor climbing walls in towns and cities, rock climbing clubs and excellent terrain to discover throughout the country. New Zealand has adopted the Australia "Ewbank" numerical grading system which uses a single numerical value to indicate route difficulty. Some of the best rock climbing areas include **Wharepapa**, south of the Waikato, which has more than 700 climbs and the **Canterbury** area which has more than 800 climbs.

For more information, contact: **Climb New Zealand**; www.climb.co.nz.

MOUNTAINEERING

Before Edmund Hillary (a New Zealander) conquered Everest, he practised in the Southern Alps. But even if your ambitions are rather less lofty, you'll find plenty of

Vital Statistics

Highest point: Mount Cook – 3,754 metres (12,313 ft)
Deepest lake: Lake Hauroko – 462 metres (1515 ft)
Largest lake: Lake Taupo – 606 km (234 miles)
Longest river: Waikato River – 425km (264 miles)
Largest glacier: Tasman Glacier – 29km (18 miles)
Deepest cave: Nettlebed, Mount Arthur – 889 metres (2916 ft)
Length of coastline: 15,811 km (9824 miles)

climbing opportunities in New Zealand. Hugh Logan's book, *Great Peaks of New Zealand*, is essential reading; packed full of useful information, it is published by John Mcintoe Ltd., Wellington.

There are numerous mountaineering and climbing clubs in New Zealand including the New Zealand Alpine Club which has a strong nationwide membership. Contact: **New Zealand Alpine Club**, P.O. Box 786, Christchurch, New Zealand, tel: 03-377 7595, fax: 03-377 7594; www.alpineclub.org.nz; e-mail: office@alpineclub.org.nz.

DIVING

Diving in New Zealand's clear waters is an absolute delight, and not surprisingly the country has more divers per head of population than anywhere else in the world. There are many shipwrecks to explore in the **Marlborough Sounds** and **Bay of Islands**, where you'll find the remains of the anti-nuclear Greenpeace ship, the *Rainbow Warrior*, which was bombed by French agents in 1985.

FISHING

From October to April, New Zealand's tranquil waters attract anglers from all over the world. One in four New Zealanders goes fishing, but there are plenty of fish to go round. The best places for trout fishing are **Lake Rotorua** and **Lake Tarawera**. In the **Nelson Lake District**, in the north of South Island, a guide will help you find eels weighing 20 kilos (44 lbs) and brown trout up to half-a-metre (2 ft) long.

GOLF

There are around 400 golf courses in New Zealand, with an average green fee of around NZ$15, and equipment for hire at low cost. The finest courses are in the Bay of Islands (Waitangi), near Taupo

Hiking Hints

Leave the land undisturbed: With an increase in the number of visitors to New Zealand, the impact on the country's natural environment has increased. There are several things you can do to protect New Zealand's environment.
● Do not damage or remove plants in the forests.
● Remove rubbish. Do not burn or bury it.
● Keep streams and lakes clean.
● Take care when building fires.
● Keep on the track when walking.
● Respect New Zealand's cultural heritage.

To find out more information about how you can protect New Zealand's environment, visit the nearest Department of Conservation office or check out the Department's website: www.doc.govt.nz.

(Wairakei International Golf Resort), in Auckland (Titirangi) and in Arrowtown (Millbrook Golf and Country Club).

HIKING

New Zealand has 14 national parks and more than five million hectares – a third of New Zealand – protected in parks and reserves. There are hundreds of walking opportunities on conservation land and other land throughout New Zealand, as well as heritage walks which explore the country's cultural and natural history.

There are nine routes, known as the **Great Walks**, for which you need a pass. These are obtainable from offices of the Department of Conservation (DOC), and cost NZ$7–35 per night if you sleep in a hut during high season (October–April), or NZ$5–10 for a serviced campground (includes flush toilets, tap water, kitchen, laundry, hot showers, rubbish collection, picnic tables and some powered sites).

If you like hot showers and other home comforts, you are best to book a guided walk. But if you don't mind "roughing it" then try independent walking, staying in basic huts and tents. For detailed maps and information on hikes and hiking passes nationwide, contact the **Department of Conservation** (DOC), Conservation Information Centre, Ferry Building, Quay Street, Auckland, tel: 09-379 6476. There are DOC offices in all the main cities or check out the DOC's website: www.doc.govt.nz or e-mail: greatwalksbooking@doc.govt.nz.

Guided walking tours of some of the country's most impressive scenery are available. Contact: **New Zealand Nature Safaris**, Lyttelton, tel: 025-360 268 or 0800-697 232 (New Zealand only), fax: 03-328 8173; www.nzsafaris.co.nz; e-mail: info@hikingnewzealand.com.

Mountain Tops

Did you know that the Southern Alps (stretching more than 700kms/435 miles) are larger than the French, Austrian and Swiss Alps combined?

HORSE-RIDING

Seeing New Zealand on horseback is an unforgettable experience, and without any doubt the best way of experiencing the country and its people at close quarters. Operators throughout the country organise treks which range from half-day to full-day and overnight trips.

RAFTING/JET-BOATING

Wild, untamed rivers and spectacular scenery provide the perfect backdrop for New Zealand's numerous wild water rafting expeditions. Many of New Zealand's rivers are ideally suited to white-water rafting.

Jet-boats, which are fast, manoeuvrable and skim the surface of the water, were invented by a New Zealand farmer. One of the best places for this activity is Queenstown's **Shotover River**. Alternatively, enjoy the thrills and spills of white-water rafting in an inflatable with up to seven other people; some of the most exciting rivers are the Shotover, the **Kawarau** (Queenstown) and the **Kaituna** (Rotorua).

For the less adventurous, try blackwater rafting through the underground caves of **Waitomo** in the Waikato. You'll discover mazes of dark caves lit by glow-worms, waterfalls and endless fun.

SAILING

The best conditions for sailing occur between October and April. You will find the widest range of sailing boats for one-day and longer trips, with or without a skipper, in the **Bay of Islands**, **Auckland** and the **Marlborough Sounds**.

Chartering a fully equipped 12-metre (40-ft) yacht costs between NZ$2,000 and NZ$3,000 a week, depending on the season. One of the most scenic trips you can make is the "coastal cruise" along the coast of Auckland into the Bay of Islands; a 10-day minimum charter fee applies. A day's sailing in a group costs around NZ$60 per person.

WHALE/DOLPHIN WATCH

You can get close to whales at **Kaikoura**, on the east coast of the South Island. Here, huge sperm whales swim barely a kilometre off the coast between April and June; orcas can also be seen during the summer, and humpbacks put in an appearance during June and July.

Rare Species

The Hector's Dolphin (the world's smallest marine dolphin) and the world's rarest sea lion, the Hooker's Sea Lion, are only found in New Zealand waters.

Heli-skiing

Heli-skiing is an affordable luxury in New Zealand: three to five runs a day cost between NZ$600 and NZ$900. There are also week-long private heli-ski charters as well as daily heli-skiing packages tailored to your skiing ability. For details contact: **Harris Mountains Heli-Ski:** The Station, corner of Shotover and Camp streets, Queenstown, tel: 03-442 6722 (year round) or 99 Ardmore Street, Wanaka, tel: 03-443 7930, fax: 03-443 8589 (NZ winters only), www.heliski.co.nz; e-mail: hmh@heliski.co.nz. Harris Mountains Heli-Ski operates in Queenstown, Wanaka and Mount Cook.
Alpine Guides: Bowen Drive, Mount Cook, tel: 03-4351 834, fax: 03-4351 898; www.alpineguides.co.nz; e-mail: mtcook@alpineguides.co.nz.

In the **Bay of Islands**, you'll encounter bottlenose dolphins, orcas and sperm whales.

KAYAKING

With so much water around, both along the coast and in inland lakes, this sport is enjoying a veritable boom in New Zealand, particularly in **Malborough Sounds** and the **Bay of Islands**. You can rent kayaks for guided or independent tours lasting one or more days.

Winter Sports
SKIING AND SNOWBOARDING

In winter, the Kiwis are magically transformed into "Skiwis". Between July and October, as soon as sufficient new snow has accumulated, snow-loving New Zealanders migrate from the water to the mountains. There are 27 peaks higher than 3,000 metres (9,843 ft), and another 140 exceeding 2,000 metres (6,562 ft),

Ski Centres

South Island ski centres are at:
Cardrona: www.cardona.com
Treble Cone:
www.treblecone.co.nz
Coronet Peak and **The
Remarkables:**
www.queenstownwinter.com
Mount Hutt:
www.nzski.com/mthutt
Ohau: www.ohau.co.nz
North Island ski centres are at
Tongariro National Park and
around Mount Ruapehu:
Whakapapa (National Park or
Whakapapa Village) and **Turoa**
(Ohakune): www.MtRuapehu.com
For more information on skiing
in New Zealand, try the following
websites: www.nzski.com;
www.nz4snow.com;
www.snow.co.nz.

and many of the ski resorts have
spectacular views of green valleys
and deep blue lakes far below. The
snowline is usually at around 1,000
metres (3,300 ft), and all the skiing
areas are above the tree-line. This
means there is plenty of space for
everyone, and conditions are
particularly ideal for the very
popular sport of snowboarding.
The main ski season runs from
July to September, though this is
often extended using artificial snow.
A day pass costs between NZ$62
and NZ$71 for adults. Multi-day
passes and season passes are
also available. Ski gear including
boots, skis and poles can be rented
for around NZ$30 a day and
snowboards and boots for around
NZ$45.

Further Reading

History & Biography

**Dictionary of New Zealand
Biography** (Dept. of Internal Affairs,
1990–1998). A three-volume
anthology covering the period
since 1769.
**Maori: A Photographic and Social
History**, by Michael King
(Heinemann, 1984).
Comprehensive illustrated history
by one of New Zealand's foremost
Maori historians.
The Old-Time Maori, by Makereti,
(New Woman's Press, 1986).The
first of its kind: this ethnographic
work, written by a Maori, was first
published in 1938.
**The Oxford Illustrated History of
New Zealand**, by Keith Sinclair
(ed.). 2nd ed. (Oxford University
Press, 1997). A complete
general history.
**Two Worlds: Meetings between
Maori and Europeans 1642–1772**,
by Anne Salmond (University of
Hawaii Press/Viking, 1991). A
fascinating account which attempts
to give both points of view.

Bookstores

Bearing in mind that New
Zealand boasts the highest per
capita readership of books and
periodicals anywhere in the
world, it is well worth paying a
visit to some of New Zealand's
fine bookshops. Whitcoull's is
the country's major bookstore
(and stationer) and offers a good
selection of quality titles. There
is a wealth of reading related to
New Zealand.

Literature/Fiction

A Good Keen Man (Reed, 1960);
Hang on a Minute Mate (Reed,
1961) and others by Barry Crump.
Popular books by Kiwi adventurer.

**Collected Stories of Katherine
Mansfield.** (Constable, 1945) by ,
Katherine Mansfield. This author is
New Zealand's best known literary
export.
Leaves of the Banyan Tree (Lane,
1979); **Ola** (Penguin, 1991), and
others by Albert Wendt. Fine
Samoan novelist, poet and short
story writer.
Once Were Warriors. (Tandem,
1990) by Alan Duff. A first novel
that has been made into an
internationally acclaimed film.
Owls Do Cry (W.H. Allen, 1961),
Living in the Maniototo (G.
Braziller, 1979) and other novels by
Janet Frame; also a fascinating
three-volume autobiography, made
into the award-winning film *An Angel
at my Table*.
Plumb (Faber and Faber, 1978);
Going West (Viking/Faber and
Faber, 1992) and others by Maurice
Gee. Critically acclaimed novels.
The Bone People (Spiral/Hodder
and Stoughton 1983) by Keri
Hulme. Winner of the British Booker
McConnell prize for fiction.
**The Oxford Book of New Zealand
Short Stories**, by Vincent O'Sullivan
(ed.) (Oxford University Press, 1992).
**The Penguin Book of New Zealand
Verse**, by Allen Curnow (ed.)
(Penguin, 1960).
**The Penguin History of New
Zealand Literature**, by Patrick
Evans (Penguin, 1990).
The Season of the Jew (Hodder and
Stoughton, 1986) by Maurice
Shadbolt. The best-known novel of
this prolific and highly regarded
contemporary writer.
The Woman Who Never Went Home
(Penguin Books, 1987); **The
Grandiflora Tree** (Viking Penguin,
1989); **Fifteen Rubies by
Candlelight** (Vintage, 1993), and
others by Shonagh Koea.
Traditional Maori Stories.
Translated by Margaret Orbell.
Edited by Ian Wedde and Harvey
McQueen (Reed, 1992).

North Island

Northland

GETTING THERE

The Bay of Islands is approximately 250km (155 miles) north of Auckland.

Air New Zealand operates daily flights from Auckland airport to **Kerikeri** airport, Northland's main city. The flight time is approximately 45 minutes. A shuttle service is available from the airport.

The **Northliner** operates a daily luxury express coach service from downtown Auckland to the Bay of Islands and to Kaitaia in the far north. Prices range from NZ$44–67 one way. Contact: **Northliner Travel Centre**, 172 Quay St, Auckland, tel: 09-307 5873, fax: 09-307 5882.

The Bay of Islands is 3½ hours' drive from Auckland via the East Coast Highway or five hours if you travel past the mighty Waipoua forest (the largest Kauri forest in New Zealand). See also *Getting Around* on pages 323–4.

CITY TRANSPORT

Northland is well serviced with buses travelling into and out of the region as well as inner-city bus and taxi services in most Northland towns. There are also shuttle services to and from the airports.

TOURISM OFFICES

Kerikeri
Information Far North, Jaycee Park, South Road, Kaitaia, tel: 09-408 0879, fax: 09-408 2546; www.northland.org.nz; e-mail: kaitaiainfo@xtra.co.nz.

Paihia
Bay of Islands Information Centre, The Wharf, Marsden Road, Paihia, tel: 09-402 7345; www.fndc.govt.nz; e-mail: visitorinfo@fdnc.govt.nz.

Whangarei
Whangarei Visitor Information Centre, Tarewa Park, tel: 09-438 1079, fax: 09-438 2943; www.whangareinz.co.nz; e-mail: whangarei@clear.net.nz.

WHERE TO STAY

Kerikeri
Kerikeri Homestead Motel, 17 Homestead Road, Kerikeri, tel: 09-407 7063, fax: 407 7656; e-mail: kerikerihomestead@xtra.co.nz. 12 boutique units (max occ. 4), all with cooking facilities. Four units have spa baths. Close to a restaurant and bar in a quiet and tranquil area. Has great views of Kerikeri Golf Course. Huge pool and outdoor spa. **$–$$**

Sommerfields Lodge, Inlet Road, Kerikeri, tel: 09-407 9889, fax: 09-407 1648; www.sommerfields.co.nz; e-mail: hosts@sommerfields.co.nz. An elegant and relaxing retreat surrounded by pine forest, fields and with unobstructed views over Kerikeri inlet. Three super-king or twin bedded guest suites, ensuite bathrooms and private balcony. **$$$$**

Paihia
Abel Tasman Lodge Motel, Waterfront, Marsden Road, Paihia, tel: 09-402 7521, fax: 09-402 7576; www.abeltasmanmotel.co.nz; e-mail: stay@abeltasmanmotel.co.nz. 25

Hotel Price Guide

Approximate prices per night (off peak) for two people in a double room, including GST:

> **$** = below NZ$100
> **$$** = NZ$100–150
> **$$$** = NZ$150–200
> **$$$$** = NZ$200–250
> **$$$$$** = over NZ$250

units (max occ. five), luxury units available, all amenities, two private spa pools. On beach front, 50 metres (164 feet) to restaurant, 100 metres (328 feet) from post office and shopping centre. **$–$$$**

Beachcomber Resort, 1 Seaview Road, Paihia, tel: 09-402 7434 or 0800-732 786 (New Zealand only), fax: 09-402 8202; www.beachcomber-resort.co.nz; e-mail: beachcomberpaihia@xtra.co.nz. A unique resort with 45 rooms (max occ. five). Near post office, town centre and restaurants. Own private beach with safe swimming, tennis courts, swimming pool and sauna. Winner of a 2000 New Zealand Tourism Award. Sea views. Has award-winning restaurant and bar. **$$$**

Blue Pacific Quality Apartments, 166 Marsden Road, Paihia, tel: 09-402 7394, fax: 09-402 7369; www.bluepacific.co.nz; e-mail: info@bluepacific.co.nz. Just minutes from Paihia township, these apartments have breathtaking views of the Bay of Islands. Each unit has full Italian-styled kitchens with whiteware, washing machine and drying facilities as well as a private balcony or courtyard. There are 12 high-quality apartments ranging from one to three bedrooms. **$$$–$$$$**

Paihia Beach Resort, 116 Marsden Road, Paihia, tel: 09-402 6140 or 0800-870 111 (New Zealand only), fax: 09-402 6026; www.paihiabeach.co.nz; e-mail: bookings@paihiabeach.co.nz. Panoramic waterfront views from every suite, studio and private patio. Heated seasonal swimming pool and spa. Spa baths, kitchen and dining facilities. **$$–$$$$**

Russell
Commodore's Lodge Motel, Russell, tel: 09-403 7899, fax: 09-403 7289; e-mail: commodores.lodge@xtra.co.nz. 12 fully self-contained, spacious and luxurious studios which open on to a sub-tropical garden (max occ. 6). There is also a solar-heated swimming pool, children's pool,

spa and barbeque. Situated on waterfront. **$–$$$**

Duke of Marlborough Hotel, The Strand, Russell, tel: 09-403 7829, fax: 09-403 7828; www.theduke.co.nz; e-mail: the.duke@xtra.co.nz. "The Duke" as the hotel is affectionately known, holds New Zealand's oldest license. It has been a haven of hospitality for more than 150 years. This elegant hotel offers 26 rooms (max occ. 3) and superb dining. All rooms have their own ensuite bathrooms and coffee/tea making facilities. There are a variety of rooms to choose from – including waterfront rooms and sundeck mini-suites. Situated on waterfront adjacent to ferry terminal. **$$–$$$$**

Tapeka on the Tide, Tapeka Point, Russell, tel: 09-407 8706; www.tapeka.co.nz; e-mail: blampied@xtra.co.nz. A large beachfront family holiday home with spectacular views. The two-storeyed home is made of cedar and has bedrooms upstairs and a living area downstairs. The house sleeps 10–12 people. **$–$$$**

Whangarei

Central Court Motel, 54 Otaika Road, Whangarei, tel/fax: 09-438 4574; www.centralcourtmotel.co.nz; e-mail: centralcourt@xtra.co.nz. 21 self-contained units close to the shops and Whangarei. Finnish sauna and private spa room available. Licence restaurant next door. **$**

Pacific Rendezvous, Tutukaka, tel: 09-434 3847, fax: 09-434 3919; www.oceanresort.co.nz; e-mail: pacific@igrin.co.nz. A world-renowned holiday resort overlooking Tutukaka Harbour. Features 30 self-contained apartments with a variety of accommodation from three-bedroom suites to one-bedroom chalets. Two private beaches, putting golf, pentaque and swimming pool. **$$**

Settlers Hotel, Hatea Drive, Whangarei, tel: 09-438 2699, fax: 09-438 0794; e-mail: settlers@ihug.co.nz. Set in the centre of the city overlooking the Hatea River and Parahaki. The

quaint Settlers Hotel has 53 ensuite bedrooms with a lounge and garden, a restaurant, spa pool and swimming pool. **$–$$**

Other Areas

Harbourside Bed & Breakfast – Omapere, State Highway 12, tel: 09-405 8246. A beachfront house within easy walking distance from restaurants. All rooms have modern facilities and private decks. The house is close to the Waipoua Forest, west coast beaches and have great views of the sand hills. **$**

Kingfish Lodge, Whangaroa Harbour, tel: 09-405 0164 or 0800-100 5464; www.kingfishlodge.co.nz; e-mail: fish@kingfishlodge.co.nz. A premiere sportfishing resort and exclusive family-owned retreat at the headland of Whangaroa Harbour in Kingfish Cove. Water access only by courtesy scenic cruise up the harbour. 12 deluxe guest rooms on the water's edge. Harbour views, luxury facilities, "dream" beds. Mouth-watering menu of fresh seafood at the Cove restaurant. **$$$$$**

Orongo Bay Homestead, Aucks Road, Orongo Bay, tel: 09-403 7527, fax: 09-403 7675; www.thehomestead.co.nz; e-mail: reserve@thehomestead.co.nz. The historic Orongo Bay homestead is set on 17 private acres (7 hectares) along the coast. Known as New Zealand's first American Consulate, the homestead was built in the 1860s. Organic, tasteful wines, a vintage Austrian grand piano, an underground wine cellar, spectacular sea views and spacious grounds are all part of the package. The lodge boasts super-king beds, private bathrooms, CD collections and gourmet meals by arrangement. **$$$$$**

Waipoua Lodge, State Highway 12, Katui, tel/fax: 09-439 0422; e-mail: tony@waipoualodge.co.nz. Located on the southern boundary of Waipoua Forest, the lodge was built over a century ago as a private residence. The present owners have restored it to include three pioneer-style fully self-

contained cottages. The cottages have super-king and queen bedrooms, ensuite bathrooms, lounge and kitchenette. Fully-licenced restaurant and bar on site. **$$**

WHERE TO EAT

Kerikeri

Redwoods Café, Kerikeri, where Hwy 1 forks to the north of town, tel: 09-407 6681. Good, healthy food from a café located in the vegetable garden of a small farm. **$**

Rocket Café, Kerikeri Road, tel: 09-407 3100; www.rocketcafe.net; e-mail: RocketCafe@xtra.co.nz. An award-winning café that boasts superior indoor and outdoor dining. The Rocket Café has placed an emphasis on family by including a children's menu and playground. There is even a delicatessen stocked with home-made sauces, dressings, mustards and fruit wines. Not open for dinner. **$**

Paihia

Bistro 40 & Only Seafood, 40 Marsden Road, tel: 09-402 7444, fax: 09-402 7908. Situated on Paihia's waterfront, Bistro 40 offers the best of New Zealand's cuisine with an emphasis on good New Zealand wines. Only Seafood, situated above Bistro 40 is a fully licensed casual restaurant, overlooking the Bay of Islands. It serves fresh local seafood. **$–$$**

Tides Restaurant, Williams Road, tel: 09-402 7557, fax: 09-402 7061; e-mail: tides_restaurant@yahoo.com. A restaurant that specialises in New Zealand cuisine. One minute from the Pahia wharfs and opposite the post office. **$**

Restaurant Price Guide

The following symbols indicate average prices per person for dinner, including service and tax:

$ = NZ$9–16
$$ = NZ$17–24
$$$ = NZ$25 and over

Twin Pines Restaurant and Bar,
Puketona Road, tel: 09-402 7195,
fax: 09-402 7193; e-mail:
enquiries@twinpines.co.nz. The
historic Twin Pines Restaurant and
bar is located adjacent to Haruru
Falls. The ultimate dining experience
with a focus on local produce. The
beautiful Kauri building was
originally a family mansion in
Auckland and was built with wood
from Northland's forests. **$$**
Waikokopu Café, Treaty Grounds,
Waitangi, tel: 09-402 6275, fax: 09-
402 6276; e-mail:
waikokopucafe@xtra.co.nz. This
award-winning café is located in a
shady garden at the entrance to the
Waitangi Treaty Grounds. Food
ranges from breakfast and light
snacks to lamb, beef and seafood
mains. Best to book ahead. **$**

Russell
The Gables, The Strand, tel: 09-403
7618; www.gablesrestaurant.co.nz;
e-mail:
book@gablesrestaurant.co.nz. One
of New Zealand's oldest buildings,
The Gables is a restaurant with a
strong Mediterranean flavour. Built
in 1847, The Gables has retained
most of its historic past including
Kauri panelling, open fires, original
maps and old photographs. Despite
the historic architectural features,
the contemporary menu includes
everything from mushroom wild rice
risotto and chicken livers sautéed in
butter and brandy to Louisiana
chicken and ostrich steak. **$$$**

Whangarei
Caffeine Espresso Café, 4 Water
Street, tel: 09-438 6925;
www.caffeinecafe.co.nz; e-mail:
shane@caffeinecafe.co.nz. Judged as
one of the best cafes in the country
for coffee, Caffeine Espresso serves
superb coffee and mouth-watering
meals in a cozy atmosphere. Imagine
sweet pancakes with creamy ricotta
and blackberries, fresh Cajun salmon
and avocado salad or grilled
vegetable and lamb salad
sandwiches. Keep an eye out for one
of their "Caffeine To Go" mobile
coffee units in the main street. Open
for breakfast and lunch. **$**

Killer Prawn, 26-28 Bank Street,
tel: 0800-661 555 (New Zealand
only), fax: 09-430 3131;
www.killerprawn.co.nz; e-mail:
info@killerprawn.co.nz. New Zealand
and Pacific Island cuisine at its
best. Try the restaurant's signature
"Killer Prawn" bowl with an
abundance of prawns and delicious
spicy sauce or a selection of other
tasty fresh seafood. Enjoy a cocktail
or cognac in the main bar or soak
up the sun in the garden bar. **$$$**
Reva's on the Waterfront, Town
Basin Marina, tel: 09-438 8969,
fax: 09-438 0172; www.revas.co.nz.
Reva's offers an extensive menu of
seafood, traditional and
contemporary cuisine as well as the
"famous original" Mexican recipes.
$$

MUSEUM AND GALLERIES

Paihia
Kelly Tarlton's Shipwreck Museum,
Paihia. The museum at the beach
houses an interesting array of relics
salvaged from wrecks around the
New Zealand coast. Decks,
swinging lanterns and sailing
ship sound effects create a seagoing illusion.

Russell
Captain Cook Memorial Museum,
York Street, Russell. Named after
Captain James Cook, the museum
houses mainly local relics of the
early European settlement. These
include specimens of Maori culture,
war exhibits, whaling gear, and
relics of the early traders and
missionaries. Open: 10am–4pm
(Mon–Sat), 2–4pm (Sun), 8am–5pm
daily during school holidays.

Whangrei
Whangarei Art Museum, Calfler
Park Rose Gardens, Water Street,
Whangarei. The only public gallery
in Northland and the permanent
home of the city art collection which
includes both heritage and
contemporary art. Open:
10am–4pm (Mon–Fri), 12–4pm (Sat
and Sun).

Other Areas
Dargaville Museum, Harding Park,
Dargaville. Explore the area's
pioneer and Maori history by visiting
the Gumdiggers Exhibition Hall with
its operational gum chip washing
plant. The museum also houses the
Rainbow Warrior masts and
extensive artefacts from
shipwrecks. Open: 9am–4pm.
Far North Regional Museum,
Centennial Buildings, South Road,
Kaitaia. Collections include a
"colonial" room, Maori artefacts,
and a reconstructed moa display,
also a large room housing the de
Surville anchor and associated
display, and the Northwood
photographic collection. Open:
10am–5pm (Mon–Fri), 1–5pm (Sat
and Sun), and 10am–7pm
Christmas–February (daily).
Kauri Museum, Church Road,

Where to Shop

Paihia
Cabbage Tree, Williams Road
and Maritime Building, Paihia,
tel: 09-402 7318; www.cabbage-
tree.co.nz; e-mail:
cabtree@voyager.co.nz. Winner of
a New Zealand Tourism Award,
this shop focuses on New
Zealand handmade products
including bone and jade carvings,
paintings, sweat shirts, pure
New Zealand wool jumpers, All
Black rugby merchandise and
handblown glass.

Russell
Blue Penguin Gallery, 22 York
Street, Russell, tel: 09-403
7300. A unique shop trading in
local and indigenous Maori arts
and crafts. The gallery stocks an
exclusive range of paintings,
greenstone, jewellery, paua shell,
pottery, books and furniture.

Whangrei
The Strand, Whangarei. This is
the city's premiere all-weather
retail therapy centre with
everything from fine food to high
fashion, gifts and a variety
of services.

Matakohe. A museum dedicated to the awesome and mighty Kauri tree, its timber and gum and to the pioneering settlers of New Zealand. Open 8.30am–5.30pm (Nov–April) and 9am–5pm (May–Oct). Admission charge.

Northland Nightlife

Nightlife is pretty relaxed in Northland but there are plenty of bars and restaurants to choose from. The town of Paihia or the trendy precinct of the Town Basin in Whangarei are probably the best place to go for live music and bars.

OUTDOOR ACTIVITIES

Diving
New Zealand's most interesting diving areas are located in Northland including the **Bay of Islands**. Here you'll find the site of the sunken Greenpeace ship, the *Rainbow Warrior*, which was towed to its present resting place from Auckland Harbour. For bookings and equipment (also covering the Three Kings diving area, 50 km/30 miles from the northern tip of New Zealand), contact **Paihia Dive**, P.O. Box 210, Paihia, tel: 09-402 7551, 09-402 7110; www.divenz.com, e-mail: divepaihia@xtra.co.nz. The **Poor Knights**, 22 km (14miles) off the east coast at Whangarei, is New Zealand's best dive site, with large numbers of mau mau fish and steep coral walls. Contact: **Poor Knights Dive Centre**, Marina Road, Tutukaka RD3, Whangarei, tel: 09-434 3867, fax: 09-434 3884; www.diving.co.nz; e-mail: info@diving.co.nz.

Golf
One of the finest golf courses with the most impressive scenery and views is the Waitangi Golf Club in the Bay of Islands. Contact: **Waitangi Golf Club**, Tau Henare Dr, Bay of Islands, tel: 09-402 7713, fax: 09-402 7713; www.waitangi.nzgolf.net/; e-mail: waitangi@golf.co.nz.

Kayaking
There are over 150 maritime and scenic islands to explore by sea kayak. Coastal Kayakers conduct guided tours of the Bay from NZ$45 to NZ$420 per person. Tours include half-day or three-day expeditions. Contact: **Coastal Kayakers**, Te Karuwha Parade, Ti Bay, Waitangi, tel: 09-402 8105, fax: 09-403 8550; www.coastalkayakers.co.nz; e-mail: kayak@coastalkayakers.co.nz.

Dolphin/Whale Watching
In the Bay of Islands, you'll encounter bottlenose dolphins, orcas and sperm whales. Dolphin Discoveries run regular trips from Paihia and Russell. Contact: **Dolphin Discoveries**, New Zealand Post Building, corner of Marsden & Williams roads, Paihia, tel: 09-402 8234, fax: 09-402 6058; www.dolphinz.co.nz; e-mail: dolphin@igrin.co.nz.

Cruising/Sailing
The Bay of Islands with its myriad of islands and crystal clear water is renowned for excellent sailing and cruising. There are a number of cruises, charters and sailing vacations available in Russell and Pahia. Contact: **Fullers Bay of Islands Cruises**, Maritime Building on the Pahia waterfront, tel: 09-402 7421, fax: 09-402 7831. Fullers conducts luxury cruises, tall ship sailing and dolphin adventures.

Auckland

GETTING THERE

The main gateway to New Zealand is the **Auckland International Airport** at Mangere, 24 km (15 miles) south-west of the city's downtown area. Bus, shuttle and taxi transfers are available into the city. You'll find them lined up outside the main terminal. Shuttles and buses cost about NZ$13–18 and take about an hour to reach the city. A taxi takes about half the time but will cost you about NZ$45.

As New Zealand's largest city, Auckland is well connected by a network of domestic flights, inter-city coaches as well as rail services. See also *Getting Around* on pages 323–4.

CITY TRANSPORT

There is a great inner city bus service and plenty of taxi services to choose from. You'll find taxi stands dotted throughout the central city. A NZ$8 Auckland Pass will give you all-day use of all **Stagecoach** buses, **Link** buses and cross-harbour **Fullers** ferries. You can buy the pass on any Stagecoach or Link bus or at the ferry office or tel: 09-366 6400. For **Auckland Co-operativeTaxis**, contact tel: 09-300 3000.

The Link bus is a convenient way to travel around the inner city. It travels both clockwise and anti-clockwise in a loop travelling through Ponsonby, K Road and the City. It's cheap too – only NZ$1.20. Auckland also has a commuter train system, the **Tranzmetro**, linking the city to the outer suburbs.

TOURISM OFFICE

Auckland Visitor Centre, 287 Queen Street, tel: 09-366 6888; www.aucklandnz.com; e-mail: reservations@aklnz.com.

WHERE TO STAY

Airport Gateway Hotel, 206 Kirkbride Road, Mangere, tel: 0800-651 110; e-mail: gatewayhotel@xtra.co.nz. 52 rooms (max occ. 4). Three km/2 miles to airport. Near town centre and winery. Conference facilities, pool, family style restaurant and lounge bar. **$–$$**
Ascott Metropolis, 1 Courthouse Lane, tel: 09-300 8800; www.theascott.com. In the heart of Auckland, the Ascott Metropolis combines the influences of cosmopolitan Manhattan and Chicago. Elegant one- and two-bedroom suites offer unashamed luxury with separate living and dining

Hotel Price Guide

Approximate prices per night (off peak) for two people in a double room, including GST:

$ = below NZ$100
$$ = NZ$100–150
$$$ = NZ$150–200
$$$$ = NZ$200–250
$$$$$ = over NZ$250

areas, a designer kitchen and breathtaking views of the harbour and nearby Albert Park. **$$$$–$$$$$**
Barrycourt Suites, Hotel and Conference Centre, 10–20 Gladstone Road, Parnell, tel: 09-303 3789, fax: 09-377 3309; www.barrycourt.co.nz; e-mail: barrycourt@xtra.co.nz. 107 units and suites (max occ. 5). Two km/1 mile to city, 1 km/½ mile to beach. Hotel rooms, motel units with full kitchens to serviced apartments, many with grand harbour and sea views. Licensed restaurant, bar and spa. **$–$$**
Carlton Hotel, corner Vincent Street & Mayoral Drive, tel: 09-366 3000, fax: 09-366 0121; www.carlton-auckland.co.nz. 286 rooms (max occ. 3). Close to waterfront. 24-hour room service, hotel shops, currency exchange, doctor. In easy walking distance to most major offices and the main entertainment area of Auckland, The Edge. Executive rooms also available. **$$$$**
Centra Auckland Airport, Corner Ascot & Kirkbride Roads, tel: 275 1059, fax: 275 7884; www.centra.com.au. 242 rooms (max occ. 3). Five km/three miles to airport and 14 km/8½ miles to city. Set in 10 acres (four hectares) of tranquil gardens, the Centra offers the perfect way to relax after a long flight. Facilities include a sauna, gymnasium, outdoor swimming pool, children's play area. **$$$**
Grand Chancellor Hotel Auckland Airport, corner Kirkbride & Ascot Roads, Mangere, tel: 275 7029, fax: 275 3322; www.granda.co.nz; e-mail: enquiries@granda.co.nz. 193 rooms (max occ. 3). Close to airport. Gymnasium, heated swimming pool, restaurant, bar, 24-

hour room service, parking, car rental. Close to golf course. **$$$**
Heritage Auckland, 35 Hobson Street, tel: 09-379 8553; www.heritagehotels.com. 467 luxurious rooms and suites. Transformed from Auckland's most significant and historic former department store, the Heritage is now a landmark building and New Zealand icon. There are two distinctive accommodation wings with full services and facilties including gymnasium, hair salon, florist and all-weather tennis court. The hotel also has a full restaurant and bar. Located downtown, near the America's Cup Village. **$$$**
Park Towers Hotel, 3 Scotia Place, tel: 09-309 2800, fax: 09-302 1964; www.parktowers-hotel.co.nz; e-mail: res@parktowers-hotel.co.nz. 80 rooms (max occ. 3). Central city location near Aotea square. Restaurant, house bar. **$**
Ranfurly Evergreen Lodge Motel, 285 Manukau Road, Epsom, tel: 09-638 9059, fax: 09-630 8374; www.ranfurlymotel.co.nz. 12 spacious self-contained units (max occ. 5). 500 metres (547 yards) to restaurants, 1 km (½ mile) to racecourse and showgrounds. On airport bus route. **$$**
Sheraton Hotel, 83 Symonds Street, tel: 09-379 5132, fax: 09-377 9367; www.sheraton.com. Situated in the heart of the city, the Sheraton has just completed a NZ$20 million dollar refurbishment of the rooms, public areas, health club and restaurants. 411 rooms (max occ. 3). Downtown location. City views, indoor swimming pool, spa, restaurants and bars. **$$$$**
Sky City Hotel, Victoria Street, tel: 09-363 6000 or 0800-759 2489 (New Zealand only), fax: 09-363 6010; www.skycity.co.nz; e-mail: enquiries@skycity.co.nz. 344 rooms including luxury and premiere suites. Heated rooftop pool and gymnasium, restaurants and bars. Located in the Sky City complex, there are a range of entertainment options to choose from, including two on-site casinos. Free parking available. **$$$$**
Villa Cambria, 51 Vauxhall Road, Devonport, tel: 09-445 7899;

www.villacambria.co.nz; e-mail: info@villacambria.co.nz. An elegant historic villa which operates as a world-class bed and breakfast. Voted as the best B&B in New Zealand. Four distinctive rooms to choose from. **$$$–$$$$**
Waitakere Park Lodge, 573 Scenic Drive, Waiatarua, Auckland, tel: 09-814 9622; www.waitakereparklodge.co.nz. A private paradise surrounded by rainforest perched at 244 metres (800 feet) above sea level. Within easy reach of the city centre. 17 suites with modern facilities, library and Kauri lounge. **$$$**

Restaurant Price Guide

The following symbols indicate average prices per person for dinner, including service and tax:
$ = NZ$9–16
$$ = NZ$17–24
$$$ = NZ$25 and over

WHERE TO EAT

Antoine's, 333 Parnell Road, tel: 09-379 8756. Elegant, highly innovative gourmet restaurant located in a busy shopping street containing many other good eateries. The menu offers New Zealand cuisine with French undertones. **$$$**
Bistro Bambina, 268 Ponsonby Road, tel: 09-378 7766. Wild breakfasts lead into good fusion cuisine throughout the day. Relaxed atmosphere, excellent service. **$**
De Post Belgian Beer Café, 466 Mt Eden Road, Mt Eden, tel: 09-630 9330. Highly popular, this bar offers a range of Belgian beers and some of the best mussel dishes you'll ever come across. **$$**
Essence, 72 Jervois Road, Herne Bay, tel: 09-376 2049. One of the city's best restaurants, featuring original "Pacific Rim" (fusion) cuisine. Encased in 19th century walls, Essence is a two-storied restaurant. Private rooms available for larger groups. **$$$**
Euro, Princess Wharf, tel: 09 309 9866. Fashionable restaurant that was *the* place to be during the

Restaurant Price Guide

The following symbols indicate average prices per person for dinner, including service and tax:

$ = NZ$9–16
$$ = NZ$17–24
$$$ = NZ$25 and over

America's Cup yachting regatta. The high-quality food and service continues with the focus on fresh New Zealand produce. **$$$**
Harbourside, Ferry Building (first floor), tel: 09-307 0556. Like the CinCin on the ground floor, this restaurant offers imaginative cooking with the accent on fish. Great view. **$$$**
Iguacu, 269 Parnell Road, tel: 09-358 4804. Large, busy bar and restaurant featuring Cajun and Italian food. **$$**
Kermadec, Viaduct Quay (opposite the Maritime Museum), tel: 09-309 0412. Very good fish dishes. **$$**
Point 5 Nine, 5-9 Pt Chevalier Road, Pt Chevalier, tel: 09-815 9595. Nice décor, extensive wine list, great cuisine and there's even a television in the toilet. **$$–$$$**
Porterhouse Blue, 58 Calliope Road, Devonport, tel: 09-445 0309. Slightly off the beaten track; specialises in fish, including Moreton Bay bug, a species of crab. **$$**
Rice, 10-12 Federal Street, CBD, tel: 09-359 9113; www.rice.co.nz; e-mail: inquiries@rice.co.nz. International cuisine. Mouth-watering recipes derived from 20 types or derivates of rice. Modern and chic, with a stylish bar attached. Try the entrée platter, especially the BBQ pork and crispy vermicelli. **$$**
Rocco, 23 Ponsonby Road, Ponsonby, tel: 09-360 6262. Intimate and cozy atmosphere, modern and healthy cuisine, extensive range of wines. **$$$**
SPQR, 150 Ponsonby Road, Ponsonby, tel: 09-360 1170. One of Auckland's most famous and loved restaurants. Great cuisine, especially the linguini and clams dish. Turns into a popular nightspot once the plates are cleared away. Dark interior, footpath tables. **$$$**

WHERE TO SHOP

Auckland's **Queen Street** is a good place to start. At the top of Queen Street is **Karangahape Road**. The word "Karangahape" translates as "winding ridge of human activity" and aptly describes the bustle of one of Auckland's busiest and oldest established commercial streets. It offers a wealth of interesting shops, together with an ethnic cross-section of Auckland's Polynesian and European communities, with small second-hand clothing and furniture shops competing for business with spacious department stores.

For mainstream international brands follow the locals to the malls, starting at **Pakuranga** shopping centre in South Auckland to **St Lukes**. The suburbs of **Parnell**, **Ponsonby** and **Newmarket** also offer a wide choice of shops. Check out some of the back streets in Newmarket where a wealth of interesting shops await.

Design stores such as **Pauanesia** in High Street, Auckland, stock jewellery and ornaments from throughout the Pacific. There are also plenty of New Zealand souvenir shops up and down Queen Street. Fashionable **High Street** and modish **Vulcan Lane** is where you'll find all the chic New Zealand designer stores including World, Stella Gregg, Ricochet and Zambesi. Don't forget to visit the **Victoria Park Market** with its distinct chimney stack on Victoria Street. This is a market filled with stalls, shops and cafés.

MUSEUMS AND GALLERIES

Auckland War Memorial Museum, Auckland Domain. Set in Auckland's best known park, the War Memorial Museum's exhibitions include a wonderful selection of Maori and Pacific artefacts and carvings. Other sections are devoted to New Zealand's natural history; applied arts (including Asian art); maritime and war history and the history of Auckland. There is also a planetarium in the complex. The Institute administers the Institute Library, Auckland Astronomical Society, an anthropology and Maori Studies section, a conchology section, and the Ornithological Society of New Zealand. Open: daily 10am–5pm.

Auckland Art Gallery, Wellesley/Kitchener Street, Auckland. First opened in 1888. Collection includes New Zealand paintings, sculpture, drawings, prints and photographs from the 1800s onwards. Also an extensive Frances Hodgkins collection; European Old Master paintings and drawings; a small Gothic collection; a collection of 19th- and 20th-century Japanese prints; plus international sculptures and prints. Open: daily 10am–4.30pm. Free guided tours at 12pm (Mon–Fri), 2pm (Sun).

Museum of Transport and Technology (Motat), Great North Road, Western Springs, 5 km (3 miles) from downtown Auckland. Displays include aircraft, a working tramway and railway, vintage cars, carriages, the development of printing and photography, calculating machines from the abacus to the computer, and a colonial village where buildings are preserved and stored. Also houses the remains of Richard Pearse's aircraft which twice flew successfully in March 1903, three months after the Wright Brothers, and "Meg Merrilees", an F-class saddle-tank locomotive constructed by the Yorkshire Engine Co. of Leeds, England, in 1874. Open: 9am–5pm (weekdays), 10am–5pm (weekends and public holidays).

New Zealand National Maritime Museum, Waterfront. First opened in 1993 and proclaimed as a "new generation" museum with no precedent in New Zealand. The museum offers a Pacific Discovery theatre and has 14 main galleries showcasing New Zealand's maritime history. Heritage vessels can also be inspected and travelled on. There are research and library facilities and school holiday programmes for children. Open:

9am–6pm (5pm from Easter to October). Admission charge.

ENTERTAINMENT

New Zealand's biggest city has started to develop its own cultural identity and is home to several dance, and theatre companies, its' own Arts Festival and a newly restored massive theatre, the **Civic**. The entertainment section of the *New Zealand Herald* is the best source of information on current performances. There are also brochures in most shops around the city. Book for major events through **Ticketek** (Aotea Centre, Aotea Square, Queen Street, tel: 09-307 5000).

THEATRE/DANCE

The 700-seat **Sky City Theatre**, which opened in 1997 in the Casino Complex (on the corner of Victoria and Albert streets, tel: 09-912 6000); **Maidment Theatre** (in the university, on the corner of Princes and Alfred streets, tel: 09-308 2383) and the **Herald and ASB Theatres** (Aotea Centre complex, tel: 09-309 2677) are three of the most popular venues for live theatre. The opulent **Civic** (tel: 09-309 2677) is usually used for touring musicals and shows.

Details of performances at various venues by the Auckland's main theatre group – **Auckland Theatre Company** – are available at tel: 09-309 3395; www.atc.co.nz. For the **Auckland Music Theatre Company**, contact tel: 09-846 7693. Amateur theatre groups perform at the **Dolphin Theatre** (Spring Street, Onehunga, tel: 09-636 7322), and also at the **Howick Little Theatre** (Lloyd Elsmore Park, Pakuranga, tel: 09-534 1406).

Auckland is also home to the all-male dance company, **Black Grace**, which boasts some of New Zealand's finest and most respected contemporary dancers, tel: 09 358 0552; www.blackgrace.co.nz.

Concert Venues

The main concert and opera venues are the modern **Aotea Centre** and the **Town Hall** (Aotea Square, Queen Street, tel: 09-309 2677). The North Shore also has a venue – the **Bruce Mason Theatre** – which tends to be used for bigger international music concerts. Bookings tel: 09-488 3133. There are a number of smaller, part-time venues, such as old theatre complexes (in the city centre) that are used for concerts and shows by international DJs and musicians.

Authentic Maori ceremonies and dances are performed daily at 11am, midday and 1.30pm in the **Auckland War Memorial Museum** (Domain, tel: 09-309 0443). Performances last approximately 45 minutes and costs about NZ$15.

BARS & NIGHTLIFE

It's hard to escape the buzz of Auckland's nightlife. Walk along Ponsonby Road, turn left into K' Road, then down Queen Street, and through to the viaduct and you'll discover music pulsating from every doorway. Most clubs have dress codes and you'll find it difficult getting in wearing shorts or gym shoes. Some clubs are discreetly hidden away up staircases or down alleyways and only the locals know they exist. But if you follow the sound of the music, you're bound to eventually discover them. Some of the popular bars include:
Crow, Basement, 26 Wyndham Street, tel: 09-366 0398. Serving the best French daiquiri in town, the Crow bar is also one of the most popular lounge bars in town. It's decked out with large brown leather couches, huge booths and tanks of bubbling water.
Fu and Fu Bar, 166 Queen Street, tel: 09-309 3079. Relaxed hideaway with friendly staff. Good venue for drum-and-bass fiends.

Additional bar space with more room called Fu.
Havana, 8 Beresford Street, tel: 09-302 3354. Latin music from Wed to Fri. Live bands on Sat.
Hobson Street Lounge, 2 Hobson Street, City, tel: 09-307 7030. A small and elegant underground bar in the heart of the city. Hip spot that plays Frank Sinatra and other lounge bar classics.
Hush Lounge Bar, Paul Matthews Road and Omega Street, North Harbour, tel: 09-414 5679. A swish watering-hole in the heart of Albany. Boasts a comprehensive cocktail list, small dinner menu and has a sunny outdoor courtyard.
Khuja Lounge, 536 Queen Street, tel: 09-377 3711. A small bar hidden away up three flights of stairs. Great DJs, soulful jazzy music and excellent Chocolate Martinis.
Temple, 486 Queen Street, tel: 09-377 4866; www.temple.co.nz. For a taste of Auckland's live original music scene, try this small venue at the top of Queen Street. Not as sophisticated as other bars in the city, but provides a relaxed and friendly atmosphere.

OUTDOOR ACTIVITIES

Auckland is the land of outdoor activities. Whether you're an adrenaline junkie or you just want to keep fit, there is something for everyone. You can hurl yourself from the Sky Tower on the end of a bungy rope, climb over the top of the harbour bridge, go sailing or play a round of golf.

Golf

There are numerous links in and around Auckland. Try the Titirangi Golf Club, a top course of tight fairways, deep gullies and subtle bunkers set in exotic trees, native bush and streams. Contact: **Titirangi Golf Club**, Links Road, New Lynn, Auckland, tel: 09-827 5749, fax: 09-827 8125; www.titirangigolf.co.nz; e-mail: manager.titirangi@golf.co.nz.

Horse Riding

On North Island, near Wellsford and 90 minutes' drive from Auckland, Sharley and Laly Haddon organise rides along the beach and also rent covered wagons: **Pakiri Beach Horse Riding**, Rahuikiri Road, Pakiri Beach, Wellsford, tel: 09-422 6275, fax: 09-422 6277; www.horseride-nz.co.nz; e-mail: pakirihorse@xtra.co.nz.

Bungy Jumping

Touting itself as a world-first adventure experience, the 192-metre (630-ft) Sky Jump is a cable controlled base jump with unbelievable views and thrills. Contact: **Sky Tower**, Central Victorian and Federal streets, Auckland, tel: 07-878 7788, fax: 07-878 6266; www.skyjump.co.nz; e-mail: bookings@skyjump.co.nz.

Bridge Climb

For a bird's eye view of the City, try a two-hour guided climb over the Auckland Harbour Bridge. A maze of catwalks and surprising twists and turns add to the thrill of this outdoor adventure. Contact: **Auckland Bridge Climb**, 70 Nelson Street, tel: 09-377 6543; www.aucklandbridgeclimb.co.nz; e-mail: info@aucklandbridgeclimb.co.nz.

Windsurfing

There are plenty of great windsurfing spots in Auckland: from the popular **Point Chevalier** near the city centre, to **Orewa Beach** (north of Auckland) and **Piha Beach** (northwest of Auckland). Winds are consistent but seldom tend to be very strong. You can hire windsurfers from: **Point Chev Sailboards**, 5 Raymond Street, Point Chevalier, tel: 09-815 0683.

Surfing

The best surf beaches in Auckland are on the west coast and include **Piha**, **Maori Bay**, **Muriwai** and **Bethells**. Up north are **Mangawhai** and **Whangaparoa**. Keep an eye on serious rips and tidal changes, especially on the West Coast, which is renowned for its danger spots. **Dial-a-forecast:** 0900-99 990 (premium rates apply).

Coromandel and Bay of Plenty

GETTING THERE

Coromandel

Located about 90 minutes from Auckland and Rotorua, the Coromandel is located on the Pacific Coast Highway. There are two daily flights to Whitianga from Auckland with **Air Coromandel**, tel: 09-256 6500, fax: 09-256 6509; www.aircoromandel.co.nz. There are also daily door-to-door shuttle services between Whitianga, Tairua, Thames and Auckland for around NZ\$55. Contact: **Go Kiwi Shuttles & Adventures**, tel: 07-866 0336, fax: 07-866 0337; e-mail: nzwild@xtra.co.nz. Or drive the 2½-hour scenic and winding route up the Pacific Coast Highway from Auckland. See also *Getting Around* on pages 323–4.

Bay of Plenty

From the Coromandel, you can take the Pacific Coast Highway to the Bay of Plenty. The trip into Tauranga takes one to two hours. Or call **Intercity** and catch a bus to Tauranga from most North Island destinations. Also try **Bayline Coaches**, tel: 07-578 3113.

CITY TRANSPORT

Coromandel

Contact **Coromandel** local visitor's information centre to get the complete list of tour operators. You can also rent a car from **The Rental Car Centre**, 32 Campbell Centre, Whitianga, tel: 07-866 5901. Otherwise both Whangamata and Mercury Bay have taxi services. Contact, **Whangamata Taxis**, tel: 07-865 8294 or **Mercury Bay Taxi**, tel: 07-866 5643.

Tourism Offices

Coromandel
Tourism Coromandel, 516 Pollen Street, Thames, tel: 07-868 5985, fax: 07-868 5968; www.thecoromandel.com; e-mail: info@coromandel.tourism.co.nz.
Bay of Plenty
Tauranga Visitors' Centre, 95 Willow Street, tel: 07-578 8103; www.tauranga.govt.nz.

Bay of Plenty

In the **Bay of Plenty**, you can hire a taxi, rent a car or catch a bus. Contact: **Tauranga Taxis**, tel: 07-578 6086; e-mail: tauranga-taxis@xtra.co.nz.

WHERE TO STAY

Coromandel

Breakers Motel, 324 Hetherington Road, Whangamata, tel: 07-865 8464, fax: 07-865 8991; www.breakersmotel.co.nz; e-mail: breakersmotel@whangamata.co.nz. Tucked away in a reserve bordering on the estuary, this attractive motel has 20 suites with all facilities

Sailing in Auckland

Auckland isn't called the City of Sails for nothing. The best conditions for sailing occur between October and April. You will find a wide range of sailing boats for one-day and longer trips. Chartering a fully equipped 12-metre (40-ft) yacht costs between NZ\$2,000 and NZ\$3,000 a week, depending on the season. Or take a daily cruise on the former America's Cup New Zealand yacht, NZL 40, for NZ\$85 for two hours. Contact: **Viking Cruises**, tel: 0800-724 569; www.sailnewzealand.co.nz; e-mail: nzl40@sailnewzealand.co.nz. Alternatively, take a 2½ hour dinner cruise on a 15-metre (49-ft) yards) yacht around the Auckland harbour. Price: NZ\$90. Contact: **Pride of Auckland**, tel: 09-373 4557; www.prideofauckland.com.

Hotel Price Guide

Approximate prices per night (off peak) for two people in a double room, including GST:

$ = below NZ$100
$$ = NZ$100–150
$$$ = NZ$150–200
$$$$ = NZ$200–250
$$$$$ = over NZ$250

including a private outside deck with furniture and spa pool. The architecture of the motel is shaped like a wave and the units overlook a swimming pool complex with waterfall and large BBQ area. **$$**
Cabana Lodge Motel, 101-103 Beach Road, Whangamata, tel: 07-865 8772. The only motel on the water's edge. Close to excellent fishing, swimming and other outdoor activities. Nine fully self-contained units. **$**
Cathedral Cove Lodge Villas, Harsant Avenue, Hahei Beach, tel: 07-866 3889, fax: 07-866 3098; www.cathedralcove.co.nz; e-mail: info@cathedralcove.co.nz. Eight sea view units (max occ: 6) and eight garden units (max occ: 3). Beachfront accommodation. Short walk to Cathedral Cove. Spa baths, dishwasher and laundry facilities.
Kuaotunu Bay Lodge, State Highway 25, Kuaotunu, Whitianga, tel: 07-866 4396; www.kuaotunubay.co.nz; e-mail: muir@kuaotunubay.co.nz. An elegant beach house located north of Whitianga with beach access. Private deck with panoramic views of the Peninsula. Three bedrooms (two queen and two single). Great winter getaway, open-fire, underfloor heating, ensuite bathrooms. **$$$**
Pacific Harbour Lodge, Tairua Beach, tel: 07-864 8581, fax: 07-864 8858; e-mail: holiday@pacificharbour.co.nz. Island-style lodges set among tropical vegetation with shell-covered pathways to the chalet, beach and nearby restaurants. Spacious units. **$$**
Palm Pacific Resort, 413 Port Road, Whangamata, tel: 07-865 9211, fax: 07-865 9237;

www.palmpacificresort.co.nz. 27 spacious units (max occ: 6), good accommodation for families and tour groups. Close to shops, cafes and a short walk to the beach. Fully equipped kitchen, patio area. **$**
Pauanui Pines Motor Lodge, 168 Vista Paku, Pauanui Beach, tel: 07-864 8086, fax: 07-864 7122; www.pauanuipines.co.nz; e-mail: pauanuipines@clear.net.nz. Located adjacent to a golf course, this award-winning motor lodge has 18 units in nine "pioneer" cottages. All units include colour TV and kitchen facilities. Tennis court and heated swimming pool. **$–$$$**
Tuscany on Thames Motel, Corner Jellicoe Crescent and Banks Street, Thames, tel: 07-868 5099, fax: 07-868 5080; www.tuscanyonthames.co.nz; e-mail: tuscanyonthames@xtra.co.nz. Italian-style motel nestled between beautiful coast and bush-covered hills. 14 luxury units with modern facilities including large ensuite bathrooms. **$$–$$$**
Waterfront Motel, 2 Buffalo Beach Road, Whitianga, tel: 07-866 4498, fax: 07-866 4494; www.waterfrontmotel.co.nz; e-mail: enquiries@waterfrontmotel.co.nz. Apartments, suites, units and a penthouse suite available. All units self-contained with private balconies and spa baths. Overlooking Buffalo Beach. Magnificent sea views. **$$–$$$$$**

Bay of Plenty

Bay Palm Motel, 84 Given Road, Mt Maunganui, tel: 07-574 5971; www.baypalmmotel.co.nz; e-mail: baypalm@clear.net.nz. 16 comfortable units with spa baths. Close to shops and beach. Heated swimming pool. **$–$$**
Oceanside Motor Lodge & Twin Tower Apartments, 1 Maunganui Road, Mt Maunganui, tel: 07-575 5371, fax: 07-575 0486; e-mail: oceanlodge@xtra.co.nz. A premier resort in Mt Maunganui with motel and apartment accommodation. The motel rooms are spacious and feature ensuite bathrooms and kitchenettes. The complex also features lap and hot pools, gym and

sauna and is located close to shops, restaurants and the beach. The apartments have impressive views and consist of ensuite baths and full kitchens (minimum two-night stay in the apartments). **$–$$**
Summit Motor Lodge, 213 Waihi Road, Tauranga, tel: 07-578 7078, fax: 07-578 1354; www.summermotorlodge.co.nz; e-mail: summit@xtra.co.nz. 25 self contained units (max occ: 6). Quiet, private and spacious. Close to the city and Mount Maunganui, surf and shops. Spa pool, games room and laundry. **$**
Te Puna Lodge Motel, Corner Minden and Waihi roads, Te Puna, Tauranga, tel: 07-552 5621; www.tepunalodge.co.nz. A comfortable motel with family-size units. Some with spa baths. Fully self-contained. **$**
The Terraces, 346 Oceanbeach Road, Mt Maunganui, tel: 07-575 6494; e-mail: theterraces@xtra.co.nz. Spacious three-level apartment with full kitchen, laundry and balcony. (Max occ: 6). Close to Bayfair, Baypark Stadium and golf courses. **$$**

WHERE TO EAT

Coromandel

Kaiaua Seafood Restaurant, Coast Road, Seabird Coast, Kaiaua, tel: 07-232 2763, fax: 07-867 3396. Famous for its award-winning fish and chips. Dine in the licensed restaurant or take-away. **$–$$**
On The Rocks, 20 The Esplanade, Whitianga, tel: 07-866 4833, fax: 07-866 4888; www.ontherocks.co.nz; e-mail: dunnland@ontherocks.co.nz. An award-winning restaurant with waterfront views, specialising in fresh seafood, venison and beef

Restaurant Price Guide

The following symbols indicate average prices per person for dinner, including service and tax:

$ = NZ$9–16
$$ = NZ$17–24
$$$ = NZ$25 and over

Restaurant Price Guide

The following symbols indicate average prices per person for dinner, including service and tax:
$ = NZ$9–16
$$ = NZ$17–24
$$$ = NZ$25 and over

cuisine. Rated by Heineken as one of the great Heineken bars of the world. **$$**
Sealey Café, 109 Sealey Street, Thames, tel: 07-868 8641. Set in a charming 1907 villa, with courtyard and verandah dining. Daily changing blackboard of Mexican, Italian, New Zealand and Lebanese dishes. **$$**
Shells Restaurant & Bar, 227 Main Road, Tairua, tel: 07-864 8811, fax: 07-864 9298. One of the peninsula's most popular restaurants and situated next to Pacific Harbour Lodge. **$–$$**
The Grange Road Café, 7 Grange Road, Hahei, tel: 07-866 3502. Mediterranean platters arranged with fresh vegetables and herbs, gorgeous tapenade, artichokes and parmesan-crusted eggplant with pita bread is one of the delicious and cheap meals offered at this laidback café. Courtyard and deck dining. **$–$$**

Bay of Plenty

Bluebiyou, 559 Papamoa Beach, Papamoa, tel: 07-572 2099, fax: 07-572 3790; e-mail: bluebiyou@xtra.co.nz. Enjoy pacific rock oysters, a platter of fresh seafood or a delicious Italian pasta dish at this popular café, bar and restaurant. **$$**
Harbourside Brasserie & Bar, South End of The Strand, Tauranga, tel: 0800-721 714; e-mail: dining@harbourside-tga.co.nz. Waterfront dining at its best. Watch the boats come in while dining on fresh imaginative cuisine. A wide range of mains from lamb shanks Provencale to apple-roasted pork rack. Or try the Symphony of New Zealand's Finest Seafoods. **$$**
Spinnakers Restaurant, Harbourside, Tauranga, tel: 07-574 4147. Set on the water's edge in

the Harbour Bridge Marina. Fine dining with a wide range of dishes from light meals to fabulous platters and a huge variety of seafood. **$$**

WHERE TO SHOP

Coromandel

Alan Rhodes Pottery, State Highway 25, Whitianga, tel: 07-866 3841, fax: 07-866 3815. You might actually catch the potter at work in the paddock at this unique shop. The pottery is made from on-site clay and fired in gas and salt kilns.
The Bone Studio & Gallery, 16 Coghill Street, Whitianga, tel: 07-866 2158; www.carving.co.nz. A comprehensive display of carving, including pieces from greenstone, bone, wood and shell. Displays of carving history, artefacts, tools and raw materials.
Weta Design Store, 46 Kapanga Road, Coromandel, tel: 07-866 8823, fax: 07-866 8060; www.wetadesign.co.nz; e-mail: info@wetadesign.co.nz. An art store with a difference. Weta stocks works by some of New Zealand's finest contemporary artists, including handcrafted timber, glass, ceramics and Maori crafts.
Wilderness Gems, 13 River Road, Ngatea, tel: 07-867 741, fax: 07-867 7884; www.wildgems.co.nz; e-mail: wildgems@wave.co.nz. A warehouse of gems and treasures from polished and carved greenstone to Kauri Gum and petrified wood.

Bay of Plenty Shops

There are several major shopping centres in the Bay from downtown Tauranga to Mount Maunganui's Phoenix Centre, Bayfair and Palm Beach Plaza. Walk the streets of yesterday at the **Compass Community Village** in 17th Avenue West and discover colonial buildings, craft shops and rest your feet at the village café. Tel: 07-571 3700.

MUSEUMS AND GALLERIES

Coromandel

School of Mines and Historical Museum, 841 Kings Road, Coromandel. The life of mining and its impact on a small town are at the heart of this museum. Open daily: 10am–4pm (Mon–Fri), 1.20–4pm (weekends–summer).
Thames Museum, Corner Pollen & Cochrane streets, Thames. Contains effects from colonial Thames and its mining days. Open daily: 1–4pm. Admission charge.
Historic Maritime Park, State Highway Two, Paeroa, tel: 07-862 7121. The history of the Hauraki area is brought to life with historic paddle steamers, working engines and World War II naval craft. Open daily.
Waihi Arts Centre & Museum, 54 Kenny Street, Waihi, tel: 07-863 8386, fax: 07-863 8426; www.waihimuseum.co.nz. The museum features the gold mining history of the Waihi district. The gallery features changing exhibitions. Souvenirs and crafts for sale. Open: 10am–4pm (Mon–Fri), 1.30–4pm (Weekends). Admission charge.

Bay of Plenty

Jenny Coker Studio, 102 Eleventh Avenue, Tauranga, tel: 07-578 8077. A fine art studio of watercolours, pastels and pencil features of gardens, landscapes and harbour scenes. Open: Wednesdays from 9am–4pm. Viewing at other times by appointment only.
Katikati Heritage Museum, 3 Wharawhara Road, Katikati, tel: 07-549 0651. A unique museum that explores the history of Katikati. Has one of the largest bottle collections in New Zealand; over a hectare (3 acres) of grounds and a pioneer kitchen selling delicious food.
Pyromania, the Art Centre, 24 Wharf Street, Tauranga. A co-operative gallery specialising in original work by New Zealand artists and craftspeople. Pottery and sculpture, hand-blown glass,

woodcrafts and jewellery are among the items on display and for sale. Open six days a week.
Tauranga Historic Village, 17th Avenue, Tauranga, tel: 07-571 3700; e-mail: thvm@tauranga-dc.govt.nz. An open-air museum dedicated to the history of the area. Vintage car rides available. Open daily.

ENTERTAINMENT

Coromandel
There are several festivals to choose from including the Keltic Fair every January in Coromandel and the annual Pohutukawa Festival every December. The annual "Coromandel Flavours" Summer Festival in February provides a platform for local produce, seafood, wines, craft stalls, live music and plenty of entertainment. The Thames Wine and Food Festival is held every March.

Bay of Plenty
Tauranga has a vast range of events from jazz festivals, arts festivals and sports marathons. It also has a vibrant nightlife and most bars around the Tauranga and Mount Maunganui region are packed with people during the weekends. The **Baycourt Theatre** in Tauranga hosts a number of exhibitions, festivals and events, tel: 07-577 7198.

OUTDOOR ACTIVITIES

Bushwalks
Kiwi Dundee Adventures, Pauanui, Tairua and Whangamata, tel: 07-865 8809; e-mail: kiwi-dundee@xtra.co.nz. Doug and Jan are regarded as two of New Zealand's foremost guides. They offer personalised walks, hikes and tours. The three-day tour from Auckland is their most popular.

For general information on walking tracks, forest parks, reserves, campgrounds and hunting permits, contact the **Department of Conservation**, tel: 07-867 9080.

Scenic Tours
Cave Cruzer Adventures, tel: 07-866 2275 or 0800-427 893 (New Zealand only); www.cavecruzer.co.nz. Explore the Coromandel's scenic coastline in an ex-Navy inflatable rescue boat. Head into the Waitaia sea cave to hear the amazing acoustics of dolphins and whales calling, live African drumming, digeridoo and Maori instrument demonstrations. A three-hour tour costs about NZ$80. Departs daily from Whitianga Wharf.
Hahei Explorer, tel: 07-866 3910, fax: 07-866 3921. Daily adventure boat trips in the Hahei Marine Reserve, viewing the world-famous Cathedral Cove, islands, reefs and sea caves. Snorkel gear also available for hire.

Fishing
Water Edge Charters, Whitianga, tel: 07-866 5760; e-mail: waters.edge@paradise.net.nz. Experienced skipper Craig Donovan will take you out for a spot of bottom fishing, game fishing, diving and/or scenic tours. Bait and tackle supplied. Toilet and shower on board.

Fly-fishing expert Scott Hollis-Johns has a wealth of knowledge about the area and can assist anyone from a novice to an expert to catch a fish in both fresh and salt water, tel: 07-543 0555; e-mail: fishart@xtra.co.nz. **Mission Charters** also offers superb fishing expeditions, tel: 07-549 0055.

Golf
Mercury Bay Golf & Country Club, Golf Road, Whitianga, tel: 07-866 5479. An 18-hole course north of Thames. Idyllic surroundings with level walking. Food and bar facilities on site.

Swimming with Dolphins
The **Tauranga Dolphin Company** offers a unique and natural experience with wild dolphins. Masks, fins, wetsuits and snorkels supplied. Expect to see huge pods of bottlenose and common dolphins and a range of whale species, tel: 07-578 3197; e-mail: taurangadolphins@clear.net.nz.

Gold-mining

Thames Goldmine & Stamper Battery, Main Road, State Highway 25, tel: 07-868 8514; e-mail: rskeet@xtra.co.nz. The heart of the gold mining district, this unique attraction offers guided tours underground and through the stamper battery, a photo museum and gold panning. Open 10am–4pm.

Waikato

GETTING THERE

Hamilton
The main city, Hamilton, is located about two hours south of Auckland. There are bus services from most cities and towns to and from Hamilton. **Hamilton International Airport** is located about 15kms (9 miles) south of Hamilton city. The airport provides daily flights to and from major New Zealand cities.

Freedom Air International flies passengers direct to Hamilton from Australia's Gold Coast. A no-frills airline, it also has regular flights to and from Auckland, Palmerston North, Wellington, Christchurch and Dunedin.

Hamilton is also on the main trunk line with daily rail services by the **Overlander** and the **Northerner** between Auckland and Wellington. Journey time is slightly over two hours. See also *Getting Around* on pages 323–4.

CITY TRANSPORT

Hamilton
Hamilton City is serviced by excellent inner city bus and taxi services. There are also plenty of rental car agencies in Hamilton. **Hamilton City Buses**, tel: 07-846 1975
Hamilton Taxis, tel: 07-847 7477, fax: 07-847 8698; www.hamiltontaxis.co.nz; e-mail: info@hamiltontaxis.co.nz

TOURISM OFFICE

Hamilton
Hamilton Visitor Information Centre, Transport Centre, Anglesea Street, Hamilton, tel: 07-839 3580, fax: 07-839 3127; e-mail: hamiltoninfo@wave.co.nz.

WHERE TO STAY

Hamilton
Anglesea Motel, 36 Liverpool Street, Hamilton, tel: 07-834 0010, fax: 07-834 3310; www.angleseamotel.co.nz; e-mail: anglesea.motel@xtra.co.nz. A five-star hotel close to the city centre and sports grounds. Studio and one-bedroom units with modern facilities. Swimming pool, gym, squash and tennis courts. **$$–$$$**
Brooklands Country Estate, Ngaruawahia, Waikato, tel: 07-825 4756, fax: 07-825 4873; www.brooklands.net.nz; e-mail: relax@brooklands.net.nz. Beautiful décor, fine paintings, alfresco dining, large open fireplaces. Brooklands was originally the gracious homestead of a pioneer farming family. Today, it has a reputation for being one of the finest lodges in New Zealand. Exceptional cuisine, 10 sumptuous rooms with French doors overlooking the garden, tennis court and swimming pool. **$$$$$**
Novotel Tainui Hamilton, Alma Street, Hamilton, tel: 07-838 1366, fax: 07-838 1367; www.novotel.co.nz; e-mail: hamilton@novotel.co.nz. A four-star international hotel located on the banks of the Waikato River in the heart of the CBD. 177 luxury

Hotel Price Guide

Approximate prices per night (off peak) for two people in a double room, including GST:
$ = below NZ$100
$$ = NZ$100–150
$$$ = NZ$150–200
$$$$ = NZ$200–250
$$$$$ = over NZ$250

accommodation rooms, restaurant and bar, gymnasium, spa and sauna. **$$$**
Quality Hotel, 100 Garnett Avenue, Hamilton, tel: 07-849 0860, fax: 07-849 0660; e-mail: qualityhamilton@xtra.co.nz. 147 rooms with air-conditioning, ensuite bathrooms and 24-hour room service. In the city centre. **$$**
Ventura Inn and Suites Hamilton, 23 Clarence Street, Hamilton, tel: 07-838 0110, fax: 07-838 0120; www.venturinns.co.nzs; e-mail: reservations@venturinns.co.nz. Central city location. 50 rooms with modern facilties (max occ. 3). Some rooms with king beds and spa baths. **$–$$**
Waitomo Caves Hotel, Lemon Point Road, Waitomo Village, tel: 07-878 8204, fax: 07-878 8205; www.waitomocaveshotel.co.nz; e-mail: waitomo_hotel@xtra.co.nz. 37 rooms (max occ. 3). Victorian-style hotel close to limestone caves. Relax in the bar or dine at the Chandelier Restaurant. 19 km/12 miles from Te Kuiti. **$$**

WHERE TO EAT

Hamilton
Montana Restaurant, 131 Victoria Street, Hamilton, tel: 07-839 3459. With an extensive menu. One of the oldest restaurants in Hamilton. Has a "cuisine courier" service available. **$$**
Out in the Styx, 2117 Arapuni Road, Te Awamutu, tel: 0800-461 559 (New Zealand only). A bed and breakfast retreat that also has a superb fully licensed restaurant focusing on New Zealand cuisine. The menu is set and consists of good stylish country fare. Three courses for NZ$35 plus coffee. **$$$**
Roselands, Fullerton Road, Waitomo Caves, tel: 07-878 7611, fax: 07-878 7610; e-mail: roselands@xtra.co.nz. An award-winning restaurant set amongst native bush in a rural landscape. The menu is mouthwatering and prepared from fresh produce. Lunch menu only. Try the Kiwi Barbeque style lunch. **$$**

Restaurant Price Guide

The following symbols indicate average prices per person for dinner, including service and tax:
$ = NZ$9–16
$$ = NZ$17–24
$$$ = NZ$25 and over

Sahara Tent Café & Bar, 254 Victoria Street, Hamilton, tel: 07-834 0409, fax: 07-834 2504; e-mail: sarahtent@xtra.co.nz. A huge range of middle-eastern dishes with authentic and western eating areas. There's even a belly dancer thrown in for good measure. **$**
Thai Village Café, The Market Place, Hood Street, Hamilton, tel: 07-834 9960. The best of Thai cuisine in authentic surroundings. Wide range of curries, rice and noodle dishes. Good servings, cheap prices. **$**
The Narrows Landing, 431 Airport Road, Hamilton, tel: 07-858 4001. Gourmet cuisine with New Zealand and European influences. A medieval feel to the restaurant is enhanced by huge wooden doors, lots of iron, a metal mesh staircase and plenty of candlelight. **$$$**

WHERE TO SHOP

Hamilton
Bel Merino New Zealand, Upstairs, Central Place Shopping Centre, Victoria Street, Hamilton, tel: 07-839 5547. Quality souvenirs ranging from sheepskin products to kauri woodware made from 100-year-swamp Kauri. The centre also stocks All Black merchandise, greenstone and paua jewellery and kids' toys.
Cambridge Country Store, 92 Victoria Street, Cambridge, tel: 07-827 8715, fax: 07-827 7247. An award-winning showcase for New Zealand craft housed in a 100-year old church in picturesque Cambridge.
Heritage Gallery, Upper Victoria Street, State Highway 1, Cambridge, tel: 07-827 4346. A unique gift gallery featuring pottery, handblown glass, souvenirs, handmade jewellery and toys.

MUSEUMS AND GALLERIES

Hamilton

Artspost, 120 Victoria Street, Hamilton. Hamilton's community arts centre located in the old Post & Telegraph Office. Extensively renovated, the building houses the Hamilton Community Arts Council, Waikato Society of Arts and a wealth of local artistic talent on display. Open: 10am–4.30pm (Mon–Fri), 10am–5pm Saturday, 11am–5pm Sunday.

New Zealand Expressions, Hillcrest Road, Tirau. An art gallery promoting art excellence in New Zealand. The exclusive unique pieces, which include paintings, carvings, handcarved whale teeth, carved gourds and scented soaps, reflect New Zealand's bi-culturalism. Goods for sale. Open daily.

Waikato Museum of Art and History, corner of Victoria and Grantham streets, Hamilton. This handsome, five-storey building takes full advantage of its riverbank location. The restored Maori war canoe, Te Winika, and contemporary Tainui carving and *tukutuku* weaving are on permanent display. A changing programme of exhibitions draws on the museum's large collection of New Zealand fine art, Tainui and Waikato history. National and international touring exhibitions also feature regularly. Open daily: 10am–4.30pm.

ENTERTAINMENT

Hamilton

Hamilton has a variety of entertainment on offer – from arts and film festivals to live theatre, music and dance. National and international touring groups visit Hamilton and have a choice of three venues to perform at – **Founders Theatre**, the **WestpacTrust Community Theatre** and **The Meteor**, tel: 07-838 6603.

Check out the Flaming Fringe Festival or the Festival of New Zealand Theatre held in Hamilton

in June. Hamilton has an abundance of nightclubs and bars. Some of the top DJs from Auckland often travel to Hamilton to perform as it is only a two-hour drive south from the Queen City.

OUTDOOR ACTIVITIES

Surfing

Raglan Beach is a popular seaside resort on the Waikato's rugged West Coast. The point breaks *Indicators* and *Manu* are the fastest and best surfing spots in Raglan while *Whale Bay* tends to provide a slower ride.

Climbing

Wharepapa, south of the Waikato, is one of the best rock climbing areas in New Zealand. There are over 800 routes, short easy walks to the climb and a nearby equipment store. Wharepapa South is located between Te Awamutu and Mangakino. For accommodation, equipment and climbing information about Wharepapa, contact the **Wharepapa Outdoor Centre**, tel: 07-872 2533 or e-mail: wharerock@xtra.co.nz.

Balloon Rides

The ultimate experience in flight. Take off after sunset and coast over the Waikato farmland and river. Flights usually take about four hours. Contact: **Max's Balloon Adventures**, tel: 549 1614, fax: 549 1638.

Rafting

Try blackwater rafting through the underground caves of **Waitomo** in the Waikato. You'll discover mazes of dark caves lit by glow-worms, waterfalls and endless fun. Contact: **Blackwater Rafting**, P.O. Box 13, Waitomo Caves, tel: 07-878 6219, fax: 07-878 5190; www.blackwaterrafting.co.nz. e-mail: info@blackwaterrafting.co.nz.

Abseiling/Caving

In the magnificent **Magapu** cave system near Waitomo, you can abseil down 100-metre (330-ft)

vertical faces. Training is provided beforehand to dispel any anxieties you may have. Contact **Waitomo Adventures Limited**, tel: 07-878 7640, fax: 07-878 6184.

Rotorua

GETTING THERE

A great way to see the countryside is to take the **Geyserland** service (a combination of train and bus) between Rotorua and Auckland. The journey takes just over four hours and departs from Rotorua and Auckland daily. Contact Tranz Scenic for more information. Otherwise, **Air New Zealand** has flights in and out of Rotorua. The airport is about 15 minutes from the centre of Rotorua. You can also catch one of a number of inter-city bus coaches in and out of all major New Zealand destinations. See also *Getting Around* on pages 323–4.

Rotorua City Transport

There are plenty of shuttle services that will take you around all the volcanic "hot spots" of Rotorua. **Carey's Sightseeing**, will take you on a morning Geothermal Wonderland Tour for about NZ$70, tel: 07-347 1197. There is a good public bus service and plenty of taxis available. Contact: **Rotorua Taxis**, tel: 07-348 1111 or **Super Shuttle Rotorua**, tel: 07-349 3444.

TOURISM OFFICE

Tourism Rotorua Travel Office, 1167 Fenton Street, Rotorua, tel: 0800 ROTORUA (New Zealand only) or 07-768 678; www.rotoruanz.com.

WHERE TO STAY

Acapulco Motel, corner Malfroy Road and Eason Street; tel: 07-347 9569, fax: 07-347 9568. 15 rooms (max occ. 5). Quiet location near city centre. 500 metres (547 yards) from restaurant and shops. **$**

Hotel Price Guide

Approximate prices per night (off peak) for two people in a double room, including GST:

$ = below NZ$100
$$ = NZ$100–150
$$$ = NZ$150–200
$$$$ = NZ$200–250
$$$$$ = over NZ$250

Birchwood Spa Motel, Corner Sala Street and Trigg Avenue, tel: 07-347 1800, fax: 07-347 1900; www.birchwoodspamotel.co.nz. 13 luxury units all with spa baths or spa pools. Close to thermal reserve and golf course. **$–$$**

Gibson Court Motel, 10 Gibson Street; tel: 07-346 2822, fax: 07-348 9481; www.gibsoncourtmotel.co.nz. 10 rooms (max occ. 4). 1 km/½ mile to thermal reserve. Private authentic mineral pools with some units. Spacious rooms, central heating. A short drive to the racecourse. **$**

Lake Plaza Rotorua Hotel, Lake end of Eruera Street; tel: 07-348 1174, fax: 07-346 0238; www.lakeplazahotel.co.nz. 250 rooms (max occ. 4). Opposite Polynesian Pools. Superb views of the lake and thermal areas. 500 metres (547 yards) to city centre. Golf packages available. **$$**

Millennium Rotorua, corner of Eruera and Hinemaru streets, tel: 07-347 1234; www.cdlhotels.com. Ask for a room overlooking the Polynesian Pools and Lake Rotorua. You get a great view from the balcony. Friendly staff and good facilities including gym and pool. **$$$**

Muriaroha Lodge, 411 Old Taupo Road, tel: 07-346 1220, fax: 07-346 1338; www.muriarohalodge.co.nz; e-mail: muriaroha_lodge@clear.net.nz. Five rooms (max occ. 4). Luxury accommodation with private mineral pools. Charming guest house set in acres of landscaped grounds, 3 km/2 miles to centre. **$$$$$**

Okawa Bay Resort, Mourea, Lake Rotoiti, tel: 07-362 4599, fax: 07-362 4594; www.okawabay.co.nz; e-mail: info@okawabay.co.nz. 42 rooms (max occ. 3). Award-winning resort on the shores of Lake Rotoiti: trout fishing, water skiing. Conference facilities. **$$$**

Quality Hotel Rotorua, Fenton Street, tel: 07-348 0199, fax: 07-346 1973; www.qualityrotorua.co.nz; e-mail: quality.rotorua@mcqhotels.co.nz. 133 rooms (max occ. 3) with modern facilities. Adjacent to racecourse, sports ground and golf courses. A famous and well-photographed bronze statue of a Maori warrior in the traditional challenge posture greets visitors at the entrance of the hotel. **$$**

Silver Fern Motor Inn, 326 Fenton Street, Rotorua, tel: 07-346 3849; www.silverfernmotorinn.co.nz; e-mail: silverfernmotorinn@xtra.co.nz. A touch of California. 20 executive suites with spa pools, modern facilities. Central city location. **$$**

Solitaire Lodge, Road 5, Lake Tarawera, tel 07-362 8208, fax: 07-362 8445; www.solitairelodge.co.nz; e-mail: solitaire@sth.com. 10 suites (max occ. 4). Luxury accommodation. Stunning lake-edge location. Superb views, timber cathedral ceilings in each suite, large beds, private deck, spacious bathroom, open fire in the main lounge. **$$$$$**

Wylie Court Motor Lodge, 345 Fenton Street, tel: 07-347 7879, fax: 07-346 1494; e-mail: wyliroto@fc-hotels.co.nz. 36 rooms (max occ. 6) with private heated pools in a resort-style complex set in park-like grounds. Modern facilities including large heated swimming pool. **$$–$$$**

WHERE TO EAT

Bistro 1284, 1284 Eruera Street, Rotorua, tel: 07-346 1284; e-mail: Bistro1284@paradise.net.nz. An award-winning restaurant set in a historic 1930s building in Rotorua. **$$–$$$**

Japanese Sushi Bar, 1139 Tutanekai Street, Rotorua, tel: 07-346 0792; e-mail: jpsushiroto@clear.net.nz. Authentic Japanese cuisine including sushi, teriyaki, tempura, miso chicken and vegetarian options. **$$**

Poppy's Villa, 4 Marguerita Street, Rotorua, tel: 07-347 1700. A fine-dining restaurant serving quality New Zealand cuisine and wine in an Edwardian villa. Has won awards for its beef and lamb dishes. **$$**

The Landing Café, Lake Tarawera, tel: 07-362 8595, fax: 07-362 8883; www.purerotorua.com. Nestled on the shores of Lake Tarawera, this famous café is heavily themed around the lake's famous Pink & White Terraces, the Tarawera eruption and trout memorabilia. Features a mouth-watering menu comprising traditional winter fare like venison, bacon & mushroom pie to more delicate summer dishes such as scallops in a boysenberry sauce. Huge open fire setting and rich interior colours. **$$$**

Zanelli's, 23 Amohia Street, tel: 07-348 4908. Deservedly popular, Italian restaurant. Famous for their mussels topped with garlic and crumb gratin. **$$$**

Restaurant Price Guide

The following symbols indicate average prices per person for dinner, including service and tax:

$ = NZ$9–16
$$ = NZ$17–24
$$$ = NZ$25 and over

WHERE TO SHOP

With attractive cobble stone paved streets, Rotorua provides an abundance of shops from clothing and fashion to souvenir, food and pharmacies. Tutanekai and Hinemoa are the streets to visit while City Focus square is within walking distance. There are souvenir shops galore in the city including **The Jade Factory** in Fenton Street, tel: 07-349 3968, which showcases quality jade from throughout New Zealand and the world; **The Souvenir Centre**, tel: 07-348 9515, also in Fenton Street, stocks a wide range of New Zealand arts and crafts.

MUSEUMS AND GALLERIES

Blue Baths, next to the Rotorua Museum. The Blue Baths are one of New Zealand's most loved buildings. Located next to the Rotorua Museum, the Spanish-style baths were opened in 1933. They were closed in 1981 after 48 years of operation and have since been meticulously restored. The pool area and café are open to visitors daily 10am–6pm. Times vary in winter.

Buried Village, tel: 07-362 8287; www.buriedvillage.co.nz. A living museum commemorated to the buried village of Te Wairoa which was destroyed when Mt Tarawera erupted in 1886. Visit the excavation sites of the village, take a guided tour with descendents of the Maori people who lived in the village prior to the eruption or wander around the world-class museum. Open daily from 9am.

Rotorua Museum, tel: 07-349 8334; www.rotoruamuseum.co.nz. Located in the world-famous Bath House building in the Government Gardens, the award-winning Rotorua Museum houses a number of collections tracing the development of painting and print making in New Zealand. On exhibit are works by famous New Zealand painters, plus an impressive collection of images of the Maori in paintings and portraits. The museum boasts a collection of 6,000 prints of the volcanic plateau area, and a colonial cottage reflecting the period 1870–1900 when Rotorua was settled by Europeans. A new wing has also been dedicated to the local Te Arawa Maori people and portrays a wide variety of their artefacts. Open daily: 9.30am–6pm. Times vary in the winter.

Tamaki Maori Village, Taupo Highway Five, tel: 07-347 2913; www.maoriculture.co.nz; e-mail: tamaki@wave.co.nz. A cultural journey back to the *marae* (Maori Village) where you'll experience the protocol and customs of Maori, including a *hangi* (food cooked in the ground) and even get to stay in a traditional *wharemoe* (sleeping house). A great way to experience Maori culture first-hand.

ENTERTAINMENT

You'll find nightclubs and bars throughout Rotorua. The most popular are **Ace of Clubs** in Ti Street, tel: 07-346 2204 and the **Lava Bar** in Arawa Street, tel: 07-348 8618. The **Civic Theatre** is a popular venue for Kapa Haka and performing arts and there are plenty of Maori concerts and shows on throughout Rotorua. Rotorua is also home to the famous **Opera In The Pa** concerts in January at Rotowhio Marae. For more information, contact the **Tourism Rotorua Travel Office**, tel: 0800 ROTORUA (New Zealand only) or 07-768 678.

OUTDOOR ACTIVITIES

Trout Fishing

There are plenty of trout fishing guides and companies to hire in Rotorua. **Down to Earth Trout Fishing** offers lake-edge and boat-fishing with a professional guide, tel: 07-362 0708. Maori guide, **Greg Tuuta**, also has plenty of local knowledge and specialises in trolling, harling and jigging. Check out his "no fish no pay" policy, tel: 07-362 7794, fax: 07-362 7792.

Hot Springs

Frying Pan Lake near Rotorua is the world's largest hot water spring, reaching a temperature of 200 ˚C (392 ˚F) at its deepest point.

Rafting/Jet boating

Kaituna Cascades, Trout Pool Road, Okere Falls, tel; 07-345 4199, fax: 07-345 9533; e-mail: kaituna@cascades.clear.net.nz. Offers day- and multi-day rafting and kayaking adventures down the Kaituna, Wairoa, Rangitaiki and Motu rivers. The company has

Zorbing

Roll downhill cushioned inside a huge inflated ball at Rotorua – the home of zorbing. Try it harnessed inside the Dry Zorb or loose in the Wet Zorb. Contact: **Agrodome Adventure Centre**, Rotorua, tel: 07-332 2768, fax: 07-357 5102; www.zorb.co.nz; e-mail: rotorua@zorb.com.

award-winning guides, custom-built rafts and first-class equipment.

You don't have to look far for the ultimate jetboating thrill. **Agrojet** offers a 450hp 4-metre (13-ft) raceboat and travels up to 100kph (62 mph) in just four seconds with no slowing for corners, tel: 07-357 2929; e-mail: agrojet@xtra.co.nz.

Mountain Biking

Rotorua has world-class mountain biking in **Whakarewarewa Forest** close to the city centre. Choose from flat, easy rides for first timers or fast, technical single-track action for the more experienced. Half-day adventures or two-day adventures on offer with Planet Bike or try a combination of mountain biking, horse riding, rafting and kayaking. A half-day single track exploration will cost about NZ$79 or take a two-hour night ride for about NZ$69. Equipment, bikes, guides and refreshments included. Contact: **Planet Bike**, tel: 07-348 9971, fax: 07-348 6812; www.planetbike.co.nz; e-mail: ride@planetbike.co.nz.

Scenic Flights

Volcanic Air Safaris conduct air tours of the Rotorua region and central volcanic plateau including Mt Tarawera and White Island, tel: 07-348 9984; www.volcanicair.co.nz; e-mail: VolcanicAir@xtra.co.nz. Cost ranges from NZ$50 for a flight (minimum four people) over the town area to a three-hour helicopter flight to White Island for NZ$725.

Central Plateau

GETTING THERE

Taupo is about four's south of Auckland and four hour's north of Wellington. It is located on the classic touring route, the Thermal Explorer Highway, which runs through Taupo en route from Auckland to Rotorua and Hawke's Bay. There are direct **Air New Zealand** flights daily from Auckland and Wellington to Taupo Airport with connections to South Island.

To get to National Park and Ohakune, take the **Overlander** train from Auckland. Taupo is also well serviced by inter-city coaches. See also *Getting Around*, pages 323–4.

CITY TRANSPORT

Alpine Scenic Tours, offer daily transport from Taupo and Turangi to Whakapapa and National Park (and vice-versa), tel: 07-386 8918, fax: 07-378 7412; e-mail: alpine-scenic@xtra.co.nz.
Taupo Taxis, Gascoigne Street, Taupo, tel: 07-378 5100 or **Go Cabs**, 67 Heu Heu Street, Taupo, tel: 07-378 5886.

TOURISM OFFICES

Taupo Visitor's Centre, Tongariro Street, Taupo, tel: 07-376 0027, fax: 07-378 9003; www.laketauponz.com; e-mail: taupovc@laketauponz.com.

WHERE TO STAY

Mt Ruapehu

The Grand Chateau, State Highway 48, Mt Ruapehu, tel: 07-892 3809; www.chateau.co.nz; e-mail: info@chateau.co.nz. Completed in 1929, this is one of New Zealand's few hotels located in the middle of a World Heritage park. Range of rooms from executive to economy. "The Grand Old Lady of the Mountain" is renowned for its style and grandeur. **$$–$$$$**

Ohakune

Powderhorn Chateau, bottom of Mountain Road, Ohakune, tel: 06-385 8888, fax: 06-385 8925; www.powderhorn.co.nz; e-mail: powderhorn@xtra.co.nz. The Chateau in the ski town of Ohakune combines the ambience of a traditional European ski chalet with the luxury of a hotel. 30 rooms with modern facilities including the Mansion luxury apartment which can sleep up to eight adults. Dine at the downstairs restaurant or enjoy a drink around the log fire in the main bar – the Powderkeg. The Powderhorn ski and board shop is right next door. **$$$**

Hotel Price Guide

Approximate prices per night (off peak) for two people in a double room, including GST:
   $ = below NZ$100
   $$ = NZ$100–150
   $$$ = NZ$150–200
   $$$$ = NZ$200–250
   $$$$$ = over NZ$250

Taupo

Baywater Motor Inn, 126 Lake Terrace, Taupo, tel: 07-378 9933, fax: 07-378 9940; e-mail: baywater.motorinn@xtra.co.nz. Magnificent lake and mountain views with large in-room spa baths. 12 fully self-contained units with balconies or patios. One kilometre from town. **$$**
Boulevard Waters Motor Lodge, 215 Lake Terrace, Taupo, tel: 07-377 3395, fax: 07-377 2241; www.boulevardwaters.co.nz; e-mail: inquiries@boulevardwaters.co.nz. Lake-edge motel with 10 suites containing luxury features including in-room spas, king-size beds, underfloor heating and sunny patios. Thermal pool also included. **$$–$$$**
Gables Motor Lodge, 130 Lake Terrace, Taupo, tel: 07-378 8030, fax: 07-378 8031; e-mail: gables@reap.org.nz. Opposite Taupo's main swimming pool. Lake and mountain views from 12, one-bedroom ground floor units – each

with own private spa pool. Close to town. **$**
Lanecove, 213 Lake Terrace, Taupo, tel: 07-378 7599, fax: 07-378 7393; www.lanecove.co.nz; e-mail: info@lanecove.co.nz. Luxury boutique hotel situated on the lake edge, 3 kilometres (2 miles) from the town edge. Lake views, restaurant with extensive menu and comprehensive wine list.
$$$$–$$$$$
Wairakei Resort, State Highway One, Taupo, tel: 07-374 8021; www.wairakei.co.nz; e-mail: resort@wairakei.co.nz. In the heart of the Wairakei Thermal Park, the resort is just 9 kilometres (6 miles) from the centre of Taupo. It has more than 180 guest rooms and villas from standard to luxury accommodation. Sauna, gym, tennis and squash courts. **$$–$$$$**

Turangi

Tongariro Lodge, Turangi, tel: 07-386 7946, fax: 07-386 8860; www.tongarirolodge.co.nz; e-mail: trout@tongarirolodge.co.nz. Internationally famous trout fishing lodge in 22 acres (9 hectares) of parklike grounds. One-bedroom and three-bedroom chalets, gourmet food and wine, resident guides and expansive views. **$$$$$**

WHERE TO EAT

Taupo

Finch's, 64 Tuwharetoa Street, Taupo, tel: 07-377 2425. Asian-influenced New Zealand cuisine using local ingredients. **$$$**
Restaurant Villino, 45 Horomatangi Street, Taupo, tel: 07-377 4478, fax: 07-377 4479; www.villino.co.nz; e-mail: villino@xtra.co.nz. A European-style

Restaurant Price Guide

The following symbols indicate average prices per person for dinner, including service and tax:
   $ = NZ$9–16
   $$ = NZ$17–24
   $$$ = NZ$25 and over

EASTLANDS AND HAWKE'S BAY ♦ 351

restaurant in the CBD of Taupo. Alex the Bavarian chef uses fresh produce to create a captivating menu which is a combination of half German and Italian cuisine. Vilino has a reputation for a wide variety of oyster dishes and delicious risottos. **$$$**

Santorini's Greek-Mediterranean Kitchen & Bar, 133 Tongariro Street, Taupo, tel: 07-377 2205. A vibrant atmosphere, authentic décor and tasty home cooking. The owners have a fondness for Greek cuisine. **$$**

The Bach, 116 Lake Terrace, Taupo, tel: 07-378 7856; www.thebach.co.nz; e-mail: daniel@thebach.co.nz. Award-winning menu prepared by an impressive line-up of international and local chefs topped with a superb wine selection. The Bach, one of New Zealand's most popular restaurants, is located inside a cozy building. Most popular dishes on the summer menu are lamb rump and maple-cured duck breast. **$$–$$$**

Walnut Keep, 77 Spa Road, Taupo, tel: 07-378 0777. New Zealand cuisine. Extensive wine list. **$$**

WHERE TO SHOP

Taupo
Spend a day on the **Lake Taupo Art's Trail** discovering some of the region's top paintings, pottery, sculpture, ceramics, jewellery and carving or just wander around the streets looking at the huge selection of shops. Book at the Visitor's Centre for the art trail. You can buy snowboard and ski equipment from a number of shops in Ohakune, Whakapapa and Taupo.

ENTERTAINMENT

The Central Plateau has numerous festivals including art festivals, sports extravaganzas, fishing tournaments and winter events.

There are numerous bars in Taupo and a few in Ohakune and Turangi. Most have open log fires

burning in the winter months – a warm respite from the cold weather. **Holy Cow**, 11 Tongariro Street, Taupo, tel: 07-378 0040; www.holycow.co.nz; e-mail: louis@holycow.co.nz. Judging from the photographs on their website, the Holy Cow is *the* place to go to if you want to drink with loads of backpackers, visiting tourists and locals. There is lots of dancing on the tables and general shenanigans. There is a huge range of shooters and drinks available. Don't expect a quiet night here.

OUTDOOR ACTIVITIES

Golf
Voted as one of the top 20 golf courses outside the USA by *Golf Digest*, the Wairakei International Golf Course is a golfer's paradise. It has magnificent fairways and large greens with 101 bunkers. Contact: **Wairakei International Golf Course**, State Highway 1, P.O. Box 377, Taupo, tel: 07-374 8152, fax: 07-374 8289.

Fishing

Famous for trout fishing, Taupo has numerous rivers and streams that are superb for fly fishing. Rainbow Trout in Lake Taupo average 2 kg (4 lbs) while brown trout average 3 kg (6 lbs). For first class fly-fishing with experienced guides, contact **Albion Fishing Guides**, 378 Lake Terrace, Two Mile Bay, Taupo, tel: 07-378 7788, fax: 07-378 2966; www.albionfishing.co.nz; e-mail: info@albionfishing.co.nz.

Kayaking
Kayak New Zealand, tel: 07-377 1236, fax: 03-3771233; www.kayaknz.com; e-mail: info@kayaknz.com.

Bungy Jumping
Taupo Bungy offers jumps from above the Waikato River. Contact: **Taupo Bungy**, Spa Road, Taupo, tel: 07-377 1135, fax: 07-377

1136; www.taupobungy.co.nz; e-mail: jump@taupobungy.co.nz.

Skiing
New Zealand's biggest ski circuit in the North Island is on Mount Ruapehu, in the **Tongariro National Park**, about 40 minutes from Taupo: **Whakapapa** (base: National Park or Whakapapa Village) or **Turoa** (base: Ohakune). Contact: **Ruapehu Alpine Lifts**, tel: 07-892 3738, fax: 07-892 3732; www.MtRuapehu.com; e-mail: info@mtruapehu.com.

Eastlands and Hawke's Bay

GETTING THERE

Gisborne is a six-hour car ride south on the Pacific Coast Highway from Auckland while **Napier** is another three hours from Gisborne. Regular flights connect major North and South island centres to Gisborne and Hawke's Bay Airports. Coaches also operate regular schedules from around the country. See also *Getting Around*, pages 323–4.

CITY TRANSPORT

Both Eastland and Hawke's Bay are well serviced by taxis, buses and shuttles. There are also numerous private tour shuttle operators in both regions. Contact the nearest Visitor's Information Centre for more details.

TOURISM OFFICES

Eastland
Tourism Eastland, 209 Grey Street, Gisborne, tel: 06-868 6139, fax: 8686 6138; www.gisbornenz..com; e-mail: info@gisbornenz.com.

Hawke's Bay
Napier Visitor Information Centre, 100 Marine Parade, Napier, tel: 06-834 1911, fax: 06-873 5529; www.hawkesbaynz.com; e-mail: info@napiervic.co.nz.

WHERE TO STAY

Eastland

Alfresco Motor Lodge, 784 Gladstone Road, Gisborne, tel: 06-863 2464, fax: 06-863 2465; e-mail: alfresco@paradise.net.nz. 14 luxurious ground-floor units with cooking facilities, some with spa baths. Located close to the airport and golf courses. **$–$$**

Cedar House, 4 Clifford Street, Gisborne, tel: 06-868 1902, fax: 06-867 1932; www.cedarhouse.co.nz; e-mail: stay@cedarhouse.co.nz. A centrally-located bed and breakfast hotel set in a restored Edwardian mansion within walking distance from the CBD, museums, restaurants and galleries. Spacious guestrooms with large beds, bathrobes, fresh flowers and nightly turn-downs. **$$–$$$**

Hotel Price Guide

Approximate prices per night (off peak) for two people in a double room, including GST:
- **$** = below NZ$100
- **$$** = NZ$100–150
- **$$$** = NZ$150–200
- **$$$$** = NZ$200–250
- **$$$$$** = over NZ$250

Champers Motor Lodge, 811 Gladstone Road, Gisborne, tel: 06-863 1515, fax: 06-863 1520. Modern complex with 14 luxurious ground-floor units and studios, some with double spa baths, heated outdoor pool, landscaped grounds. Two minutes from airport and city centre. **$–$$**

Ocean Beach Motor Lodge & Sandbar Restaurant, Wainui Beach, Gisborne, tel: 06-868 6186, fax: 06-868 3653; e-mail: motorlodge@oceanbeach.co.nz. Mediterranean-style luxury motor lodge located at Wainui Beach. 1–2 bedroom apartments with spacious private courtyards, designer kitchens, leather furniture. **$$**

The Quarters, Te Au Farm, Nuhaka, Mahia, tel: 06-837 5751, fax: 06-837 5721; www.quarters.co.nz; e-mail: m.rough@xtra.co.nz. Self-contained, modern and stylish cottage with stunning ocean views. Complimentary crayfish and homemade bread, scenic walks, bush reserve, swimming, hunting, surfing or just relaxing. Sleeps six to eight people. **$$**

Hawke's Bay

Aladdin Lodge Motel, 120 Maddison Street, Hastings, tel: 06-876 6322, fax: 06-876 6736; www.aladdins.co.nz; e-mail: lodge@aladdins.co.nz. 11 ground-floor fully self-contained units close to city centre. Swimming pool and spa pools. **$**

The Woolshed Apartments, 106 Te Mata Road, Havelock North, tel: 06-877 0031, fax: 06-877 0032; www.woolshedapartments.co.nz; e-mail: info@woolshedapartments.co.nz. Unique accommodation. Nine apartments, fully equipped, two bedrooms, tastefully furnished. Five-minute walk from Havelock North village. **$$$**

Tuscany Motor Lodge, 271 Kennedy Road, Napier, tel: 06-843 9129, fax: 06-843 9227; www.tuscanymotorlodge.co.nz; e-mail: tuscanymotorlodge@xtra.co.nz. Architecturally-stunning, Mediterranean style accommodation with spa bath suites, private courtyards, tasteful furnishings. **$–$$**

WHERE TO EAT

Eastland

C-View Restaurant, Salisbury Street, Waikanae Beach, Gisborne, tel: 06-867 5861. **$$**

The Colosseum, 4 River Point Road, Matawhero, Gisborne, tel: 06-867

Restaurant Price Guide

The following symbols indicate average prices per person for dinner, including service and tax:
- **$** = NZ$9–16
- **$$** = NZ$17–24
- **$$$** = NZ$25 and over

4733. Country café cuisine in a vineyard setting. **$$**

The Fettucine Brothers, 12 Peel Street, Gisborne, tel: 06-868 5700. Fine pasta restaurant in the heart of the city. **$$**

Trudy's Restaurant, Gisborne Hotel, Corner Huxley and Tyndall roads, tel: 06-868 4109. Specialising in lamb, beef and seafood cuisine. **$**

Wharf Café Bar, on the Waterfront, Gisborne, tel: 06-868 4876. **$**

Hawke's Bay

Pierre sur le Quai, 62 West Quay, Ahuriri, tel: 06-834 0189. Excellent French fish dishes served in an old warehouse in the fishing port. **$$–$$$**

Thorps Coffee House, 40 Hastings Street, Hastings, tel: 06-835 6699. An Art Deco coffee house, ideal for either an inexpensive lunchtime snack or something more substantial. **$**

Ujazi, 28 Tennyson Street, Napier, tel: 06-835 1490. Cosy café featuring exhibitions by local artists. **$**

Westshore Fish Café, 112A Charles Street, Westshore, Napier, tel: 06-834 0227. Slightly outside the centre of town, but worth it for the fresh and inexpensive fish. **$$**

Where to Shop

Eastland

Gisborne has a full range of retail shops including most of the national chain stores. There is a busy downtown scene with boutique-style fashion outlets, gift shops, book stores, bars and cafés.

Hawke's Bay

The inner city of Napier buzzes with shopping activity. The city's palm-lined streets, unique architecture and street fiestas make shopping in the city a delightful experience. There are plenty of boutique and designer shops, art galleries, art deco furniture, antique and crafts shops to investigate.

MUSEUMS AND GALLERIES

Eastland

Tairawhiti Museum, Stout Street, Gisborne, tel: 06-867 3832; e-mail: tairawhitimuseum@clear.net.nz. A variety of galleries displaying the region's history, art and Maori artefacts. It also houses an extensive photographic collection showing the changing faces of Gisborne between the late 1800s and today. Nearby is the Star of Canada Maritime Museum and the colonial Wyllie Cottage. Open: 10am–4pm (Mon–Fri), 1.30–4pm (weekends).

Hawke's Bay

Hawke's Bay Exhibition Centre, 201 Eastbourne Street, Hastings, tel: 06-876 2077; e-mail: hbec@inhb.co.nz. The region's venue for short-term national and international exhibitions of art, craft, science and history as well as works by renowned and emerging local and regional artists. Open: 10am–4.30pm (weekdays) and 11am–4pm (weekends).
Hawke's Bay Museum, 65 Marine Parade, Napier, tel: 06-835 7781; e-mail: info@hbct.co.nz. Hawke's Bay regional museum features a wide range of specialist exhibits relating to the area such as the 1930 earthquake, dinosaurs in Hawke's Bay as well as art, craft and social history. Open: 10am–4.30pm. Admission charge.

ENTERTAINMENT

Hawke's Bay and Eastland have some of the finest wineries in the country and there are plenty of wine tours, conferences, festivals and special events happening at the larger vineyards. There are numerous bars and nightclubs in both Hawke's Bay and Eastland to choose from. **The Smash Palace Wine Bar and Winery** in Banks Street in Gisborne is more unusual. The wine bar is a corrugated iron shed with a full size DC 3 aircraft on the roof and a dinosaur on the door, tel: 06-867 7769.

OUTDOOR ACTIVITIES

Walking

The East Coast has a selection of excellent walking tracks to explore from beach walks, privately-owned walkways and old piers. Enjoy a leisurely historic walk through Gisborne city or take an early morning Alpine climb to the top of Mount Hikurangi, which at 1,752 metres (5,748 ft) is the first point on mainland New Zealand to see the sunrise, tel: 06-867 9960. For other scenic walks, visit the nearest Department of Conservation office or Visitor Information Centre.

Fishing

Charter or cruise Poverty Bay with an experienced skipper on a 10.34 metre (33 ft) Bruce Farr designed sloop. Contact: **Sail-A-Bay Yacht Charters & Cruises**, Harbour Marina, Gisborne, tel: 06-868 4406; e-mail: sailabay@clear.net.nz.

Gannet Safaris

Ride in style and comfort in 4-wheel drive vehicles for the unique experience of visiting the largest mainland colony of gannets in the world. Contact: **Gannet Safaris Overland**, Summerlee Station, Hastings, tel: 06-875 0888, fax: 06-875 0893; www.gannetsafaris.com; e-mail: gannetsafaris.@xtra.co.nz.

Surfing

There are plenty of good surf spots along the East Coast to choose from including beach breaks, point breaks and exposed offshore reef surf. For more information about surf breaks of the East Coast, ask at any local surf shop.

Taranaki/Manawatu and Wanganui

GETTING THERE

These regions all have their own airports and are serviced daily by **Air New Zealand**. Inter-city coaches also run services to all three regions. **Taranaki**, a little off the beaten track, is about a five-hour drive from Auckland along State Highway 43. **Wanganui** is a three-hour drive from Wellington, New Plymouth, Napier or Taupo. You can also reach Wanganui from Auckland (six-hour drive) via Taranaki or along State Highway 4. **Palmerston North**, the heart of the Manawatu, is about another hours' drive south of Wanganui. Palmerston North is also on the main trunk line with daily rail services by the **Overlander** and the **Northerner** between Auckland and Wellington. See also *Getting Around*, pages 323–4.

CITY TRANSPORT

You'll find excellent taxi, bus and shuttle services in all three regions. Check the White Pages for contact details or visit your nearest tourism office.
New Plymouth Taxis, tel: 06-757 5665
Taxis Palmerston North, tel: 06-355 5333
Wanganui Taxis, tel: 06-343 5555

TOURISM OFFICES

Palmerston North

Palmerston North Visitor Information Centre, 52 The Square, Palmerston North, tel: 06-354 6593, fax: 06-356 9841; www.manawatunz.co.nz; e-mail: manawatu.visitor-info@xtra.co.nz.

Taranaki

New Plymouth Information Centre, Corner Leach and Liardet streets, New Plymouth, tel: 06-759 6080, fax: 06-759 6073; www.newplymouthnz.com; e-mail: info@newplymouth.govt.nz.

Wanganui

Wanganui Visitor Information Centre, 101 Guyton Street, Wanganui, tel: 06-349 0508; www.wanganuinz.com.

WHERE TO STAY

Palmerston North
Chancellor Motor Lodge, 131 Fitzherbert Avenue, Palmerston North, tel: 06-354 5903, fax: 06-354 5083; www.chancellormotel.co.nz; e-mail: chancellor@xtra.co.nz. With 18 quality units, some with fully equipped kitchens and spa baths. Close to the city centre. **$$**
Rose City Motel, 120-122 Fitzherbert Avenue, Palmerston North, tel: 06-356 5388, fax: 06-356 5085; e-mail: bookings@rosecitymotel.co.nz. Mezzanine, studio units and one- to two-bedroom suites available. Close to the city. Sauna, spa pool and squash court. **$**

Taranaki
Brougham Heights Motel, 54 Brougham Street, New Plymouth, tel: 06-757 9954, fax: 06-757 5979. With 34 executive suites, spa bath units, business lounge and conference facilities. **$$**
Grand Central Hotel, 42 Powderham Street, New Plymouth, tel: 06-758 7495, fax: 06-758 7496; www.grandcentralhotel.co.nz; e-mail: office@grandcentralhotel.co.nz. Centrally located, 60 rooms and suites from premiere to executive, first class café, spa baths in most rooms. **$$-$$$**
Nice Hotel & Bistro, 71 Brougham Street, New Plymouth, tel: 06-758 6423; www.nicehotel.co.nz; e-mail: info@nicehotel.co.nz. Eight luxury individual bedrooms with contemporary art, designer bathrooms, double spa baths. The hotel, a former small hospital, is in the heart of New Plymouth.

Hotel Price Guide

Approximate prices per night (off peak) for two people in a double room, including GST:
$ = below NZ$100
$$ = NZ$100–150
$$$ = NZ$150–200
$$$$ = NZ$200–250
$$$$$ = over NZ$250

Fantastic street-level bistro. **$$-$$$**

Wanganui
Arlesford House, 202 State Highway Three, Westmere, Wanganui, tel: 06-347 7751, fax: 06-347 7561; www.arlesfordhouse.co.nz; e-mail: arlesford.house@xtra.co.nz. A country homestay set in six acres offering elegant and spacious accommodation. All rooms have private bathrooms. Swimming pool, flood-lit tennis court. **$$$-$$$$**
The Avenue, 379 Victoria Avenue, Wanganui, tel: 06-345 9070, fax: 06-345 3250; www.theavenuewanganui.com; e-mail: theavenue@xtra.co.nz. An extensive range of accommodation, international cuisine, conference centre and swimming pool. **$-$$**

WHERE TO EAT

Palmerston North
Roma Italian Ristorante & Uno Basement Bar, 51 The Square, tel: 06-356 1853; e-mail: bathhouse@xtra.co.nz. Fine traditional and modern Italian cuisine. The downstairs bar transforms into a late-night club with local and touring DJs. **$$**
The Bathhouse Restaurant & Bar, 161 Broadway Avenue, Palmerston North, tel: 06-355 0051. Mediterranean-marbled walls and an earthen fireplace complete the atmosphere. Enjoy alfresco dining year round in the all-weather courtyard. Extensive menu drawing on the delights of the meditteranean. **$$**

Taranaki
L'Escargot Restaurant & Bar, 37-43 Brougham Street, New Plymouth, tel: 06-758 4812. Run by Frenchman Andre Teissonniere, L'Escargot has a definite French feel, including the namesake dish – baked French burgundy snails – and the music playing in the bar. **$$**
Nice Hotel & Bistro, 71 Brougham Street, New Plymouth, tel: 06-758 6423; www.nicehotel.co.nz; e-mail: info@nicehotel.co.nz. An award-

Restaurant Price Guide

The following symbols indicate average prices per person for dinner, including service and tax:
$ = NZ$9–16
$$ = NZ$17–24
$$$ = NZ$25 and over

winning bistro set in the gorgeous Nice Hotel. Range of menus for all occasions, light and airy dining room, huge selection of wines, superb service. **$$**

Wanganui
Legends Café & Restaurant, 25 Somme Parade, tel: 06-348 7450, fax: 06-348 7451; www.legendscafe.co.nz. Set on the western banks of the Wanganui River, this restaurants offers an extensive menu and also features a café and cigar lounge. **$-$$$**
Victoria's Restaurant, 13 Victoria Avenue, Wanganui, tel: 06-347 7007. This award-winning restaurant offers a la carte or café dining with a menu comprising mostly traditional kiwi fare. The café's menu is a bit more European and offers a variety of dishes from fettucine to paninis. **$$**

WHERE TO SHOP

New Plymouth, Wanganui and Palmerston North all have a huge range of stores stocking everything from arts and crafts, fashion and jewellery including most of the national chain stores. Check out Centre City shopping complex in New Plymouth, Mainstreet Wanganui and The Plaza in Palmerston North.

MUSEUMS AND GALLERIES

Palmerston North
Manawatu Art Gallery, 398 Main Street, Palmerston North. Gallery collection concentrating on New Zealand works from 1880, including works by all major contemporary

painters. It houses two large collections of drawings by James Cook, and oils, watercolours and drawings by H. Linley Richardson. Open: 10am–4.30pm (Tues–Fri), 1–5pm (Sat, Sun and public holidays). **Te Manawa**, 398 Main Street, Palmerston North, tel: 06-355 5000. The only regional museum complex in New Zealand to combine art, science and history experiences. Galleries show a mix of interactive science exhibitions and display art from New Zealand and around the world. In the courtyard stands two historic buildings, Totaranui Settlers Cottage and Awahou South Schoolhouse. Open daily: 10am–5pm. Admission charge.

Taranaki

Govett-Brewster Art Gallery, Queen Street, New Plymouth. One of the best collections of contemporary art in New Zealand. Most New Zealand artists of note are represented, with works by Patrick Hanly, Michael Illingworth, Colin McCahon and Brent Wong. Also an important collection of Len Lye kinetic sculptures, paintings and films. Open: 10.30am–5pm (Mon–Fri), 1–5pm (Sat and Sun).

Wanganui

Sargeant Gallery, Queen's Park, Wanganui. This has a permanent New Zealand collection, which includes oils, watercolours and prints from the 19th- and 20th-centuries. Also holds 19th- and 20th-century British and European works including drawings by Poccetti, the Denton Collection of 19th- and 20th-century photography, and an exhibition of World War I posters and cartoons. Open: 10.30am–4pm (Mon–Fri), 10.30am–12pm (Sat), 1.30–4pm (Sun).

ENTERTAINMENT

There are a variety of bars throughout New Plymouth, Palmerston North and Wanganui. Palmerston North, being a university town, has plenty of student bars.

Salvation Café and Lounge Bar in New Plymouth is an oasis of contemporary culture offering Thai and Japanese snacks, coffee, cutting-edge music from local and touring DJs, tel: 06-759 1626.

Windsurfing/surfing

Windsurfing and surfing conditions similar to Hawaii can be found in Taranaki. There are numerous spots to choose from up and down the coast from Awakino in the North to Wanganui in the south. To find out about local windsurfing and surfing spots, contact your nearest surf shops. There is also plenty of accommodation for surfers and windsurfers to utilise along the Taranaki coast.

OUTDOOR ACTIVITIES

Walking/Tramping/Climbing

There are fabulous walks both in the **Egmont** and **Whanganui** National Parks. It's best to check local weather before you embark on a walk or tramp, especially if you intend to climb **Mount Taranaki**. Talk to your nearest Department of Conservation office to find out about weather and tramping conditions. Professional guiding services are also available in Taranaki. There are also many fabulous river and coastal walks to be found throughout both regions.

Mountain Biking

Within minutes from Wanganui are some of the best mountain biking trails in the region. Recommended areas to visit include Lismore Forest. Contact: **Rayonier NZ**, Hylton Park and Whanganui River Road, tel: 06-347 1774.

Fishing

Wanganui, Manawatu and Taranaki offer great fishing and boating. Both regions have lakes with excellent trout and perch fishing. Licences must be purchased for sport fishing. Contact: **Taranaki Fish and Game Council**, tel: 06-345 4908.

Wellington

GETTING THERE

Wellington International Airport is the country's newest airline terminal. It has services from Australia and some South Pacific islands as well as a strong regional and national transport focus. The airport is about half-an-hour away from the city centre. Taxis cost about NZ$20 and take 25 minutes, a shuttle will cost about NZ$8 and will take about 35 minutes. There is also a bus service from the airport to the city and Lower Hutt which costs a mere NZ$1.50 and takes about 45 minutes.

Wellington is also well serviced by inter-city coaches and is connected by train services from Auckland.

Ferry services also link Wellington with Picton in the South Island. See also *Getting Around*, pages 323–4.

Tourism Office

Wellington Visitor Information Centre, corner Wakefield Street and Civic Square, tel: 04-804 4860; www.wellingtonnz.com.

CITY TRANSPORT

There are numerous bus services in Wellington including **Stagecoach Flyer** from the airport into the city and out to Lower Hutt, and the **City Circular**, a bus that loops the city every 10 minutes, tel: 04-801 7000; www.stagecoach.co.nz. There are plenty of taxi stands dotted around the inner city. However Wellington is compact enough that it's easy to walk from one end of Lambton Quay to Courtenay Place.

Visit the historic Somes Island or Eastbourne by ferry on the **Evening Post**, tel: 04-499 1282 or catch the unique **Cable Car**, tel: 04-472 2199 from Cable Car Lane off Lambton Quay, to the suburb of Kelburn and the top of the Botanic Gardens. Wellington also has a commuter train system, the **Tranzmetro**, linking the city to the outer suburbs.

WHERE TO STAY

Adelaide Motel, 209-211 Adelaide Road, tel: 04-389 8138; www.adelaidemotel.co.nz. A few minutes from Wellington Hospital in Newtown. Ten units with basic facilities. Off-street parking. **$**

Apollo Lodge Motel, 49 Majoribanks Street, tel: 04-385 1849, fax: 04-385 1849. 35 units (max occ. 5). Selection of motel units, executive suites and apartments. Five minutes to Oriental Bay and only 300 metres (328 yards) to the shopping centre. **$–$$**

Hotel Price Guide

Approximate prices per night (off peak) for two people in a double room, including GST:

    $ = below NZ$100
   $$ = NZ$100–150
  $$$ = NZ$150–200
 $$$$ = NZ$200–250
$$$$$ = over NZ$250

Hotel Inter-continental Wellington, Corner of Grey and Featherston streets, tel: 04-472 2722; www.interconti.com. Excellent location by the waterfront, the hotel is a good base for both business and leisure. Has 232 rooms and suites, restaurant, bars and room service and a good fitness centre with a heated pool. **$$$$**

James Cook Hotel Grand Chancellor, 147 The Terrace, tel: 04-499 9500; www.grandchancellor.co.nz. Top management and service in this landmark central hotel; ideal location for shopping. One of the first grand hotels built in Wellington but has kept up with the times. Joseph Banks restaurant and wine bar is popular. **$$$**

Novotel Wellington, 345 The Terrace, tel: 385 9829, fax: 385 2119; www.accorhotels.com. 108 rooms with swimming pool. **$$$**

Quality Hotel Oriental Bay, 73 Roxburgh Street, Mt Victoria, tel: 04-385 0279; www.qualityoriental.co.nz. 117 rooms (max occ. 3). Close to city centre. **$$$**

Quality Hotel Willis Street, 355 Willis Street, tel: 04-385 9819, fax: 04-385 9811; www.qualitywillis.co.nz. 84 rooms (max occ. 3). Restaurant, bar, gymnasium. **$$$**

The Duxton, 170 Wakefield Street, tel: 04-473 3900; www.duxton.co.nz. A favourite hotel of business travellers who want to make a good impression. Modern facilities with good views from spacious rooms. Good mid-town location near Michael Fowler Centre and the waterfront. Burbury's restaurant on the top floor offers fine silver service dining. **$$$$**

Tinakori Lodge Bed & Breakfast, 182 Tinakori Street, tel: 04-473 3478. Close to rail, botanic gardens and restaurants in historical Thorndon. Scrumptious breakfast buffet. **$$**

Victoria Court Motor Inn, 201 Victoria Street, tel: 04-472 4297; www.victoriacourt.co.nz. Located near the city centre, the quality units and off-street parking make it a good option for the traveller. From here it is only a short stroll to the eateries of Cuba Street and the shopping of Manners Mall. **$$$**

WHERE TO EAT

Brava, 2 Courtenay Place, tel: 04-384 1159. A popular restaurant with excellent breakfast menu and inspiring cuisine. Politicians, actors and film stars have been spotted in this restaurant which is located beneath Downstage Theatre. **$$**

Brooklyn Café and Grill, 1 Todman Street, tel: 04-385 9592. Belongs to the restaurant critic of a leading listings magazine, and is good by anyone's standards. **$$**

Restaurant Price Guide

The following symbols indicate average prices per person for dinner, including service and tax:

  $ = NZ$9–16
 $$ = NZ$17–24
$$$ = NZ$25 and over

Café L'Affare, 27 College Street, tel: 04-385 9748. Serves excellent breakfasts, and roasts its own coffee. Very popular so arrive early to avoid disappointment. **$**

Logan Brown Restaurant, 192 Cuba Street, tel: 04-801 5114. Book in advance to secure a table at arguably the city's hottest restaurant. **$$**

One Red Dog, 9-11 Blair Street, tel: 04-384 9777. Wellington's leading gourmet pizza restaurant, bubbly atmosphere, over 50 wines by the glass and award-winning naturally brewed beers on tap. **$**

Paradiso, 20 Courtenay Place, tel: 04-384 2675. One of many trendy restaurants around Courtenay Place, with a popular bar and highly imaginative Pacific Rim cuisine. **$$**

Shed 5, Queens Wharf, tel: 04-499 9069. Lunch and dinner in a converted warehouse opposite the Maritime Museum. **$$**

Siows, 41 Vivian Street, tel: 04-801 7771. Renowned for its excellent curries and grilled Malaysian dishes. **$$**

The Grain of Salt, 232 Oriental Parade, tel: 04-384 8642. A restaurant with a long-established reputation among gourmets. **$$$**

Zibibbo, 25-29 Taranaki Street, tel: 04-385 6650, fax: 04-385 9660; e-mail: dine@zibibbo.co.nz. Contemporary Spanish and Italian cuisine in luscious lounge bar and restaurant. Resident DJ on Friday and Saturday nights. Excellent cuisine upstairs. **$$**

WHERE TO SHOP

Wellington City is divided into several distinct shopping precincts – **Cuba Quarter** is where you'll find the more alternative, funky stores and second-hand shops. **Lambton Quarter** is home to the five shopping centres including the famous Kirkcaldie & Stains – the oldest classic department store in New Zealand while **Willis Quarter** has local design stores, sports shops and plenty of stylish cafes. For antique shops head to the character filled streets of

Wellington's historical district **Thorndon**.

For an interesting shopping experience, nip over to the **Wairarapa** where you'll discover amazing wineries, antique shops, crafts stores and beautiful historic houses and buildings.

MUSEUMS AND GALLERIES

Cable Car Museum, 1 Upland Road, www.cablecarmuseum.co.nz. One of very few cable car museums left in the world, this museum is housed in the original Winding House and features an original grip cable car built in 1901. Open daily: 9.30am–5.30pm (Mon–Fri) and 10am–4.30pm (weekends).
Capital E, Civic Square, 101 Wakefield Street, www.capitale.org.nz. A creative technology and performance facility aimed at children, young people and their families. Features a children's professional theatre, exhibition floor, hands-on creative technology learning experiences through a children's television studio, and a music development facility. Opening hours vary.
Dowse Art Gallery, Civic Centre, Lower Hutt. This gallery concentrates on New Zealand art, mainly contemporary, with some earlier works. Open: 10am–4pm (Mon–Fri), 1–5pm (weekends).
Museum of Wellington City & Sea, Bonds Store, Queens Wharf, www.bondstore.co.nz. Housed in

the restored Bond Store, this museum tells historical tales from social and maritime events. Open: 10am–5pm (Mon–Fri) and 10am–5.30pm (weekends). Admission fee.
Te Papa, the National Museum of New Zealand, The Waterfront, Wellington, www.tepapa.govt.nz. The NZ$280 million building replaces the old and cramped quarters on Buckle Street – revamped displays feature traditional Maori art and culture, one of the best collections of Polynesian art and artefacts in the world, and there are also Micronesian and Melanesian collections and many exhibits from South-East Asia. Other exhibits are: Awesome Forces, Mountain to Sea and Bush City, European discovery and settlement in New Zealand; geological history of the region; and collections of flora and fauna, including the remains of the moa, the large flightless bird which once inhabited New Zealand. Open daily: 10am–6pm, (open late on Thurs).
The Film Centre, Corner Jervois Quay and Cable streets. New Zealand's museum of moving images. Also home to the Rialto Cinema. Exhibitions, screenings and special events. Open daily.
Wellington City Gallery, Civic Square, 101 Wakefield Street, www.city-gallery.co.nz. This inner-city, contemporary gallery concentrates less on collecting work than on mounting temporary New Zealand art and design shows. It has a reputation for challenging and innovative exhibitions and is

located in a prime spot at Civic Square. Open daily: 10am–5pm.

ENTERTAINMENT

As well as being the national capital, Wellington is also New Zealand's city of culture. It has three repertory theatres, a wide range of musical events, various music, arts and theatre festivals including the famous New Zealand Festival. It's also home to the Royal New Zealand Ballet, New Zealand Symphony Orchestra, the New Zealand String Quartet, Chamber Music New Zealand, Wellington Sinfonia and NBR New Zealand Opera. At the end of the year, there are performances at various venues by the New Zealand School of Dance and the New Zealand Drama School, Toi Whakaari (details from Visitor Information).

The new stadium built on surplus rail land on the waterfront hosts major sporting events and concerts.

FILM

Wellington has a strong film audience and boasts more screens per capita than anywhere else in the country. From mainstream to arthouse, cinemas in Wellington showcase the best in international and local films and there is a strong Film Festival every year. The **Embassy Theatre**, at the end of Courtenay Place, is Wellington's grandest cinema and was the site

Theatre and Ballet in Wellington

Bats Theatre, 1 Kent Terrace, tel: 04-802 4175. This small but cozy venue has the courage to experiment with lesser-known works, which means you can often book tickets at short notice.
Circa Theatre, 1 Taranaki Street, tel: 04-801 7992. This theatre, which is managed by the actors themselves, offers a stimulating range of drama in a waterside location by Te Papa Museum.

Downstage Theatre, 2 Courtenay Place, tel: 04-801 6946. A comprehensive variety of plays from Shakespeare to modern authors, as well as performances by the leading Maori theatre company, Taki Rua. The theatre is located at the heart of the restaurant and café district.
Royal New Zealand Ballet, 77 Courtenay Place, tel: 04-381 9000; www.nzballet.org.nz. The

country's principal ballet company was formed in 1953, and is based at the St James Theatre. Tickets from Ticketek, tel: 04-384 3840.
St James Theatre, 77-87 Courtenay Place, tel: 04-802 4060. The finest lyric theatre in New Zealand. This fully restored heritage building is *the* Wellington venue for opera, ballet and major musical shows. Also the site of the Ticketek box office agency.

for the world premiere of the New Zealand-made film, *Lord of the Rings* in 2001.

NIGHTLIFE

Bouquet Garni, 100 Willis Street, tel: 04-499 1095. Perfect for a glass of wine in what are now plush surroundings. The stunning wooden building used to be a brothel; now it is upmarket and all class.

CO2, 28 Blair Street, tel: 04-384 1064. A small champagne bar, great for a special occasion or a romantic night out.

Hummingbird, 22 Courtenay Place, tel: 04-801 6336. A stylish place in a great location that attracts a more mature crowd than some of the other establishments along Courtenay Place. Try the tapas menu or a drink at the bar while you people watch.

Studio Nine, 9 Edward Street, tel: 04-384 9976. A rave-style dance club that features guest DJ's playing the latest house and drum-and-bass music. Also sometimes a venue for overseas acts. Filled to capacity on most nights.

Tatou, Cambridge Terrace, tel: 04 384 3112. Offers upstairs/downstairs options for a young and trendy crowd. Heavy dance music gets the most airtime. Gets moving late and doesn't stop.

The Opera, corner of Courtenay Place and Blair Street, tel: 04-382 8654. In the centre of the action, just opposite Hummingbird. Downstairs is where the dancing happens – especially on a Friday or Saturday night. Go upstairs for a more relaxed lounge bar atmosphere.

Concerts

Wellington Festival & Convention Centre, features the Michael Fowler Centre, a major concert hall and the venue for performances by major musical names and classical artists. For bookings, tel: 04- 472 3088.

OUTDOOR ACTIVITIES

Fly By Wire

State Highway 1, Paekakariki, tel: 0800-FLY BY WIRE; www.flybywire.co.nz. A self-controlled adventure flight. Experience exhilarating speeds, huge adrenaline rush, total weightlessness and serenity as the high-speed plane glides gently for the six-minute flight.

Mountain Biking

Scores of mountain bike tracks around the city means you don't have to travel far to enjoy the outdoors. Classic rides including the town belt on **Mount Victoria**, the **Rollercoaster** from the Wellington wind turbine to Highbury, the **Te Kopahau Reserve** and the **Makara Peak Mountain Track**.

Walking

There are plenty of parks, reserves, rivers and forests to walk on the outskirts of Wellington. Head to **Makara Beach**, 35 minutes west of Wellington city for a three- or four-hour stroll along the coast, or take a two-hour coastal walk to **Red Rocks** and visit the colony of New Zealand fur seals that live there (May–October). There are also plenty of heritage walks that retrace Wellington's history. Free brochures can be obtained from the Wellington Visitor's Information Centre.

South Island

Nelson/Marlborough Sounds/Kaikoura

GETTING THERE

Nelson Regional Airport is the fourth busiest in New Zealand, with regular flights to and from Auckland, Wellington and Christchurch as well as a range of provincial centres. There are two terminals, one for **Air New Zealand** and the other for Nelson-based airline, **Origin Pacific Airways**, tel: 0800-302 302.

Ferry services between Wellington and Picton are frequent. *The Interislander* and *The Lynx* will get you across the Cook Strait in one to three hours. The world's whale watching capital, Kaikoura, is halfway between Blenheim and Christchurch and can be reached by road or rail. The journey down the east coast to Kaikoura is picturesque and magnificent. See also *Getting Around*, pages 323–4.

CITY TRANSPORT

There are plenty of coach services within the Nelson region that connect Nelson city with Moteuka and the southern entrance of the Abel Tasman Park. Contact: **Abel Tasman Coachlines**, tel: 03-548 0285. You can also rent a car or motor home and drive to most surrounding towns in under two hours. Contact your nearest Visitor Information Centre for more details.

Numerous shuttle, coach and train services also link Kaikoura to Christchurch, Blenheim, Picton and Hanmer Springs.

TOURISM OFFICES

Kaikoura
Kaikoura Visitor Centre, West End, Kaikoura, tel: 03-319 5641, fax: 03-319 6819; www.kaikoura.co.nz; e-mail: info@kaikoura.co.nz.

Marlborough Sounds
Marlborough Information and Travel Centre, State Highway 1, Blenheim, tel: 03-577 8080; www.destinationmarlborough.com; e-mail: mvic@destinationmarlborough.co.nz

Nelson
Nelson, corner Halifax and Trafalgar streets, tel: 03-548 2304; www.nelsonnz.com; e-mail: vin@nelsonnz.com.

WHERE TO STAY

Kaikoura
Admiral Court Motel, 16 Avoca Street, tel/fax: 03-319 5525; e-mail: admiralcourt@xtra.co.nz. In a quiet location with mountain and sea views. Fully equipped kitchens, off-road parking, courtesy car to bus or rail stations, spa pool. **$**
Panorama Motel, 266 Esplanade, tel: 03-319 5053, fax: 03-319 6605; e-mail: panorama.motel@xtra.co.nz. Beachfront location with sea and mountain views from all units. 22 units, all fully equipped. Plenty of off-street parking for boats and cars. **$**
The Old Convent B&B, Mt Fyffe Road, tel: 03-319 6603, fax: 03-319 6690; e-mail: o.convent@xtra.co.nz. Set in a beautifully renovated 1911 homestead, the Old Convent serves up an atmosphere of French charm.

Hotel Price Guide

Approximate prices per night (off peak) for two people in a double room, including GST:

$ = below NZ$100
$$ = NZ$100–150
$$$ = NZ$150–200
$$$$ = NZ$200–250
$$$$$ = over NZ$250

With the majestic Kaikoura Mountains as the backdrop, the Convent is fully licensed and offers superb French cuisine cooked by the French owner. There are family rooms, double and twin rooms available. Murder mystery weekends, French cooking classes and petanque also available. **$$–$$$**

Marlborough Sounds
Gem Resort, Bay of Many Caves, tel: 03-579 9771, fax: 03-579 9771; www.gemresort.co.nz. 11 rooms (max occ. 10). In the heart of Marlborough Sounds. Quiet. Lovely holiday retreat. **$**
Portage Resort, Kenepuru Sound, tel/fax: 03-573 4309; www.portage.co.nz. A famous resort in the beautiful Marlborough Sounds. Facilities include swimming pool, spa and leisure activities, superb Portage Restaurant. Hillside and garden rooms, bunk rooms, and lodges available. **$–$$$$**
Punga Cove Resort, Endeavour Inlet, tel: 03-579 8561. Chalets nestled in the bush with superb views of the surrounding bay. Each chalet has ensuite bathrooms, modern facilities, sun deck and barbeque on request. The Punga Lodge sleeps 10 people while the studio chalets can accommodate two to three people. Own private beach. Good swimming and excellent fishing. **$$**
Raetihi Lodge, Kenepuru Sound, tel: 03-573 4300, fax: 03-573 4300; www.raetihi.co.nz; e-mail: hotel@raetihi.co.nz. Luxury lodge with 14 theme rooms, all with ensuites and elegant furnishings. Large guest lounge, licensed bar, restaurant, games room and plenty of outdoor activities. **$$–$$$$**

Nelson
Beachside Villas, 71 Golf Road, tel: 03-548 5041; www.beachsidevillas.co.nz; e-mail: enquiries@beachsidevillas.co.nz. A Mediterranean-style boutique motel in a beautiful garden setting. Six luxury fully self-contained apartments. These impressive apartments were apparently where

the *Lord of the Rings* cast and crew stayed while filming in the Nelson region. **$–$$**
Bella Vista Motel, 178 Tahunanui Drive, tel: 03-548 6948. 18 units serviced daily. A bit of a walk from the main city centre (30 minutes) but close to beautiful beach and the harbour entrance. Good cafés and shops nearby. Some units with spa baths. **$–$$**
DeLorenzo's Motel & Apartments, 51 Trafalgar Street, tel: 03-548 9774; www.delorenzos.co.nz; e-mail: delorenzos@ts.co.nz. Luxury apartments furnished in a contemporary style with ensuite bathrooms, super king beds, spa bath and Sky TV. Only 200 metres (219 yards) from city, business and shopping areas. Modern and business facilities available. Room service available. **$$–$$$**
Kimi Ora Spa Resort, Kaiteriteri, tel: 0508-546 4672; www.kimiora.co.nz; e-mail: info@kimiora.com. 20 Swiss-style chalet apartments with sea views. Features a health centre with an extensive range of spa treatments, heated indoor and outdoor pool with unique swim channel, sauna, steam room, spa, tennis courts and fully licensed restaurant with panoramic ocean views. Packages available. **$$–$$$$** (includes meals, accommodation and spa treatment).
Tuscany Gardens Motor Lodge, 80 Tahunanui Drive, tel: 03-548 5522. 12 luxury units, some with spas and air conditioners. Full kitchens. Only five-minute walk to restaurants and beach. Ranges from one- and two-bedroom family units to executive suites. **$$**

WHERE TO EAT

Kaikoura
The Craypot Café and Bar, 70 West End Road, Kaikoura., tel 03-319 6027, fax: 03 319 6041. Centrally-located, this restaurant offers an open fire, mulled wine and fresh crayfish as well as a range of other menu options. Caters for vegetarians. **$$$**

Restaurant Price Guide

The following symbols indicate average prices per person for dinner, including service and tax:

$ = NZ$9–16
$$ = NZ$17–24
$$$ = NZ$25 and over

Finz of South Bay, South Bay Parade, Kaikoura, tel:03-319 6688, fax: 03-319 6687. A seafood restaurant and bar located on the water's edge with magnificent views of the ocean and mountains. The menu speciality is fresh seafood, including Kaikoura Crayfish, although meat lovers and vegetarians are also catered for. **$$$**

Marlborough Sounds

Hotel d Urville Restaurant, 52 Queen Street, Blenheim, Marlborough, tel: 03-577 9945, fax: 03-577 9946; www.durville.com; e-mail: hotel@durville.com. A world-acclaimed restaurant and accommodation set in a historic building in Blenheim. The restaurant also transforms into an international cooking school with a difference. Fresh produce from the Marlborough Sounds is used to create an innovative menu including local Greenshell mussels, lamb, venison, fish, crayfish and organic specialty produce. Hotel d Urville, described as an urban lodge , features 11 unique bedrooms. **$$$**
Rocco's Italian Restaurant, 5 Dodson Street, Blenheim, Marlborough, tel/fax: 03-578 6940; e-mail: RoccoRest@yahoo.it. Italian cuisine combined with fresh Marlborough produce, Rocco's specialises in home-made fresh pasta and prosciutto as well as New Zealand seafood, lamb and chicken cooked in the traditional Italian way. The menu is extensive as is the wine list. Run by the Rocco brothers from Northern Italy. **$$**

Nelson

Boat Shed Café, 350 Wakefield Quay, Nelson, tel: 03-546 9783; e-mail: the.Boatshed@xtra.co.nz. Very pleasant and popular restaurant with view of the water and imaginative seafood dishes. Bookings are essential, especially during the Nelson Arts Festival and Wearable Arts Awards. **$$–$$$**
Chez Eelco, 296 Trafalgar Road, tel: 03-548 7595; e-mail: chezeelco@hotmail.com. New Zealand's oldest outdoor café, famous for its fish soup, which is also sold tinned in supermarkets. Simple food, good coffee. Try the chunky mussel chowder, Marlborough mussels and Tasman scallops. **$**
The Honest Lawyer, 1 Point Road, tel: 03-547 8850; www.honestlawyer.co.nz. Old-style country pub in historic building just outside Nelson, with a large beer garden and accommodation. Delicious New Zealand and English cuisine, a wide-ranging wine list and selection of tap beers. **$$**
The Smokehouse, Shed Three, Mapua Wharf, Mapua, Nelson, tel: 03-540 2280; www.smokehouse.co.nz. A unique smokehouse and café utilising the best and freshest local seafood. The menu is based on fish, mussels and vegetables delicately hot-smoked on site using a traditional brick kiln and manuka shavings. Located on the edge of the Waimea Estuary flowing into Tasman Bay, the Smokehouse has it's own mascot – a beautiful white Kotuku (White Heron) called Hamish. **$$**

Where to Shop

There are more than 350 fulltime artists and craftspeople in the Nelson region so expect to see plenty of crafts shops and stores in the centre of town. The Saturday morning Nelson market in Montgomery Square is popular and you'll discover everything from arts and crafts to regional produce and gourmet foods. There are also weekend markets in Motueka and Golden Bay.

MUSEUMS AND GALLERIES

Nelson

Hoglund Art Glass, Lansdowne Road, Richmond, www.hoglund.co.nz. Visit the world-famous glass blowing studio in Richmond and watch these master artists create beautiful, individual pieces of glassware. There is also a café and galleries to explore. Open daily.
Nelson Provincial Museum, Isel Park, Stoke, Nelson, e-mail: musemnp@iconz.co.nz. The region's principal museum of social history. Exhibitions include treasures and stories from the region, from Maori settlement to the present day. Open: 10am–4pm (weekdays) or weekends (12–4pm).
Rutherford Gallery, 42 Halifax Street Nelson and 250a Queen Street, Richmond. A gallery offering a wide selection of paintings and sculptures. Everything from traditional to contemporary. Includes works by well-known artists from Nelson and New Zealand. Open daily.
The Suter, 208 Bridge Street, Nelson, www.thesuter.org.nz. The region's main public art museum. Has a permanent collection of historical and contemporary works by important Nelson and New Zealand artists. Showcases local art and craft, stages performances, lectures and floortalks. Open daily: 10.30am–4.30pm. Admission fee.
World of WearableArt & Collectable Car Complex, 95 Quarantine Road, Annesbrook, Nelson, www.worldofwearableart.com. Two galleries that showcase garments from the spectacular World of WearableArt fashion shows held in Nelson and an array of collectable cars from around the world. Open daily. Admission fee.

NIGHTLIFE

Nelson

Little Rock, 165 Bridge Street, Nelson, tel: 03-546 8800.

Restaurant, bar and dance club. Stylish cocktail bar, gourmet pizzas, bar nibbles, live music, DJs. **The Victorian Rose Pub & Café**, 281 Trafalgar Street, Nelson, tel: 03-548 7631; e-mail: vicrose@xtra.co.nz. Voted best bar 2001 by the Taste Nelson Awards, it is a well-known venue for jazz and blues. Huge variety of beer on tap.

OUTDOOR ACTIVITIES

Fishing

In the **Nelson Lake District**, a guide will help you find eels weighing 20 kilos and brown trout up to half a metre (2 ft) long. Contact: **Tony Entwistle's Fly Fishing**, 5 Mason Place, Richmond, tel: 063-544 4565; www.tonyentwistlesflyfishing.co.nz; e-mail: tony@tonyentwistlesflyfishing.co.nz.

Fresh Water Springs

The clearest fresh water springs in the world are reputed to be the Waikoropupu Springs near Nelson.

Sailing

Explore the magical Marlborough Sounds on a yacht, runabout or launch with **Compass Charters**, Beach Road, Waikawa Marina, Picton, tel: 03-573 8332; www.compass-charters.co.nz; e-mail: directors@compass-charters.co.nz. You can charter a yacht for between NZ$230 and NZ$670, depending on size and make, for 24 hours. Expect to pay around NZ$25 an hour for a skipper. Cheaper rates for longer hours.

Kayaking

You can explore the beautiful Abel Tasman Park or Marlborough Sounds in rented kayaks. Go on a guided or independent tour and spend one day or an overnight soaking up the overwhelming sights of New Zealand's incredible coastline. Contact: **Abel Tasman Kayaks**, Marahau RD2, Motueka 7161, tel: 03-527 8022;

Walking/Tramping

There are three national parks in the Nelson region that provide excellent walking and tramping tracks. The Abel Tasman Coastal Track is one of New Zealand's Great Walks. The length of the track takes three to five days. There are Department of Conservation huts along the track for hire. The Kahurangi National Park has a network of tracks offering short walks or multi-day wilderness trips, including the famous four- to five-day Heaphy Track. Contact the nearest Visitor's Information Centre for details.

www.kayaktours.co.nz; e-mail: atk@kayaktours.co.nz or **Marlborough Sounds Adventure Company**, The Waterfront, Picton, tel: 03-573 6078 or 0800-283 283; www.marlboroughsounds.co.nz; e-mail: adventure@marlboroughsounds.co.nz

Whale/Dolphin Watch

Kaikoura is world famous for its whale and dolphin population. Huge sperm whales swim barely a kilometre off the coast between April and June; orcas can also be seen during the summer, and humpbacks put in an appearance during June and July. **Whale Watch**, Kaikoura, tel: 03-319 6767 or 0800-655 121 (New Zealand only), fax: 09-319 6545; www.whalewatch.co.nz; e-mail: res@whalewatch.co.nz (Bookings are essential). **Dolphin Encounter**, 58 West End, Kaikoura, tel: 03-319 6777, fax: 03-319 6534; www.dolphin.co.nz; e-mail: info@dolphin.co.nz. Whale-watching tickets should be booked a few days in advance.

Note: Resist any offers to swim with the endangered Hector's Dolphin. This practice is fast bringing about the animal's demise.

Horse Trekking

Cape Farewell Horse Treks in Golden Bay near Nelson. McGowan

Street, Puponga, Collingwood, tel/fax: 03-524 8031; www.horsetreksnz.com; e-mail: fun@horsetreksnz.com.

The West Coast

GETTING THERE

If you drive, access is either through the Buller Gorge from Nelson, through the Lewis Pass via historic Reefton, over the high alpine Arthur's Pass from Christchurch or via Haast Pass from Queenstown. Driving time takes about 3–5 hours.

There are airports at Hokitika and Westport with regular scheduled services. Or take the **Tranz Alpine** train through the Southern Alps from Christchurch to Greymouth (or vice versa). The West Coast is also well served by inter-city coaches. See also *Getting Around*, pages 323–4.

TRANSPORT

Greymouth Travel can assist with all transport information from rail, land, air and sea. The centre is situated at the Greymouth Railway Station, 164 Mackay Street.

TOURISM OFFICES

Fox Glacier

Fox Glacier Visitor Centre, Department of Conservation, State Highway 6, Fox Glacier, tel: 03-751 0807, fax: 03-751 0858; www.west-coast.co.nz.

Franz Josef Glacier

Franz Josef Glacier Visitor Centre, Department of Conservation, State Highway 6, Franz Josef Glacier, tel: 03-752 0796, fax: 03-752 0797; www.west-coast.co.nz.

Greymouth

Greymouth Information Centre, corner Mackay and Herbert streets, Greymouth, tel: 03-768 5101, fax: 03-768 03017; e-mail: vingm@minidata.co.nz.

WHERE TO STAY

Fox Glacier

A1 Motel, Lake Matheson Road, Fox Glacier, tel: 03-751 0804, fax: 03-751 0706. 10 rooms (max occ. 8). Close to post office, restaurant and beaches. **$**

Fox Glacier Hotel, corner Cook Flat Road and State Highway 6, Fox Glacier, tel: 03-751 0839, fax: 03-751 0868; e-mail: fox.resort@xtra.co.nz. Originally built in 1928, the Fox Glacier Hotel has been refurbished to retain its charm and atmosphere. 49 rooms (max occ. 4). Facilities include restaurant, lounge bar, guest lounge and internet services. **$–$$**

Glacier Country Hotel, Fox Glacier, tel: 03-751 0847, fax: 03-751 0822; e-mail: glacier_country@xtra.co.nz. Situated in Westland's World Heritage Park in the Fox Glacier township. 51 serviced rooms (max occ. 4). Facilities include guest laundry, room service and restaurant. **$$**

Franz Josef Glacier

A1 Rata Grove Motel, 6 Cron Street, tel: 03-752 0741. Seven studio units and three family units. 50 metres (164 ft) to the local shops, restaurant and post office, 6 km (4 miles) from Franz Josef Glacier. Basic facilities. Glacier and mountain views. **$**

Franz Josef Glacier Hotel, State Highway 6, tel: 03-752 0729, fax: 03-752 0709; www.scenic-circle.co.nz; e-mail: franz.Josef@scenic-circle.co.nz. 177 rooms, all have basic facilities, some with mini bars and Sky TV. Two spa pools. Guest laundry, restaurant, bar and room service available. **$$$$**

Glacier Gateway Motor Lodge, Main Road, tel: 03-752 0776, fax: 03-752 0732; e-mail: glacier.gateway@xtra.co.nz. 23 units (max occ. 5), two units with baths. Basic facilities, spa and sauna. 500 metres (547 yards) to restaurants and shops, glacier access by road. One of the closest accommodation to any glacier in New Zealand. **$**

Hotel Price Guide

Approximate prices per night (off peak) for two people in a double room, including GST:

- **$** = below NZ$100
- **$$** = NZ$100–150
- **$$$** = NZ$150–200
- **$$$$** = NZ$200–250
- **$$$$$** = over NZ$250

Glacier View Motel, Franz Josef Glacier, tel: 03-752 0705, fax: 03-752 0761. 14 units (max occ. 6). Close to restaurant. Bush-lined setting with spectacular mountain and glacier views. **$**

Karamea Bridge Farm Motels, 1RD, Westport, tel: 03-782 6955, fax: 03-782 6748; www.karameamotels.co.nz; e-mail: info@karameamotels.co.nz. Six 1–2 bedroom units on a private farm looking across the wilderness of Kahurangi National Park and beyond. Each unit has a large private lounge. Only 400 metres (437 yards) from the centre of Karamea. **$**

The Chalet, Main Road, Arthur's Pass, tel: 03-318 9236, fax: 03-318 9200; e-mail: thechalet@arthurspass.co.nz. Great alpine scenery in a true chalet-style accommodation. An la carte restaurant specialising in lamb, salmon, venison and beef; 10 rooms with elegant furnishings, ensuite bathrooms. **$$**

Greymouth

Aachen Place Motel, 50 High Street, Greymouth, tel: 03-768 6901, fax: 03-768 6958; www.aachenmotel.co.nz; e-mail: aachenmotel.grey@netaccess.co.nz. Award-winning studio apartments and units with great views of the sea and mountains. Centrally located. Self-contained. Supermarket nearby. **$–$$**

Gables Motor Lodge, 84 High Street, Greymouth, tel: 03-768 9991, fax: 03-768 9992; e-mail: gables@xtra.co.nz. Luxury units with fully equipped kitchens, large beds. Some rooms have spa baths, while others have showers. Very close to supermarket and shops. **$–$$**

Hokitika

Fitzherbert Court Motel, 191 Fitzherbert Street, Hokitika, tel: 03-755 5342, fax: 03-755 5343; e-mail: fitzherbert.court@xtra.co.nz. Luxury units with self-contained kitchens. Some units have spa baths. Close to town, airport and beach. **$–$$**

Shining Star Log Chalets, 11 Richards Drive, Hokitika, tel: 03-755 8921, fax: 03-755 8653; e-mail: shining@xtra.co.nz. Set within a stone's throw from the beach, these natural timber chalets have their own decks and direct beach access. All units are fully self-contained and are centrally-located. **$**

WHERE TO EAT

Fox Glacier

Café Neve, Main Road, Fox Glacier, tel: 03-751 0110, fax: 03-751 0020; e-mail: cafe.neve@xtra.co.nz. Café situated in the heart of Fox Glacier township. Offers inside and outside dining (summer months only). The menu features fresh seafood, lamb, beef, vegetarian meals and a selection of pasta dishes and salads. **$$–$$$**

High Peaks Restaurant, 163 Cook Flat Road, Fox Glacier, tel: 03-751 0131; e-mail: a1motel@xtra.co.nz. The venison hot pot is one of the most popular dishes of this restaurant's menu. With mountain and sea views from every table and a café and bar, High Peaks is *the* place to sample authentic west coast cuisine. The restaurant has an extensive wine list while the café offers a selection of bistro meals. **$$**

Restaurant Price Guide

The following symbols indicate average prices per person for dinner, including service and tax:

- **$** = NZ$9–16
- **$$** = NZ$17–24
- **$$$** = NZ$25 and over

Franz Josef Glacier

Beeches Restaurant, State Highway 6, Franz Josef Glacier, tel: 03-752 0721; e-mail: beeches@xtra.co.nz. A gas fire and huge stone pillars at the front of the building make it easy to find. Specialising in authentic West Coast cuisine from venison to beef, Beeches also has an extensive wine list and offers light meals. **$$**

Blue Ice Café, State Highway 6, Franz Josef Glacier, tel: 03-752 0707; e-mail: blueicecafe2000@yahoo.com. An eclectic menu ranging from Italian and Indian dishes to New Zealand cuisine. Specialises in pizzas. Extensive selection of wines. Have a game of pool upstairs after your meal. **$$**

Greymouth

Café 124 On Mackay, 124 Mackay Street, Greymouth, tel: 03-768 7503; e-mail: cameo@wave.co.nz. Situated in newly built premises. Great food and coffee. Indoor and outdoor dining. **$$**

The Smelting House Café, 102 Mackay Street, Greymouth, tel: 03-768 0012, fax: 03-768 0075. Set in a converted historic West Coast bank building and run by a registered dietician. Specialising in delicious home-style food. **$$**

Hokitika

Stumpers Bar And Café, 2 Weld Street, Hokitika, tel: 03-755 6154, fax: 03-755 6137; www.stumpers.co.nz; e-mail: enquiries@stumpers.co.nz. This warm and cozy café offers a basic but tantalising menu featuring fresh pasta, locally-caught whitebait (during the whitebait season) and venison, to name a few. Check out the copper art work, designed by local artists, on the walls. **$$**

Trappers Restaurant, 79 Revell Street, Hokitika, tel: 03-755 5133, fax: 03-755 6068; e-mail: trappers@xtra.co.nz. Specialising in wild and exotic food and fresh seafood. **$$**

WHERE TO SHOP

Hokitika

The West Coast is home to numerous arts and crafts stores from jade and bone to glass and wood. Check out the **Gray Fur Trading Co Ltd**, in Hokitika, a

Outdoor Activities

Walking

Experience the beauty and history of the West Coast on the many walks and hiking trails the region offers. There are numerous great tracks to choose from, including the Heaphy Track, Wangapeka Track and Charming Creek Walkway. Check with the local information office or Department of Conservation for track conditions.

Glacier Walks

Hire a guide and explore spectacular icefall terrain normally only seen by experienced mountaineers. There are guided walks, helihikes, mountaineering trips and instruction courses. Contact: **Alpine Guides Fox Glacier**, tel: 03-751 0825, fax: 03-751 0857; www.foxguides.co.nz or **Franz Josef Glacier Guides**, tel: 03-753 0763, fax: 03- 752 0102; www.franzjosefglacier.com.

Fishing

Moana Trout Fishing Safaris offers guided fishing trips in streams, creeks and lakes as well as a water taxi service and scenic lake tours from Lake Brunner, tel: 03-738 0086, fax: 03-738 0087; e-mail: browntrout@minidata.co.nz.

Rafting

Explore the Castles of the Underworld, slide down subterranean waterfalls and discover amazing cave formations with the **Wild West Adventure Company** in Clifton Road, Greymouth, tel: 0800-142 283. Choose from a variety of options including cave rafting and hot-rock rafting. Bookings are essential.

business that specialises in making items from possum and sheep skins, tel: 03-756 8949, fax: 03-756 8092.

Greymouth

See jade carvers at work at the Jade Boulder Gallery in Greymouth. The gallery has a range of jade jewellery and sculpture for sale as well as a Jade Boulder Discovery Walk, a recreated riverbed with the discovery of jade as the theme, tel: 03-768 0700.

MUSEUMS AND GALLERIES

Black Points Museum, State Highway 7, Reefton. Housed in a former church of pitsawn timber, the collection centres on Reefton in the days of the quartz gold mines. Photographs, equipment, maps of claims, a model of a shaft mine are displayed. Open daily except Monday (1–4pm). Closed in June and July.

West Coast Historical Museum, Carnegie Building, corner Tancred and Hamilton streets, Hokitika, e-mail: hokimuseum@xtra.co.nz. A celebration of the unique culture of the West Coast, including greenstone and gold audio-visual shows, displays, research centres, panning for gold and more. Open daily: 9.30am–5pm.

Christchurch and Canterbury

GETTING THERE

Christchurch is serviced by a busy international airport, has comprehensive road and rail links and a thriving deep water port. A public bus from the airport to the city will cost about NZ$4 and takes 30–40 minutes, a shuttle will take around 20–30 minutes at a cost of NZ$12–18 per person. The more expensive option of a taxi will cost NZ$25–30 but will only take about 12–20 minutes.

If travelling from Greymouth in the West Coast, take the scenic

City Transport

There are plenty of inner-city bus and taxi services, but for a chance to experience some olde world charm, take one of Christchurch's historic trams. The tram does a circuit from Worcester Street, past the arts centre, museum and Christ's College. You can hop off and on at any of the stops, tel: 03 366 7511; www.tram.co.nz.

There is a dedicated shuttle/coach service to Hanmer Springs, which leaves the Christchurch Information Service at 9am every day and arrives in Hanmer Springs two hours later. Contact: **Hanmer Connection**, tel: 800-377 378, **Blue Star Taxis**, tel: 03-3799 799 or **Gold Band Taxis**, tel: 03-379 5795.

Tranz Alpine train which cuts across some spectacular scenery. Christchurch is also well-served by inter-city coaches from other New Zealand destinations. See also *Getting Around*, pages 323–4.

Mount Cook Airline (operated by Air New Zealand), Mount Cook Alpine Village, tel: 0800-737 000, fax: 03-435 1886; www.airnz.co.nz, operates daily flights from Christchurch to Mount Cook.

TOURISM OFFICES

Christchurch
Christchurch & Canterbury Visitor Centre, Cathedral Square, Christchurch, tel: 03-379 9629; www.christchurchnz.net.

Hanmer Springs
Hurunui Visitor Centre, 42 Amuri Avenue, Hanmer Springs, tel: 03-315 7128; www.hurunui.com.

Methven
Methven Travel and Information, Main Street, Methven, tel: 0800-764 444, fax: 03-302 9367; e-mail: methven@clear.net.nz.

WHERE TO STAY

Christchurch
Admiral Motel, 168 Bealey Avenue, tel: 03-379 3554, fax: 03-379 3272; e-mail: admiral.motel@xtra.co.nz. 9 units (max occ. 6). Near Cathedral Square and town hall. **$**

Airport Gateway Motor Lodge, 45 Roydvale Avenue, Burnside, tel: 03-358 7093, fax: 03-358 3654; www.airportgateway.co.nz; e-mail: info@airportgateway.co.nz. 30 motel suites (max occ. 6). Close to airport. Restaurant and conference facilities. **$**

Ashleigh Court Motel, 47 Matai Street West, Lower Riccarton, tel: 03-348 1888, fax: 03-348 2973. A short walk to museum, shopping centre, gardens. Full kitchen facilities, bathroom ensuite. **$–$$**

Belmont Motor Inn, 172 Bealey Avenue, tel: 03-379 4037, fax: 03-366 9194; www.belmontmotorinn.co.nz; e-mail: belmont@clear.net.nz. Situated only 10 minutes from the city centre. 18 rooms (max occ. 6). **$$**

Centra Hotel, corner Cashel and High Street, tel: 03-365 8888, fax: 03-365 8822; www.centra.com.au. Central location, close to retail and business districts. Restaurant and bar within hotel. 146 guest rooms and suites. **$$–$$$**

Cotswold Hotel, 88 Papanui Road, tel: 03-355 3535, fax: 03-355 6695; e-mail: cotswold.hotel@xtra.co.nz. Modern-style comfort with old worlde charm. Five minutes from the city. 87 rooms including suites and motel inns. Nearby restaurant offers continental cuisine. Authentic period furnishings and decor. **$$**

Hotel Price Guide

Approximate prices per night (off peak) for two people in a double room, including GST:

$ = below NZ$100
$$ = NZ$100–150
$$$ = NZ$150–200
$$$$ = NZ$200–250
$$$$$ = over NZ$250

Country Glen Lodge, 107 Bealey Avenue, tel: 03-365 9980; e-mail: countryglenlodge@xtra.co.nz. Luxurious apartments close to the city centre. Extensive facilities including luxury spa bath units. **$–$$**

Gothic Heights Motel, 430 Hagley Avenue, tel: 03-366 0838, fax: 03-366 0188. 15 rooms (max occ. 5). Situated opposite Hagley Park. Walking distance to museum, arts centre, restaurants and botanical gardens. **$**

Hotel Grand Chancellor, 161 Cashel Street, tel: 03-379 2999; www.grandchancellor.com. Excellent location in downtown Christchurch and only a short walk from Cathedral Square. Comfortable rooms matched by prompt service. **$$$**

Latimer Motor Lodge, 30 Latimer Square, tel: 03-379 6760, fax: 03-366 0133; e-mail: enquiries @latimerlodge.co.nz. Low-rise traveller's lodge near city centre with good value rooms and off-street parking. 90 rooms (max occ. 4). 500 metres (547 yards) to city centre. **$$**

Millennium Christchurch, 14 Cathedral Square, tel: 03-365 1111, fax: 03-365 7676; www.cdlhotels.com. 179 rooms (max occ. 3) with modern facilities. Features include, restaurant, bar, gymnasium, sauna, business centre. In centre of city. **$$$–$$$$$**

Parkroyal Christchurch, corner Kilmore and Durham Streets, tel: 03-365 7799, fax: 03-365 0082; www.parkroyal.com.au. Magnificent location on Victoria Square in the central city. Immaculate rooms, spacious corridors and top-class amenities. 297 rooms (max occ. 4). Connected to town hall and convention centre. **$$$$**

The George Hotel, 50 Park Terrace, tel: 03-379 4560, fax: 03-366 6747; www.thegeorge.com. A low-rise luxury hotel on a great site across the road from the Avon River and Hagley Park. Nice willow-shaded rooms with balconies. Ten-minute walk to the city centre. Top-rated fine dining restaurant. 54 rooms (max occ. 4). **$$$$**

Windsor Court Motel, 136 New Brighton Road, Shirley, tel: 03-385 8032, fax: 03-385 7544; e-mail: siddells@xtra.co.nz. 7 rooms (max occ. 8). Quiet, well off the road. 10-minute drive to seven golf courses. **$**

Windsor Private Hotel, 52 Armagh Street, tel: 03-366 1503. Bed and breakfast style accommodation in an old Victorian villa. Share facilities, basic but good. Central location. **$$**

Hanmer Springs

Alpine Lodge, corner Amuri Drive and Harrogate Street, tel/fax: 03-315 7311. 28 rooms, traditional chalets and luxurious tower suites available. Facilities vary in each suite. Close to shops and pool complex. **$–$$$**

Greenacres Chalets and Apartments, 86 Conical Hill Road, tel/fax: 03-315 7125. Separate units in parklike setting overlooking the Hanmer Basin. Chalets and apartments have decks and balconies and full kitchen facilities. Close to Hanmer Township, 800 metres (875 yards) from thermal pools. **$–$$**

Hanmer Resort Motel, 7 Cheltenham Street, tel: 0800-114 511, fax: 03-315 7471. 15 rooms (max occ. 6). Next to hot mineral pools. **$–$$**

Hanmer Springs Larchwood Motels, 12 Bath Street, tel/fax: 03-315 7281. 16 rooms (max occ. 6). Handy to squash courts, hot pools and forest walks. **$–$$$**

Methven

Canterbury Hotel, Mt Hutt Village, tel: 03-302 8045, fax: 03-302 8085; e-mail: canterburyhotel@xtra.co.nz. This historic hotel has been a haven for travellers for more than 50 years. Basic but comfortable facilities. **$**

Mount Hutt Motel, State Highway 77, tel: 03-302 8382, fax: 03-302 8382. 10 units (max occ. 6). Closest motel to Mt Hutt. Units with separate kitchens and apartments available. Basic facilities. **$**

Powderhouse Country Lodge, 3 Cameron Street, Mt Hutt, Methven, tel: 03-302 9105; www.powderhouse.co.nz; e-mail: stay@powderhouse.co.nz. A beautifully restored Edwardian villa with classic antiques and collection of early skiing, fishing and climbing memorabilia. Fine accommodation, relaxed atmosphere. Five luxurious bedrooms with private bathrooms. Eight-person spa and foot spas available. **$$$$**

Mount Cook

Mount Cook Chalets and Motels, Mount Cook, tel: 03-435 1809, fax: 03-435 1879. 18 rooms (max occ. 6). Accommodation for the budget conscious traveller. All chalets have bathrooms, telephones and kitchen facilities. **$**

The Hermitage and Mount Cook Complex, Mount Cook, tel: 03-435 1809, fax: 03-435 1879; www.mount-cook.com. Luxurious accommodation with amazing scenery at the foot of New Zealand's tallest mountain in the Aoraki Mount Cook National Park. 143 rooms (max occ. 3). Sauna facilities, souvenir shop, clothing outlet, coffee shop, two restaurants and a bar. 50 km (30 miles) from Twizel. Excellent views. **$$$$**

WHERE TO EAT

Christchurch

Dux de Lux, The Arts Centre, corner of Montreal and Hereford Streets, tel: 03-366 6919. Laid back dining in a restaurant/bar complex that overflows with activity. The menu is extensive and includes a large number of seafood and vegetarian options. Try the brewed-on-the-premises beer. There's a great outdoor garden bar which can be used in all seasons. **$$$**

Honeypot Café, 114 Lichfield Street, tel: 03-366 5853. Casual eatery serving full meals as well as a selection of delicious sandwiches and pizzas with

innovative toppings like tandoori chicken and Cajun with sour cream sauce. Great desserts and coffee too. **$**

Il Felice, 56 Lichfield Street, tel: 03-366 7535. A very popular Italian BYO restaurant. The owners pride themselves in recreating the full Italian experience from fresh pasta to passionate ambience. **$$**

Kanniga's Thai, Carlton Courts, corner of Bealey Avenue & Papanui Road, tel: 03-355 6228. Good Thai food and simple decor. **$$**

La Bamba, 4 Papanui Road, tel: 03-3555 3633. Serves excellent Cajun food. **$**

Panini Bar and Internet Café, 223 High Street, tel: 03-377 5543. Small on-line café-bar serving panini (filled rolls) and excellent coffee. **$**

Pedro's, 143 Worcester Street, tel: 03-379 7668. Pedro comes from the Basque country, and is a popular local figure. Superb Basque cuisine served in a relaxed atmosphere. **$$**

Restaurant Price Guide

The following symbols indicate average prices per person for dinner, including service and tax:

$ = NZ$9–16
$$ = NZ$17–24
$$$ = NZ$25 and over

Tiffany's Restaurant, corner of Oxford Terrace and Lichfield street, tel: 03-379 1380. Fine wines and the best of regional cuisine. Tiffany's has a picturesque riverside location but is still close to the centre of town. Top-class service. Their al fresco lunches are recommended. **$$**

The Blue Note, 20 Regent Street, tel: 03-379 9674. Offers great food with a Mediterranean influence washed down by live jazz. The ambience is warm and welcoming, the setting on the pedestrian-only New Regent Street is superb. **$$**

WHERE TO SHOP

Christchurch

Christchurch offers the best prospects for shopping. There are design stores, nationwide chain stores, souvenir shops and shopping malls throughout the city. The **Arts Centre** in Worcester Boulevard has over 40 craft studios, galleries and shops all offering unique New Zealand-made souvenirs. **Canterbury Museum** specialises in paua shell jewellery and souvenirs, New Zealand-designed pottery, glass, stone and wood pieces. It also features a great selection of Maori carvings. For New Zealand-made products with a wintery theme, check out the **Antarctic Shops** at the International Antarctic Centre and Christchurch International Airport.

ENTERTAINMENT

Christchurch

Christchurch is a fairly laid-back city, and many artists and crafts-people have settled here. The theatre and concert scene is varied, and events are listed in the Christchurch and Canterbury Visitors' Guide. The Press newspaper also has details of current arts events. Christchurch is also home to the yearly Arts Festival, the Festival of Romance and the Winter Carnival which all saturate the city when they are on.

THEATRE

Christchurch

Court Theatre, Arts Centre, 20 Worcester Boulevard, tel: 03-366 6992; www.courtheatre.org.nz. Regarded as New Zealand's leading theatre, with a small, high-quality ensemble and guest actors from Britain playing middle-of-the-road modern drama. Also home to the Southern Ballet and Dance Theatre, tel: 03-379 7219.
Theatre Royal, 145 Gloucester Street, tel: 03-366 6326, is an Edwardian-style lyric theatre built in 1908. It seats about 1,300 people

and hosts concerts, performances, comedy and a whole host of events and arts performances.

CONCERTS

Christchurch

Convention Centre, Town Hall, and **WestpacTrust Centre**, 95 Kilmore Street, tel: 03-366 8899. This modern building near the casino plays host to major musical events ranging from classical to pop. It is also the headquarters of a leading nationwide theatre and concert ticket agency as well as New Zealand's largest indoor sport and entertainment stadium. Credit card bookings available.

NIGHTLIFE

Christchurch

On Fridays and Saturdays, nearly all

pubs have live bands, some of them surprisingly good. The **Christchurch Casino**, tel: 03-365 9999 in Victoria Street is also a hive of activity.
All Bar One, 130 Oxford Street, tel: 03-377 9898. One of several similar establishments along Oxford Terrace that are cafés by day and heaving bars by night. Start here and work your way along.
The Club, 88 Armagh Street, Christchurch, tel: 03-377 1007. Attracts an up-market clientele and has stricter dress code than most other clubs.
The Dux de Lux, 299 Montreal Street, tel: 03-379 8334. Trendy but laid-back crowd. Drink in either one of the two bars or outside. Live music, often folk and blues. Brews its own beers.
The Loaded Hog, corner of Cashel and Manchester streets, tel: 03-366 6674. The premier bar on a busy corner. Like its Auckland

Museums and Galleries in Christchurch

Aigantighe Art Museum, 49 Wai-iti Road, Timaru. Founded as a public museum in 1956, the Aigantighe (pronounced 'egg' and 'tie'), is the South Island's largest art museum. It holds a permanent collection and exhibits New Zealand and European art works. Open: 10am–4pm (Tues–Fri) and 12–4pm (weekends). The sculpture garden attached to the museum is always open.
Canterbury Museum, Rolleston Avenue, Christchurch. Opened in 1870, the museum is the world's largest display hall on Antarctica. Exhibits include a 27-metre (87-ft) skeleton of an Antarctic blue whale and equipment used in various expeditions. There is an associated reference library and theatre where films are shown. Other features include a hall of oriental art, an ornithological display, a costume gallery, a street of shops, and a Maori cultural section including artefacts from the moa hunting era. Open daily: 10am–4.30pm.

Robert McDougall Art Gallery, Botanic Gardens, Rolleston Avenue, Christchurch. This gallery houses representative works of Dutch, French, Italian and British work, including, drawing, printmaking and sculpture. Its New Zealand collection is one of the most comprehensive in the region, especially of the Canterbury works. Open daily: 10am–4.30pm.
The Ferrymead Trust is situated on a 40-hectare (16-acre) site alongside the Heathcote River, Christchurch. The trust's historic park includes many historical exhibits including vintage machinery, cars, bicycles, gigs, fire engines, tramcars, railway engines, aeroplanes, home appliances, and agricultural and printing equipment. Special features include rides on a 2-km (1-mile) tramway and a 1-km (½-mile) railway. The last Kitson steam tram locomotive with trailers built in Leeds, England, in 1881 can also be seen. Open daily: 10am–4.30pm.

counterpart it is big, bold and a popular place to be seen.

The Ministry, 90 Lichfield Street, tel: 03 379 2910. Plays the latest sounds from around the world to a crowd often happy and often gay. Big dance floor and great sound system adds to the frenetic atmosphere late at night.

OUTDOOR ACTIVITIES

Horse Riding

Tours in the farmland of North Canterbury are run by **Hurunui Horse Treks** (Rob and Mandy Stanley), Ribbonwood, Hawarden (between Hammer Springs and Christchurch), tel/fax: 03-314 4204; www.horseback.co.nz; e-mail: info@hurunui.co.nz.

Cycling

Adventure South, in Christchurch, tel: 03-332 1222; www.advsouth.co.nz, offers tours of South Island lasting between five and 22 days.

Skiing

Christchurch is a good base to plan your skiing holiday. It is close to Mount Hutt and Porter Heights. Mount Hutt, Methven and Canterbury are a 90-minute drive from Christchurch.

Contact: **Mt Hutt Ski Area**, tel:

Mountaineering

Alpine Guides, the only resident guide company in Aoraki/Mount Cook National Park, offers alpine touring, mountaineering courses, private instruction, mountain expeditions and guiding programmes through the Southern Alps. The cost for a seven-day expedition up Mount Cook (3,754 metres/12,348 ft) is NZ$3,995. Aircraft access is included in the price. Contact: **Alpine Guides**, Bowen Drive, Mount Cook, tel: 03-4351 834, fax: 03-4351 898; www.alpineguides.co.nz; e-mail: mtcook@alpineguides.co.nz.

03-308 5074, fax: 03-308 5076; www.nzski.com/mthutt; e-mail: service@mthutt.co.nz or.

Windsurfing/Surfing

Pegasus and Sumner bays near Christchurch offer the best windsurfing and surfing conditions. The water is freezing so it is advisable to wear a wetsuit.

Queenstown and Otago

GETTING THERE

Queenstown

Air New Zealand has regular flights to Queenstown. You can reach Queenstown directly from Christchurch and Auckland, and daily flights also operate to and from Sydney, Australia. Coach and shuttle services operate daily to and from Mount Cook, Dunedin, Te Anau, Wanaka, Franz Josef and Milford Sound.

Dunedin

Dunedin has an international airport with flights direct from Sydney and Brisbane in Australia as well as Auckland, Wellington, Christchurch and Rotorua. Airport shuttles to the city cost around NZ$12 per person and taxis are also available. The airport is about half an hour from the city. You can also drive, catch a train or take a bus from anywhere around the country. Driving from Dunedin to Christchurch takes about five hours while Dunedin to Queenstown is about 4 hours.

Wanaka

Wanaka is about an hour's drive north from Queenstown. Alternatively, take a shuttle service or inter-city bus or scenic flight. The flight from Queenstown to Wanaka takes about 20 minutes.

Te Anau

Te Anau is about a two-hour drive south of Queenstown. Shuttle services and inter-city buses travel between the two towns. **Top Line Tours** in Te Anau (tel: 03-249 7959) travels from Te Anau to Queenstown

every day. You can also take a 45-minute flight from Queenstown to Te Anau. See also *Getting Around*, pages 323–4.

CITY TRANSPORT

Queenstown

In Queenstown, you can reach most places by walking or taking a short taxi ride. To really get out and see the countryside, a rental car is a great idea. You'll find plenty of rental car companies in Queenstown. Getting to and from Arrowtown is also easy with a regular coach service.

Dunedin

Dunedin, like Queenstown, is easily accessed by foot or taxi: **Southern Taxis**, tel: 03-476 6400. There are also regular city bus services in Dunedin. For all shuttle, rail, coach and domestic flight bookings, go to the **Dunedin Railway Station** in lower Stuart Street, tel: 03-477 4449.

Wanaka and Te Anau

Both are small towns and easily covered on foot.

TOURISM OFFICES

Queenstown

Queenstown Travel and Visitor's Centre, Clock Tower Building, corner of Shotover and Camp streets, tel: 03-442 4100; www.queenstown-vacation.com; e-mail: qvc@xtra.co.nz.

Dunedin

Dunedin Visitor Centre, 48 The Octagon, tel: 03-474 3300, fax: 03-474 3311; www.cityofdunedin.com; e-mail: visitor.centre@dcc.govt.nz.

Wanaka

Lake Wanaka Visitor's Information Centre, Waterfront Log Cabin, Ardmore Street, tel: 03-443 1233; www.lakewanaka.co.nz; e-mail: info@lakewanaka.co.nz.

WHERE TO STAY

Dunedin

Abbey Lodge, 900 Cumberland Street and 680 Castle Street, tel: 03-477 5380, fax: 03-477 8715; www.abbeylodge.co.nz. Rooms are spacious and comfortable with basic facilities. Central location. Other facilities include indoor heated pool, sauna and spa. **$–$$$$$**

Cargill's Hotel, 678 George Street, tel: 477 7983, fax: 477 8098; www.cargills.co.nz; e-mail: cargills@es.co.nz. Central location. Perfect for the business traveller. Basic facilities but comfortable rooms. Adjacent restaurant. **$$**

Hotel Price Guide

Approximate prices per night (off peak) for two people in a double room, including GST:

$ = below NZ$100
$$ = NZ$100–150
$$$ = NZ$150–200
$$$$ = NZ$200–250
$$$$$ = over NZ$250

Hulmes Court Bed & Breakfast, 52 Tennyson Street, Dunedin, tel: 0800-448 563, fax: 03-447 5310; www.hulmes.co.nz; e-mail: normwood@earthlight.co.nz. A beautiful 1860s Victorian Mansion located in the heart of Dunedin. Plenty of off-street parking. A large marble fireplace to sit in front of during winter and a relaxed Victorian drawing room. Authentic furnishings. **$–$$**

Larnach Lodge, Camp Road, Otago Peninsula, tel: 03-476 1616; www.larnachcastle.com; e-mail: larnach@larnachcastle.co.nz. Close to Royal Albatross Sanctuary. There are 12 bedrooms with private facilities, each individually decorated in period style. Each room has an amazing view of the ocean 305 metres (1,000 feet) below. Lodge guests allowed to dine in the historic Larnach Castle dining room. **$$$$**

Skyline Leisure Lodge, Duke Street, Dunedin North, tel: 03-477 5360,

fax: 03-477 5460; e-mail: skyline.leisure@xtra.co.nz. Close to shopping centre and adjacent to the Botanical Gardens. The lodge occupies the original location of McGavin's Brewery and still retains the original stonework and theme. **$$**

Southern Cross Hotel, 118 High Street, tel: 03-477 0752, fax: 03-477 5776; www.scenic-circle.co.nz; e-mail: cross@es.co.nz. Plenty of superior and premium rooms to choose from. Central location, spacious and welcoming lobby. Great café attached to the hotel. Excellent service. Some rooms by the road can be a bit noisy. **$$$–$$$$$**

The Chancellor, 310 Princes Street, Dunedin, tel: 03-477 1155, fax: 03-477 7737; www.thechancellor.co.nz. Bohemian Victorian Hotel, central location. Part of the Grand Hotel's International Group. **$**

Queenstown

Alpine Sun Motel, 14 Hallenstein Street, tel: 0800-10 1914, fax: 03-442 6432; e-mail: alpine.sun@xtra.co.nz. 10 units (max occ. 5). Located in central business district. Basic facilities including guest laundry, activities desk, spa pool. **$**

Ambassador Motor Lodge, 2 Man Street, tel: 03-442 8593. Good value for money. Basic facilities but most rooms have lake views. Located at the start of town as you come in from the airport. **$$**

Copthorne Lakefront Resort, corner of Adelaide and Frankton Roads, tel: 03-442 8123; www.copthornelakefront.co.nz. Four-star accommodation with 241 cosy rooms, many with views of the lake and mountains. Not in the centre of Queenstown but within walking distance of the main shopping area. Shuttle service available. **$$$**

Gardens Park Royal, corner of Marine Parade and Earl Street, tel: 03-442 7750; www.parkroyal.com.au. A modern hotel on the lakefront about 200 metres (219 yards) from the city. Spacious and welcoming foyer gives a hint of the nature of the rooms. Management and staff are top class and unobtrusive. **$$$$**

Millennium Queenstown, corner Frankton Road & Stanley Street, tel: 03-441 8888, fax: 03-441 8889; www.cdlhotels.com; e-mail: central.res@cdlhms.co.nz. 220 rooms (max occ. 3) at this top class hotel with tasteful rooms. Restaurant, bar, car parking, gymnasium, spa. **$$$**

Millbrook Resort, Malaghans Road, Arrowtown, tel: 03-441 7000, fax: 03-441 7007; www.millbrook.co.nz. A world-class famous luxury resort with various style of accommodation from country-style rooms and cottages to hotel villas. Facilities include excellent a superb golf course, restaurant, health and fitness spa, gymnasium. **$$$$$**

Novotel Queenstown, Sainsbury Road, tel: 03-442 6600. Overlooking the Remarkables mountain range with expansive lake views. Five minutes from the town. Facilities include 24-hour room service, spa, tennis courts and a tour observation deck. **$$**

Nugget Point Resort, Arthur's Point, tel: 03-442 7273, fax: 03-442 7308; www.nuggetpoint.co.nz. Award-winning boutique property only 10 minutes drive from Queenstown. The suites are impeccably furnished with the more expensive ones featuring stunning views of the Shotover River and Coronet Peak. Competent staff magically appear when you need them. Birches restaurant is highly recommended. **$$$$**

Quality Resort Terraces, 88 Frankton Road, tel: 03-442 7950, fax: 03-442 8066; e-mail: quality.terraces@cdlhms.co.nz. Only 10 minutes walk from the town centre. 85 rooms (max occ. 5) including studios and apartments, all with magnificent views of the lake and mountains. Some rooms with cooking facilities, complimentary private spa pool. **$$$**

The Heritage Queenstown, 91 Fernhill Road, tel: 03-442 4988; www.heritagehotels.co.nz; e-mail: res.heritagezqn@dynasty.co.nz. A unique European-style lodge with forest and waterfall rooms and lakeside suites. Crafted from centuries-old schist stone and cedar. Facilities include comprehensive day spa, sauna, gymnasium, swimming pool. **$$$**

Te Anau

Aden Motel, 59 Quintin Drive, tel: 03-249 7748, fax: 03-249 7434. 12 self-contained units with kitchen facilities (max occ. 7). Close to lake and shops. **$**

Explorer Motel, 6 Cleddau Street, tel: 03-249 7156, fax: 03-249 7149. 11 rooms (max occ. 6). 500 metres (547 yards) to town centre. **$–$$**

Lakeside Motel, Lake Front Drive, tel: 03-249 7435, fax: 03-249 7529. 13 units (max occ. 8). Centrally located in a garden setting. 100 metres (109 yards) to restaurant. Spectacular views of the lake and mountains. **$**

Luxmore Hotel, Main Street, tel: 03-249 7526, fax: 03-249 7272. 105 rooms (max occ. 4). Within 300 metres (328 yards) of all services and attractions. And only 100 metres (109 yards) from the lake front. **$$**

Quality Hotel Te Anau, 20 Lake Front Drive, tel: 03-249 7421, fax: 03-249 8037. 105 rooms (max occ. 3). Lake-front garden setting. Restaurant and bar. **$$**

Te Anau Downs Hotel, Milford Highway, tel: 03-249 7811, fax: 03-249 7753; www.tenau-milfordsound.co.nz. 25 rooms (max occ. 4). Situated on the highway to Milford Sound. Quiet location. Licensed restaurant. Closed 20 May–10 Sept. **$**

Wanaka

Alpine Motel Apartments, 7 Ardmore Street, Lake Wanaka, tel: 03-443 7950, fax: 03-443 9031; www.alpinemotels.co.nz; e-mail: alpinemotel@lakewanaka.co.nz. Centrally located and within walking distance to the town centre, lake and nearby golf course. Basic family and studio serviced suites. Self-contained and comfortable. **$–$$**

Brook Vale Manor Motels, 33 Brownston Street, Wanaka, tel: 0800-438 333 (New Zealand only), fax: 03-443 9040; e-mail:

info@brookvale.co.nz. Close to the centre of town. Very private with views to the Southern Alps. Close to shops and restaurants. All units have kitchen facilities. Other guest facilities include spa pool and outdoor pool, boat ramp, BBQ area and guest laundry. **$**

Edgewater Resort, Sargood Drive, Lake Wanaka, tel: 03-443 8311, fax: 03-443 8323; www.edgewater.co.nz; e-mail: reservations@edgewater.co.nz. Modern luxurious apartments and hotel rooms available in this aptly named resort, located on the edge of Lake Wanaka. Hotel rooms have modern facilities including large bathrooms. Apartments are fully self-contained. Some apartments and rooms can be configured to provide full family accommodation. Excellent lake and mountain views. **$$$$–$$$$$**

Mount Aspiring Hotel, 109 Mt Aspiring Road, Lake Wanaka, tel: 03-443 8216, fax: 03-443 9108; www.wanakanz.com; e-mail: info@wanakanz.com. Built in natural stone and wood, this picturesque hotel is family-owned and consists of 32 studio rooms and four superior suites. All rooms have private bath and shower facilities. The superior suites have a spa bath. The Tilikum Restaurant, attached to the hotel, offers seasonal menus and a range of wines. **$$$**

WHERE TO EAT

Dunedin

2 Chefs, 428 George Street, tel: 03-477 9117. Gourmet restaurant; contemporary New Zealand cuisine. **$$$**

Bell Pepper Blues, 474 Princes Street, tel: 03-474 0973. Pleasant, high-quality restaurant with fireside atmosphere and outstanding food. Always very full. **$$$**

Bennu, 12 Moray Place, tel: 03-474 5055. Imaginative brasserie meals including pizza, pasta and tacos, amid the stylish decor of the old Savoy building. **$$**

Etrusco, 8 Moray Place, tel: 03-477 3737. The interior is Edwardian, the food pure Italian. Extensive spaghetti menu. **$$**

Ombrellos, 10 Clarendon Street, tel: 03-477 8773. Highly imaginative cuisine in an attractive, wood-panelled interior. Excellent wine list. **$$**

Queenstown

Lone Star, 14 Brecon Street, tel: 03-442 9995. As the name implies, a Western-style restaurant; the portions are huge, and the food good. **$$**

Minami Jujisei, 45 Beach Street, tel: 03-442 9854. Award-winning Japanese cuisine; particularly good for those who have never tried Japanese food before. Traditional cuisine mixed with modern influences. **$$**

Roaring Megs Restaurant, 57 Shotover Street, tel: 03-442 9676; e-mail: roaringmegs@xtra.co.nz. Award-winning restaurant set in a historic gold miner's cottage dating back to the late 1800s. Features candle-lit dining in a relaxed, cozy atmosphere and unique European/Pacific Rim-influenced dishes. **$$**

Solera Vino, 25 Beach Street, tel: 03-442 6082. A very attractive place serving Spanish cuisine; range of wines. **$$–$$$**

The Bathhouse, Marine Parade, tel: 03-442 5625; www.bathhouse.co.nz. An authentic Victorian bathhouse built in 1911 that offers nostalgic indoor and awe-inspiring outdoor dining, right on the beach with amazing lake and mountain views. Award-winning menu. **$$–$$$**

The Bunker, Cow Lane. Dark interior but fantastic food and great wine selection. One of the hottest bars in Queenstown. **$$**

Restaurant Price Guide

The following symbols indicate average prices per person for dinner, including service and tax:

   $ = NZ$9–16
   $$ = NZ$17–24
   $$$ = NZ$25 and over

Te Anau
Kepler1s Restaurant, Town Centre, Te Anau, tel: 03-249 7909. Sauteed baby octopus and grilled prawns share the limelight with traditional New Zealand favourites such as Pavlova and fish and chips on this eclectic menu. Located in the centre of Te Anau, Kepler1s has excellent food and good service. **$$**
La Toscana, 108 Milford Road, Te Anau, tel: 03-249 7756. If you fancy some good Italian fare with excellent service, then the menu at La Toscana will whet your appetite. Word from the locals is that the al nonno pasta and cheesecake are divine. **$$**

Wanaka
Calaboose Restaurant and Bar, 2 Dunmore Street, Wanaka, tel: 03-443 6262, fax: 03-443 6263. Built on the old 1880 Wanaka jail site, this spacious upmarket but casual restaurant offers an inviting atmosphere in rustic stone, wood and iron surroundings. The open fireplace is a drawcard. Extensive menu and wine list. Large secluded sundeck and even a grand piano indoors. **$$**
Kai Whakapai Café and Bar, Lakefront, Wanaka, tel: 03-443 7795. Not hard to find on the edge of Lake Wanaka, this café has panoramic views and prides itself on its freshly baked breads, pies and fresh pasta, vegetarian selection and popular gourmet pizzas. **$**

MUSEUMS AND GALLERIES

Dunedin
Otago Early Settlers Museum, 220 Cumberland Street, Dunedin. First opened in 1908. Collections include records and documents of emigration and early settlement in the Otago area, and a wide range of pioneer relics, including folk crafts, costumes, whaling relics, gold relics and household devices. Paintings and photographs depicting early settlers and settlements can also be seen. Open: 8.30am–4.30pm

(Mon–Fri), 10.30am–4.30pm (Sat), 1.30–4.30pm (Sun).
Otago Museum, Great King Street, Dunedin. Houses excellent collections and displays including Pacific collections, halls of Melanesia and Polynesia, a Maori hall, halls of maritime history and marine life, ceramics including Greek pottery and sculpture, New Zealand birdlife and an Otago historical collection. Open: 10am–5pm (weekdays), 1–5pm (weekends).
Dunedin Public Art Gallery, Logan Park, Dunedin. Established in the 1880s. The large collection comprises 18th- and 19th-century English watercolours, as well as major oil portrait and landscape artists from the 16th to the 19th centuries. The New Zealand collection ranges from the mid-19th century, and includes a retrospective collection of Frances Hodgkins. Open: 10am–4.30pm (Mon–Fri), 2–5pm (Sat, Sun and public holidays).

Queenstown
Lakes District Museum, Buckingham Street, Arrowtown. The collection is housed in a two-storey, renovated, former bank built in 1875. It comprises mining and geological items such as gold and mineral specimens, gold-miner's tools, and relics belonging to the Chinese miners. Domestic and agricultural items, old implements and machinery, and a collection of horse-drawn vehicles are also on display. A collection of 3,000 early photographs, books and documents portrays local history from 1862 to the 1920s. Open daily: 9am–5pm.
Queenstown Motor Museum, Brecon Street, Queenstown. This museum complex contains more than 60 exhibits which, though they periodically change, always include veteran and vintage cars and motorcycles, as well as post-vintage and post- World War II models and aero engines. Some of the many makes on display are Bentley, Rolls-Royce, Aston Martin, Maserati, Mercedes, and many other European specialist cars. Included is a range

of American cars including Model T Fords. Open daily: 9am–5.30pm.

Wanaka
Fighter Pilot's Museum, Wanaka Airport. Established by aviation enthusiast Sir Tim Wallis, the museum and alpine fighter collection provides an insight into an era that has since passed. Aircraft replicas, war memorabilia, photographs and computered combat games are on offer. Open: 9am–4pm. Admission charge.

ENTERTAINMENT/ NIGHTLIFE

Dunedin
Behind the facades of its once elegant buildings, Dunedin is still a youthful town. It is the home of New Zealand's oldest university, and the

Where to Shop

Dunedin
Shopping in Dunedin is relaxed and unhurried. The main shopping centre is located around the Octagon, Lower Stuart Street, Princes Street, George Street and St Andrews. There are also a number of suburban centres with good shops at Mornington, The Gardens, Andersons Bay Road and Mosgiel.
Queenstown
Visitors to Queenstown can be rest assured that the streets bristle with souvenir shops. Prices are usually fixed but bargaining is becoming increasingly common. Queenstown is the exception to normal retail hours – most shops are open seven days a week for extended hours.
Wanaka
Everything you need is within walking distance in Wanaka. You ll find shops selling local arts and crafts, plenty of souvenir stores and basic amenities such as pharmacies, hardware and stationary stores.

large numbers of students give it a relaxed atmosphere, with plenty of pub music and theatre on offer. Dunedin has a vibrant live music scene and a number of excellent Kiwi bands have originated from the city. **The Fortune Theatre**, 231 Stewart Street, tel: 03-477 83 23 has a particularly good reputation and hosts both local and touring performances. The **Summer Arts Festival** takes place in February and early March. The **Dunedin Casino**, 118 High Street, tel: 03-477 4545 is also worth a look.

Queenstown

The **Queenstown Winter Festival** in July is one not to be missed. Highlights include the Festival Parade, opening party, jazz nights, the winter beer festival, celebrity ski race and Queenstown Mardi Gras. More information at tel: 03-442 2453; www.winterfestival.co.nz.

Queenstown has plenty of superb bars and nightclubs that are often packed with international travellers and backpackers as well as local skiers and adventurers.

Lone Star Café and Bar, 14 Brecon Street, tel: 03-442 9995. A busy Texas-style restaurant and bar that plays predominantly 60s and 70s music.

McNeill's Cottage Brewery, 14 Church Street, tel: 03-442 9688. Queenstown's only brewery, bar and restaurant. Its open fires and relaxed atmosphere are great in the winter, its garden bar equally welcoming in the summer.

Pog Mahone's, 14 Rees Street, tel: 03-442 5328. As Irish as they come in Queenstown. The Guinness flows smoothly and it packs out when live bands are playing – usually Wednesday and Sunday. Also functions as a restaurant.

The World, 27 Shotover Street, tel: 03-4426 757. Often filled with backpackers and young adventurers. This is a lively and often very noisy venue renowned for its very happy hours that go on till late.

Surreal, 7 Rees Street, tel: 03-441 8492. It's a restaurant in the early evening but as the night goes on techno music takes hold and this

venue transforms into one of the cooler nightspots in town.

Wanaka

Like Queenstown, the nightlife and entertainment in Wanaka tends to centre around the après-ski crowd in winter and adventure bunnies in summer. There are plenty of bars and a few nightclubs to choose from. Check out the **Slainte Irish Bar** in Helwick Street, which offers a huge variety of New Zealand and Irish beers, tel: 03-443 6755 or the **Kingsway Bar** in Helwick Street – formerly the local tearooms but now converted into a bar with guest DJs and pool tables, tel: 03-443 7663.

OUTDOOR ACTIVITIES

Jet boating/Rafting

One of the best places for jet boating is the **Shotover River**. For more information, contact: **Shotover Jet**, Shotover Jet Beach, Arthurs Point, Queenstown, tel: 03-442 8570, fax: 03-442 7467; www.shotoverjet.co.nz; e-mail: reservations@shotoverjet.co.nz.

Alternatively, enjoy the thrills and spills of white-water rafting in an inflatable with up to seven other people; some of the most exciting rivers are the **Shotover** (Queenstown), the **Kawarau** and the **Kaituna** (Rotorua). **Challenge Rafting**, Queenstown Information Centre, corner Shotover and Camp streets, tel: 03-442 7318, fax: 03 441 8563; www.raft.co.nz; e-mail: challenge@raft.co.nz.

Horse Riding

Backcountry Saddle Expeditions, Cardrona Valley, Wanaka, tel: 03-443 8151, fax: 03-443 1712; e-mail: backcountry@kiwiadv.co.nz, organise tours in the mountains of South Island.

Paragliding

Paragliding is the simplest way of taking to the air, and with the impressive backdrop of Lake Wanaka it becomes a breathtaking experience. A one-day session

Bungee Jumping

Queenstown is where the international bungee-jumping craze began. Skippers Canyon alone has three bridges, ranging from 43–102 metres (140–335 ft) in height, from which you can hurl yourself into the void. There are four official A.J Hackett bungy jump sites including the world's first 43-metre (47-yard) site at Kawarau Bridge near Queenstown. Contact: **A.J Hackett Bungy**, The Station, corner of Camp and Shotover streets, Queenstown, tel: 03-411 8735; www.ajhackett.com.

costs around NZ$120. Contact the **School of Paragliding**, Wanaka, tel: 03-443 9193.

Climbing/Mountaineering

New Zealand Wild Walks, based in **Wanaka**, specialises in tramping and climbing in Mount Aspiring National Park and guides small groups on day and overnight climbing trips up the mountain and on treks over glaciers. Contact: **New Zealand Wild Walks**, 10a Tenby Street, Wanaka, tel: 03-443 4476; www.wildwalks.co.nz; e-mail: info@wildwalks.co.nz.

Skiing

The best-organised ski centres in the **South Island** are Cardona, Treble Cone, Coronet Peak and The Remarkables, all close to Queenstown and Wanaka. For more details on **Cardrona** check www.cardona.com and for **Treble Cone**, www.treblecone.co.nz. Also contact **Wanaka Visitors Centre**, tel: 03-443 1233, fax: 03-443 1290; e-mail: info@lakewanaka.co.nz.

For **Coronet Peak** and **The Remarkables** (www.queenstownwinter.com) contact **Queenstown Travel & Visitor Centre**, corner of Camp and Shotover streets, tel: 03-442 4100; www.queenstown-vacation.com; e-mail: qvc@xtra.co.nz. The club field, **Ohau** in Twizel, North Otago, also provides excellent skiing facilities. Contact: **Lake Ohau Lodge & Snow Field**, Lake Ohau, tel/fax: 03-438 9885; www.ohau.co.nz; e-mail: ohau@ohau.co.nz.

Heli-skiing

Harris Mountains Heli-Ski offer a range of packages including private heli-ski weeks and charters as well as daily heli-skiing packages tailored to your skiing ability. Skiers get to explore the vast terrains of the Southern Alps with its untracked powder, massive peaks, stunning valleys and challenging chutes The best time for heli-skiing is July–September. Contact: **Harris Mountains Heli-Ski**, The Station, corner of Shotover and Camp streets, Queenstown, tel: 03-442 6722 (year round) or 99 Ardmore Street, Wanaka, tel: 03-443 7930, fax: 03 443 8589 (NZ winters only), www.heliski.co.nz; e-mail: hmh@heliski.co.nz. Harris Mountains Heli-Ski operates in Queenstown, Wanaka and Mount Cook.

Hiking

Guided walking tours of some of the country's most impressive scenery are available. Contact: **New Zealand Nature Safaris**, Lyttelton, tel: 025-360 268 or 0800-697 232 (New Zealand only), fax: 03-3288 173; www.nzsafaris.co.nz; e-mail: info@hikingnewzealand.com.

Surfing

For those brave enough to handle the freezing cold ocean, Dunedin offers some of the best waves in the country. There are 47 km (29 miles) of beach within the city boundaries. Popular surf spots include **St Clair**, **St Kilda** and **Brighton**. Just make sure you have a thick wetsuit, hat and booties in winter.

Scenic Flights

Should you wish to spread your wings and see what lies beyond the beautiful mountains that surround Queenstown, try **Milford Sound Fly & Cruise** which operates from the Queenstown Airport, tel: 0800-789 999. The **Helicopter Line**, tel: 03-442 3034 in Queenstown also

offers flights over Mount Cook, West Coast glaciers and Queenstown.

Golf

Experience a round of golf at the Millbrook Resort's spectacular par 72 championship golf course in Arrowtown. The course was designed by New Zealand's renowned master golfer, Sir Bob Charles. Contact: **Millbrook Resort**, Malaghans Road, Arrowtown, tel: 03-411 7010; www.millbrook.co.nz; e-mail: marketing@millbrook.co.nz.

Southland and Stewart Island

GETTING THERE

Invercargill Airport is a five-minute drive west from the city centre and is serviced by **Air New Zealand** flights. Coach services also connect Invercargill with other points in New Zealand. The **Foveaux Express ferry** service links Invercargill with Stewart Island, and operates daily from Bluff, tel: 03-212 7660; www.foveauxexpress.co.nz; e-mail: foveauxexpress@southnet.co.nz. **Stewart Island Flights** also fly directly from Invercargill Airport to Stewart Island, tel: 03-218 9129; www.stewartislandflights.com; e-mail: sif@xtra.co.nz. See also *Getting Around*, pages 323–4.

TOURISM OFFICE

Stewart Island

Main Road, P.O. Box 3, Stewart Island, tel: 03-219 1218, fax: 03-219 1555; www.stewartisland.co.nz; e-mail: stewartislandfc@doc.govt.nz.

WHERE TO STAY

Invercargill

Ascot Park Hotel/Motel, corner Racecourse Road and Tay Street, Invercargill, tel: 03-217 6195, fax: 03-217 7002; www.ilt.co.nz; e-mail: ascot@ilt.co.nz. A large complex in quiet surroundings. Facilities include indoor swimming pool, spa, sauna and gym and restaurant. **$–$$**

Hotel Price Guide

Approximate prices per night (off peak) for two people in a double room, including GST:

$ = below NZ$100
$$ = NZ$100–150
$$$ = NZ$150–200
$$$$ = NZ$200–250
$$$$$ = over NZ$250

Birchwood Manor, 189 Tay Street, Invercargill, tel: 03-218 8881, fax: 03-218 8880; www.birchwoodmanor.co.nz; e-mail: birch@birchwood.co.nz. Award-winning motel. Good family and business accommodation. Spacious and affordable units and rooms. Located close to central city. **$–$$**

Stewart Island

Nadia Outpost, Slope Point, The Catlins, tel: 03-246 8544. A range of accommodation from tent sites to bed and breakfast. The Outpost is at the southernmost tip of the South Island. Set amongst forested trees with spectacular views. Facilities are basic but include small souvenir and supplies shop. **$**
South Sea Hotel, tel: 03-219 059; www.stewart-island.co.nz; e-mail: southsea@stewartisland.co.nz. A friendly country-style hotel with fully licenced restaurant featuring local seafood on the menu. Also features motel units adjacent to the hotel. Great views, close to Mill Creek and 25-minute walk from town. **$–$$**
Stewart Island Lodge, tel: 03-219 1085; www.StewartIslandLodge.co.nz; e-mail: Doug&Margaret@xtra.co.nz. Nestled in the natural beauty of the a bush setting. Each suite has large beds, central toilet and ensuite bathrooms. Gourmet meals, featuring fresh local seafood. Fantastic views of Halfmoon Bay. **$$$**

WHERE TO EAT

Invercargill

Frog n' Firkin Café Bar, Dee Street, Invercargill, tel: 03-214 4001, fax:

Restaurant Price Guide

The following symbols indicate average prices per person for dinner, including service and tax:

$ = NZ$9–16
$$ = NZ$17–24
$$$ = NZ$25 and over

03-214 0661. Has an old English pub theme, with great atmosphere and affordable pub meals. Late night entertainment in the weekends. **$**
The Cabbage Tree, 379 Dunns Road, Otatara, Invercargill, tel: 03-213 1443, fax: 03-213 1108; www.thecabbagetree.com; e-mail: cabbage.tree@xtra.co.nz. A European-inspired restaurant and wine bar set in a cozy and warm atmosphere (there are four fireplaces) and featuring a delicious European and New Zealand menu using local seafood and ingredients. There is a choice of a la carte or set menus. **$$**

MUSEUMS AND GALLERIES

Invercargill

Southland Museum and Art Gallery, 108 Gala Street, Invercargill. The region's main museum holds collections by international, national and regional artists. Includes Maori and social history galleries and you'll even get to see the remains of the extinct New Zealand bird, the Moa. Open daily.

Stewart Island

Rakiura Museum, Ayr Street (opposite the Community centre), Stewart Island. Run by volunteers, the museum houses a vast collection of items and photographs of Stewart Island's early history. Open: 10am–noon (Mon–Sat), noon–2pm (Sun).

Walking in Southland and Stewart Island

There are rainforest retreats, coastal tracks and beach ecotours to explore as well as vast tracks of national park around Southland. The 53.5-km (33-mile) Milford Track is one of the most popular. Contact: **Fiordland National Park Visitor Centre** in Te Anau, tel: 03-249 8514, fax: 03-249 8515.

Foveaux Walkway near Bluff is a walk along rugged coastline below the bluff. It's about 7 kilometres (4 miles) in length and provides excellent views of the coast and bush. Or explore New Zealand's latest national park, the **Catlins**, where you might be lucky enough to spot seals, sea lions and dolphins.

Try the new **Tuatapere Hump Ridge Track** at the south-eastern end of Fiordland National Park. The track is a 53-kilometre (33-mile) circuit that starts and finishes at the western end of Blue Cliffs Beach on Te Wae Wae Bay.

Contact: **Great Walks Booking Desk**, Lakefront Drive, P.O. Box 29, Te Anau 9681, tel: 03-249 8514, fax: 03-249 8515; www.doc.govt.nz; e-mail: greatwalksbooking@doc.govt.nz.

There are numerous tracks on **Stewart Island** to explore with some walks taking as little as 15 minutes while others, as long as three days.

The **Rakiura Track**, the most popular, crosses rimu and kamahi forest and is suitable for anyone with moderate fitness. It takes three days and provides a good introduction to Stewart Island. Travellers are bound to see and hear Stewart Island's massive population of native birds from tuis and fantails to cape pigeons and blue penguins.

For all walks in Southland and Stewart Island, contact the nearest Department of Conservation office or Visitors' Information Centre.

Petrified Forest

Curio Bay in Southland is one of the most extensive and least disturbed examples of a petrified forest. The forest is believed to be about 180 million years old.

ENTERTAINMENT

Invercargill

The Bluff Oyster and Southland Food Festival is an annual event and a chance for locals to show off their fine Southland hospitality with seafood, fine wine and entertainment. Local restaurants and community groups offer a vast selection. Entertainment is provided all day by bands, local performers and celebrities, tel: 0800-CITY EVENTS; e-mail: bluffoysterfest@icc.govt.nz.

OUTDOOR ACTIVITIES

Fishing

The Southland region abounds with numerous quality rivers, lakes and streams. The Mataura River in Gore is famous as one of the best brown trout fishing rivers in the world. For a guided fishing tour, contact: **Riverside Guides in Gore**, tel: 03-208 4922; e-mail: fishing@esi.co.nz.

Kayaking

Kayaking is another great way to see Stewart Island. **Stewart Island Sea Kayaking Adventures**, tel: 03-219 1080 offer a range of guided adventures.

Charters

There are numerous charter outfits on Stewart Island including adventure cruises and diving and fishing excursions. For a real sense of adventure, head out on the 17-metre (56-ft) steel motorised ketch called *Talisker* and explore Stewart Island and the Fiordland. Contact: **Talisker Charters**, tel: 03-219 1151; www.taliskercharter.co.nz; e-mail: tait@taliskercharter.co.nz.

ART & PHOTO CREDITS

Cartographic Editor **Zoë Goodwin**
Design Consultants
Klaus Geisler, Graham Mitchener
Picture Research **Hilary Genin**

Index

Note: *Page references in italics refer to illustrations*

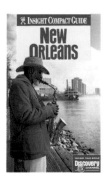

INSIGHT GUIDES

The classic series that puts you in the picture

Alaska
Amazon Wildlife
American Southwest
Amsterdam
Argentina
Arizona & Grand Canyon
Asia, East
Asia, Southeast
Australia
Austria
Bahamas
Bali
Baltic States
Bangkok
Barbados
Barcelona
Beijing
Belgium
Belize
Berlin
Bermuda
Boston
Brazil
Brittany
Brussels
Buenos Aires
Burgundy
Burma (Myanmar)
Cairo
California
California, Southern
Canada
Caribbean
Caribbean Cruises
Channel Islands
Chicago
Chile
China
Continental Europe
Corsica
Costa Rica
Crete
Cuba
Cyprus
Czech & Slovak Republic
Delhi, Jaipur & Agra
Denmark

Dominican Rep. & Haiti
Dublin
East African Wildlife
Eastern Europe
Ecuador
Edinburgh
Egypt
England
Finland
Florence
Florida
France
France, Southwest
French Riviera
Gambia & Senegal
Germany
Glasgow
Gran Canaria
Great Britain
Great Railway Journeys
 of Europe
Greece
Greek Islands
Guatemala, Belize
 & Yucatán
Hawaii
Hong Kong
Hungary
Iceland
India
India, South
Indonesia
Ireland
Israel
Istanbul
Italy
Italy, Northern
Italy, Southern
Jamaica
Japan
Jerusalem
Jordan
Kenya
Korea
Laos & Cambodia
Las Vegas
Lisbon

London
Los Angeles
Madeira
Madrid
Malaysia
Mallorca & Ibiza
Malta
Mauritius Réunion
 & Seychelles
Melbourne
Mexico
Miami
Montreal
Morocco
Moscow
Namibia
Nepal
Netherlands
New England
New Orleans
New York City
New York State
New Zealand
Nile
Normandy
Norway
Oman & The UAE
Oxford
Pacific Northwest
Pakistan
Paris
Peru
Philadelphia
Philippines
Poland
Portugal
Prague
Provence
Puerto Rico
Rajasthan

Rio de Janeiro
Rome
Russia
St Petersburg
San Francisco
Sardinia
Scandinavia
Scotland
Seattle
Sicily
Singapore
South Africa
South America
Spain
Spain, Northern
Spain, Southern
Sri Lanka
Sweden
Switzerland
Sydney
Syria & Lebanon
Taiwan
Tenerife
Texas
Thailand
Tokyo
Trinidad & Tobago
Tunisia
Turkey
Tuscany
Umbria
USA: On The Road
USA: Western States
US National Parks: West
Venezuela
Venice
Vienna
Vietnam
Wales
Walt Disney World/Orlando

INSIGHT GUIDES

The world's largest collection of visual travel guides & maps